Shojo Beat

kimi ni todoke
From Me to You

Vol. 26
Story & Art by
Karuho Shiina

Volume 26

Contents

Story Thus Far

Sawako Kuronuma has always been a loner. Though not by choice, this optimistic 16-year-old girl can't seem to make any friends. Stuck with the unfortunate nickname "Sadako" after the haunting movie character, rumors about her summoning spirits have been greatly exaggerated. With her shy personality and scary looks, most of her classmates will barely talk to her, much less look into her eyes for more than three seconds lest they be cursed. Thanks to Kazehaya, who always treats her nicely, Sawako makes her first friends at school, Ayane and Chizu. Eventually, Sawako finds the courage to date Kazehaya.

The time has come for Sawako and her friends to think about their futures after high school. Everyone is struggling towards their dreams and a happy future. Yano and Kento have broken up, and Yano takes Pin's advice to follow her dream to go to a school in Tokyo. Chizu, who was initially unsure if she could go along with Ryu's decision to leave her and play baseball, decides she's willing to support him and wait for him to return to her. Meanwhile, although Sawako initially decided to go to the same university as Kazehaya, she doesn't want to give up on her dream school. Knowing how she feels, Kazehaya tells her not to worry about him and to do what she wants, but Sawako fights back for the first time! Summer vacation is about to begin, and Kazehaya and Sawako are in the middle of their first fight!

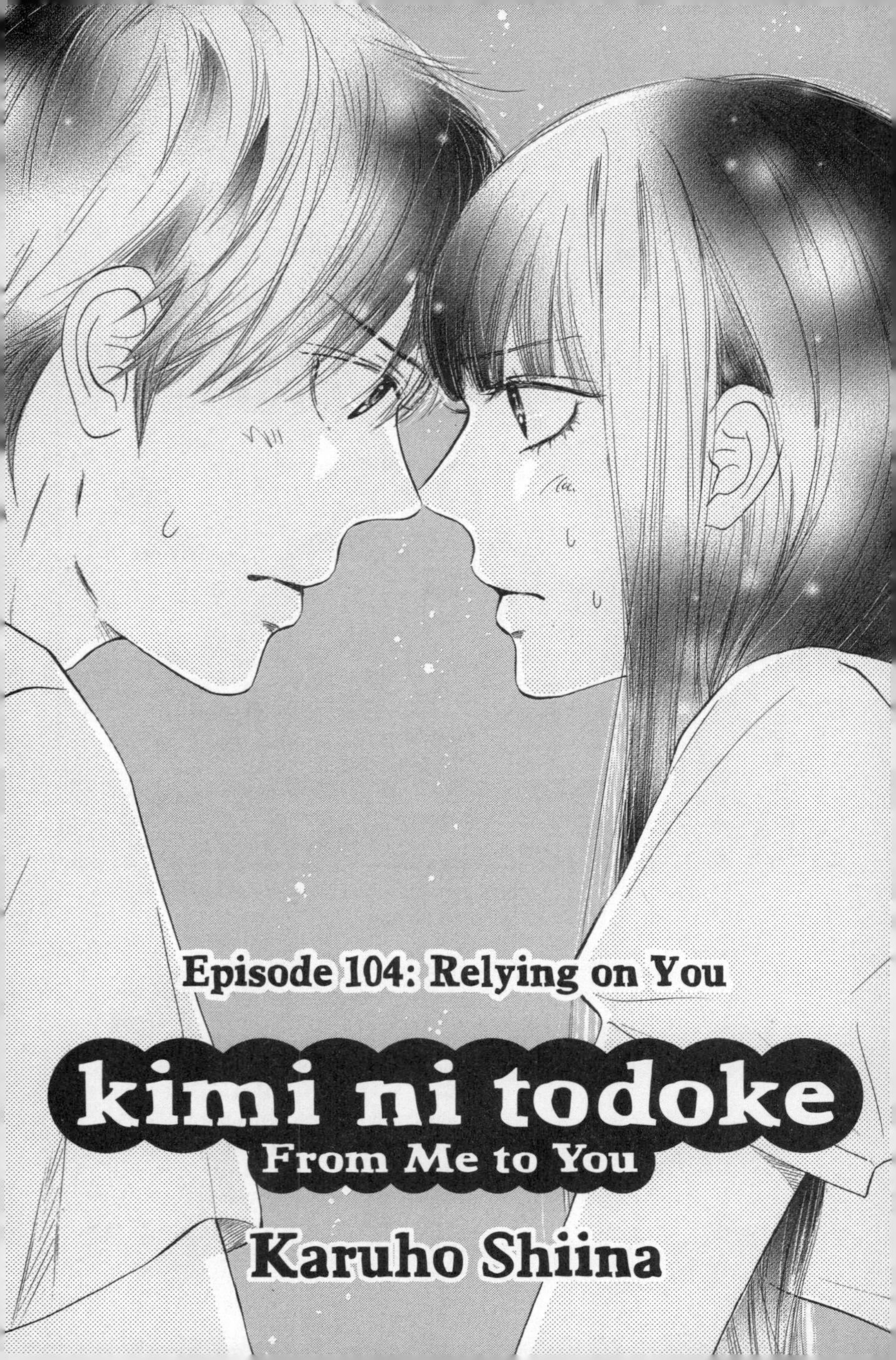
Episode 104: Relying on You
kimi ni todoke
From Me to You
Karuho Shiina

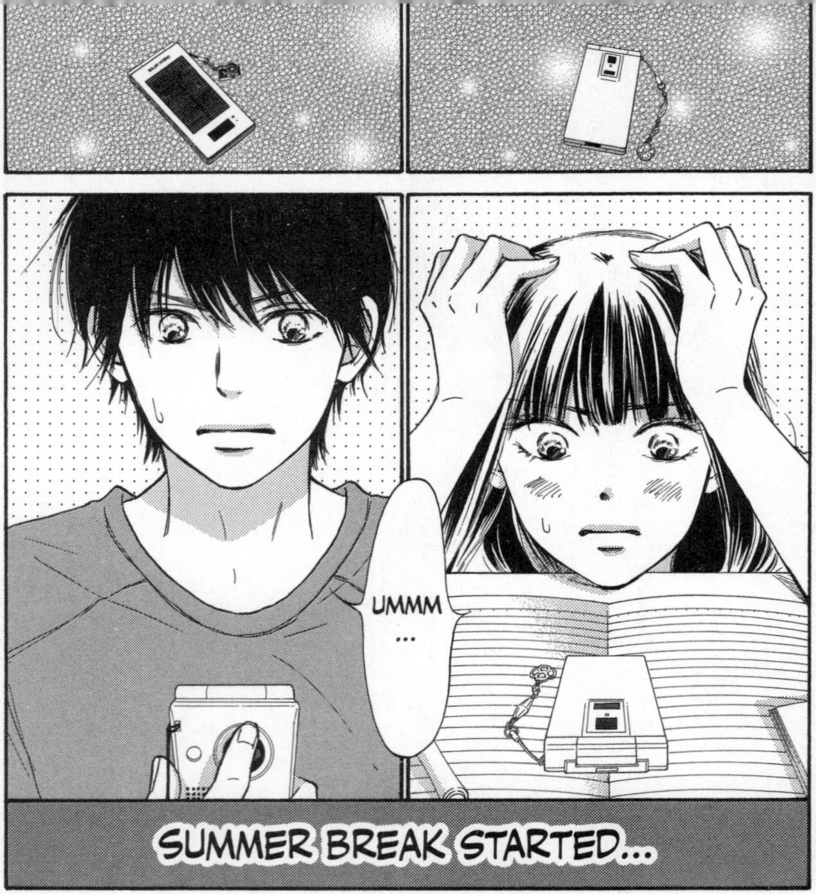
UMMM ...
SUMMER BREAK STARTED...
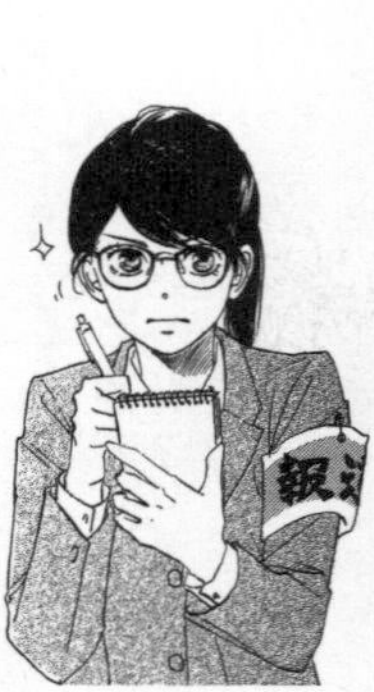

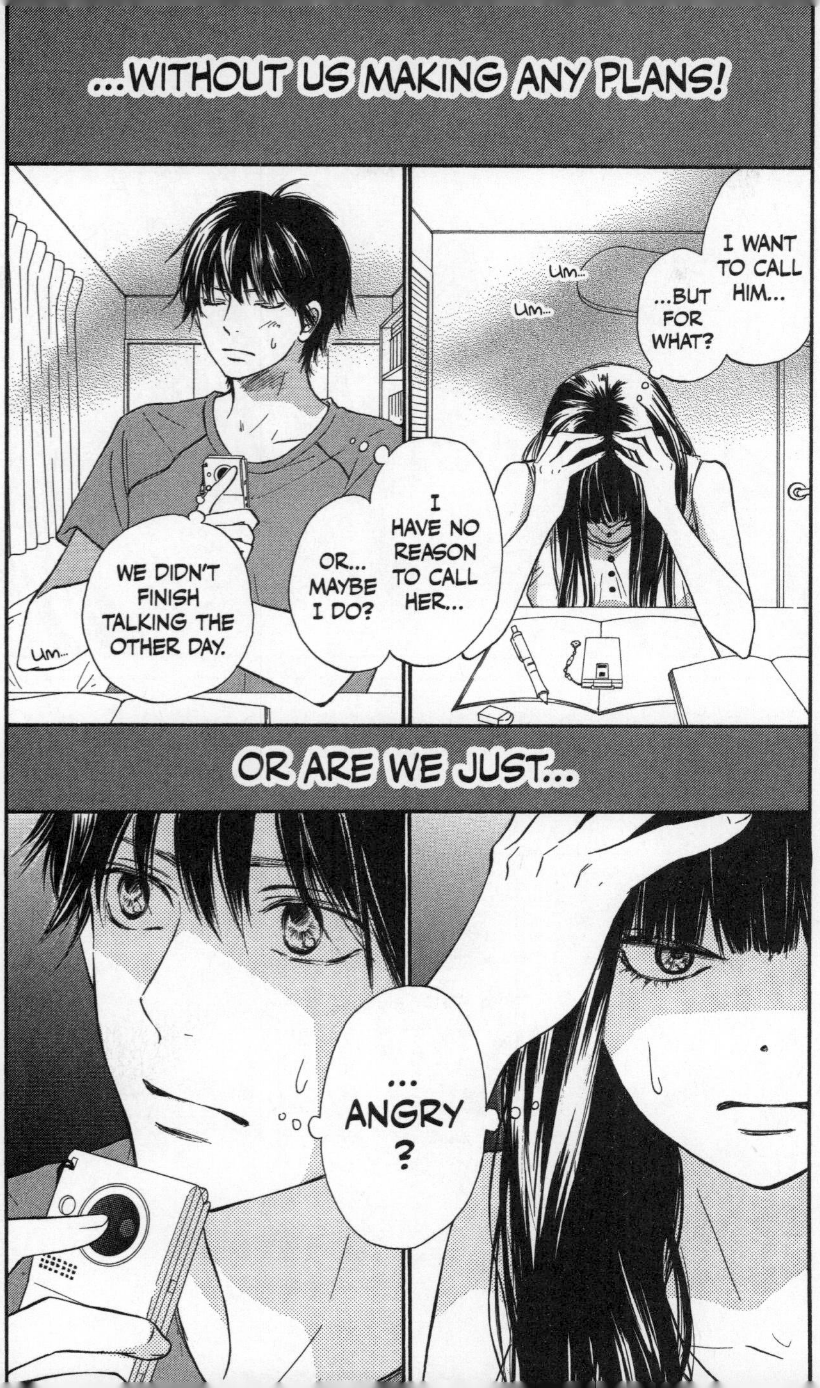
...WITHOUT US MAKING ANY PLANS!
I WANT TO CALL HIM...
...BUT FOR WHAT?
Um...
Um...
I HAVE NO REASON TO CALL HER...
OR... MAYBE I DO?
WE DIDN'T FINISH TALKING THE OTHER DAY.
Um...
OR ARE WE JUST...
... ANGRY ?

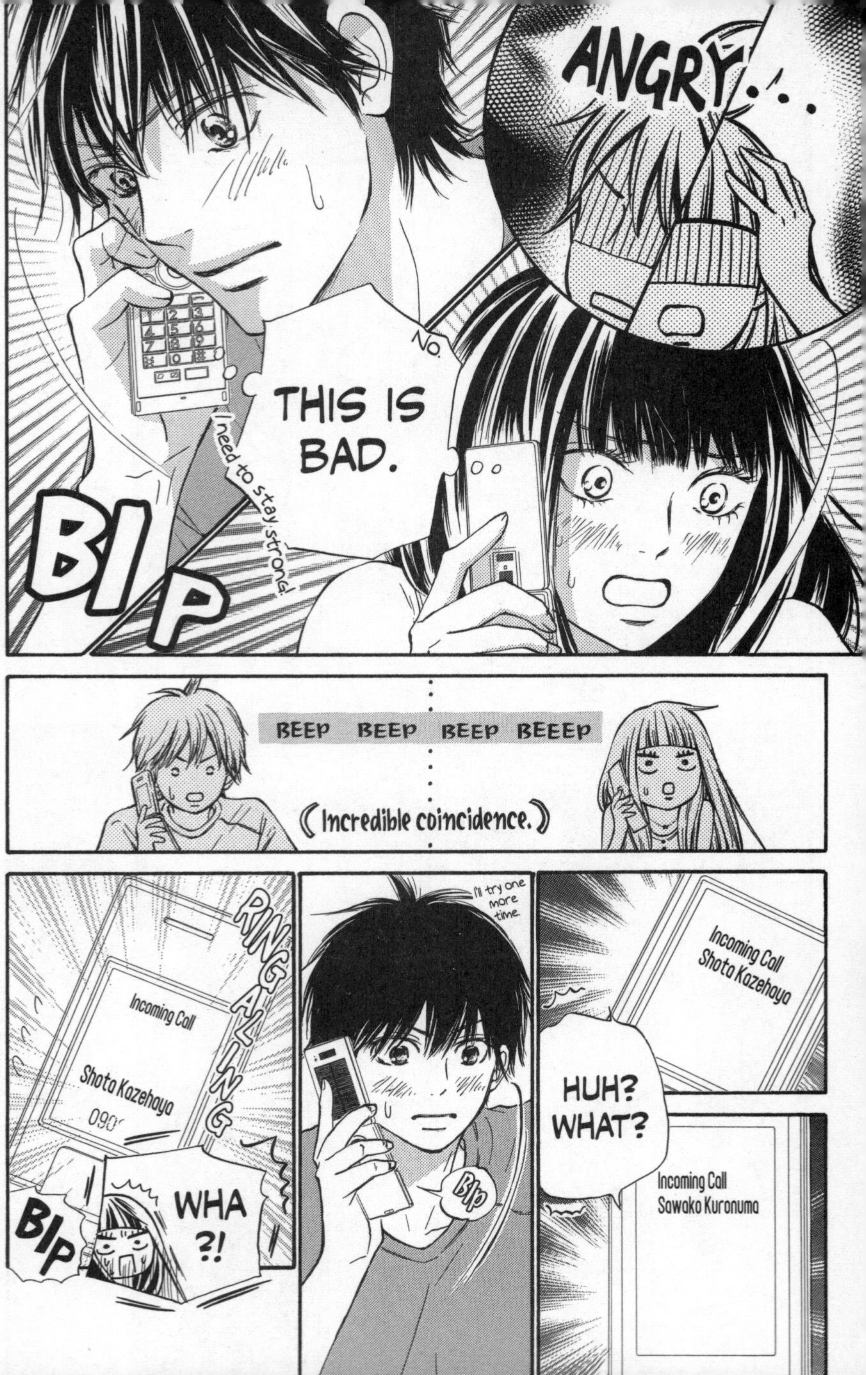
ANGRY...
No.
THIS IS BAD.
I need to stay strong!
BIP
BEEP BEEP BEEP BEEEP
Incredible coincidence.
Incoming Call
Shota Kazehaya
HUH? WHAT?
Incoming Call
Sawako Kuronuma
I'll try one more time.
Bip
RINGALING
Incoming Call
Shota Kazehaya
090
WHA?!
BIP

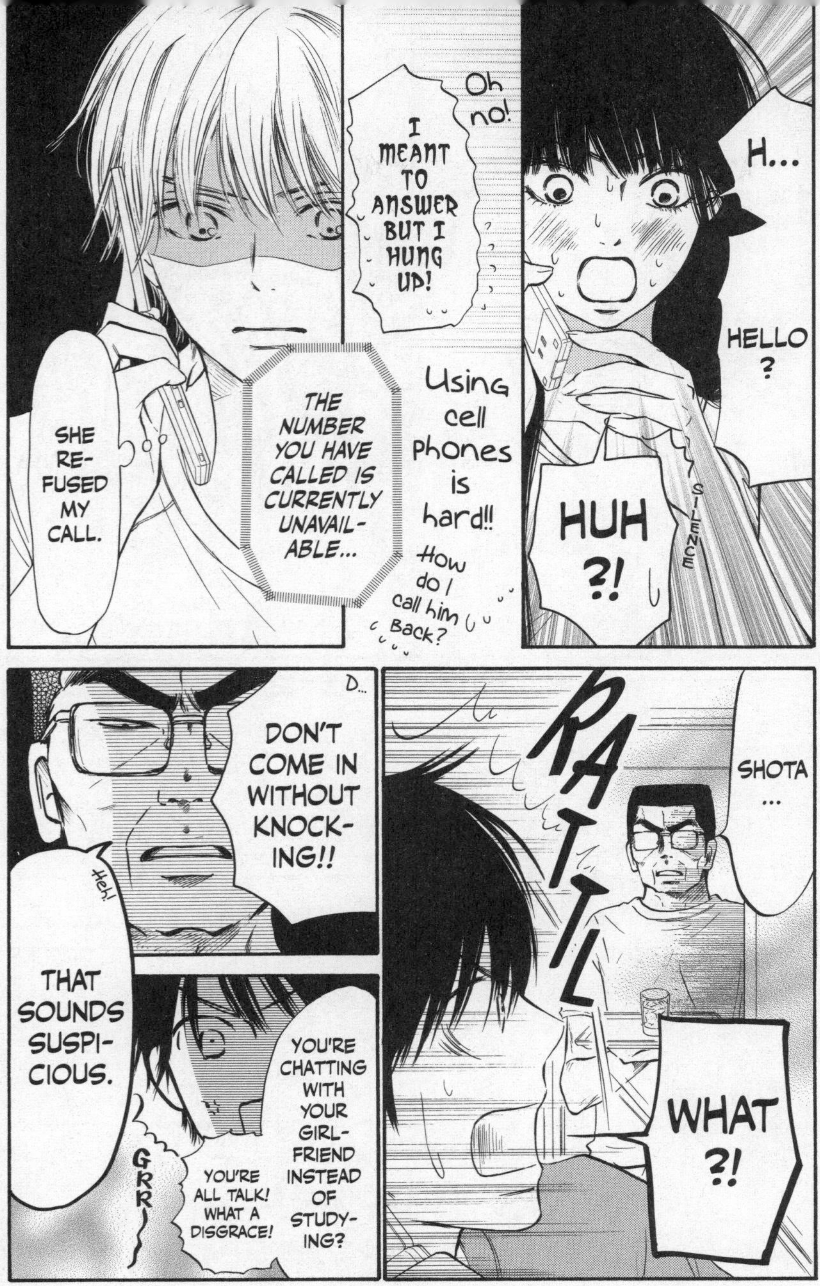
H...
HELLO ?
HUH ?!
SILENCE
Oh no!
I MEANT TO ANSWER BUT I HUNG UP!
Using cell phones is hard!!
How do I call him back?
THE NUMBER YOU HAVE CALLED IS CURRENTLY UNAVAIL-ABLE...
SHE RE-FUSED MY CALL.
SHOTA ...
RATTL
WHAT ?!
D...
DON'T COME IN WITHOUT KNOCK-ING!!
Heh!
YOU'RE CHATTING WITH YOUR GIRL-FRIEND INSTEAD OF STUDY-ING?
YOU'RE ALL TALK! WHAT A DISGRACE!
GRR
THAT SOUNDS SUSPI-CIOUS.

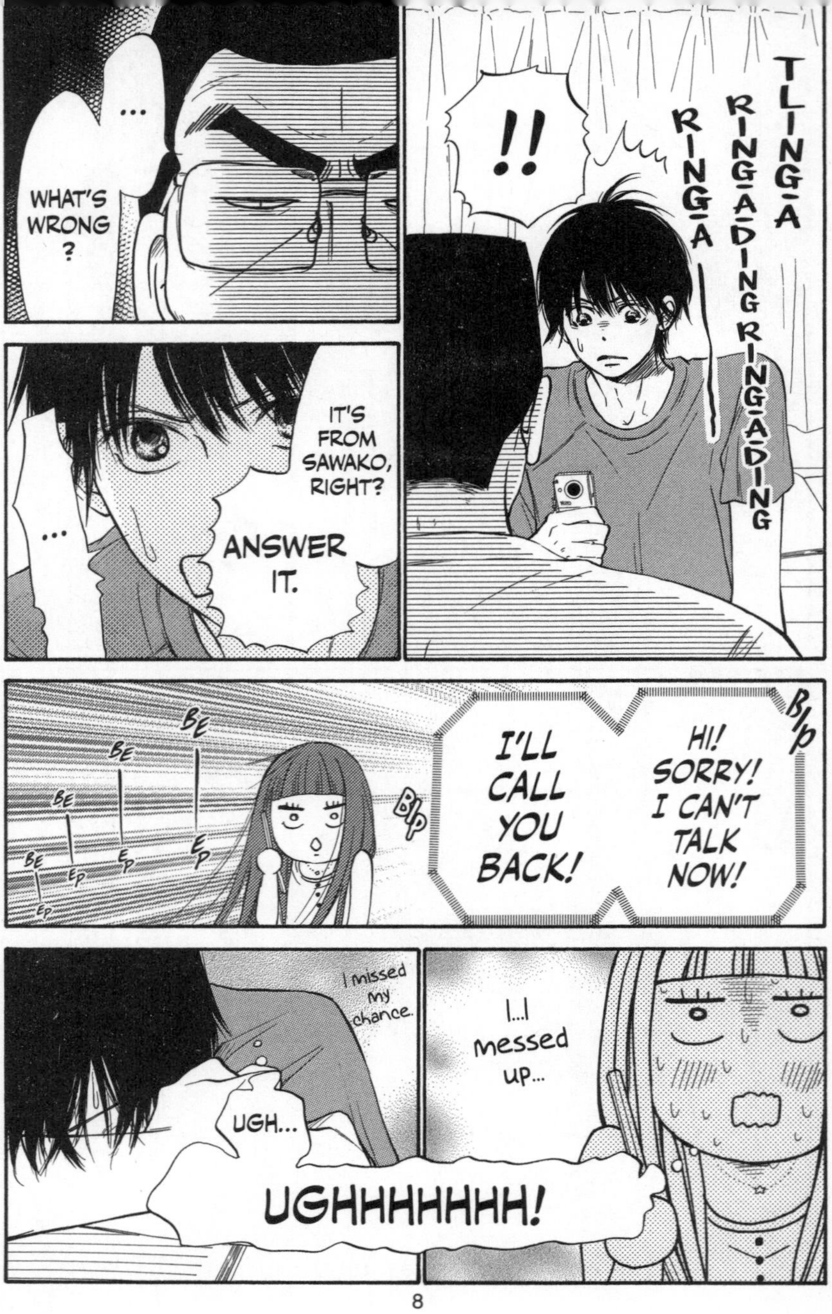
TLING-A RING-A-DING RING-A-DING
RING-A
!!
...
WHAT'S WRONG?
IT'S FROM SAWAKO, RIGHT?
ANSWER IT.
...
BIP
HI! SORRY! I CAN'T TALK NOW!
I'LL CALL YOU BACK!
BIP
BEEP BEEP BEEP BEEP
I...I messed up...
I missed my chance.
UGH...
UGHHHHHHH!

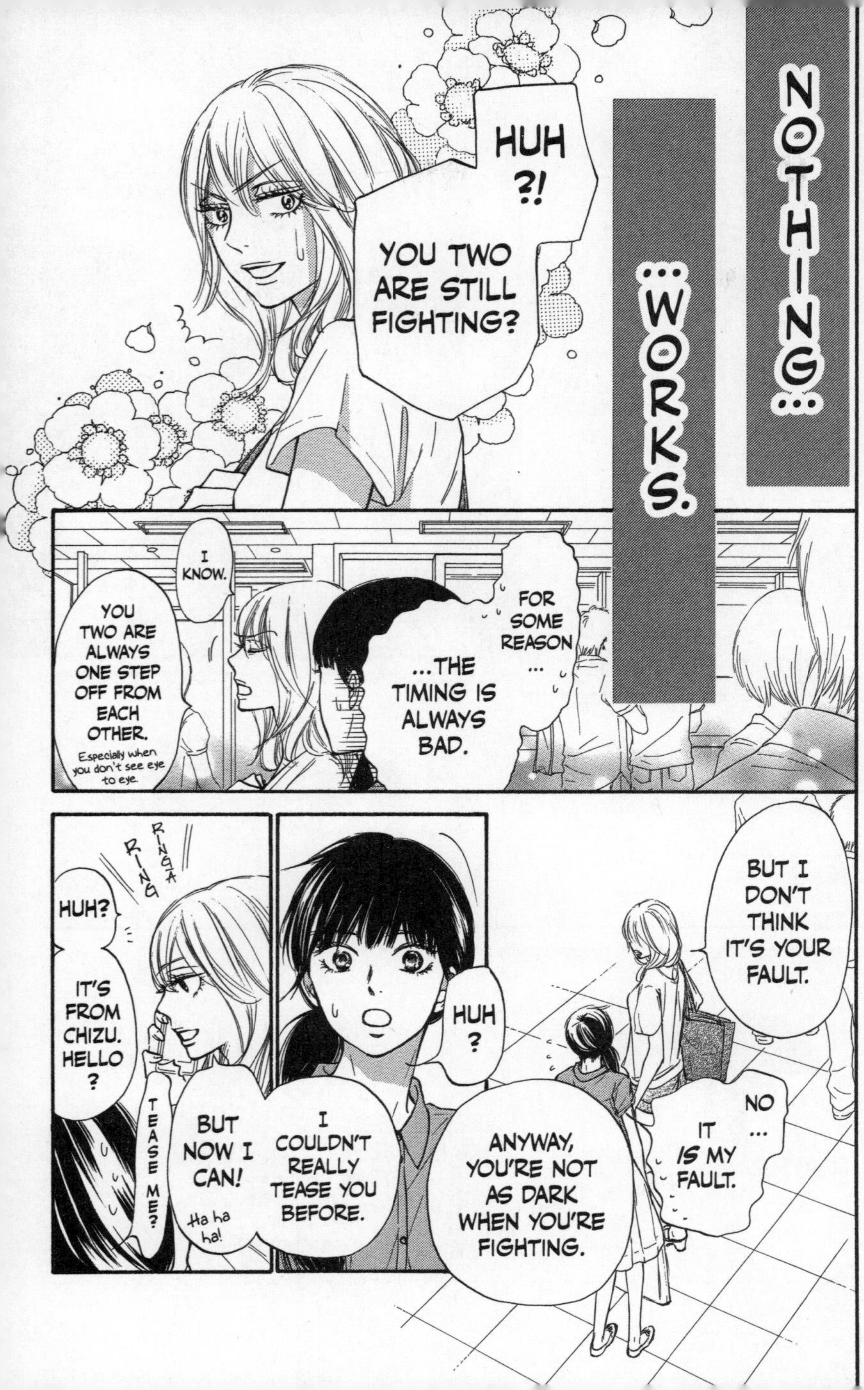
NOTHING...
...WORKS.
HUH?!
YOU TWO ARE STILL FIGHTING?
FOR SOME REASON...
...THE TIMING IS ALWAYS BAD.
I KNOW.
YOU TWO ARE ALWAYS ONE STEP OFF FROM EACH OTHER.
Especially when you don't see eye to eye.
BUT I DON'T THINK IT'S YOUR FAULT.
NO...
IT IS MY FAULT.
ANYWAY, YOU'RE NOT AS DARK WHEN YOU'RE FIGHTING.
HUH?
I COULDN'T REALLY TEASE YOU BEFORE.
BUT NOW I CAN!
Ha ha ha!
TEASE ME?
RINGA RING
HUH?
IT'S FROM CHIZU. HELLO?

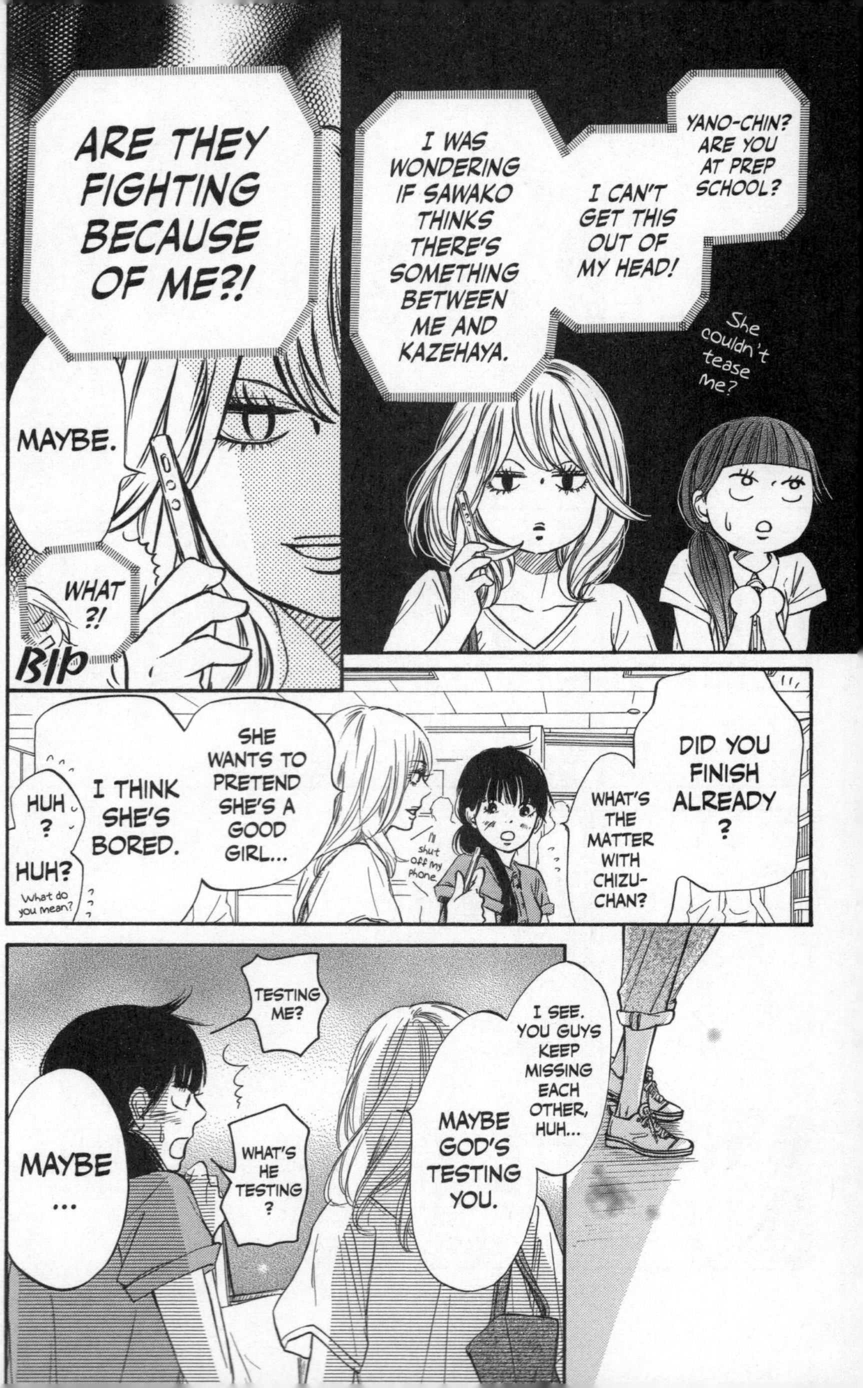
YANO-CHIN? ARE YOU AT PREP SCHOOL?
I CAN'T GET THIS OUT OF MY HEAD!
I WAS WONDERING IF SAWAKO THINKS THERE'S SOMETHING BETWEEN ME AND KAZEHAYA.
She couldn't tease me?
ARE THEY FIGHTING BECAUSE OF ME?!
MAYBE.
WHAT?!
BIP
DID YOU FINISH ALREADY?
WHAT'S THE MATTER WITH CHIZU-CHAN?
I'll shut off my phone.
SHE WANTS TO PRETEND SHE'S A GOOD GIRL...
I THINK SHE'S BORED.
HUH?
HUH?
What do you mean?
I SEE. YOU GUYS KEEP MISSING EACH OTHER, HUH...
MAYBE GOD'S TESTING YOU.
TESTING ME?
WHAT'S HE TESTING?
MAYBE...

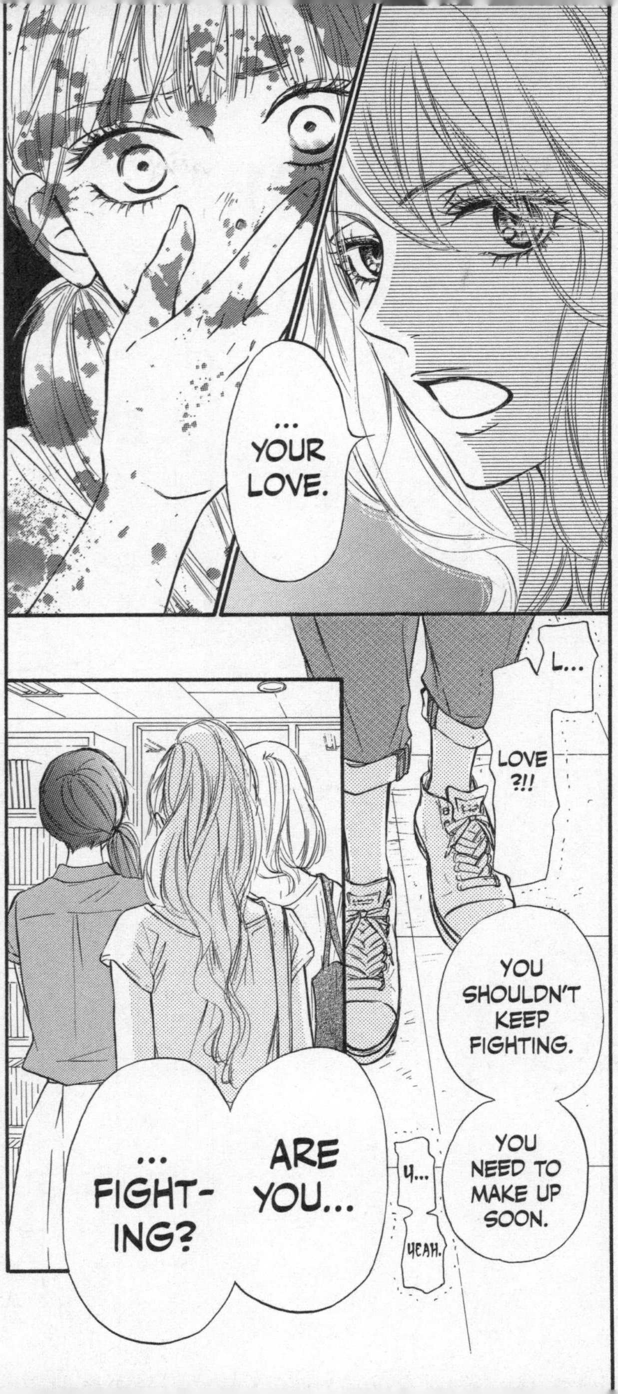
... YOUR LOVE.
L...
LOVE ?!!
YOU SHOULDN'T KEEP FIGHTING.
YOU NEED TO MAKE UP SOON.
Y... YEAH.
ARE YOU...
... FIGHT-ING?

KARUPIN on JAPAN 1

Hi! It's Shiina! How are you?

It's been a long time since I wrote sidebars.

It's March 2016. I had an autograph event for My Margaret in Sapporo last December.

Thank you to everyone who applied for tickets and showed up! I had a great time.

In the previous volume I wrote about aromatherapy and on Twitter I talked about tea, so some people brought me teas, scented items, handmade goods, flowers and letters!! Thank you all so much! For all the bath items...

I love taking baths! Thank you!

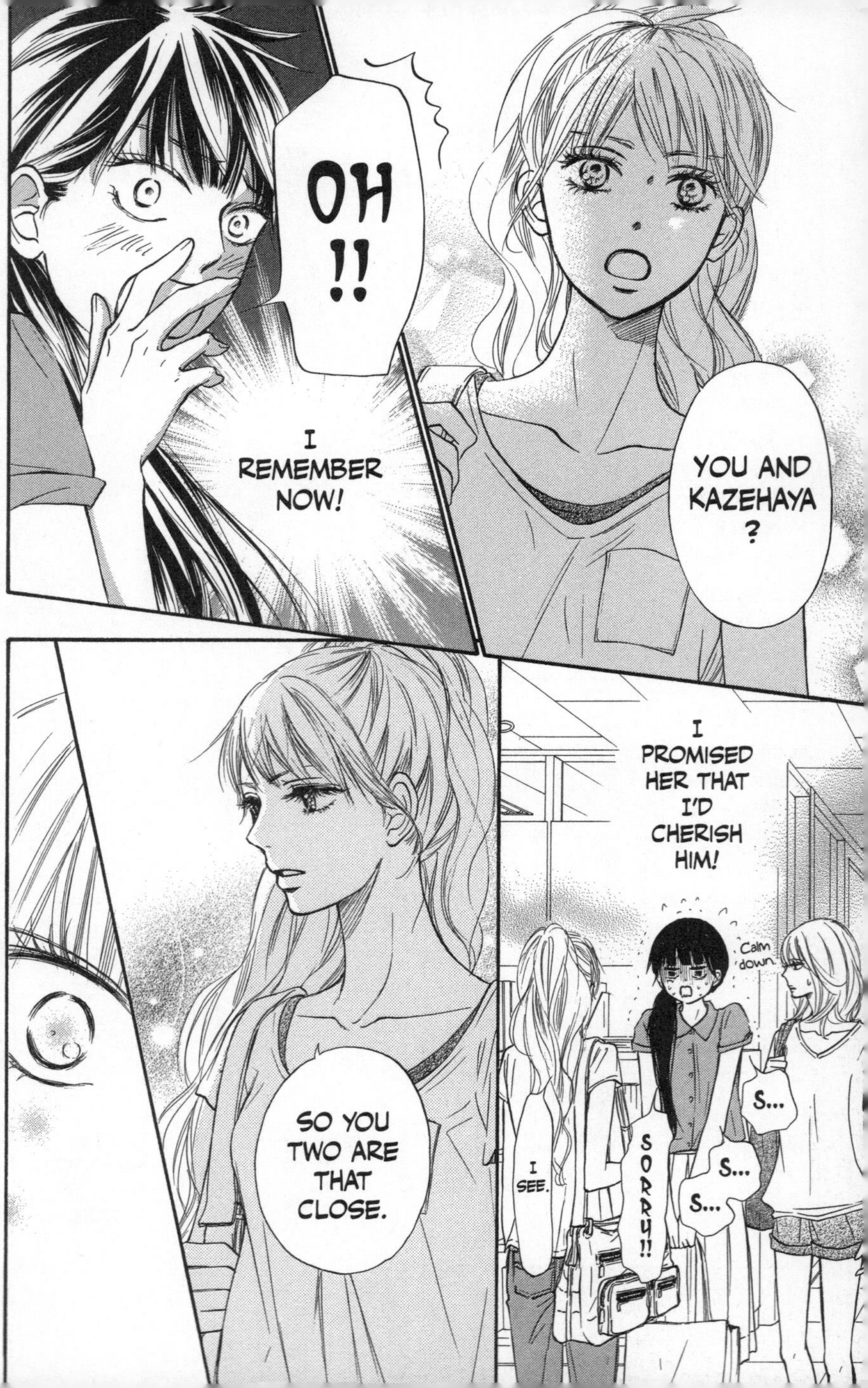
YOU AND KAZEHAYA?
OH!!
I REMEMBER NOW!
I PROMISED HER THAT I'D CHERISH HIM!
Calm down.
S...
S...
S...
SORRY!!
I SEE.
SO YOU TWO ARE THAT CLOSE.

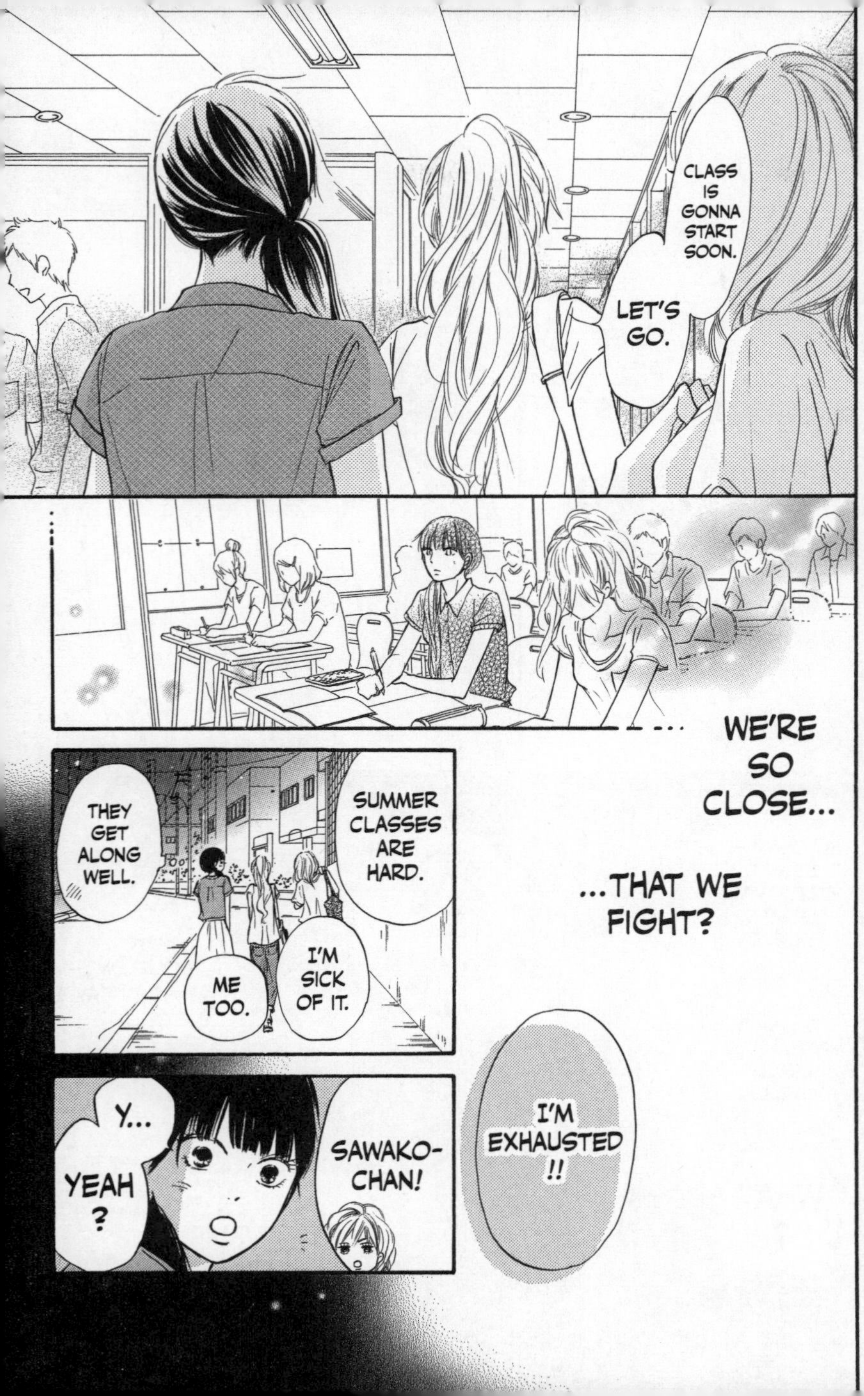
CLASS IS GONNA START SOON.
LET'S GO.
......
WE'RE SO CLOSE...
...THAT WE FIGHT?
SUMMER CLASSES ARE HARD.
I'M SICK OF IT.
ME TOO.
THEY GET ALONG WELL.
I'M EXHAUSTED!!
SAWAKO-CHAN!
Y... YEAH?

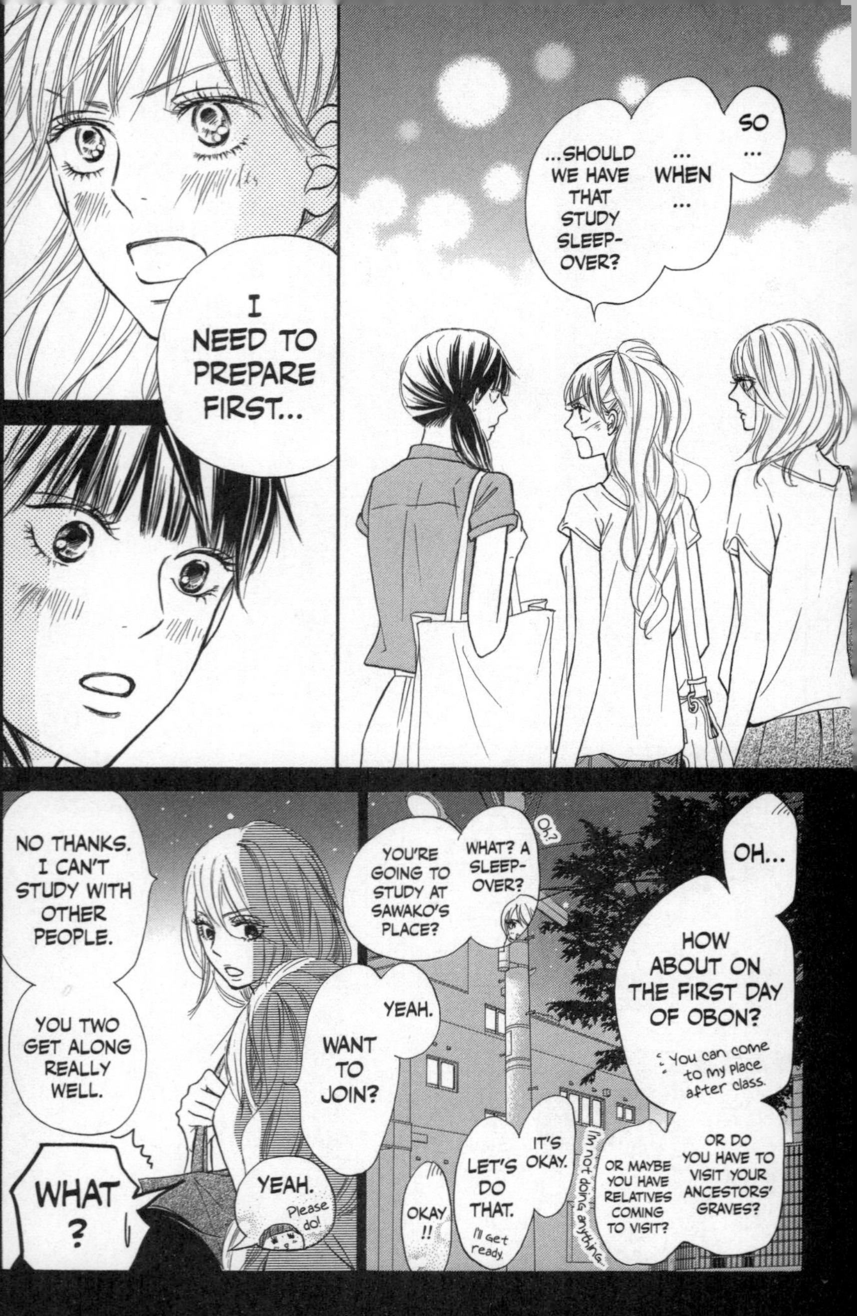
SO ...
... WHEN ...
...SHOULD WE HAVE THAT STUDY SLEEP-OVER?
I NEED TO PREPARE FIRST...
OH...
HOW ABOUT ON THE FIRST DAY OF OBON?
You can come to my place after class.
OR DO YOU HAVE TO VISIT YOUR ANCESTORS' GRAVES?
OR MAYBE YOU HAVE RELATIVES COMING TO VISIT?
I'm not doing anything...
IT'S OKAY.
LET'S DO THAT.
I'll get ready.
OKAY !!
Oh?
WHAT? A SLEEP-OVER?
YOU'RE GOING TO STUDY AT SAWAKO'S PLACE?
YEAH.
WANT TO JOIN?
YEAH.
Please do!
NO THANKS. I CAN'T STUDY WITH OTHER PEOPLE.
YOU TWO GET ALONG REALLY WELL.
WHAT ?

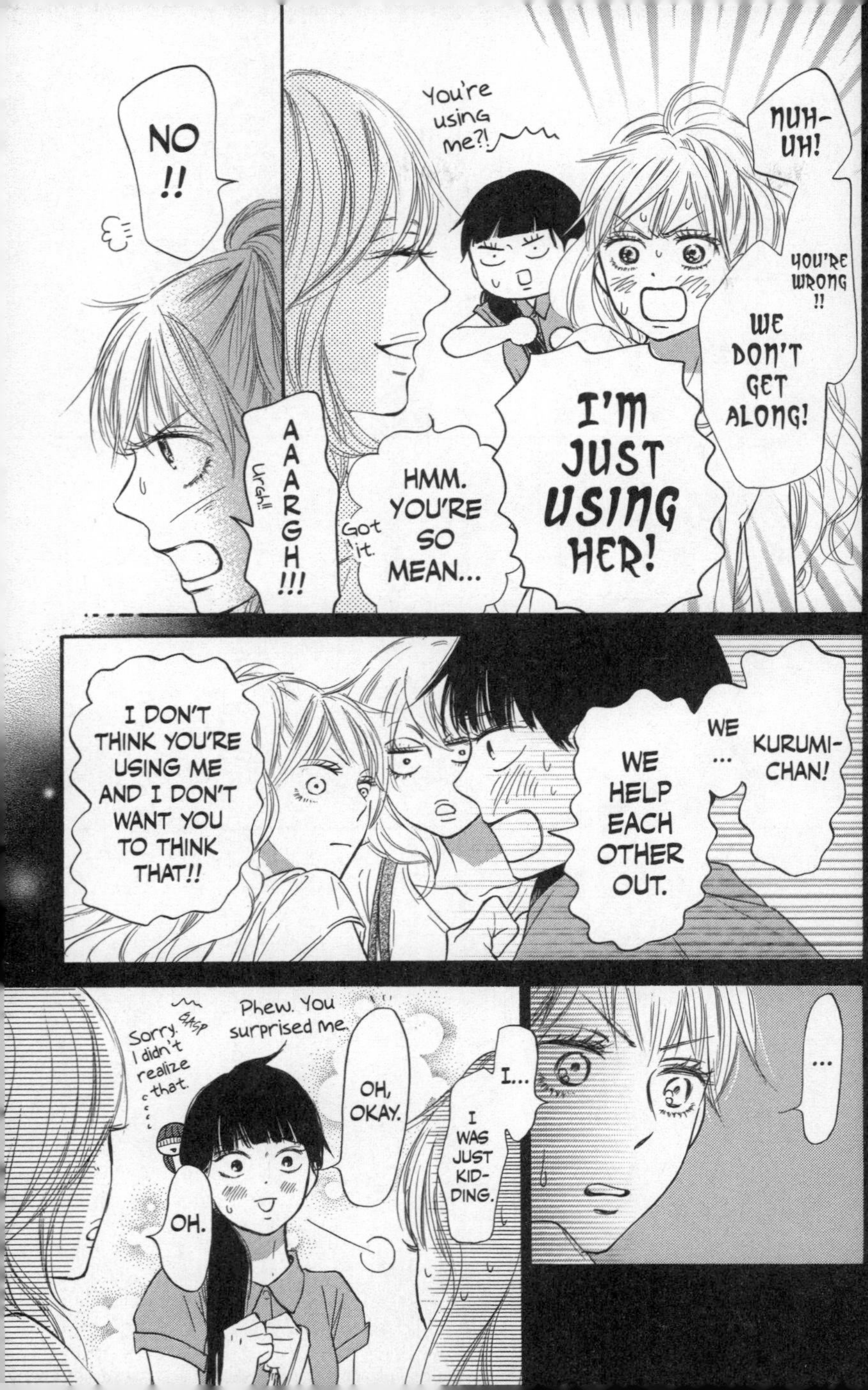
NUH-UH!
YOU'RE WRONG !!
WE DON'T GET ALONG!
You're using me?!
I'M JUST USING HER!
HMM. YOU'RE SO MEAN...
Got it.
NO !!
AAAARGH!!!
Urgh!!
KURUMI-CHAN!
WE ...
WE HELP EACH OTHER OUT.
I DON'T THINK YOU'RE USING ME AND I DON'T WANT YOU TO THINK THAT!!
...
I...
I WAS JUST KID-DING.
OH, OKAY.
Phew. You surprised me.
OH.
GASP
Sorry. I didn't realize that.

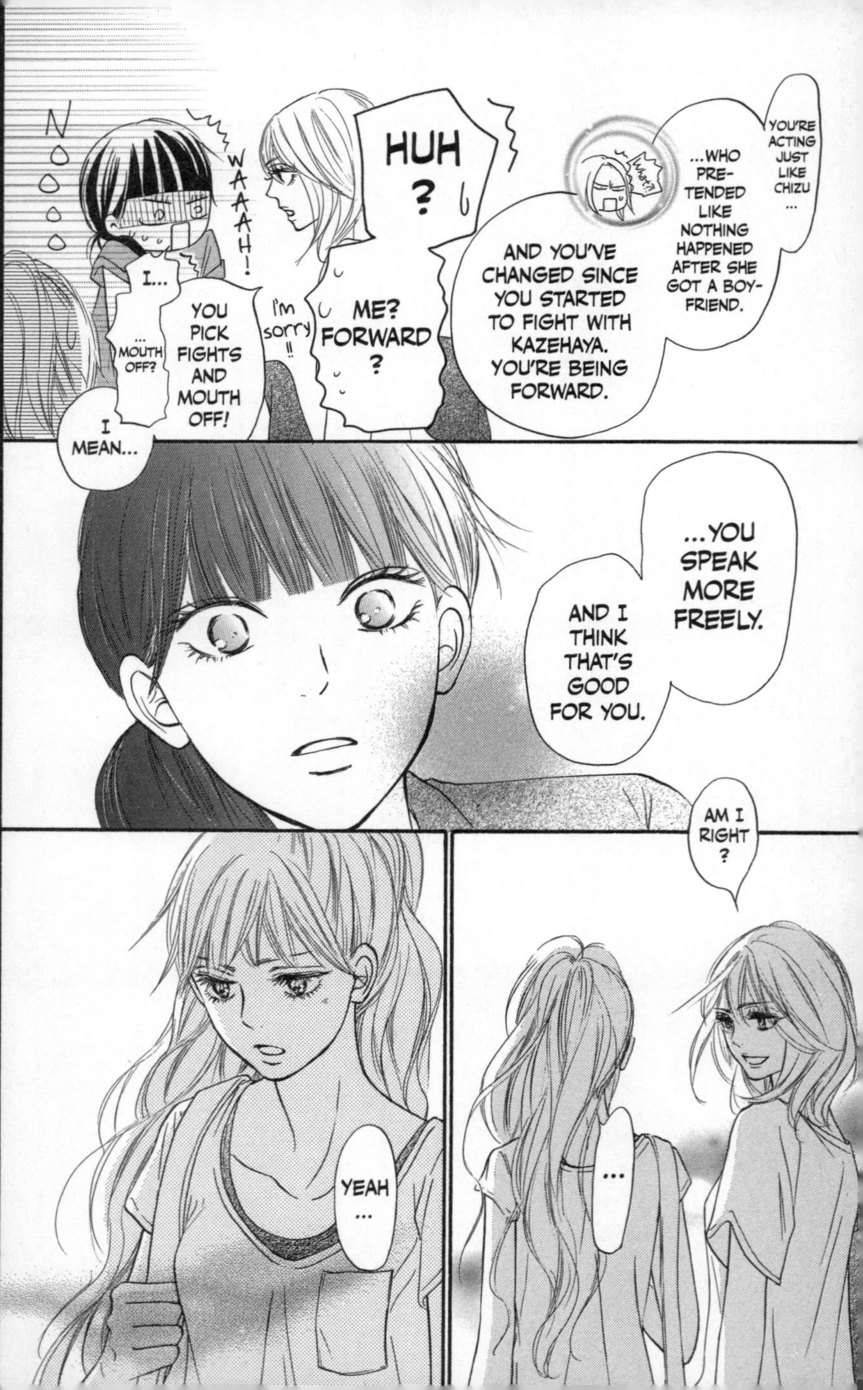
YOU'RE ACTING JUST LIKE CHIZU...
...WHO PRE-TENDED LIKE NOTHING HAPPENED AFTER SHE GOT A BOY-FRIEND.
What?!
AND YOU'VE CHANGED SINCE YOU STARTED TO FIGHT WITH KAZEHAYA. YOU'RE BEING FORWARD.
HUH?
ME? FORWARD?
I'm sorry!!
WAAAAH!
YOU PICK FIGHTS AND MOUTH OFF!
I...
...MOUTH OFF?
NOOOOO
I MEAN...
...YOU SPEAK MORE FREELY.
AND I THINK THAT'S GOOD FOR YOU.
AM I RIGHT?
...
YEAH...

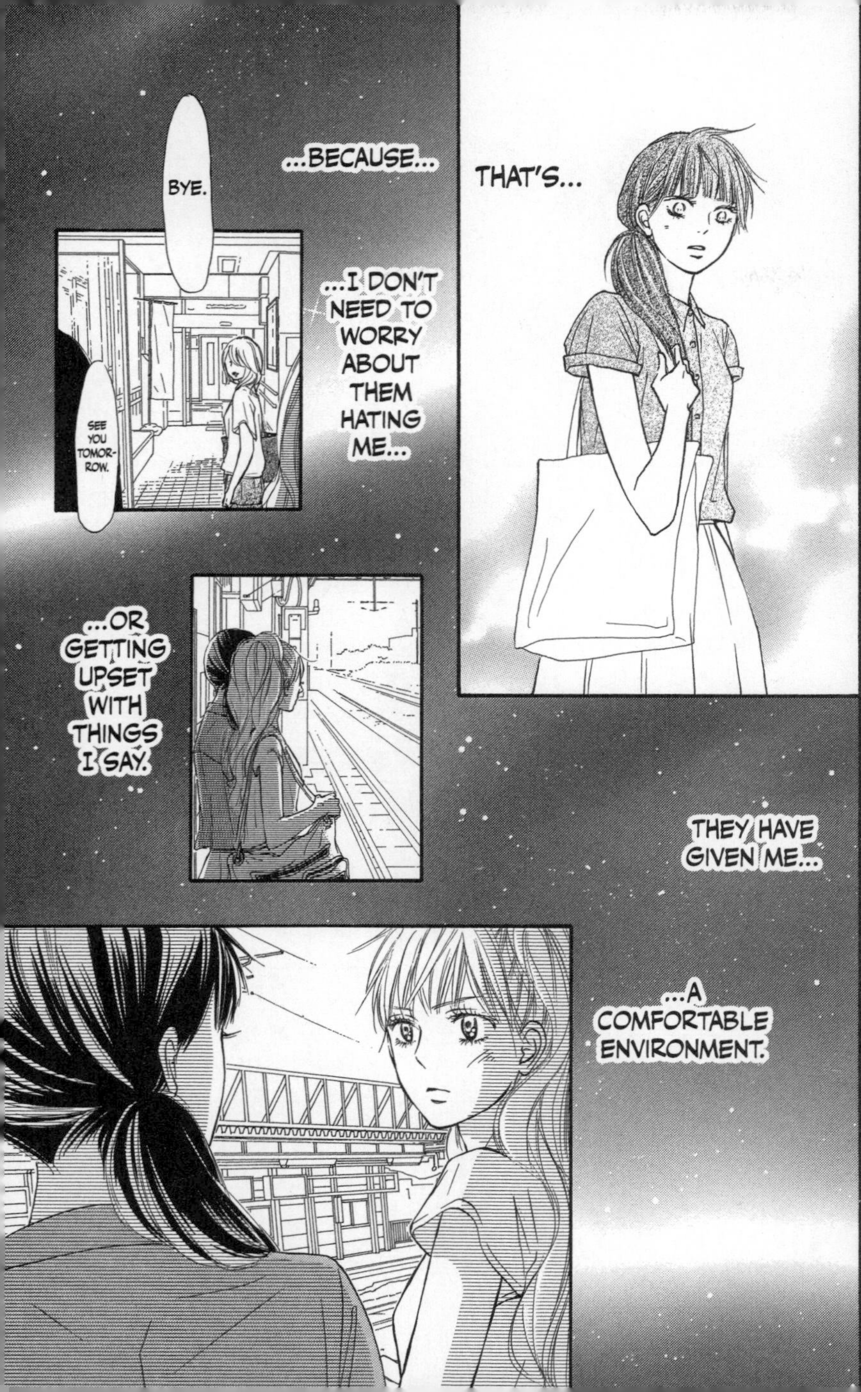
THAT'S...
...BECAUSE...
BYE.
SEE YOU TOMORROW.
...I DON'T NEED TO WORRY ABOUT THEM HATING ME...
...OR GETTING UPSET WITH THINGS I SAY.
THEY HAVE GIVEN ME...
...A COMFORTABLE ENVIRONMENT.

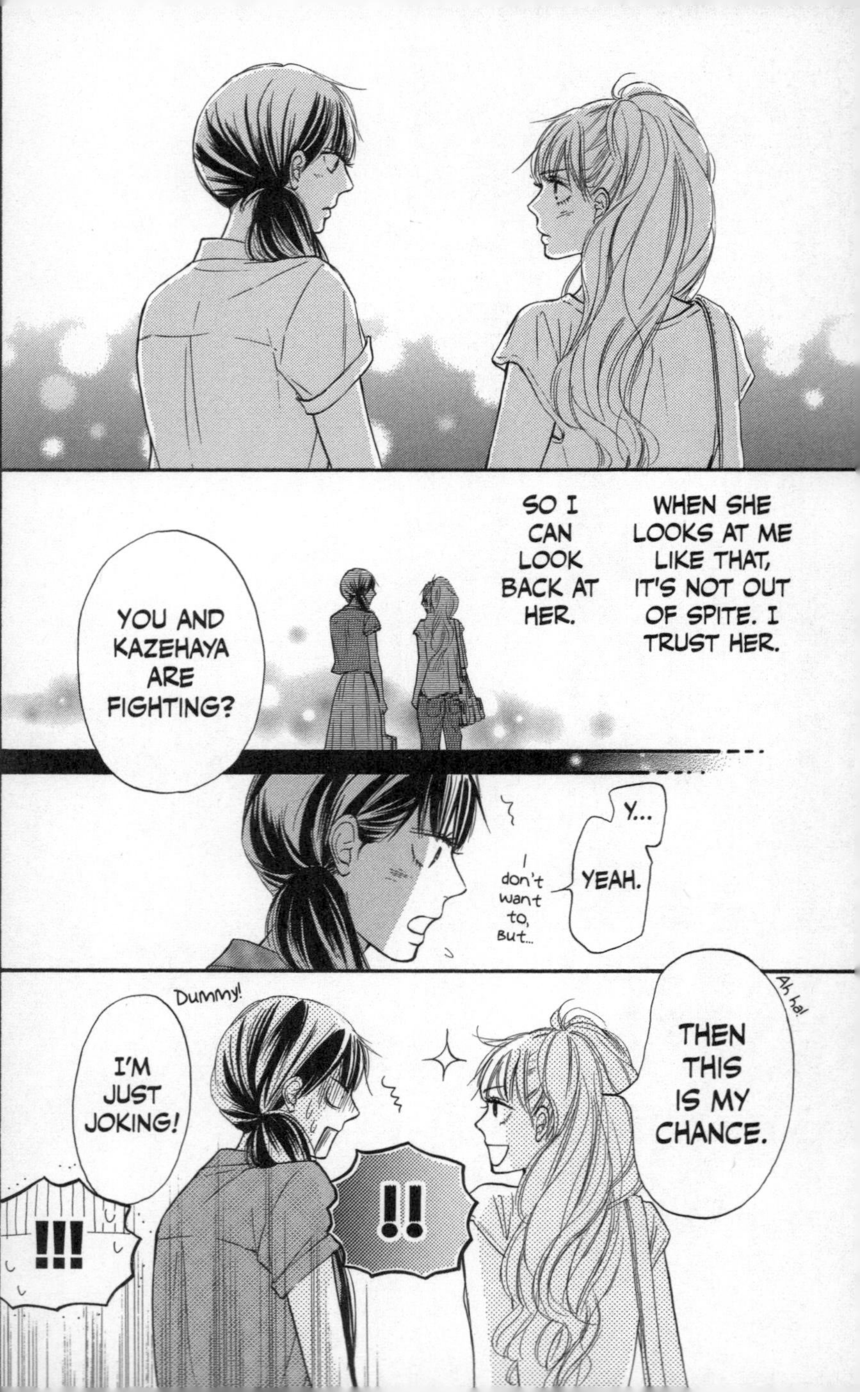
WHEN SHE LOOKS AT ME LIKE THAT, IT'S NOT OUT OF SPITE. I TRUST HER.
SO I CAN LOOK BACK AT HER.
YOU AND KAZEHAYA ARE FIGHTING?
Y... YEAH.
I don't want to, but...
Ah ha!
THEN THIS IS MY CHANCE.
!!
Dummy!
I'M JUST JOKING!
!!!

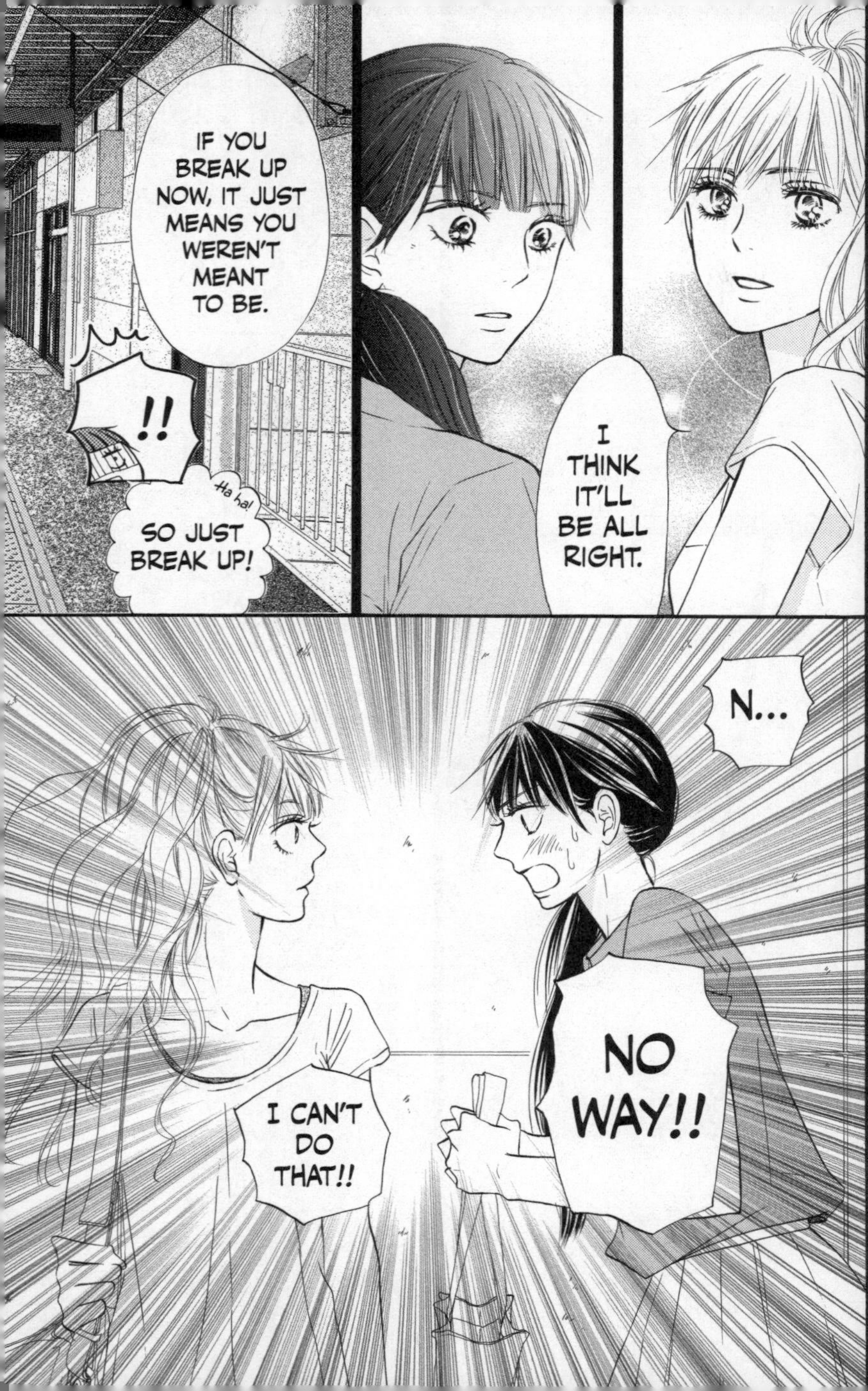
I THINK IT'LL BE ALL RIGHT.
IF YOU BREAK UP NOW, IT JUST MEANS YOU WEREN'T MEANT TO BE.
!!
Ha ha!
SO JUST BREAK UP!
N...
NO WAY!!
I CAN'T DO THAT!!

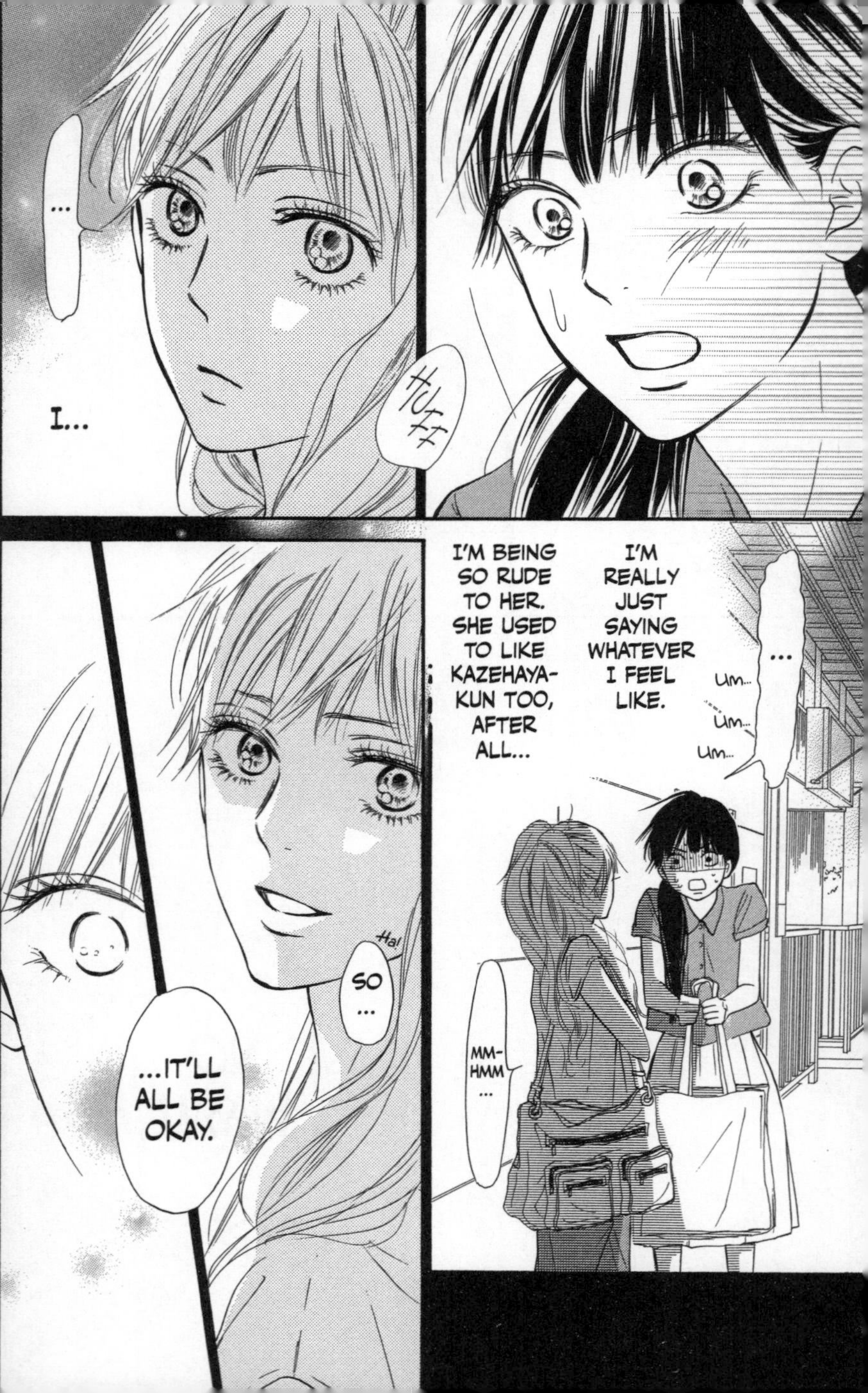
HUFF
...
I...
I'M REALLY JUST SAYING WHATEVER I FEEL LIKE.
I'M BEING SO RUDE TO HER. SHE USED TO LIKE KAZEHAYA-KUN TOO, AFTER ALL...
...
Um...
Um...
Um...
MM-HMM ...
Ha!
SO ...
...IT'LL ALL BE OKAY.

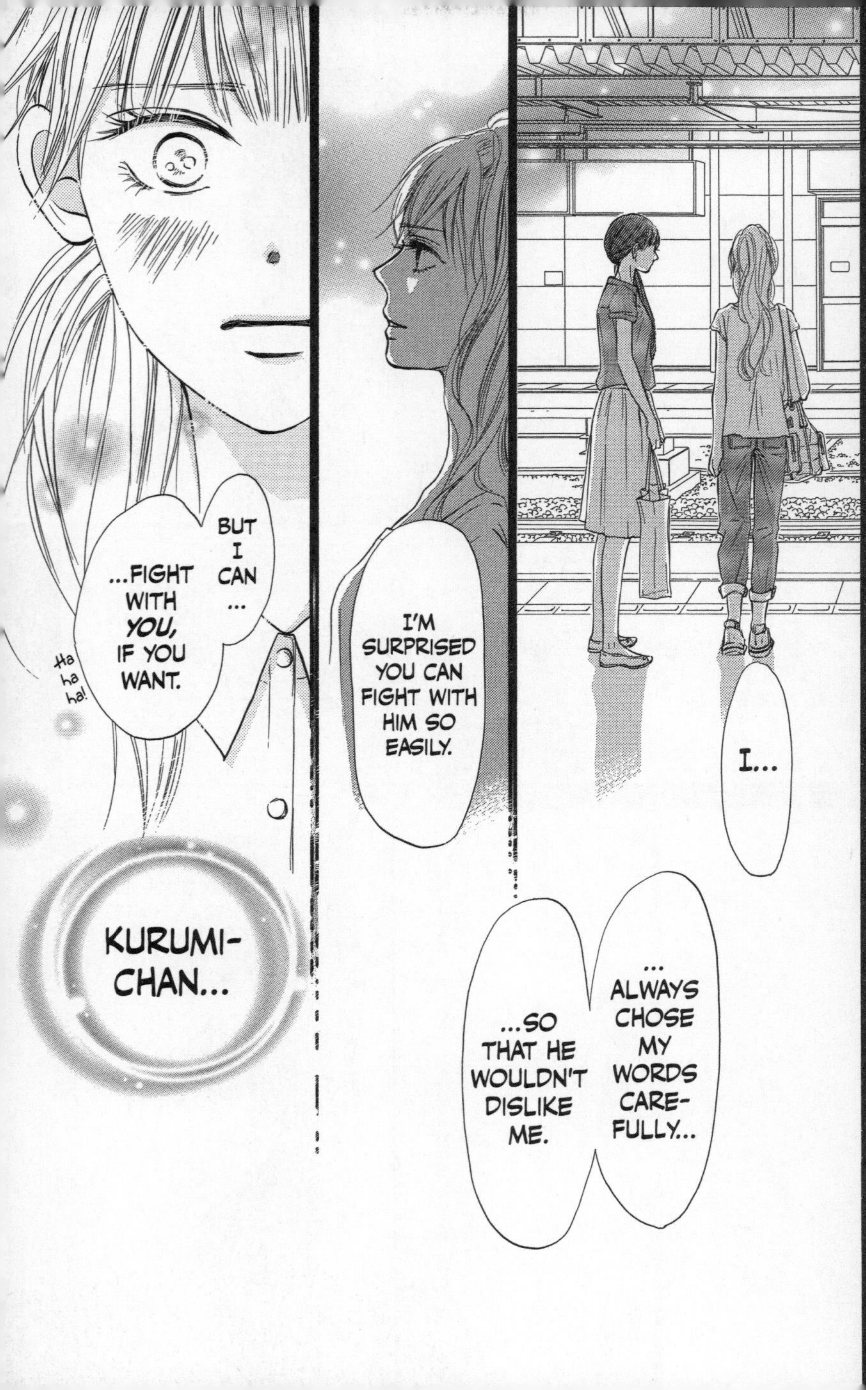
I...
...ALWAYS CHOSE MY WORDS CAREFULLY...
...SO THAT HE WOULDN'T DISLIKE ME.
I'M SURPRISED YOU CAN FIGHT WITH HIM SO EASILY.
BUT I CAN...
...FIGHT WITH *YOU,* IF YOU WANT.
Ha ha ha!
KURUMI-CHAN...

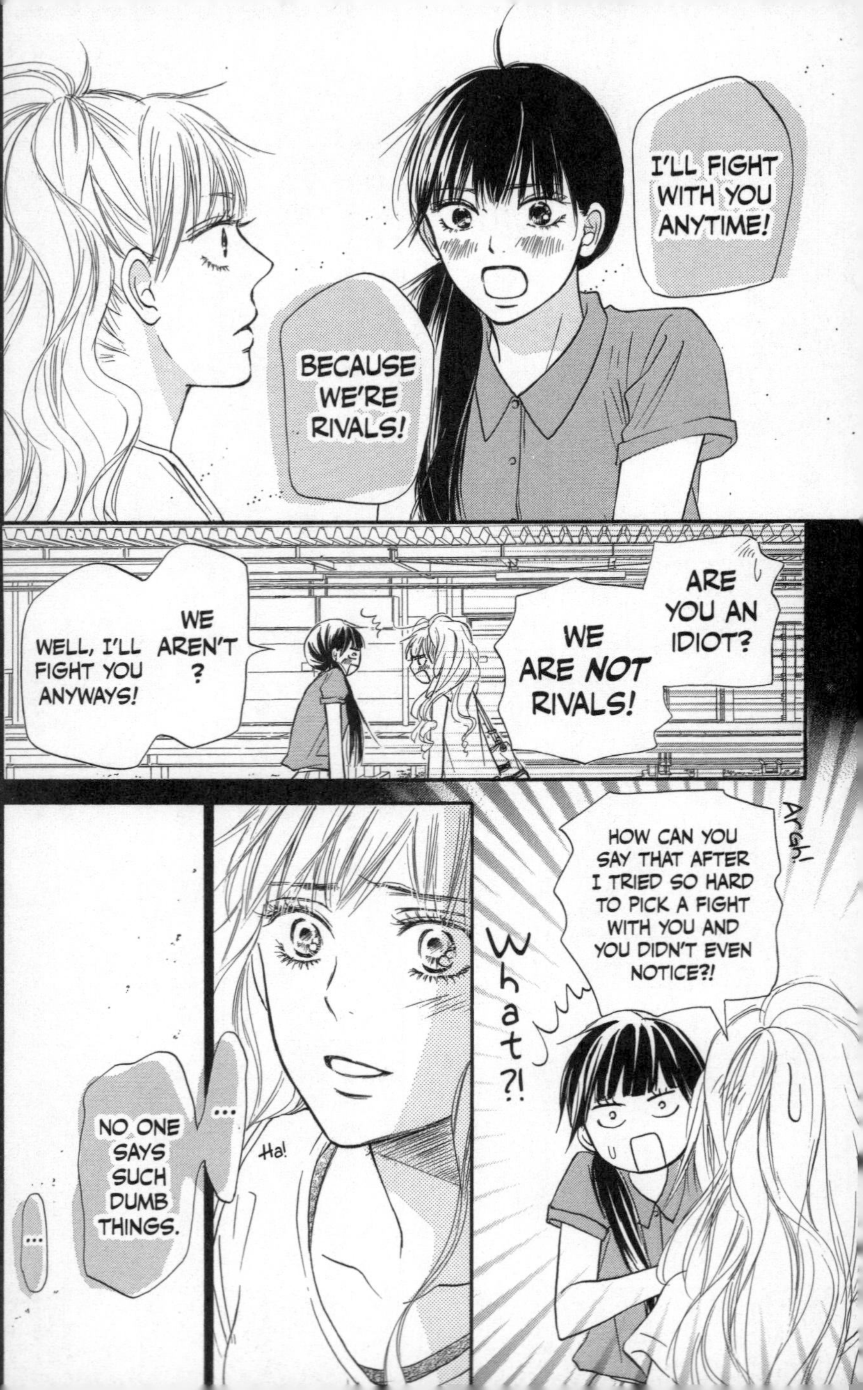

I'LL FIGHT WITH YOU ANYTIME!
BECAUSE WE'RE RIVALS!
ARE YOU AN IDIOT?
WE ARE *NOT* RIVALS!
WE AREN'T ?
WELL, I'LL FIGHT YOU ANYWAYS!
Argh!
HOW CAN YOU SAY THAT AFTER I TRIED SO HARD TO PICK A FIGHT WITH YOU AND YOU DIDN'T EVEN NOTICE?!
What?!
...
Ha!
NO ONE SAYS SUCH DUMB THINGS.
...

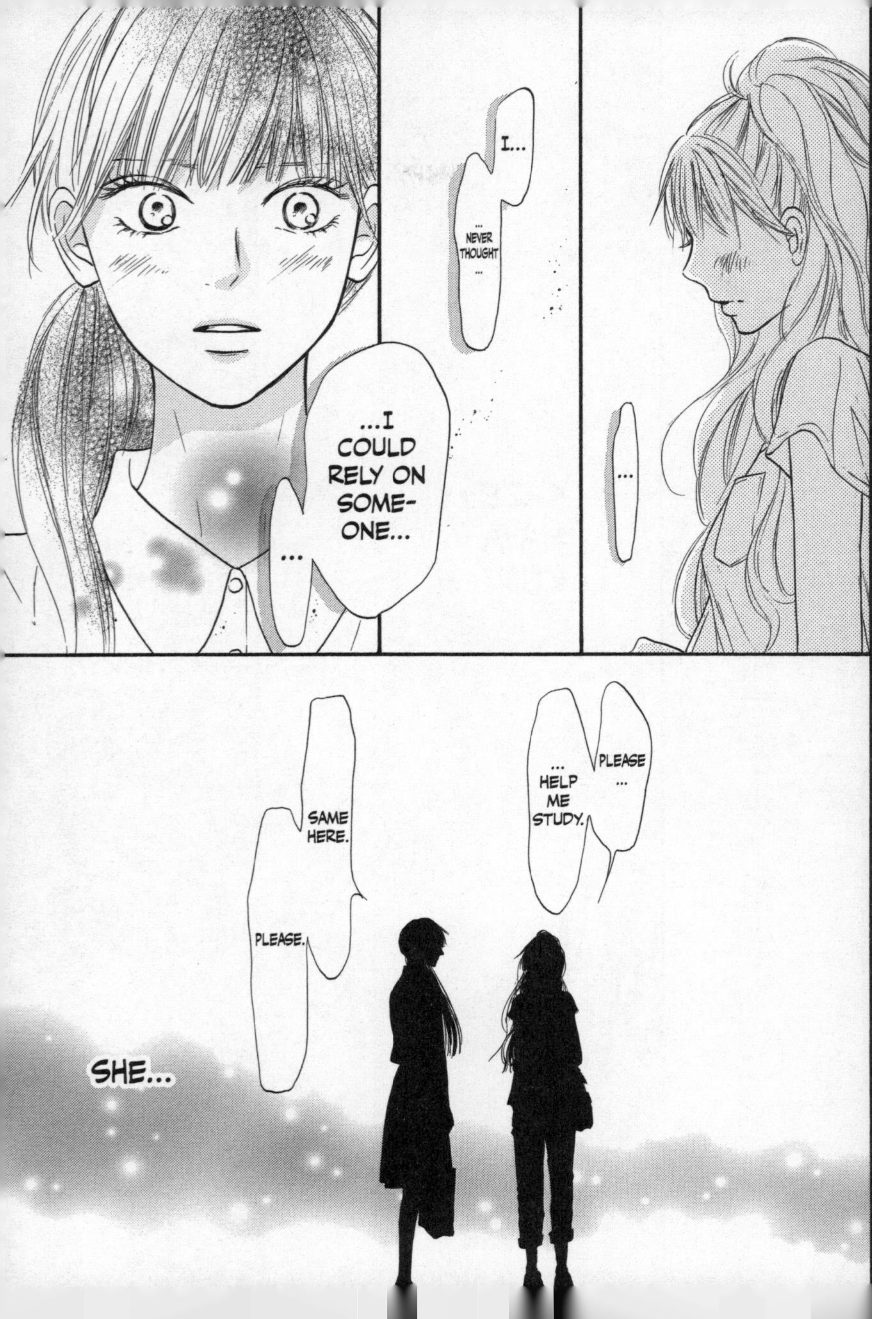
...
I...
...NEVER THOUGHT...
...I COULD RELY ON SOME-ONE...
...
PLEASE...
...HELP ME STUDY.
SAME HERE.
PLEASE.
SHE...

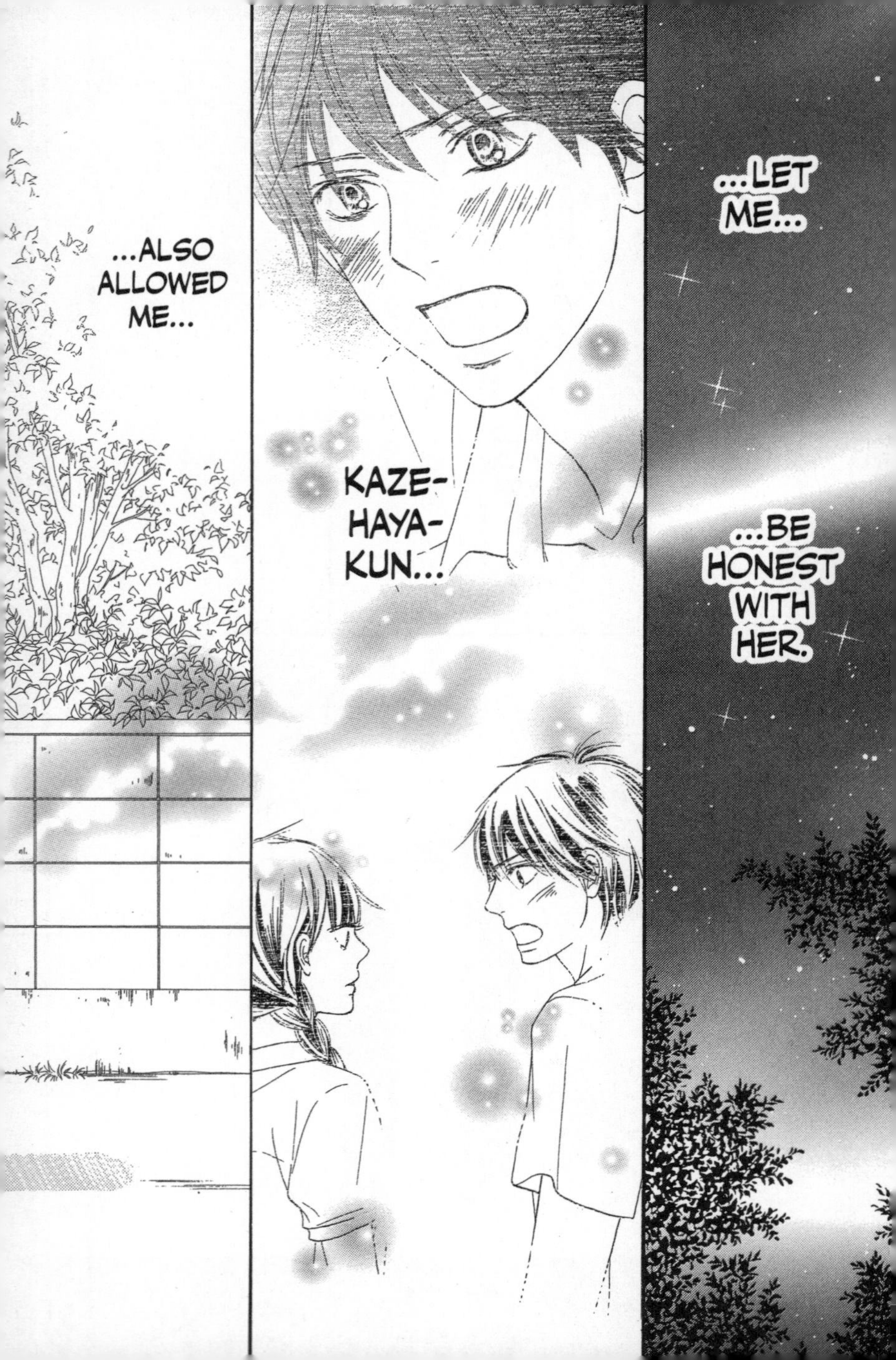
...LET ME...
...BE HONEST WITH HER.
KAZE-HAYA-KUN...
...ALSO ALLOWED ME...

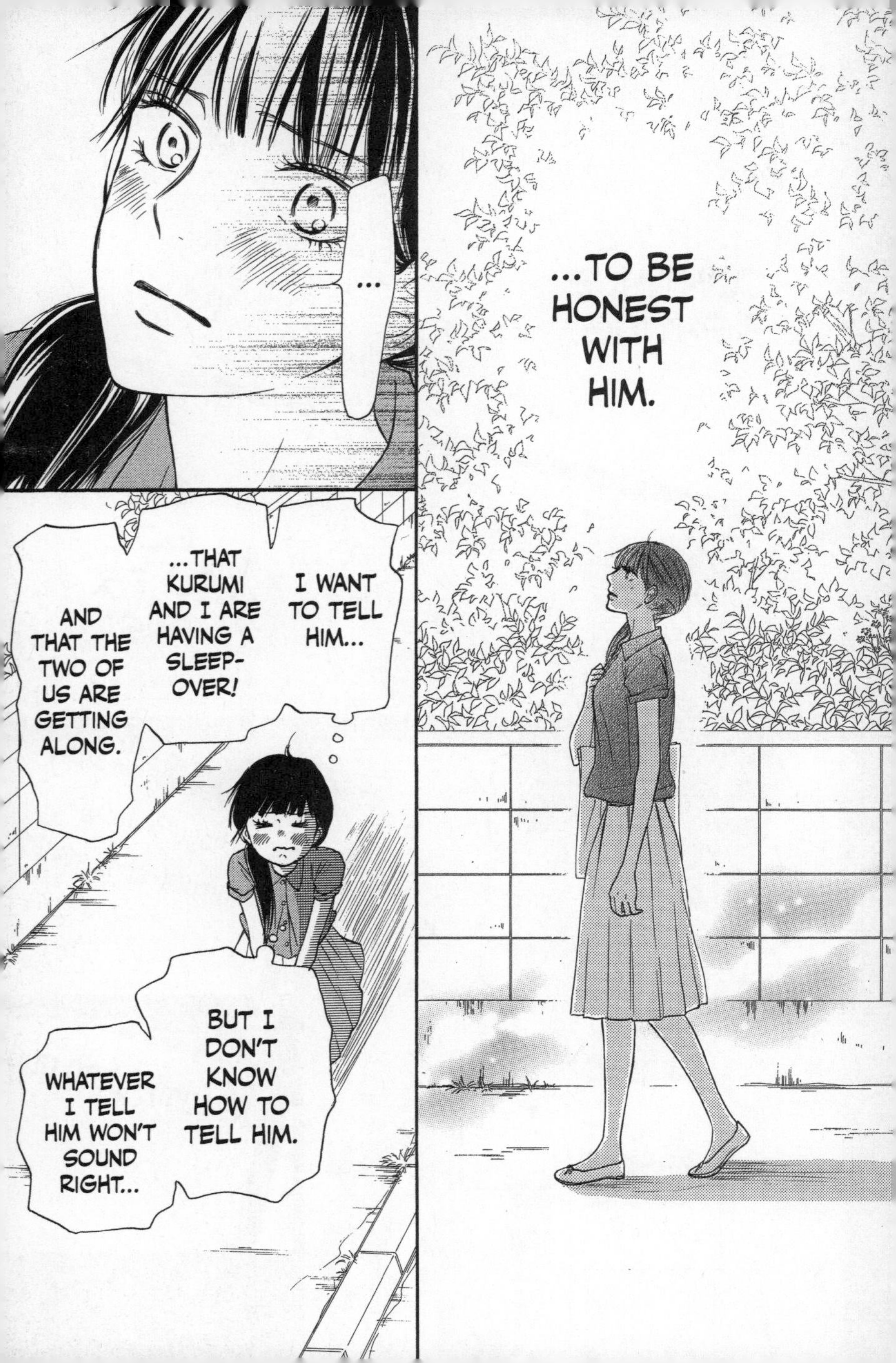
...TO BE HONEST WITH HIM.
...
I WANT TO TELL HIM...
...THAT KURUMI AND I ARE HAVING A SLEEP-OVER!
AND THAT THE TWO OF US ARE GETTING ALONG.
BUT I DON'T KNOW HOW TO TELL HIM.
WHATEVER I TELL HIM WON'T SOUND RIGHT...

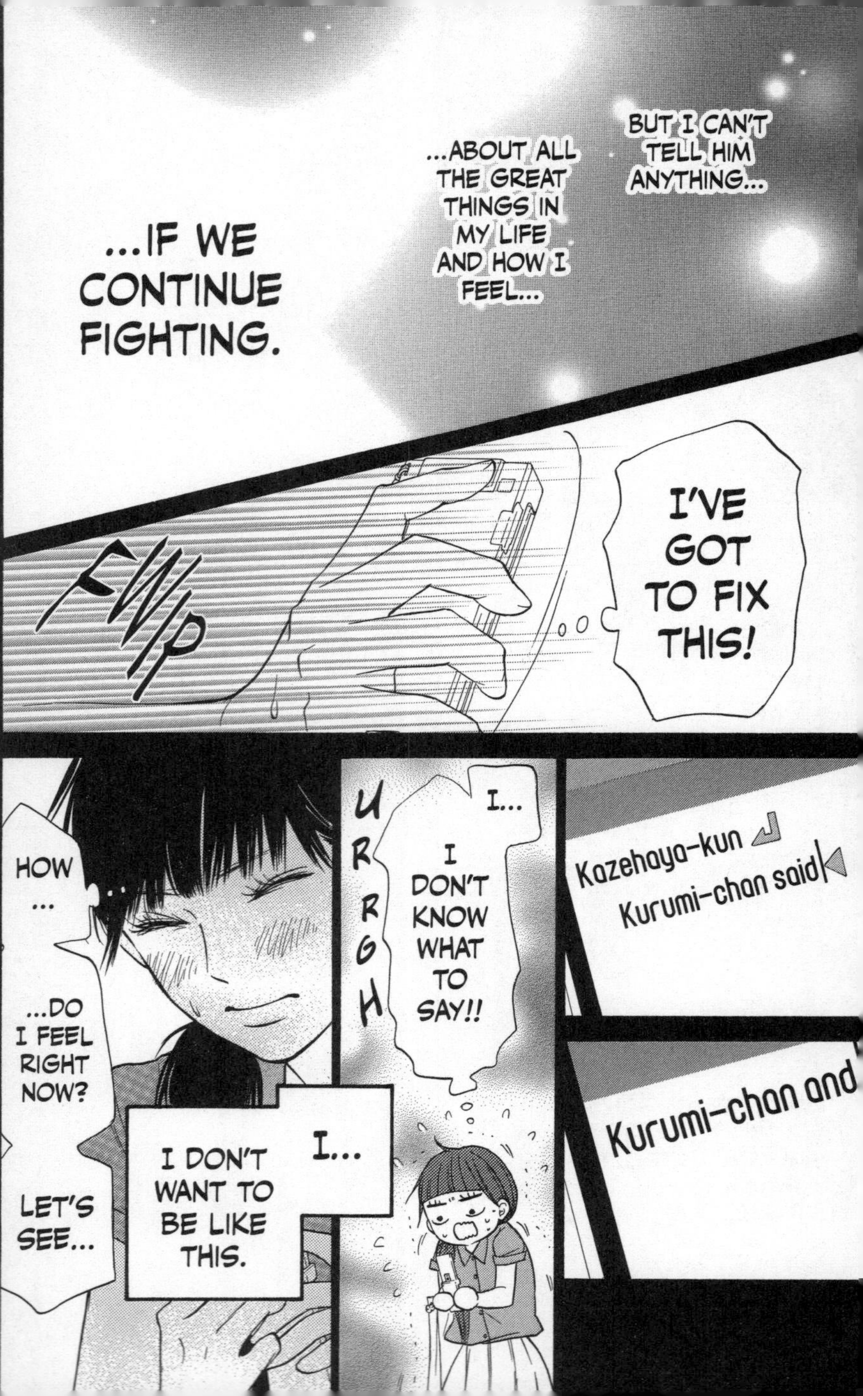
BUT I CAN'T TELL HIM ANYTHING...
...ABOUT ALL THE GREAT THINGS IN MY LIFE AND HOW I FEEL...
...IF WE CONTINUE FIGHTING.
I'VE GOT TO FIX THIS!
FLIP
Kazehaya-kun
Kurumi-chan said
Kurumi-chan and
URRGH
I...
I DON'T KNOW WHAT TO SAY!!
HOW...
...DO I FEEL RIGHT NOW?
LET'S SEE...
I...
I DON'T WANT TO BE LIKE THIS.

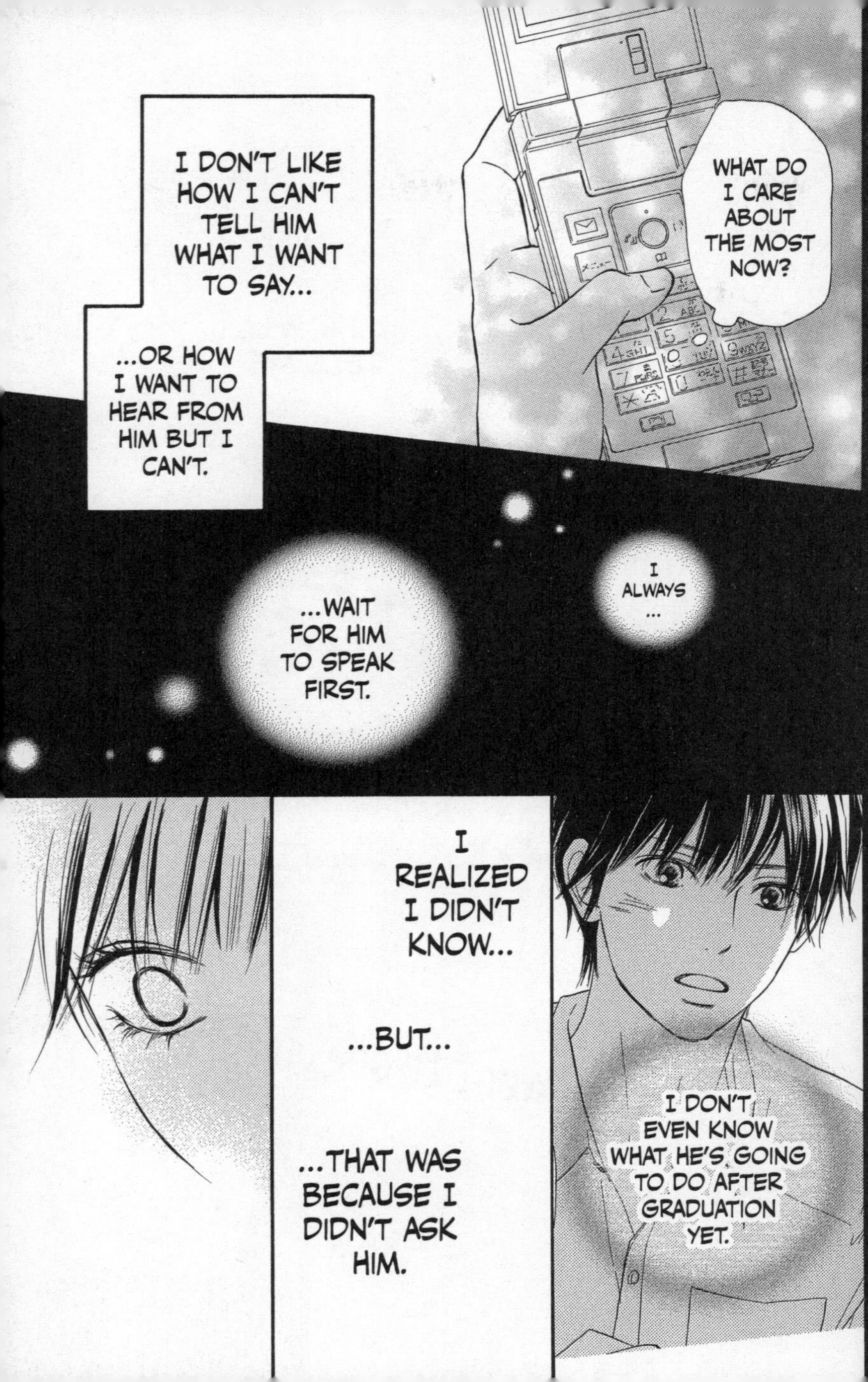
WHAT DO I CARE ABOUT THE MOST NOW?
I DON'T LIKE HOW I CAN'T TELL HIM WHAT I WANT TO SAY...
...OR HOW I WANT TO HEAR FROM HIM BUT I CAN'T.
I ALWAYS...
...WAIT FOR HIM TO SPEAK FIRST.
I DON'T EVEN KNOW WHAT HE'S GOING TO DO AFTER GRADUATION YET.
I REALIZED I DIDN'T KNOW...
...BUT...
...THAT WAS BECAUSE I DIDN'T ASK HIM.

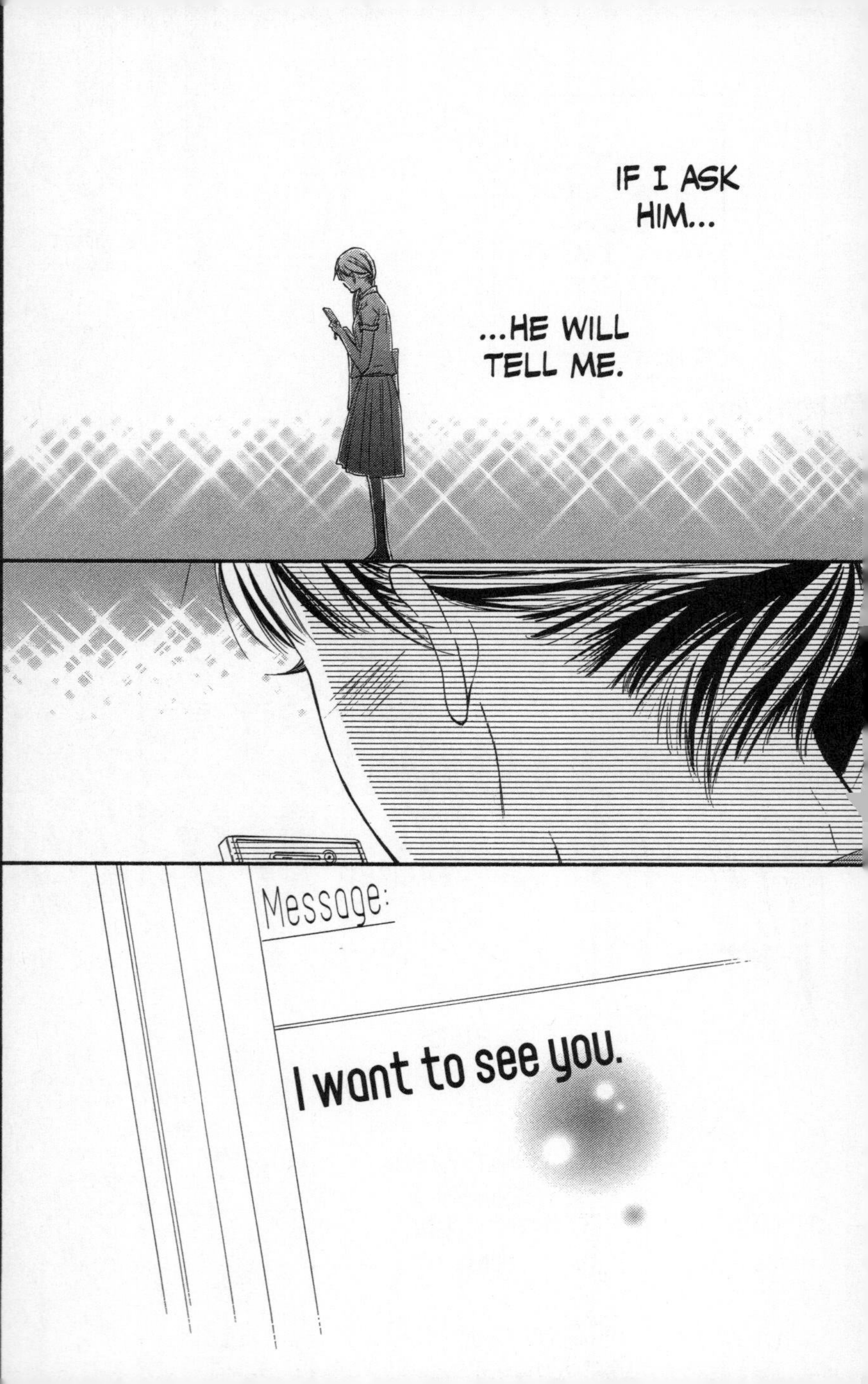
IF I ASK HIM...
...HE WILL TELL ME.
Message:
I want to see you.

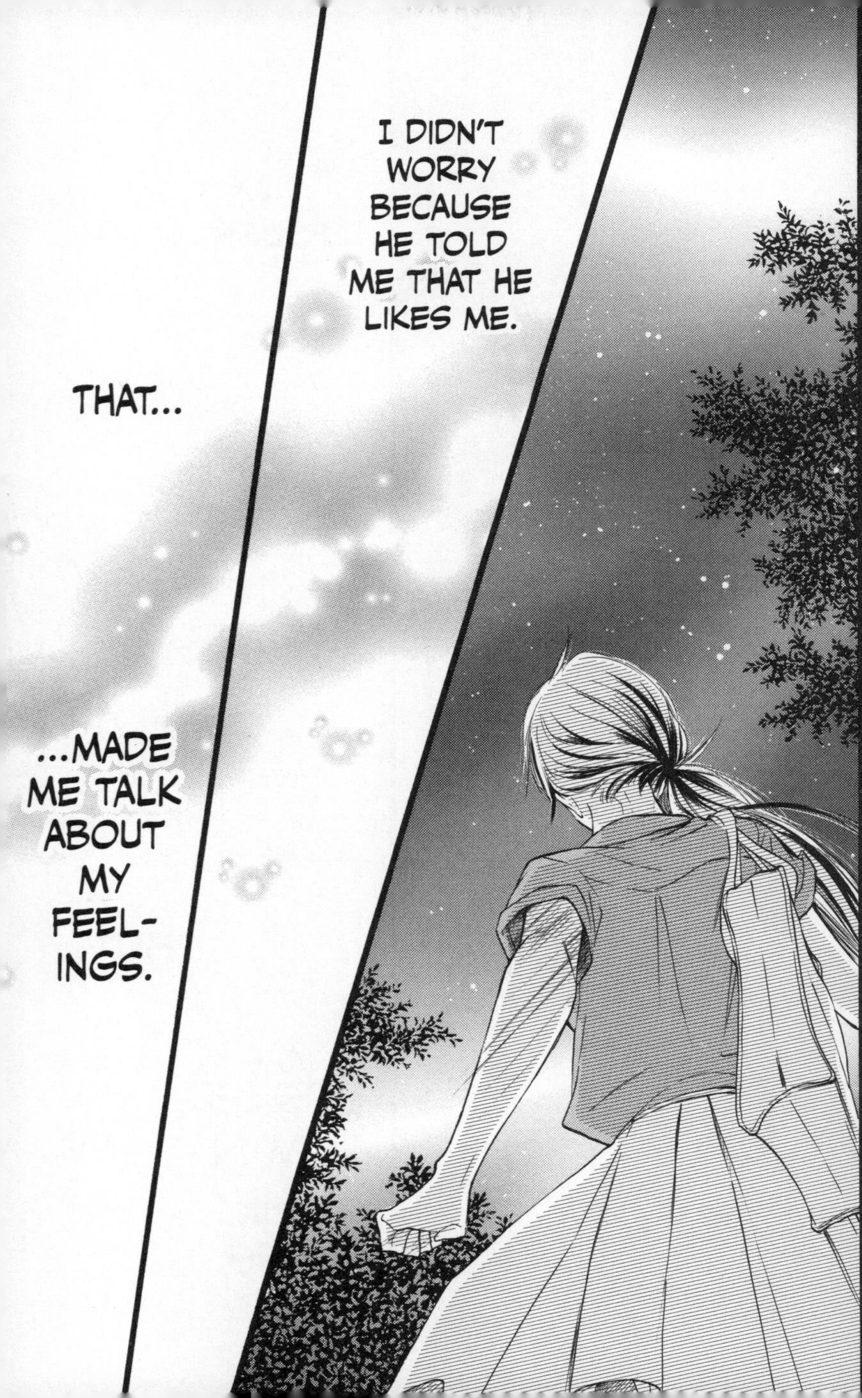
I DIDN'T WORRY BECAUSE HE TOLD ME THAT HE LIKES ME.
THAT...
...MADE ME TALK ABOUT MY FEEL-INGS.

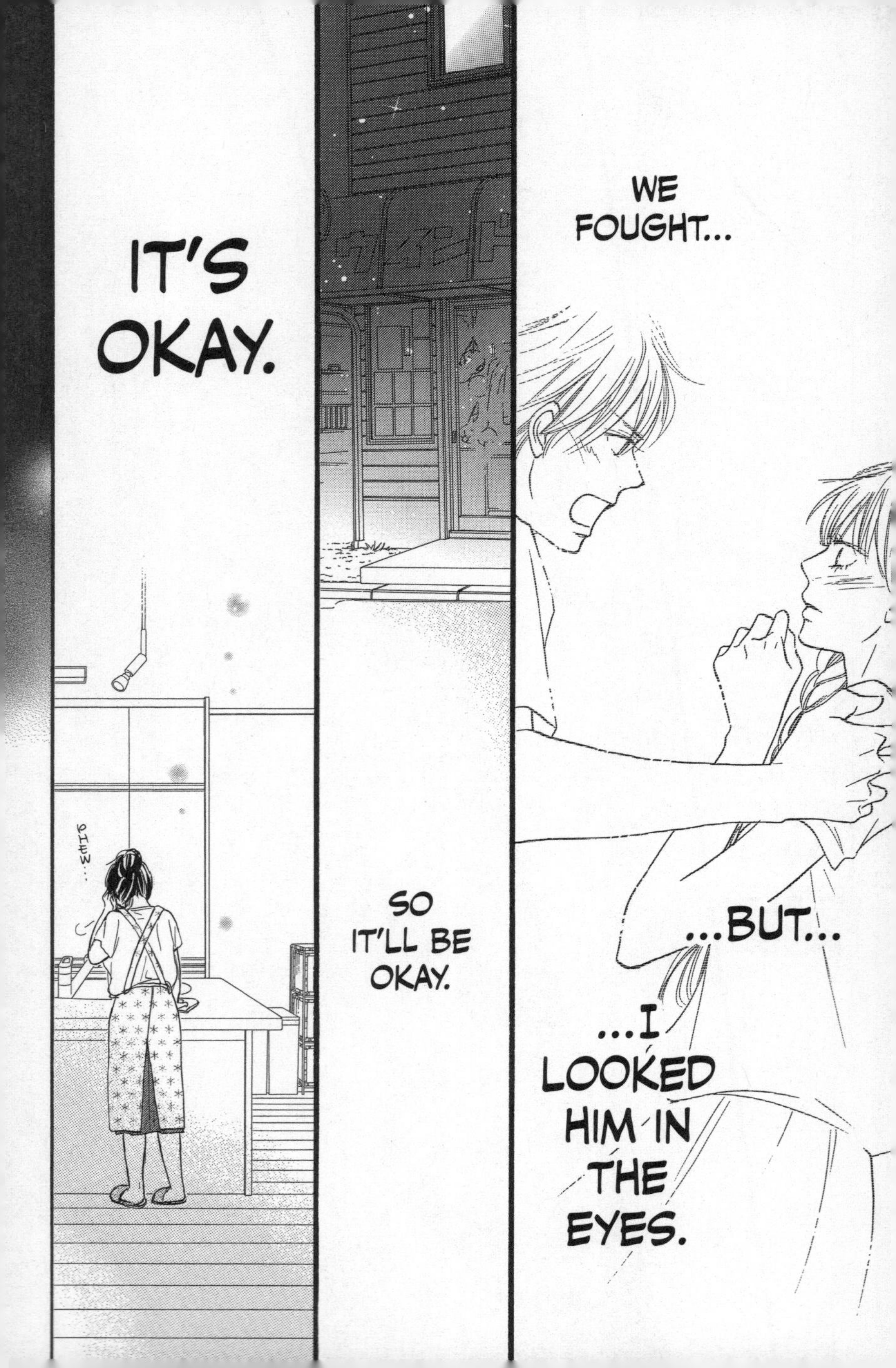
WE FOUGHT...
...BUT...
...I LOOKED HIM IN THE EYES.
SO IT'LL BE OKAY.
IT'S OKAY.
PHEW...

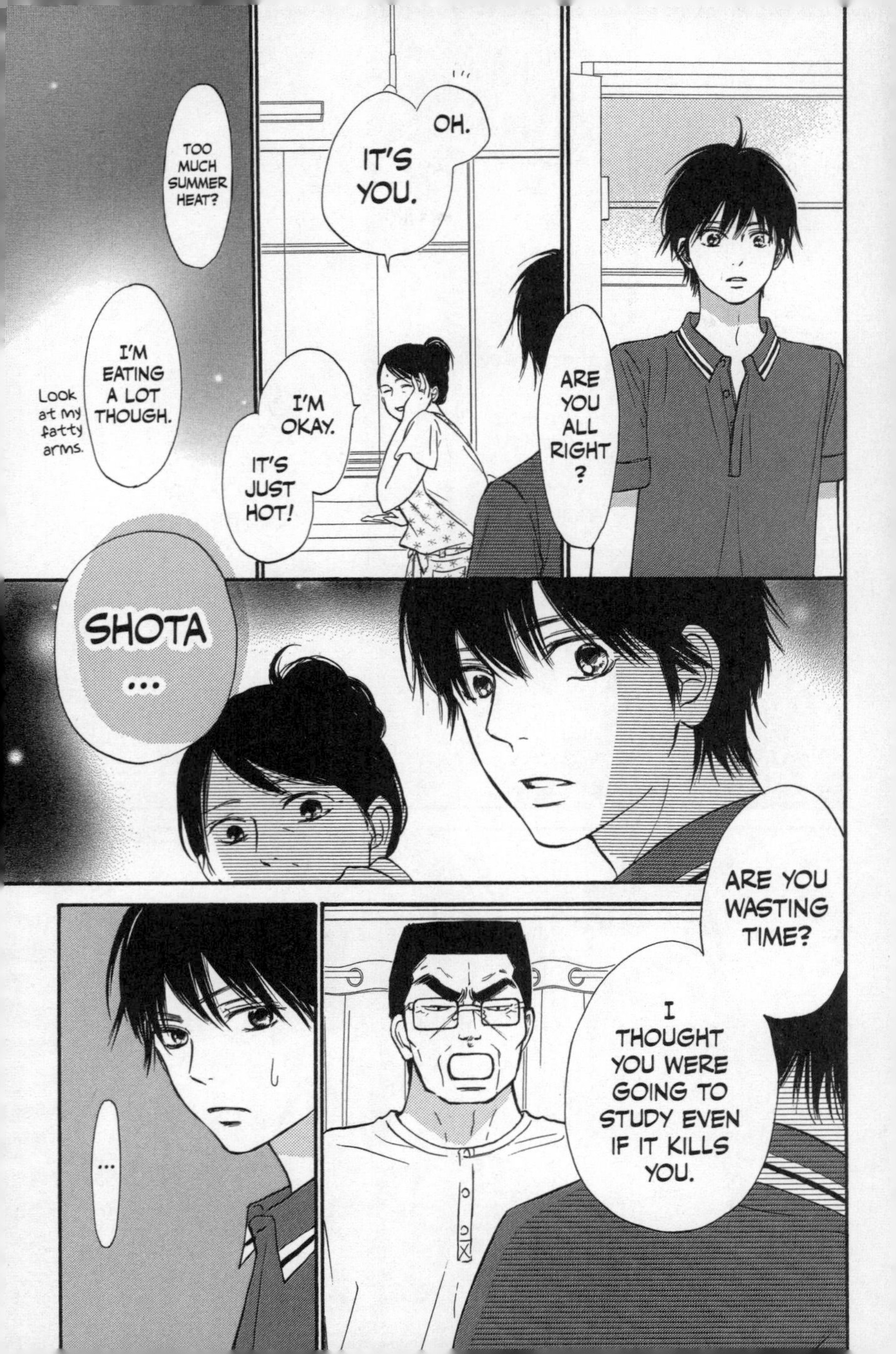

ARE YOU ALL RIGHT?
OH. IT'S YOU.
I'M OKAY.
IT'S JUST HOT!
TOO MUCH SUMMER HEAT?
I'M EATING A LOT THOUGH.
Look at my fatty arms.
SHOTA ...
ARE YOU WASTING TIME?
I THOUGHT YOU WERE GOING TO STUDY EVEN IF IT KILLS YOU.
...

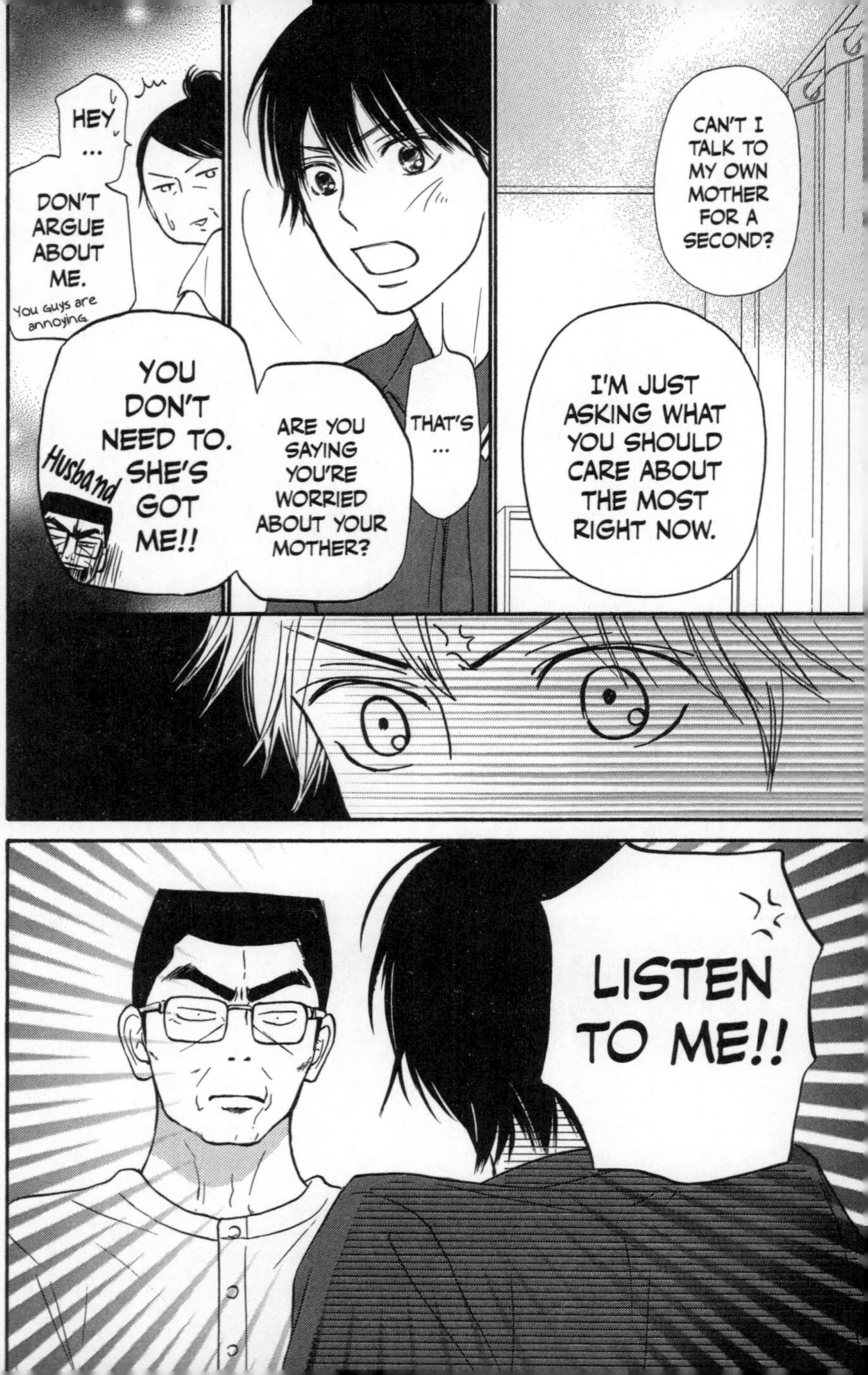
CAN'T I TALK TO MY OWN MOTHER FOR A SECOND?
I'M JUST ASKING WHAT YOU SHOULD CARE ABOUT THE MOST RIGHT NOW.
THAT'S ...
ARE YOU SAYING YOU'RE WORRIED ABOUT YOUR MOTHER?
HEY ... DON'T ARGUE ABOUT ME.
You guys are annoying.
YOU DON'T NEED TO. SHE'S GOT ME!!
Husband
LISTEN TO ME!!

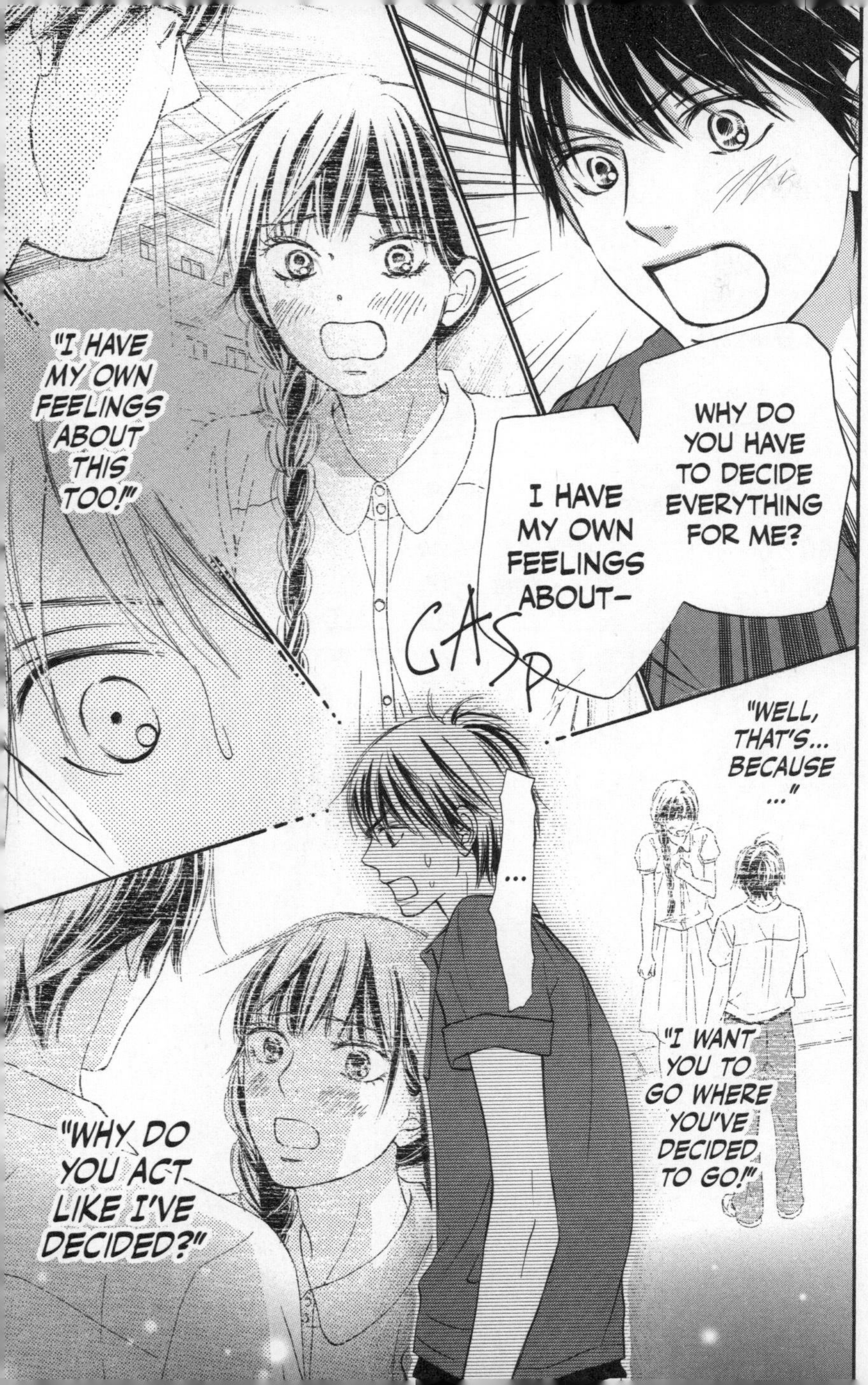
WHY DO YOU HAVE TO DECIDE EVERYTHING FOR ME?
I HAVE MY OWN FEELINGS ABOUT-
GASP
"I HAVE MY OWN FEELINGS ABOUT THIS TOO!"
"WELL, THAT'S... BECAUSE ..."
...
"I WANT YOU TO GO WHERE YOU'VE DECIDED TO GO!"
"WHY DO YOU ACT LIKE I'VE DECIDED?"

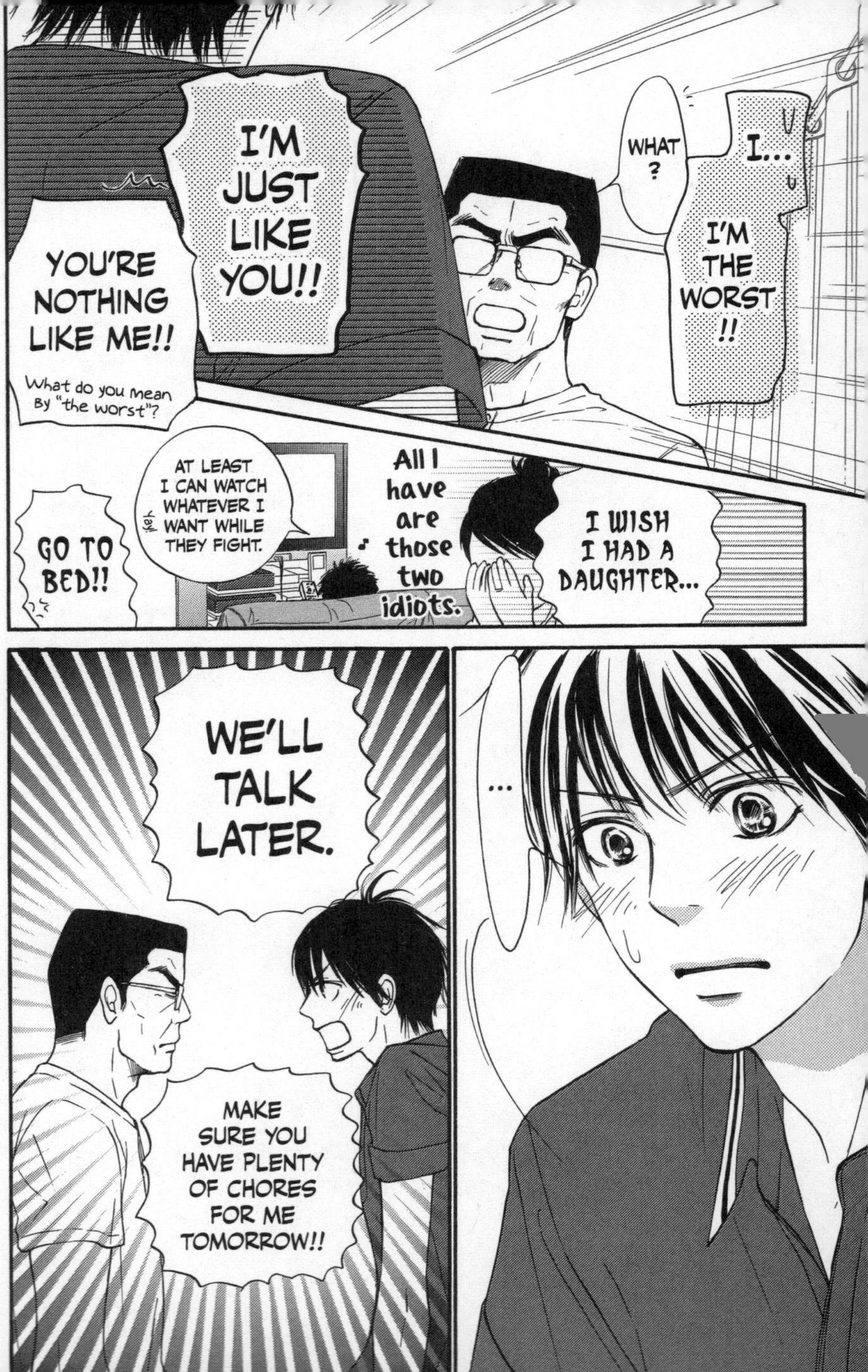
I... I'M THE WORST!!
WHAT?
I'M JUST LIKE YOU!!
YOU'RE NOTHING LIKE ME!!
What do you mean by "the worst"?
I WISH I HAD A DAUGHTER...
All I have are those two idiots.
AT LEAST I CAN WATCH WHATEVER I WANT WHILE THEY FIGHT.
Yay!
GO TO BED!!
...
WE'LL TALK LATER.
MAKE SURE YOU HAVE PLENTY OF CHORES FOR ME TOMORROW!!

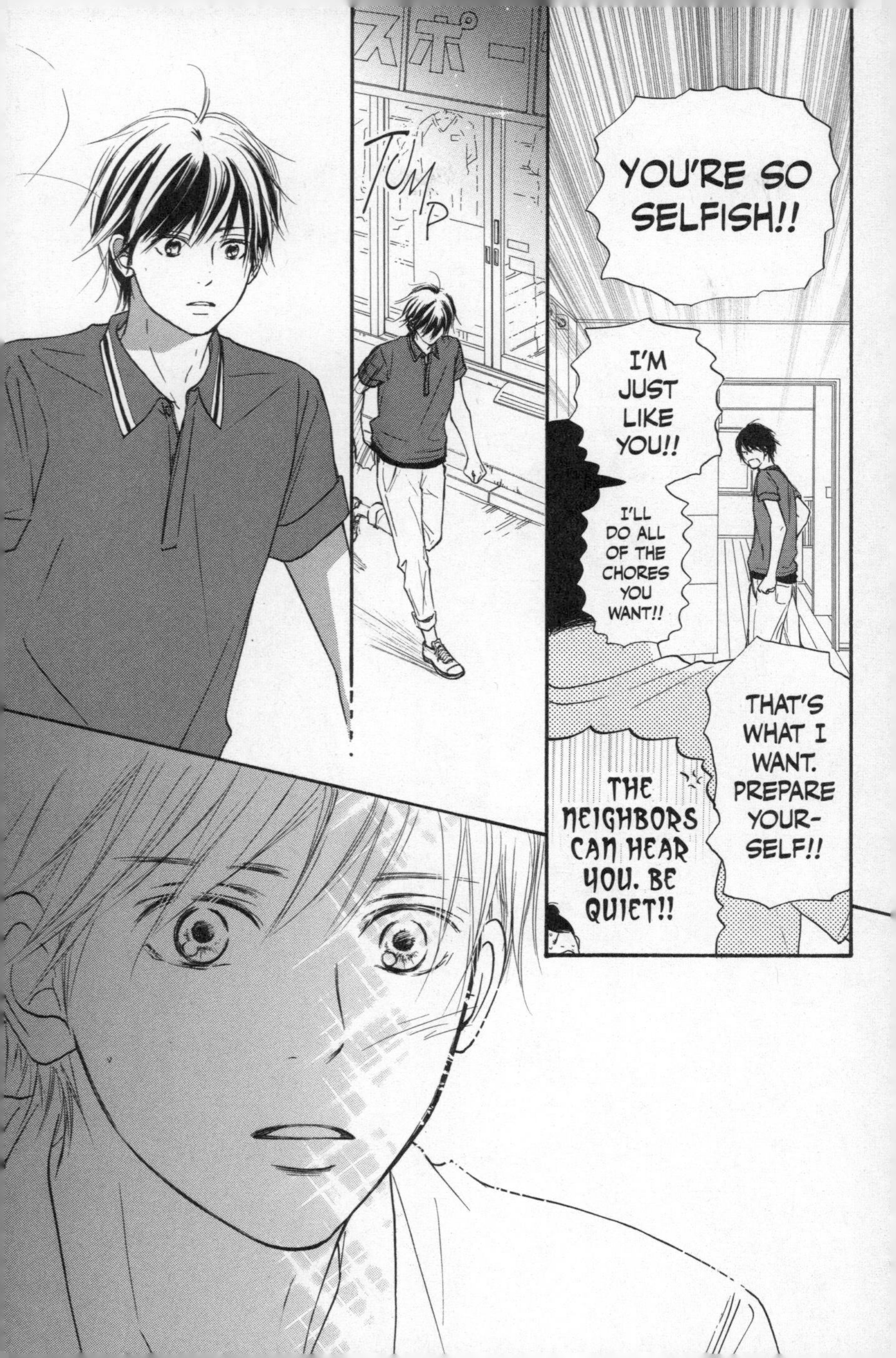
YOU'RE SO SELFISH!!
I'M JUST LIKE YOU!!
I'LL DO ALL OF THE CHORES YOU WANT!!
THAT'S WHAT I WANT. PREPARE YOUR-SELF!!
THE NEIGHBORS CAN HEAR YOU. BE QUIET!!
スポー
TUMP

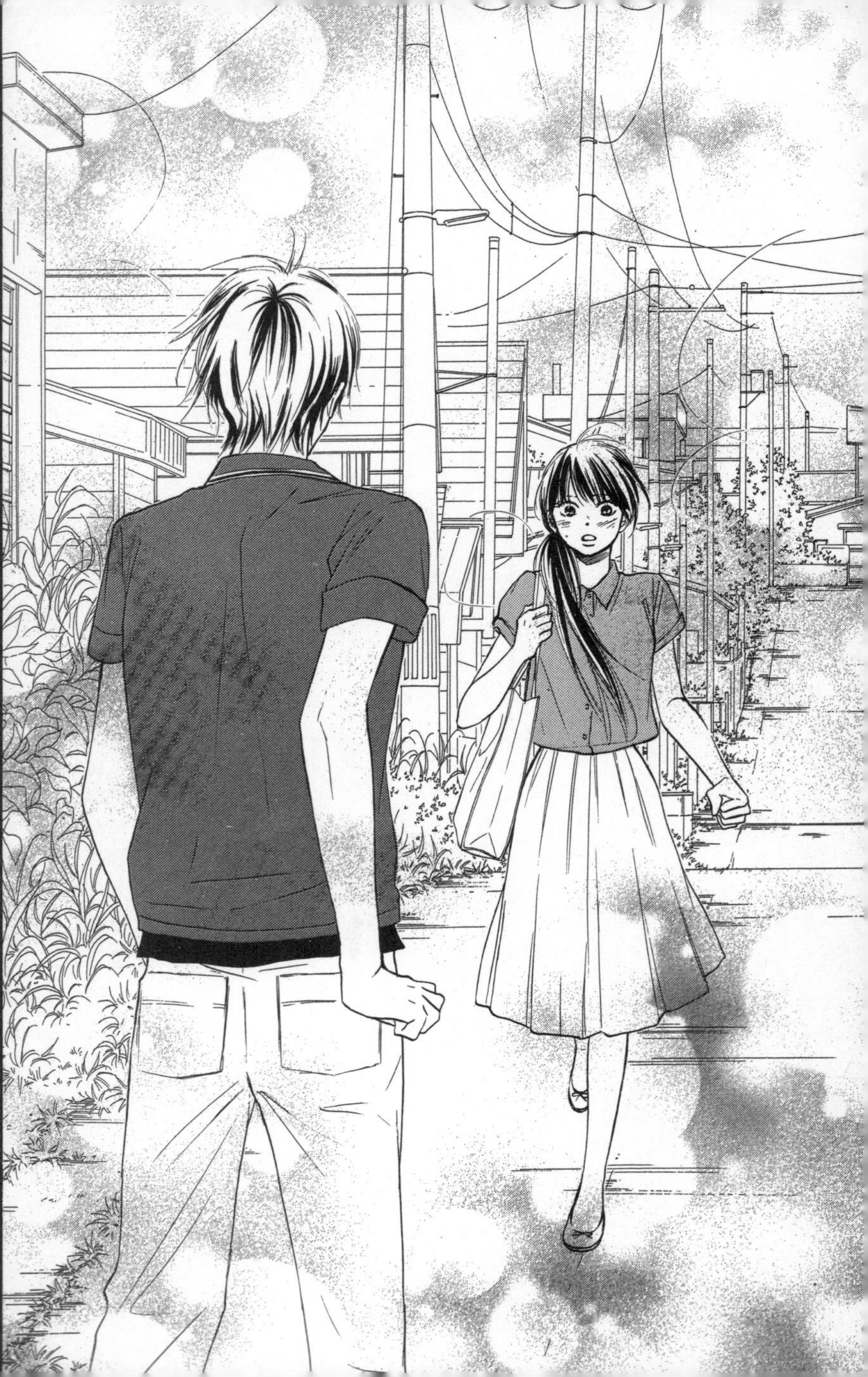

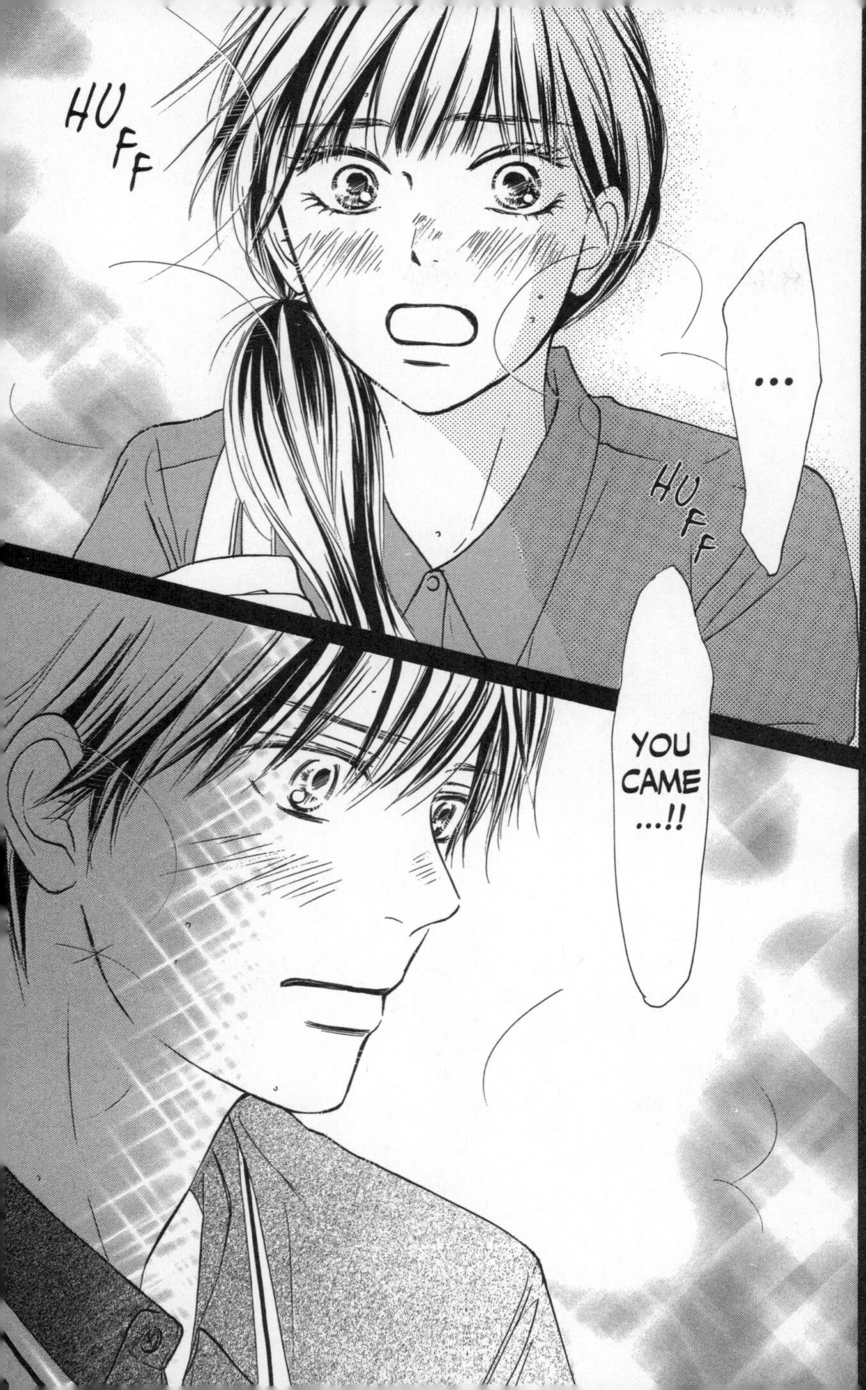

...
HUFF
HUFF
YOU CAME ...!!

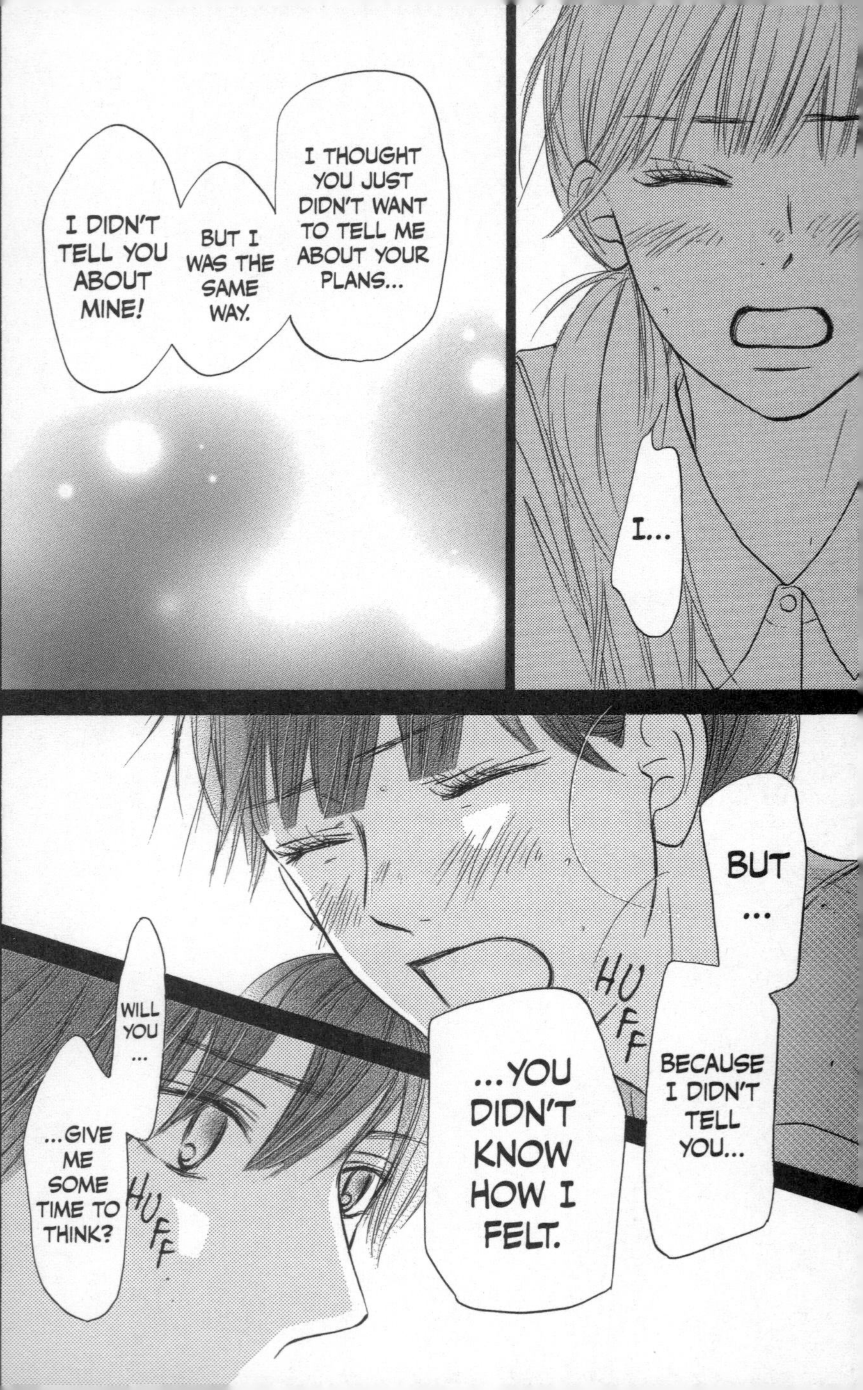
I...
I THOUGHT YOU JUST DIDN'T WANT TO TELL ME ABOUT YOUR PLANS...
BUT I WAS THE SAME WAY.
I DIDN'T TELL YOU ABOUT MINE!
BUT ...
BECAUSE I DIDN'T TELL YOU...
HUFF
...YOU DIDN'T KNOW HOW I FELT.
WILL YOU ...
HUFF
...GIVE ME SOME TIME TO THINK?

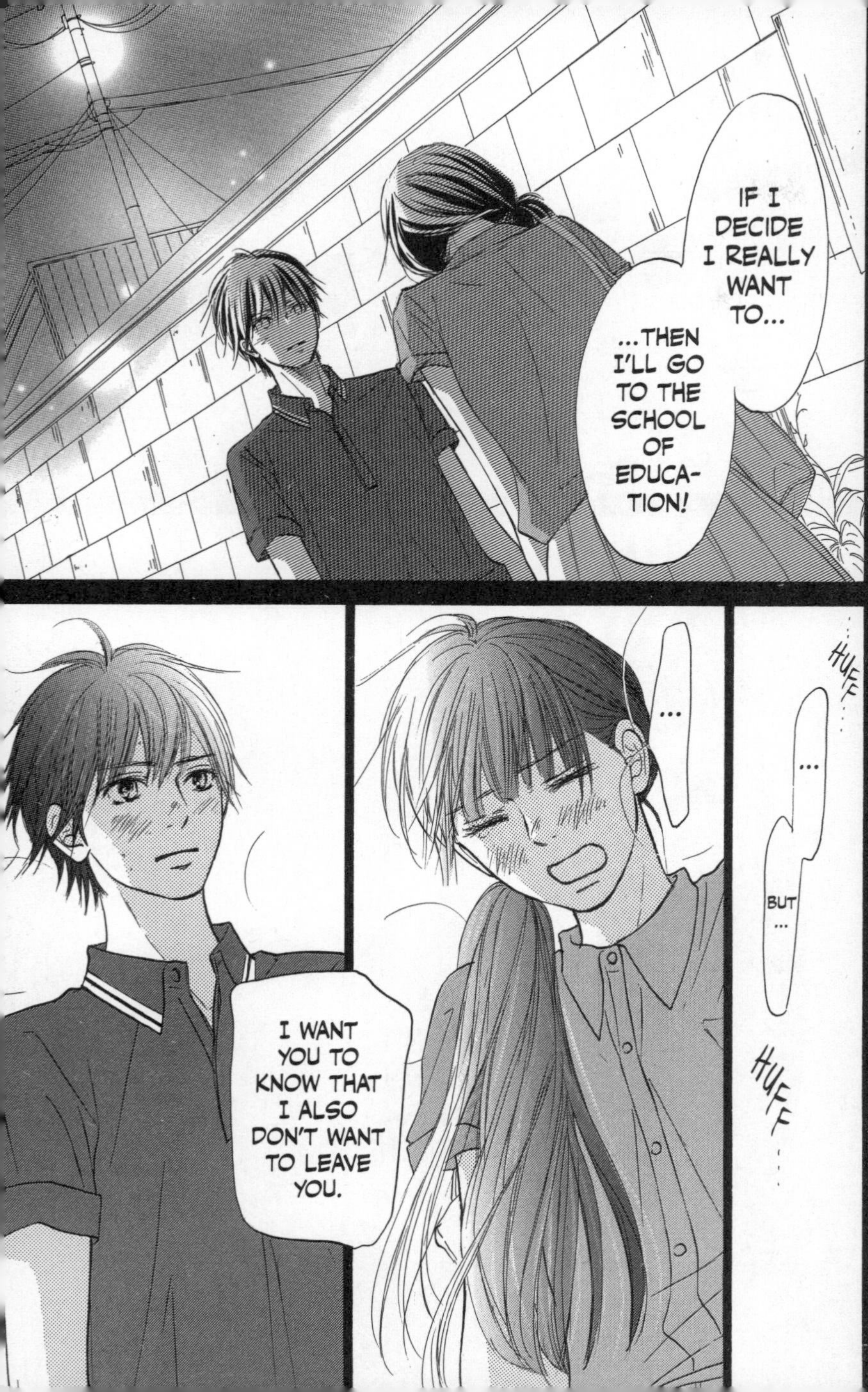
IF I DECIDE I REALLY WANT TO...
...THEN I'LL GO TO THE SCHOOL OF EDUCATION!
...HUFF...
...
BUT...
HUFF...
...
I WANT YOU TO KNOW THAT I ALSO DON'T WANT TO LEAVE YOU.

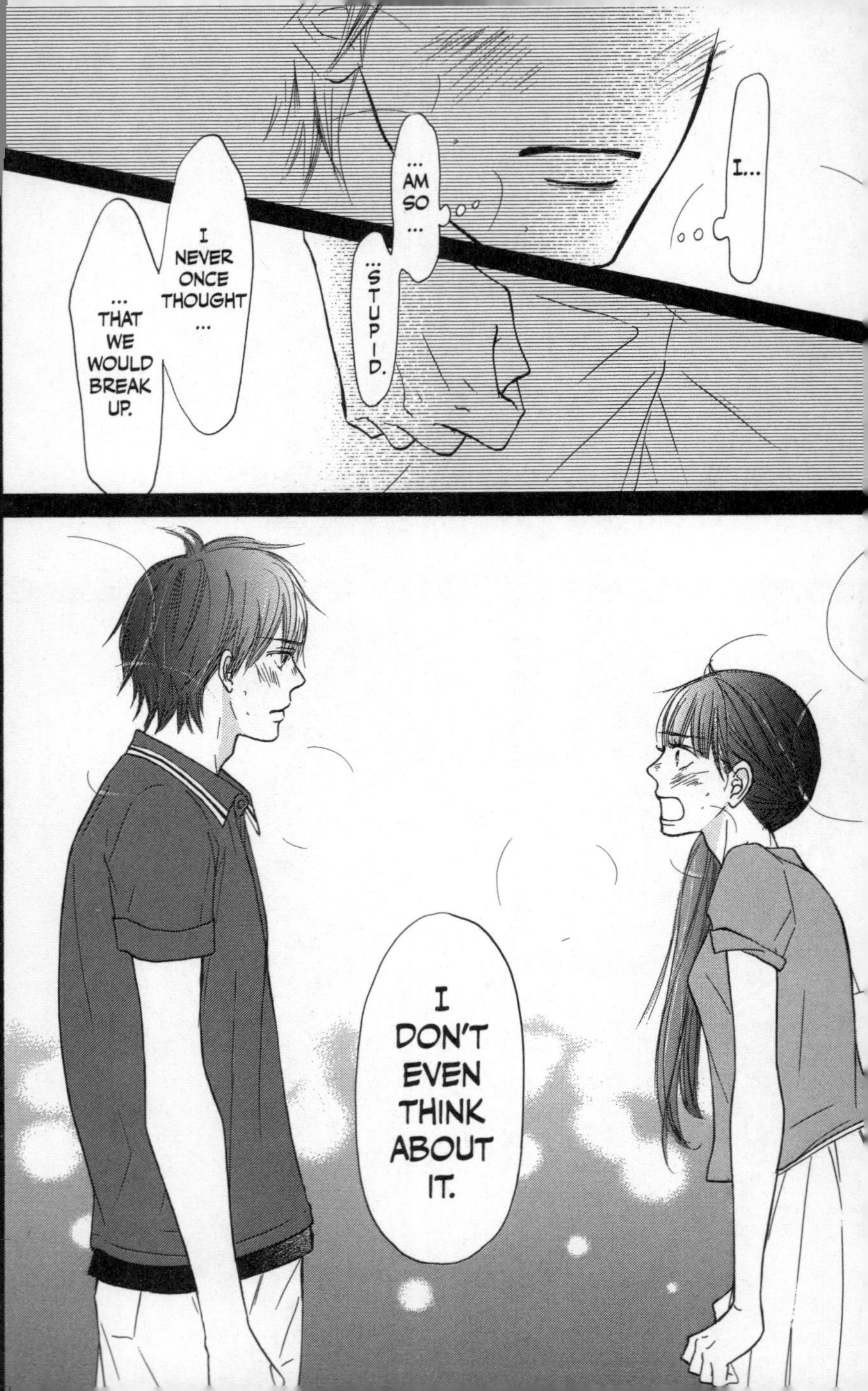
I...
...AM SO ...
...STUPID.
I NEVER ONCE THOUGHT ...
... THAT WE WOULD BREAK UP.
I DON'T EVEN THINK ABOUT IT.

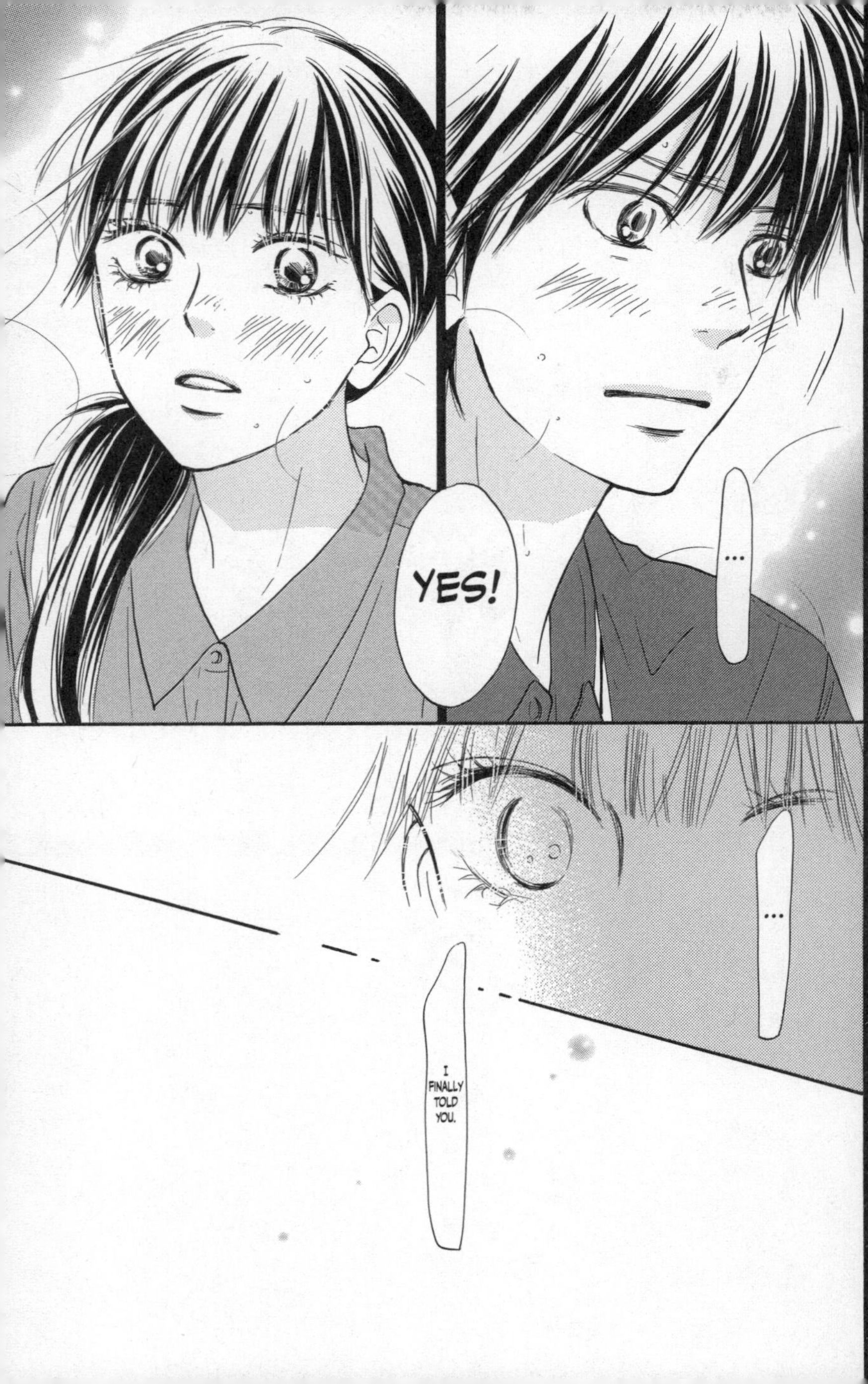
...
YES!
...
I FINALLY TOLD YOU.

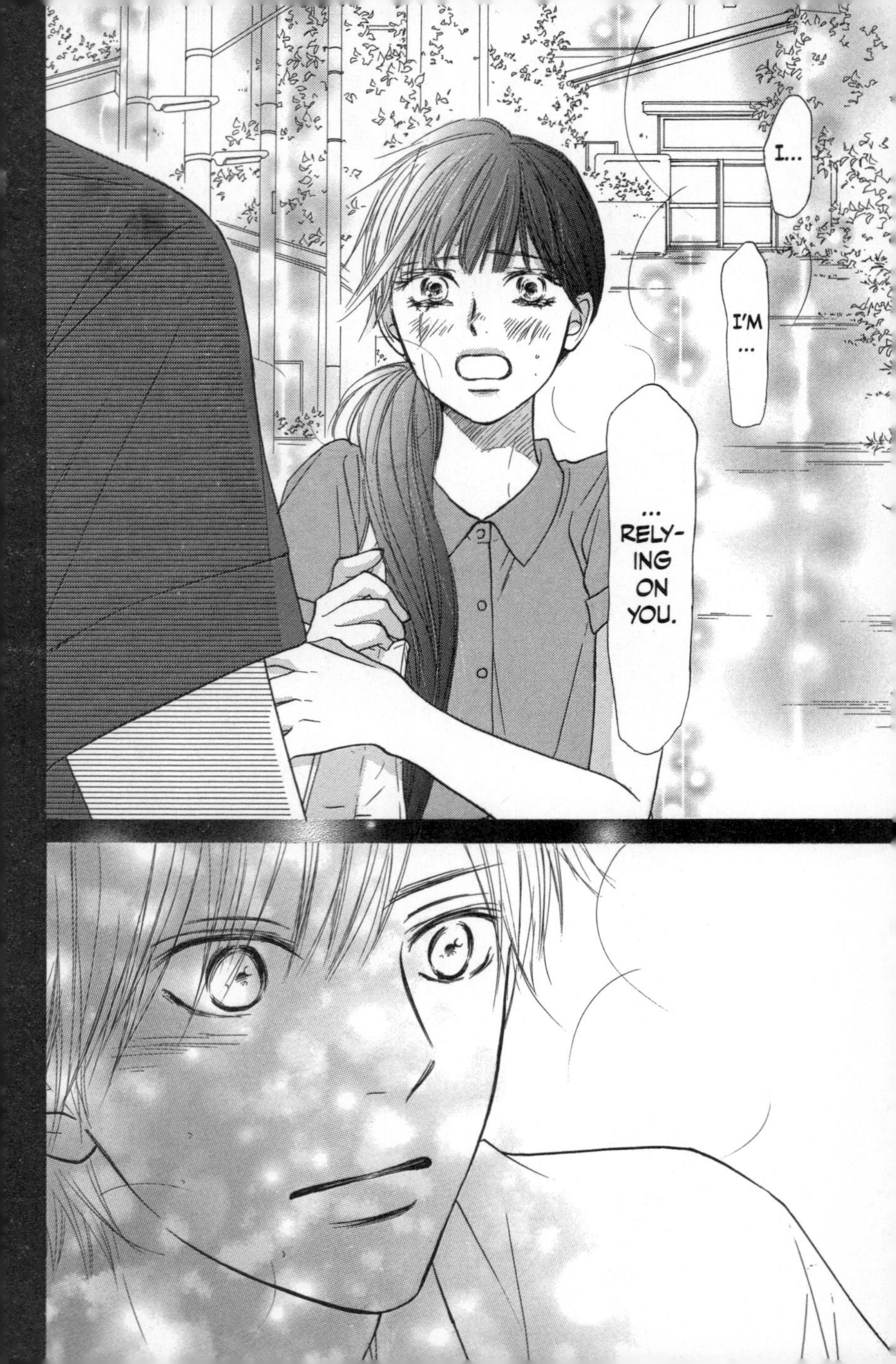
I...
I'M ...
... RELY-ING ON YOU.

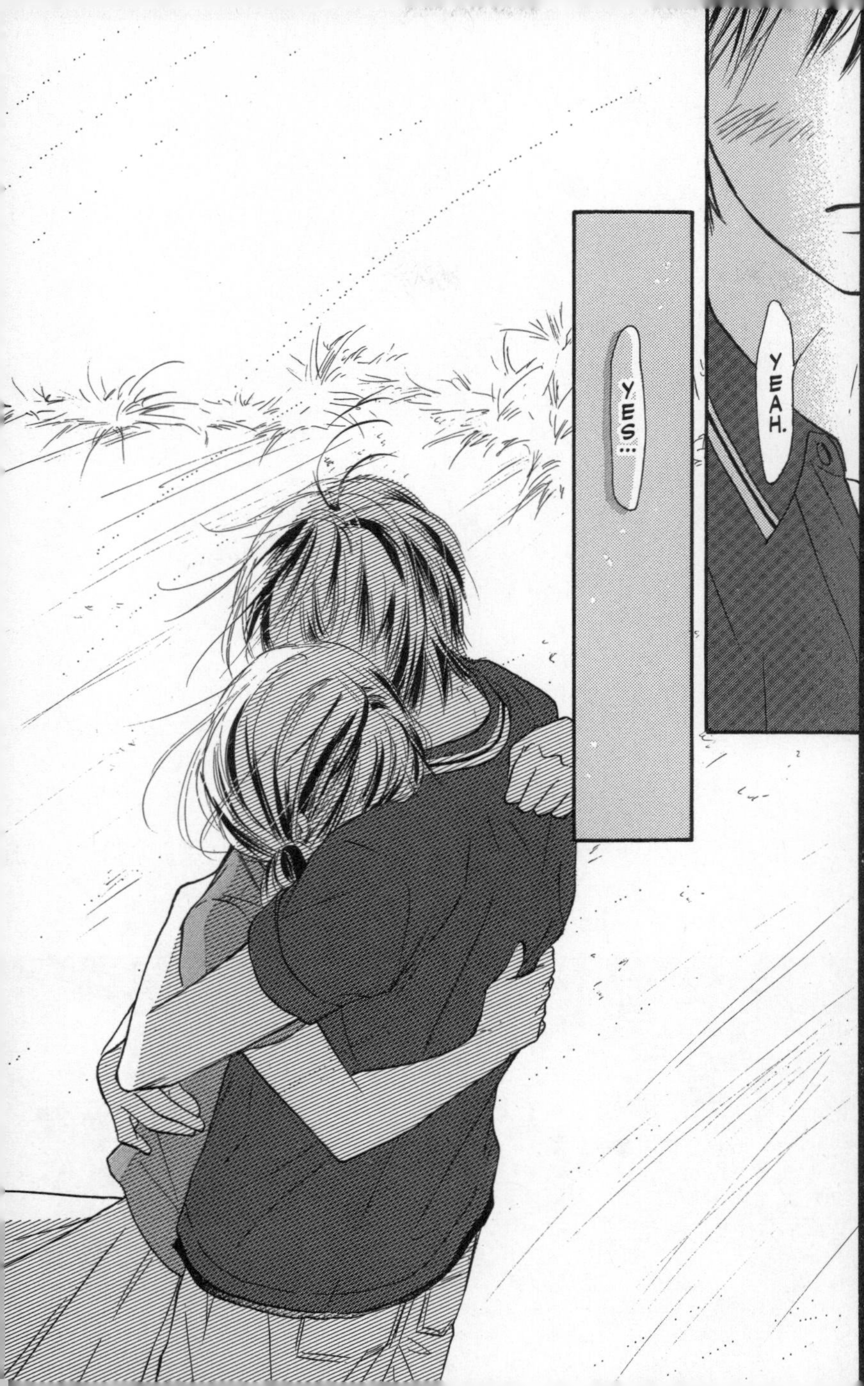
YEAH.
YES...

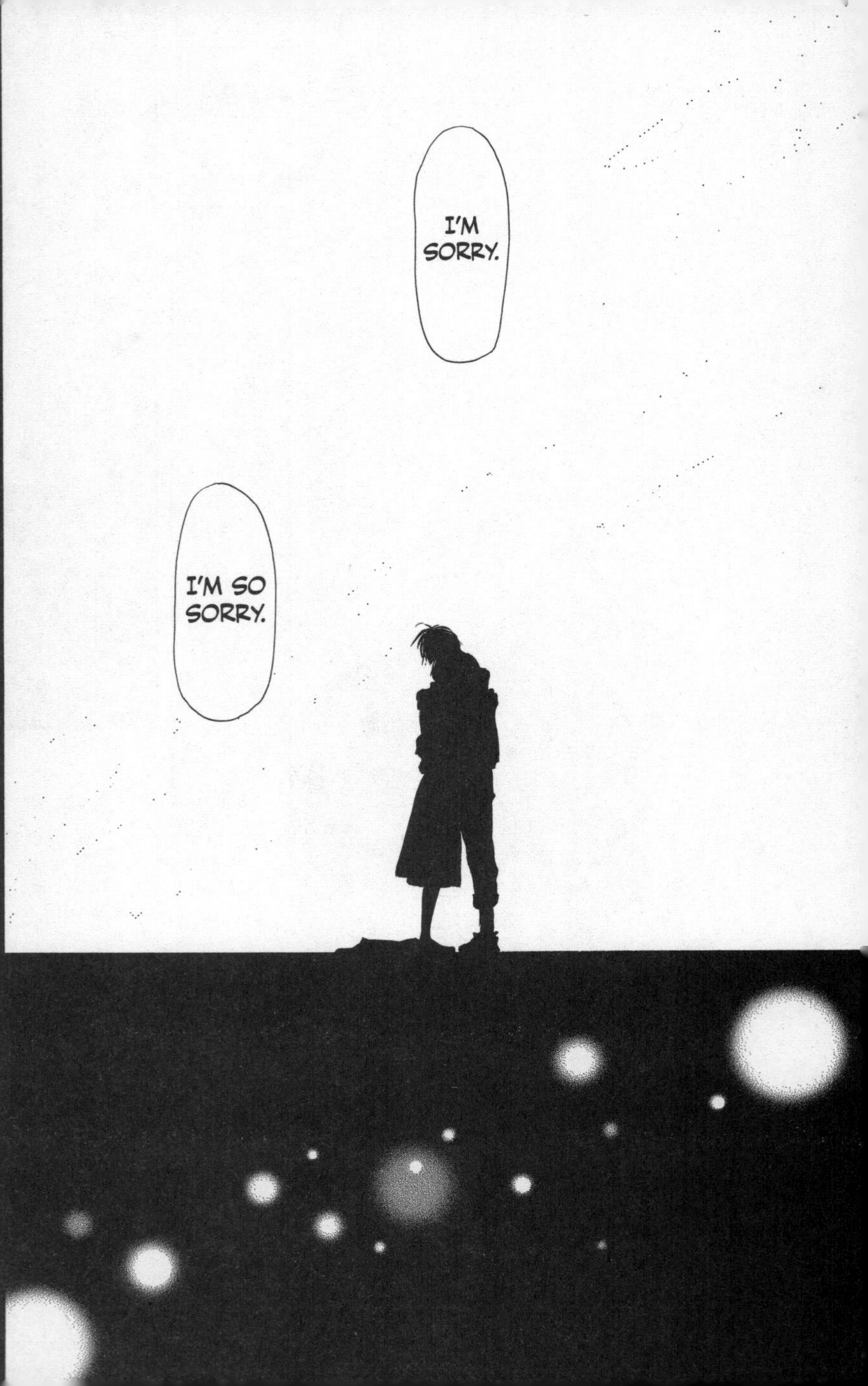
I'M SORRY.
I'M SO SORRY.

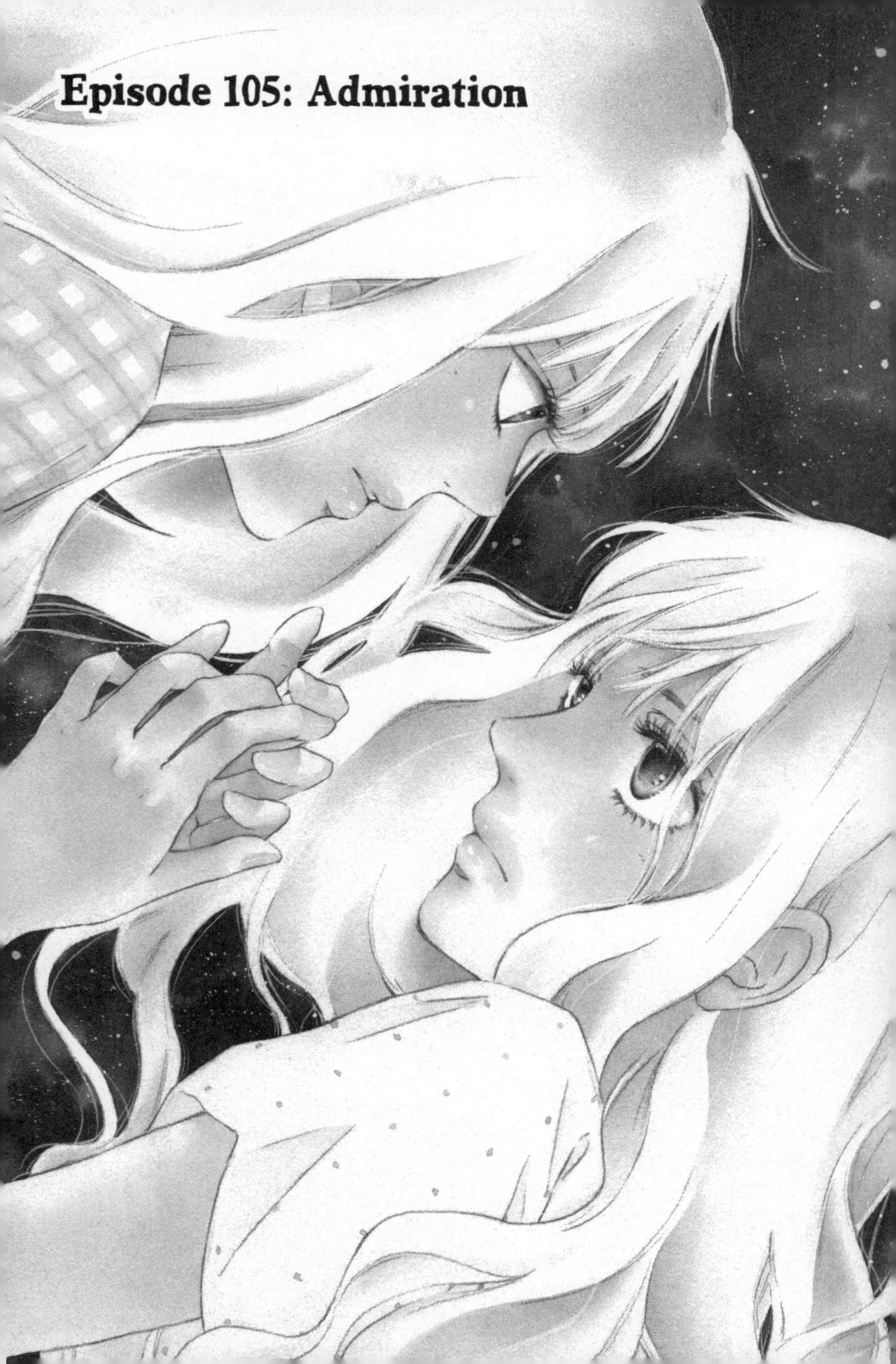
Episode 105: Admiration

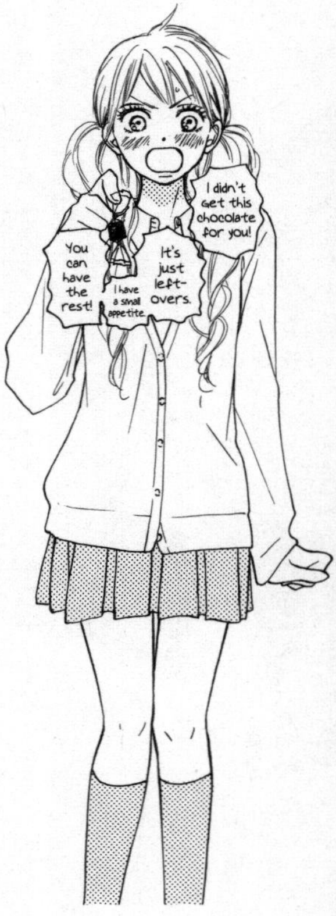
I didn't get this chocolate for you!
It's just left-overs.
I have a small appetite.
You can have the rest!

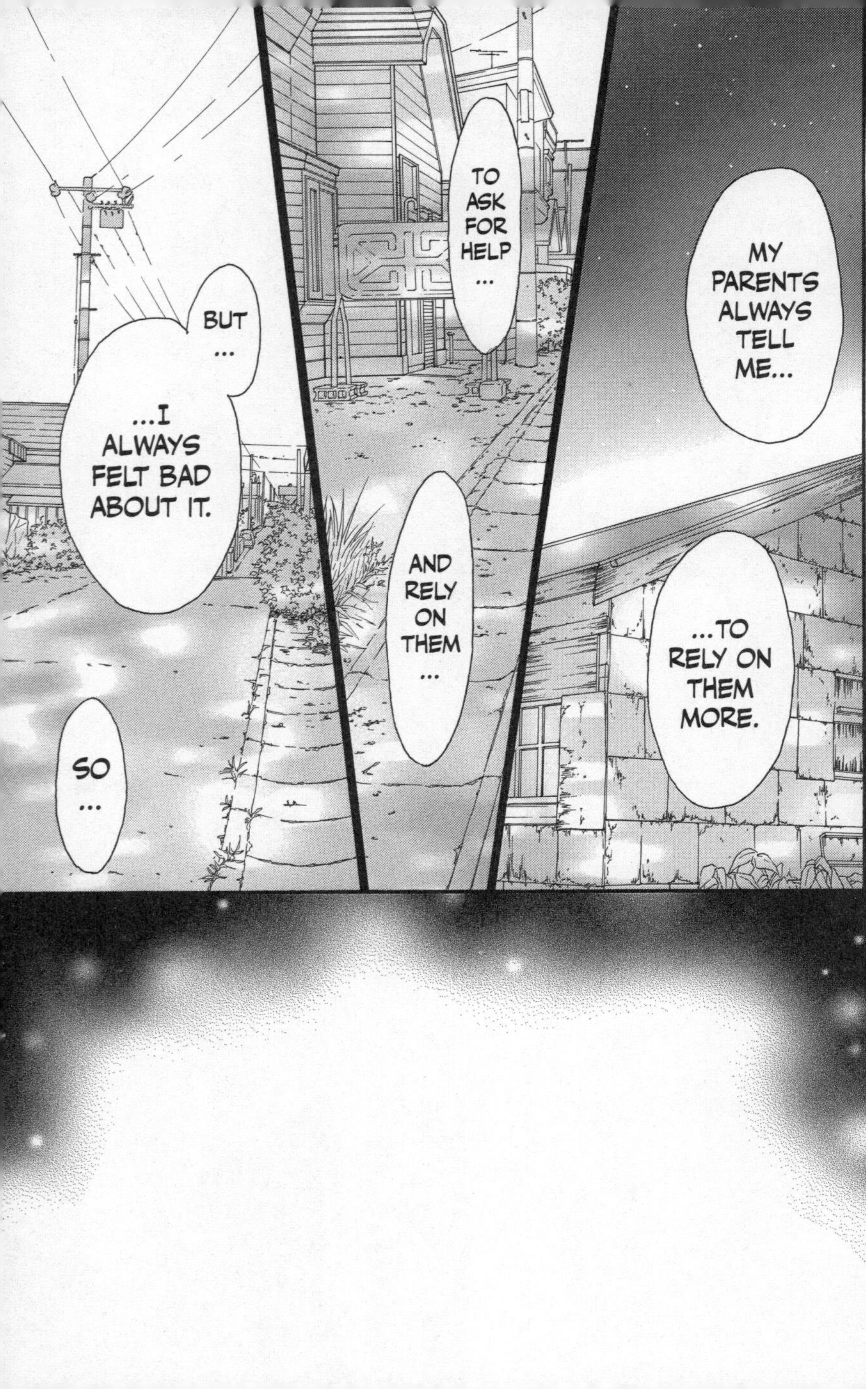
MY PARENTS ALWAYS TELL ME...
...TO RELY ON THEM MORE.
TO ASK FOR HELP...
AND RELY ON THEM...
BUT...
...I ALWAYS FELT BAD ABOUT IT.
SO...

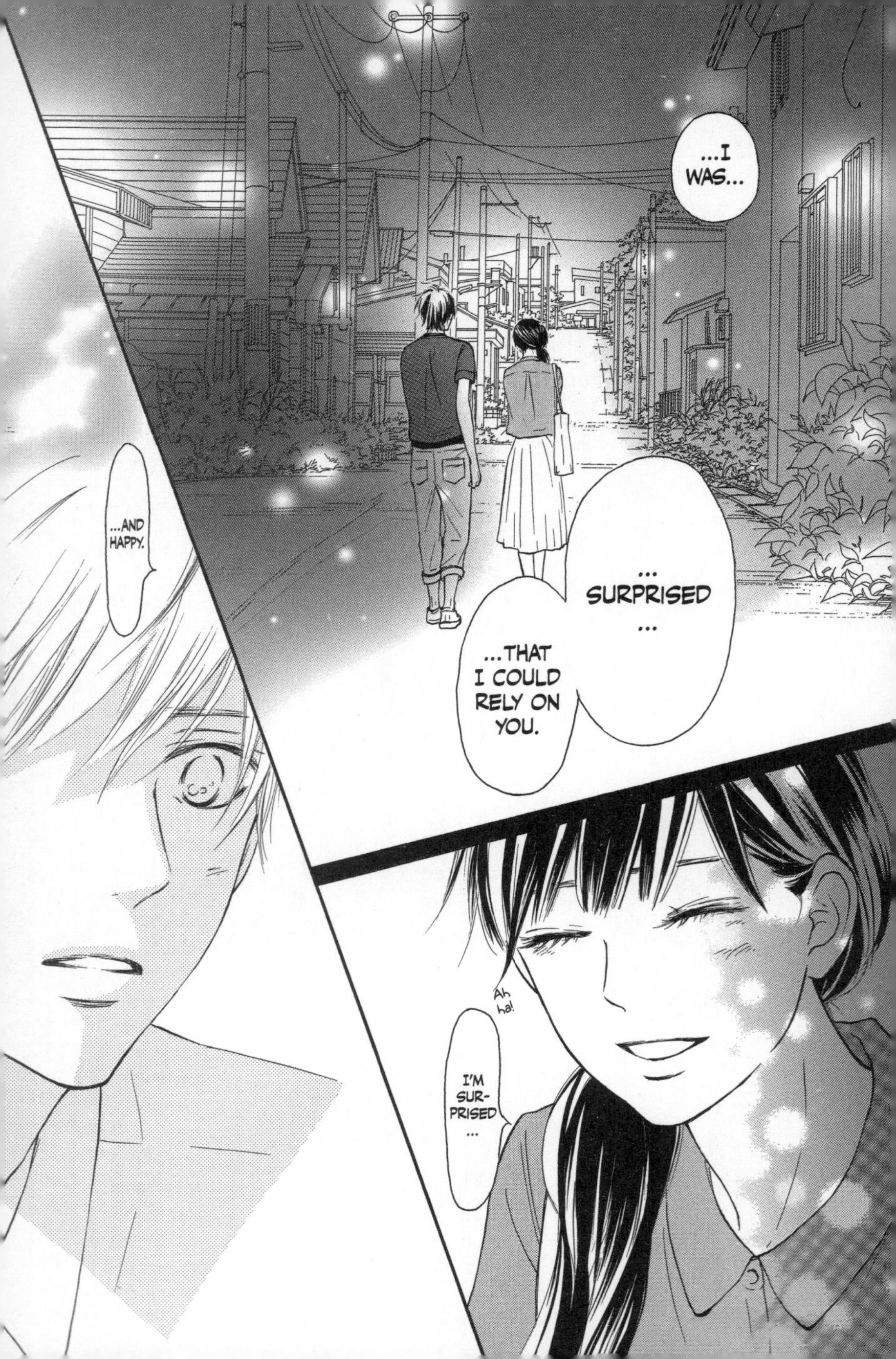
...I WAS...
...SURPRISED...
...THAT I COULD RELY ON YOU.
Ah ha!
I'M SUR-PRISED...
...AND HAPPY.

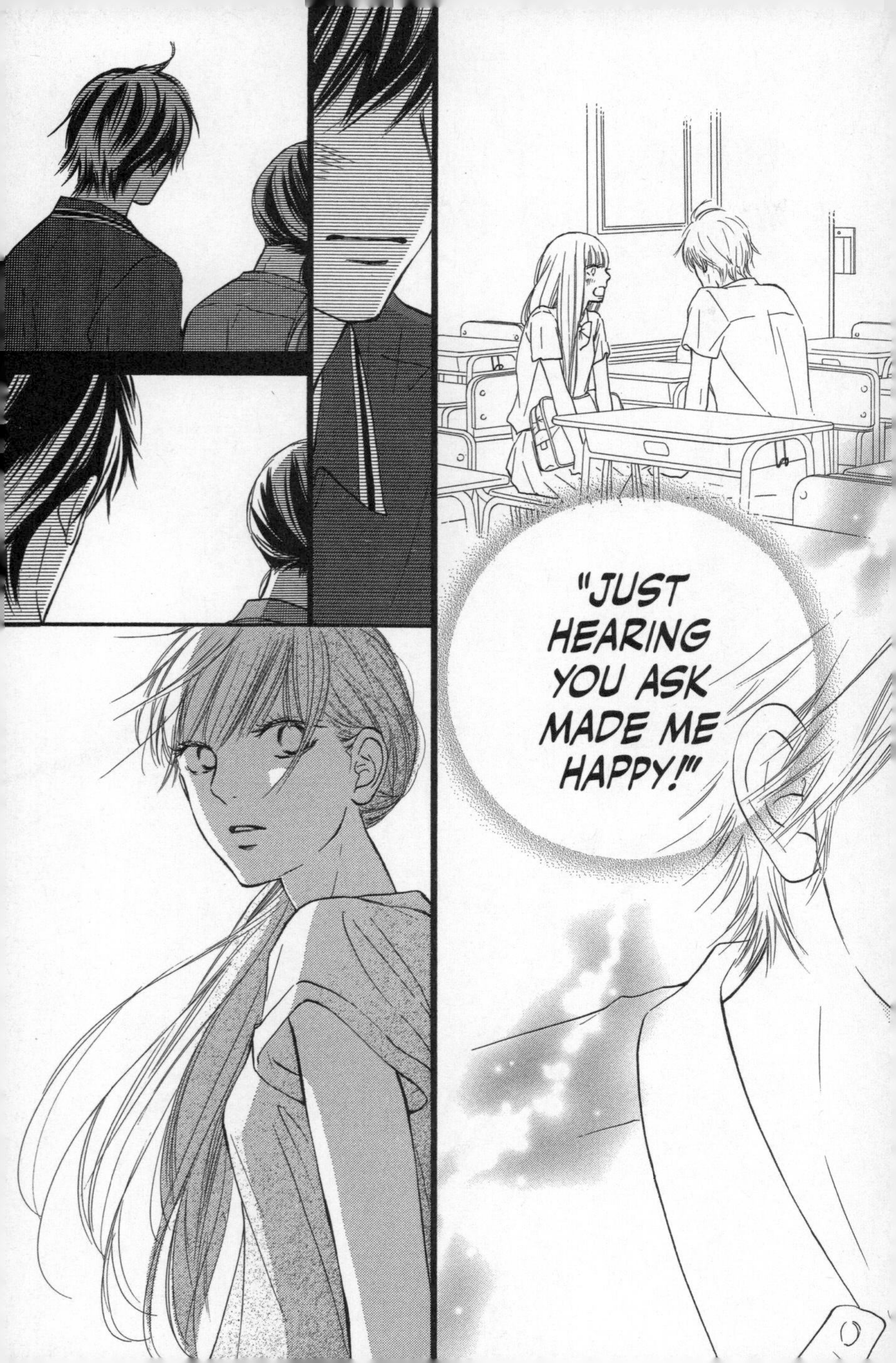
"JUST HEARING YOU ASK MADE ME HAPPY!"

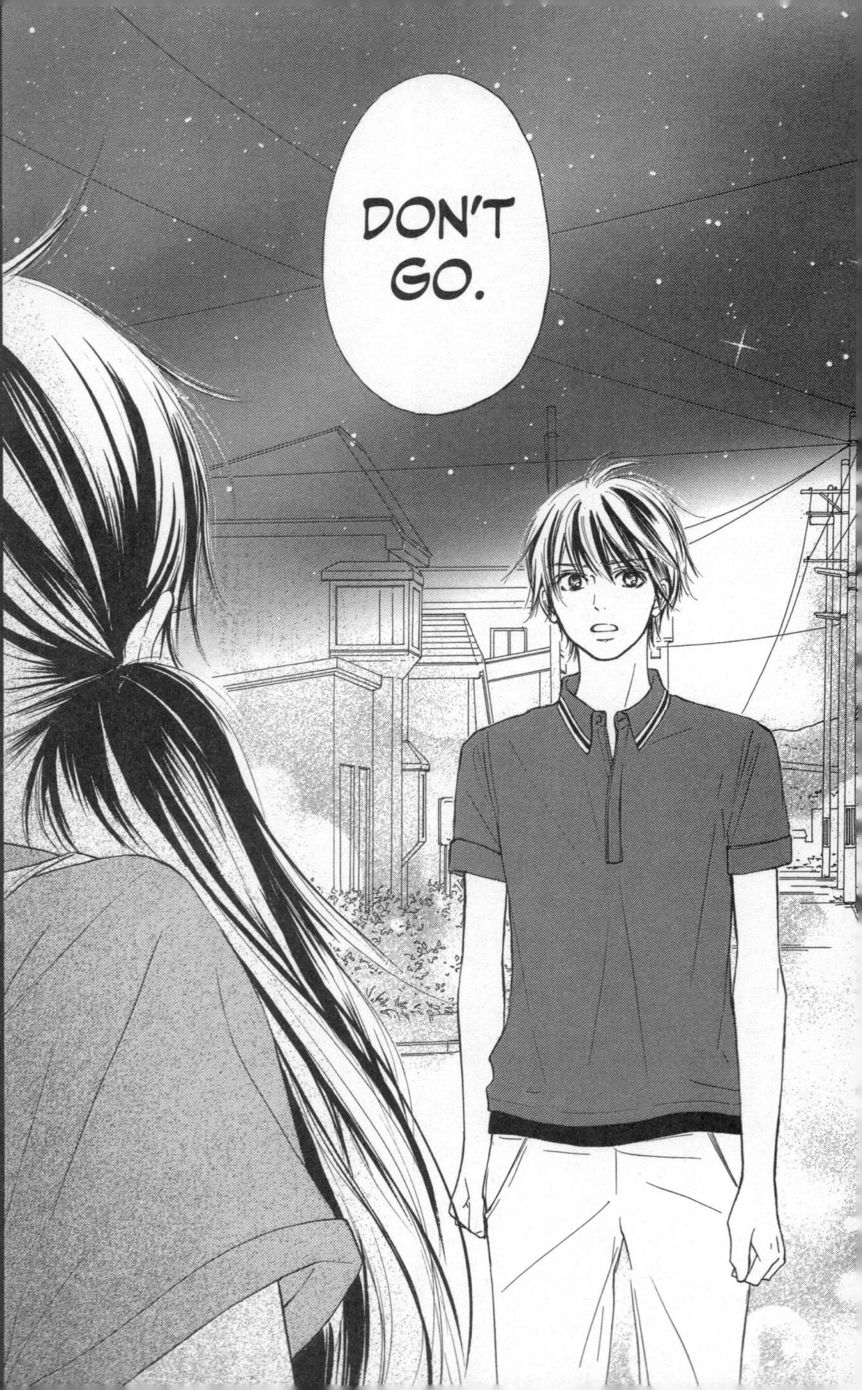
DON'T GO.

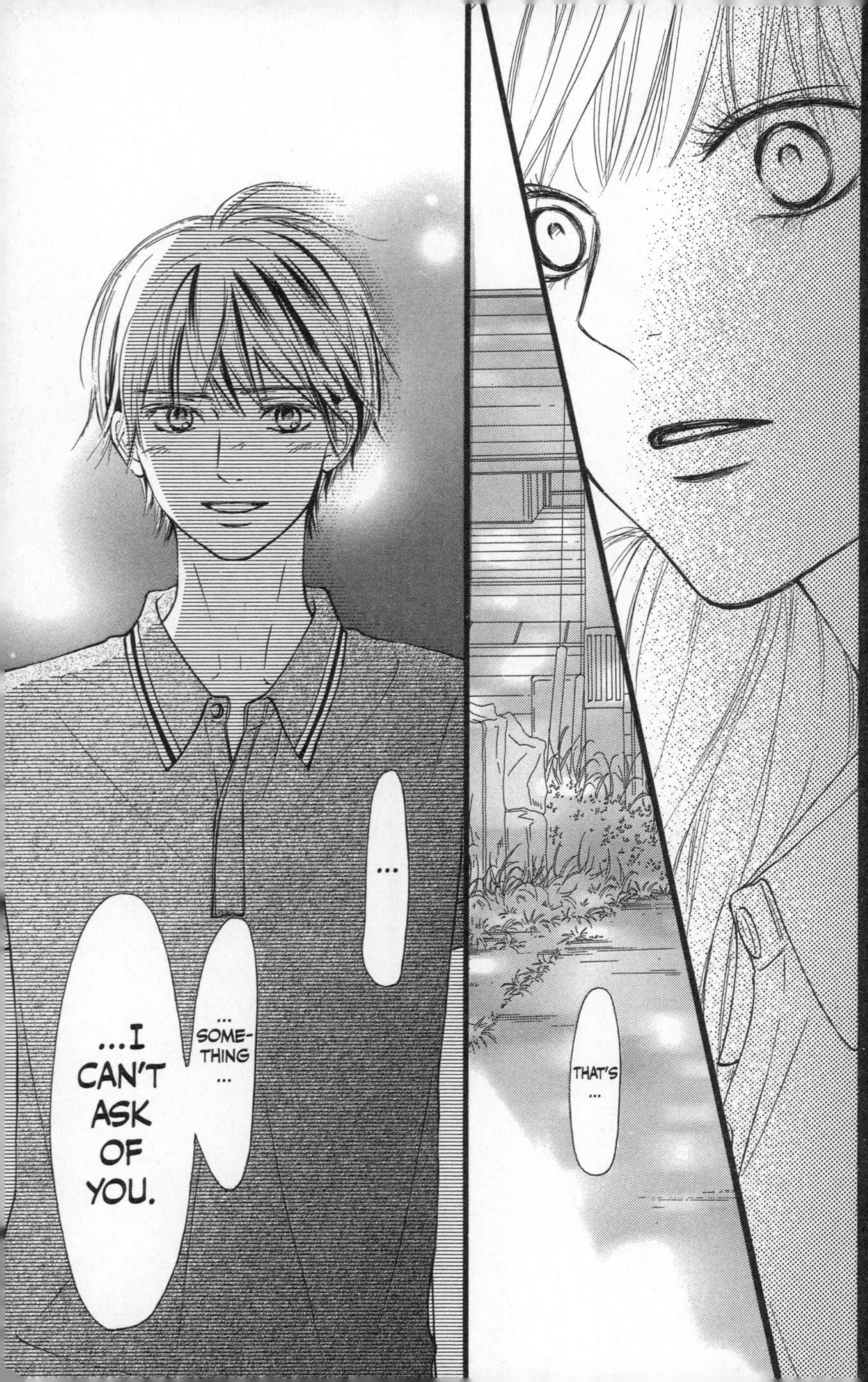
THAT'S ...
...
... SOMETHING ...
...I CAN'T ASK OF YOU.

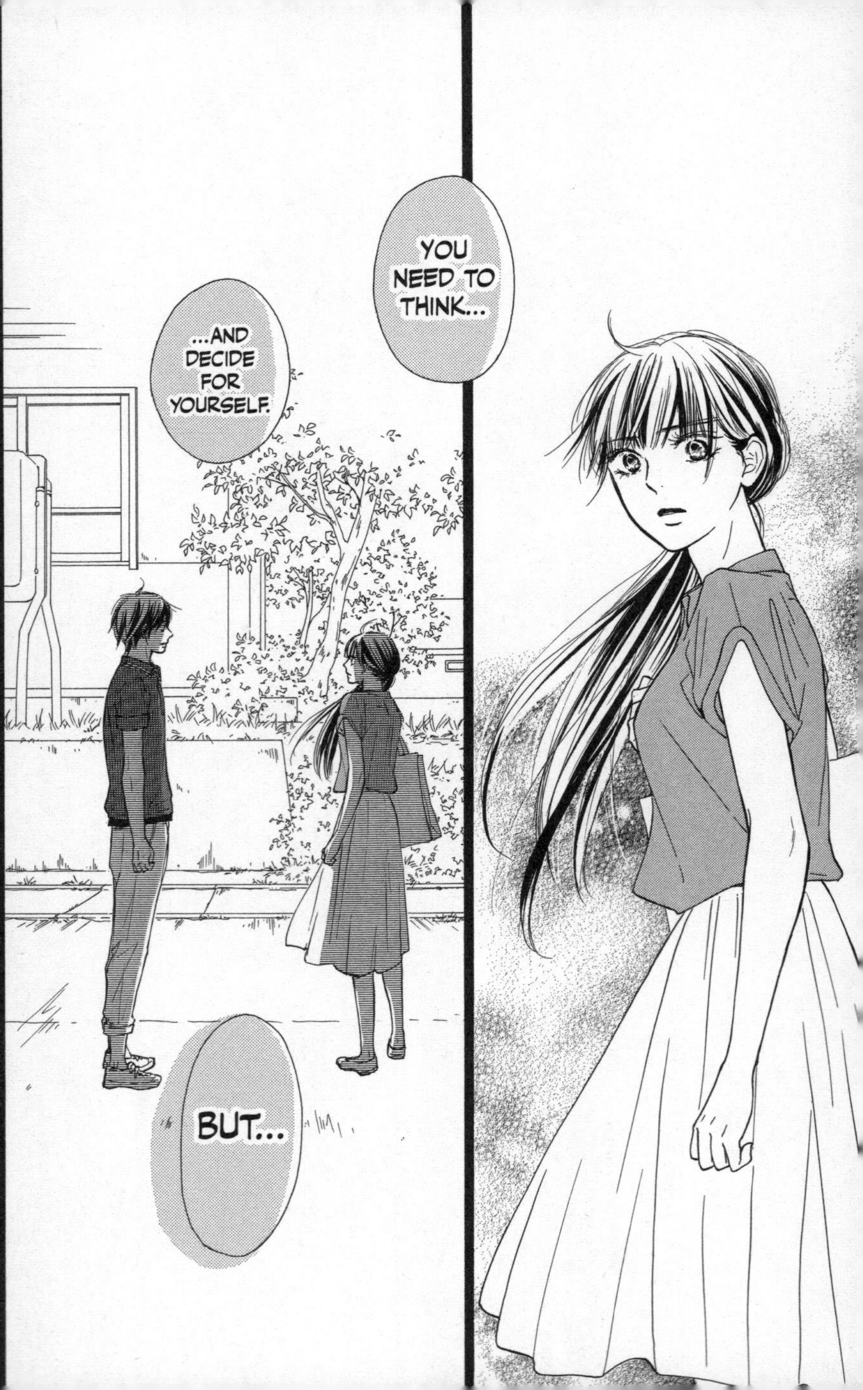
YOU NEED TO THINK...
...AND DECIDE FOR YOURSELF.
BUT...

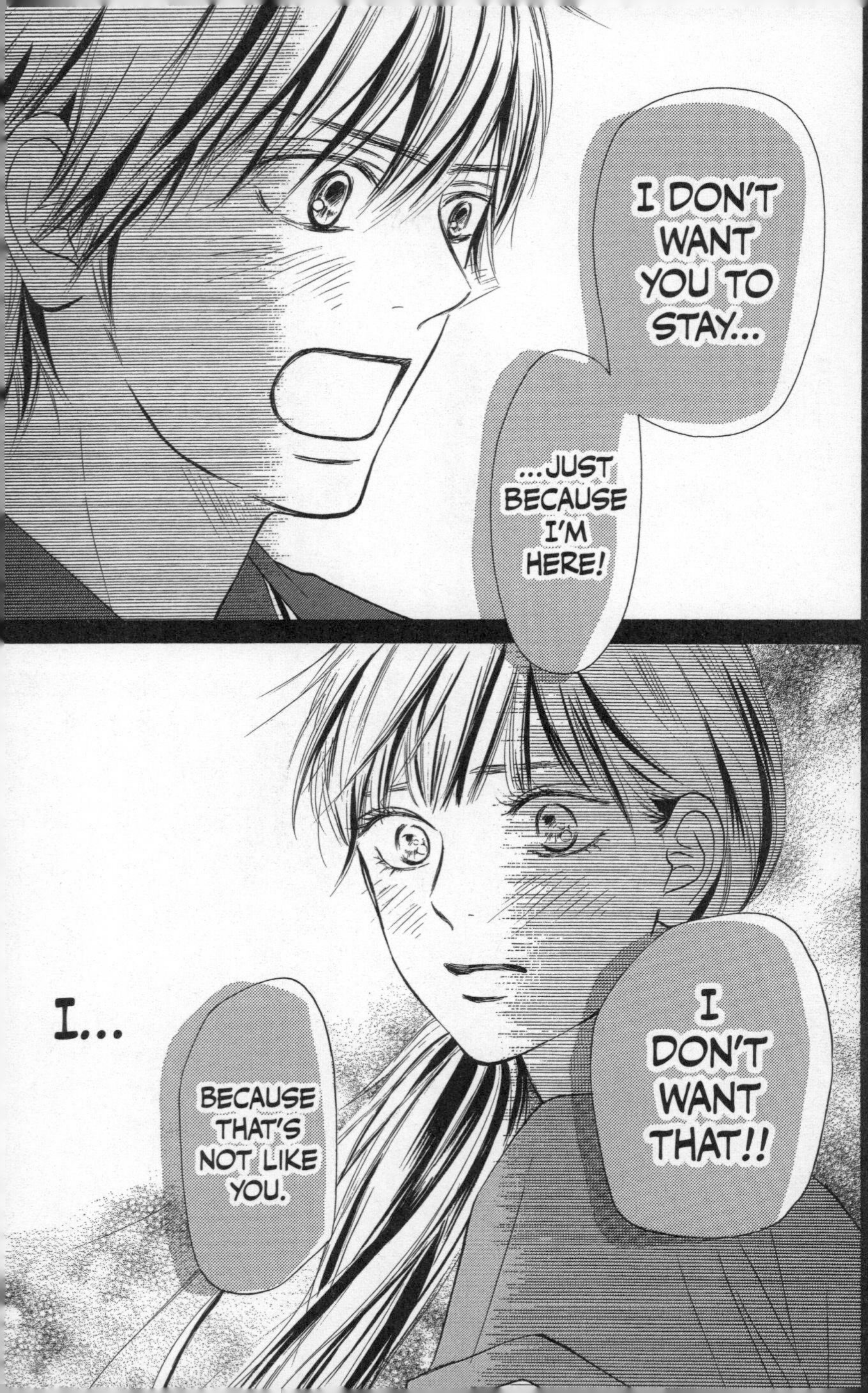
I DON'T WANT YOU TO STAY...
...JUST BECAUSE I'M HERE!
I DON'T WANT THAT!!
BECAUSE THAT'S NOT LIKE YOU.
I...

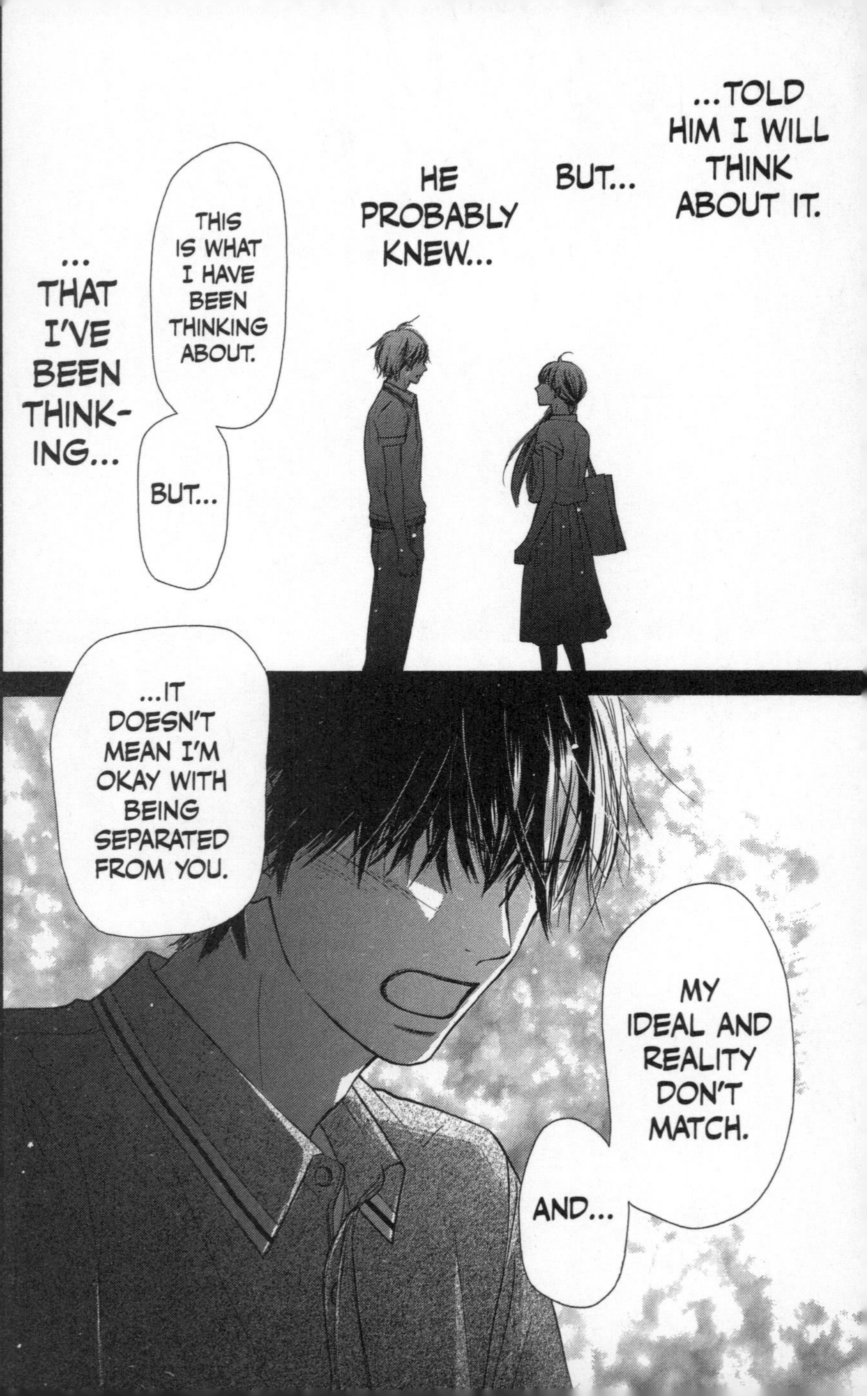
...TOLD HIM I WILL THINK ABOUT IT.
BUT...
HE PROBABLY KNEW...
...THAT I'VE BEEN THINKING...
THIS IS WHAT I HAVE BEEN THINKING ABOUT.
BUT...
MY IDEAL AND REALITY DON'T MATCH.
AND...
...IT DOESN'T MEAN I'M OKAY WITH BEING SEPARATED FROM YOU.

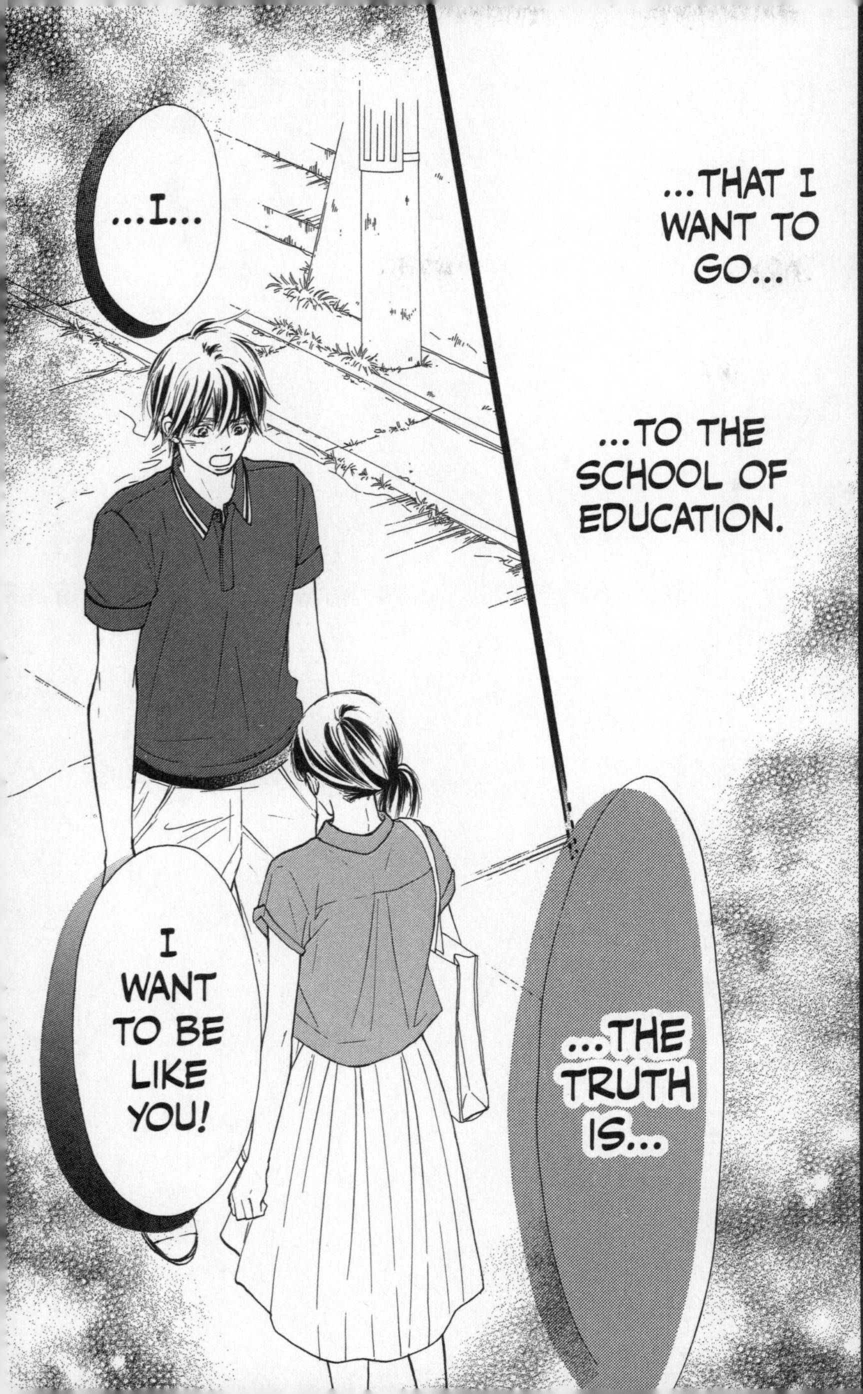
...THE TRUTH IS...
...THAT I WANT TO GO...
...TO THE SCHOOL OF EDUCATION.
...I...
I WANT TO BE LIKE YOU!

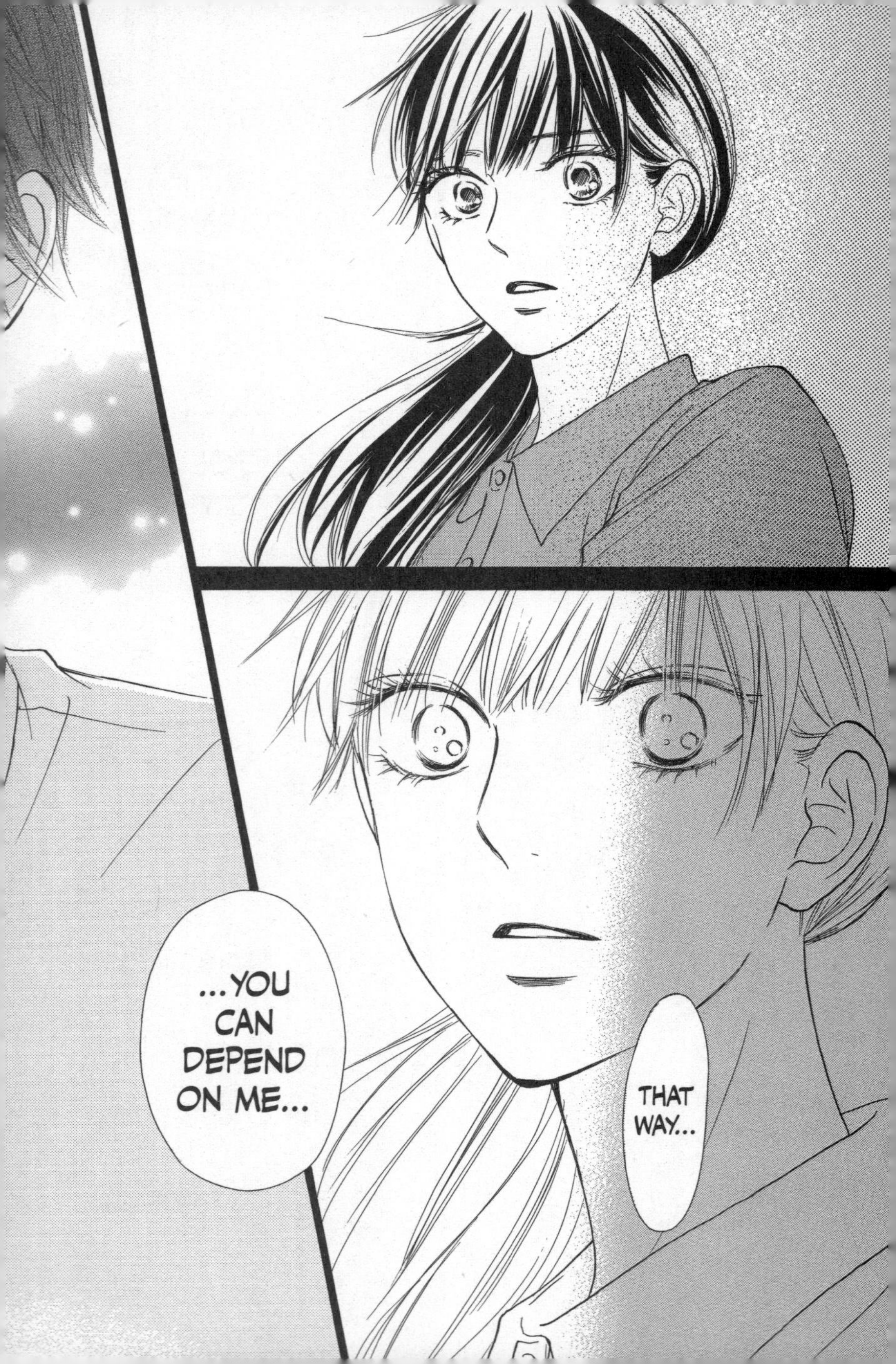
THAT WAY...
...YOU CAN DEPEND ON ME...

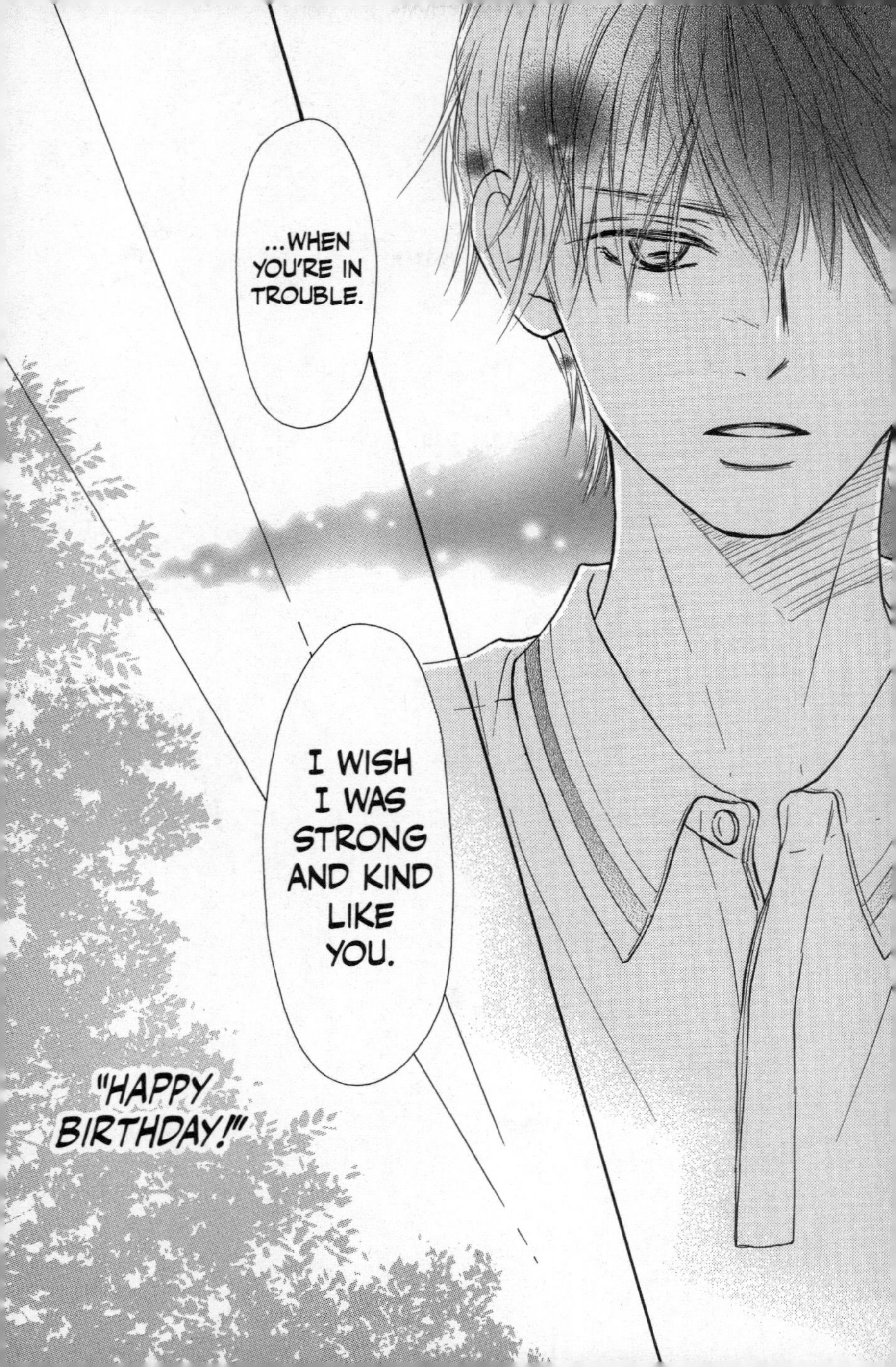
...WHEN YOU'RE IN TROUBLE.
I WISH I WAS STRONG AND KIND LIKE YOU.
"HAPPY BIRTHDAY!"

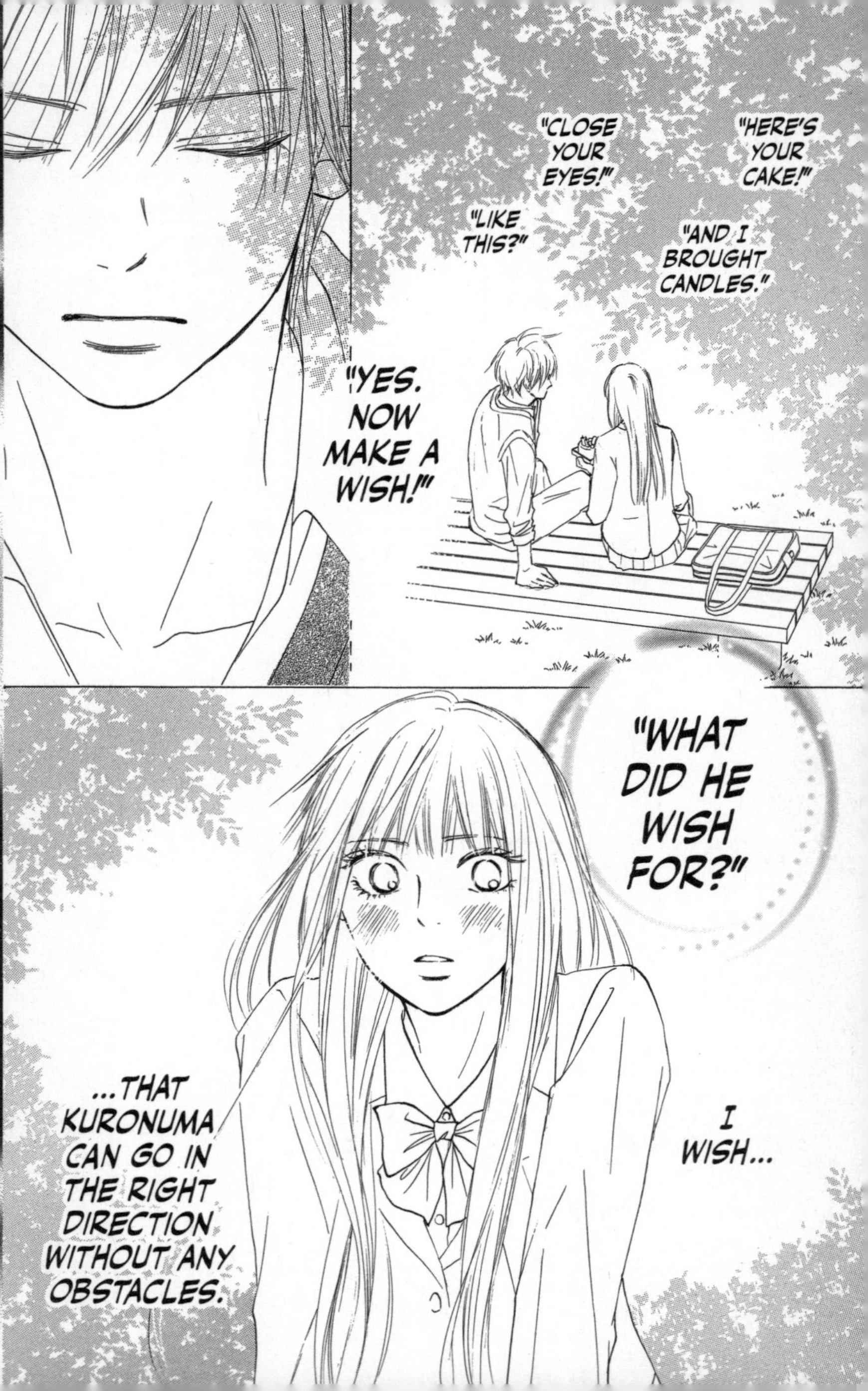
"HERE'S YOUR CAKE!"
"AND I BROUGHT CANDLES."
"CLOSE YOUR EYES!"
"LIKE THIS?"
"YES. NOW MAKE A WISH!"
"WHAT DID HE WISH FOR?"
I WISH...
...THAT KURONUMA CAN GO IN THE RIGHT DIRECTION WITHOUT ANY OBSTACLES.

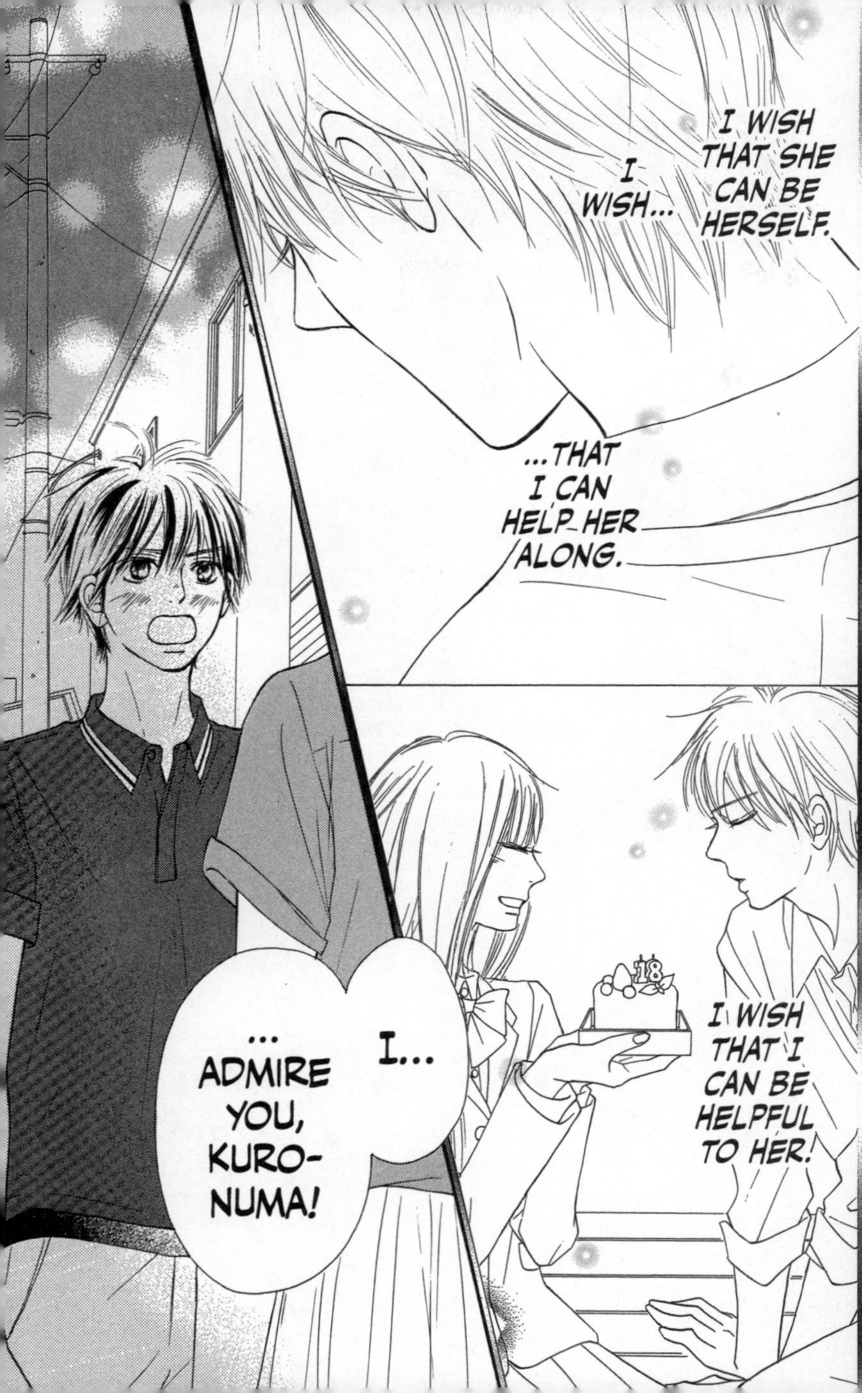
I WISH THAT SHE CAN BE HERSELF.
I WISH...
...THAT I CAN HELP HER ALONG.
I WISH THAT I CAN BE HELPFUL TO HER!
I...
...ADMIRE YOU, KURO-NUMA!

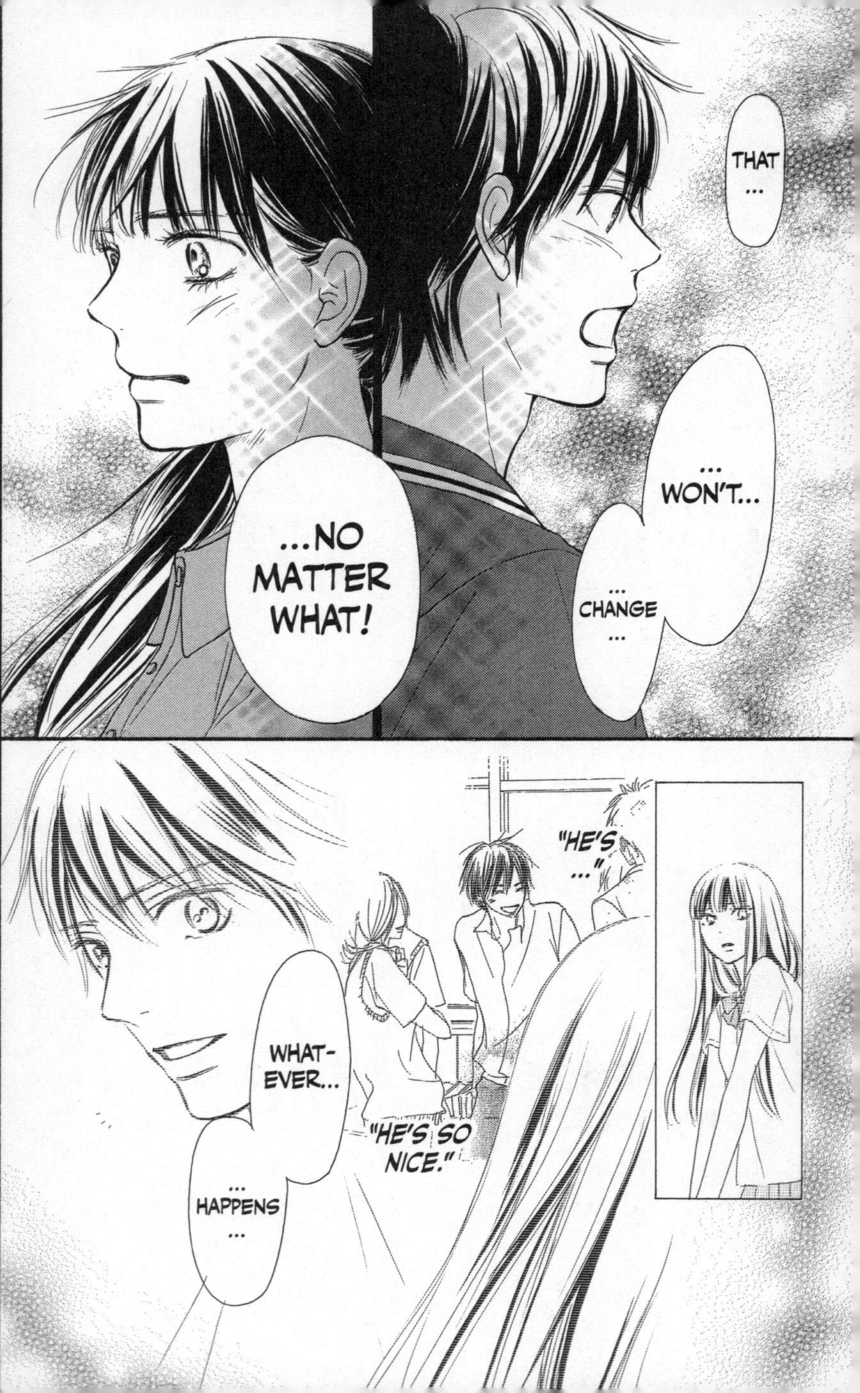
THAT ...
... WON'T...
... CHANGE ...
...NO MATTER WHAT!
"HE'S ..."
"HE'S SO NICE."
WHAT-EVER...
... HAPPENS ...

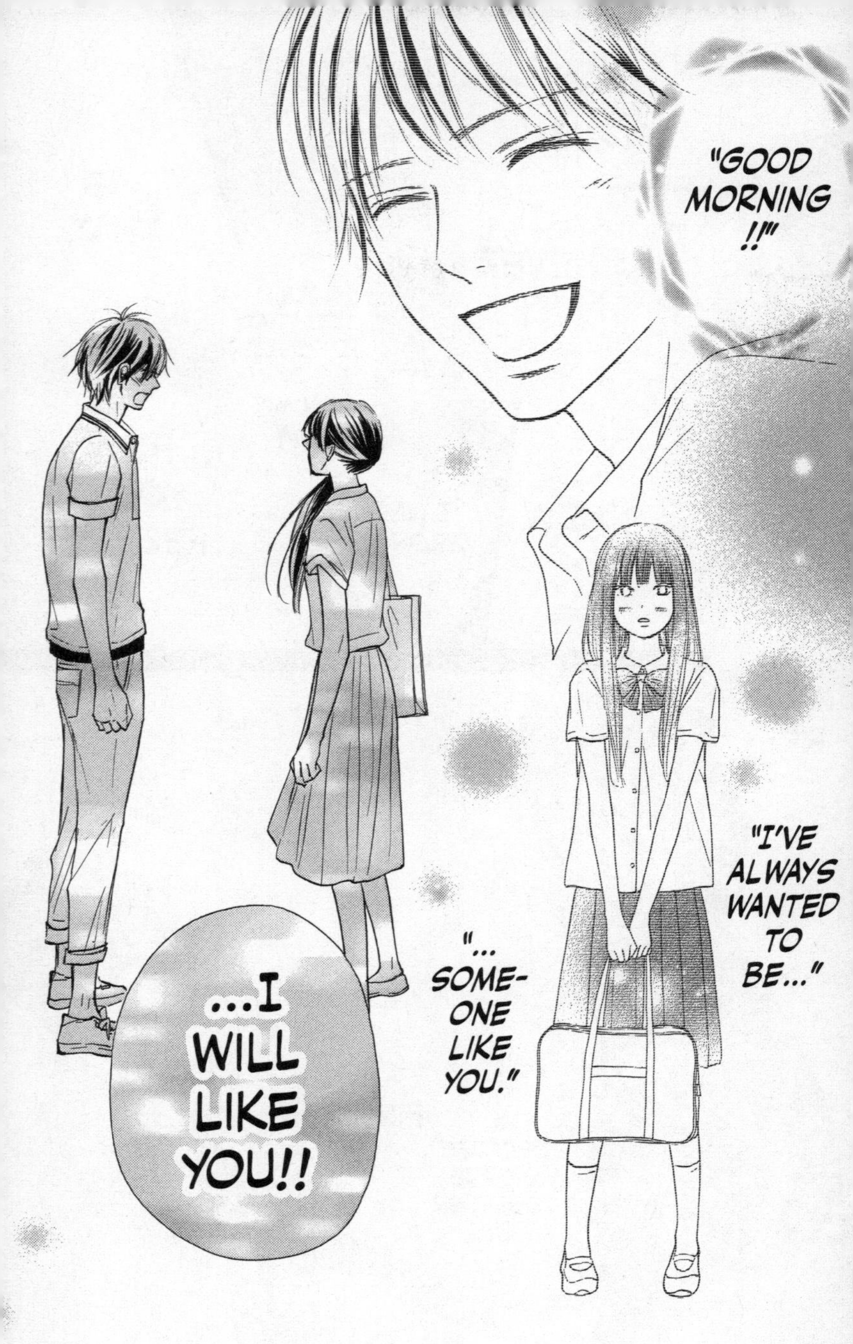
"GOOD MORNING!!"
"I'VE ALWAYS WANTED TO BE..."
"...SOMEONE LIKE YOU."
...I WILL LIKE YOU!!

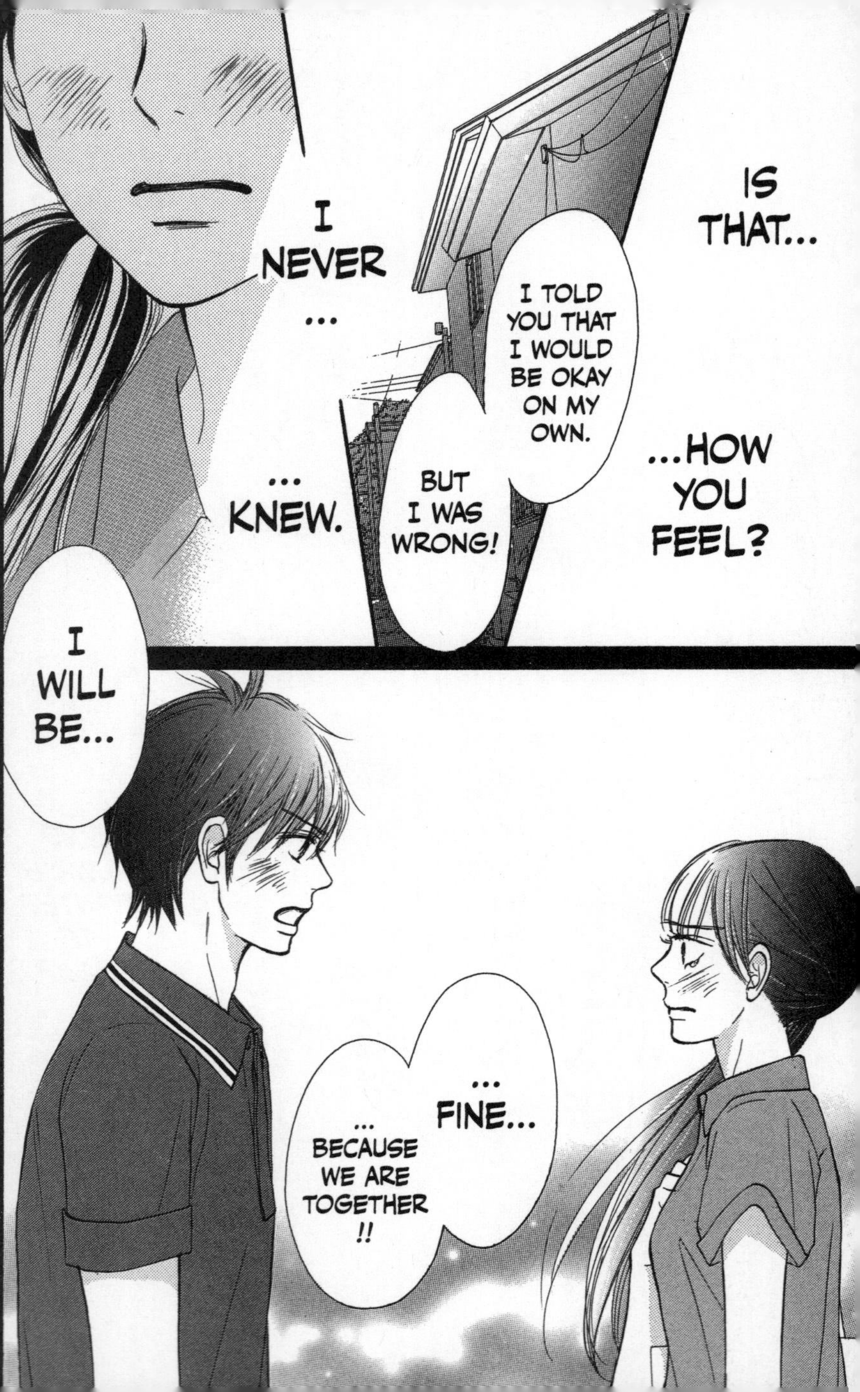
IS THAT...
...HOW YOU FEEL?
I TOLD YOU THAT I WOULD BE OKAY ON MY OWN.
BUT I WAS WRONG!
I NEVER ...
... KNEW.
I WILL BE...
... FINE...
... BECAUSE WE ARE TOGETHER !!

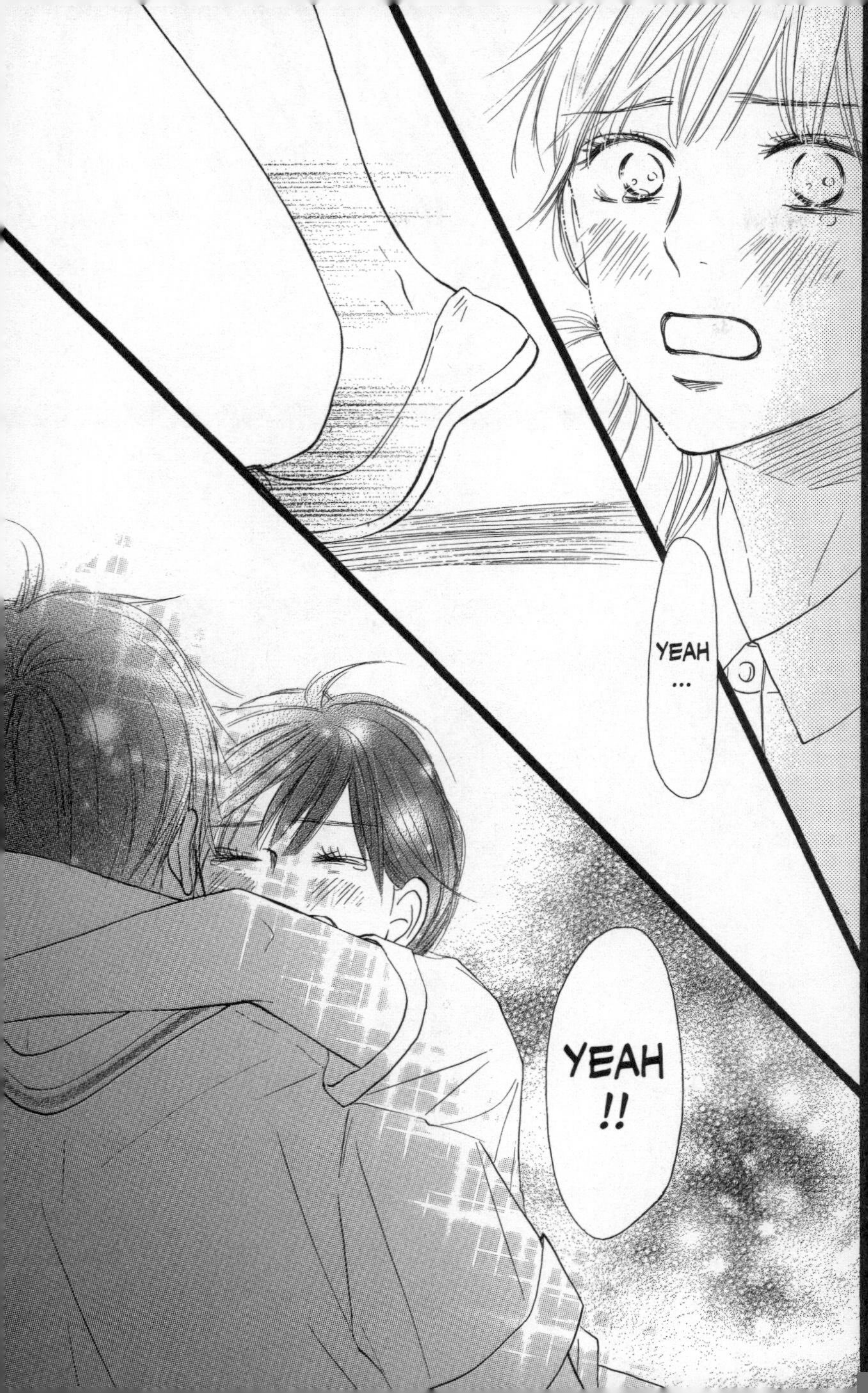
YEAH ...
YEAH !!

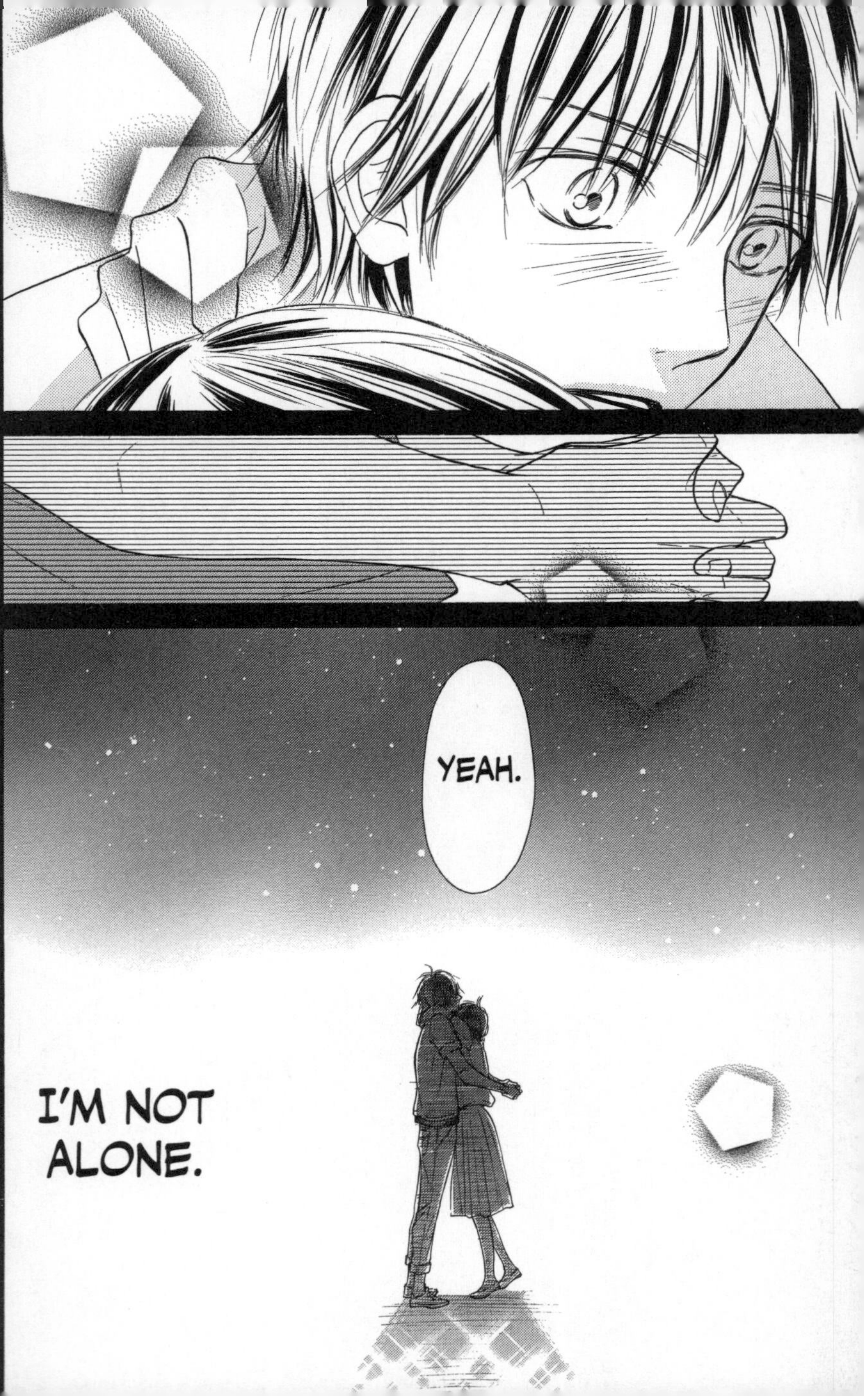
YEAH.
I'M NOT ALONE.

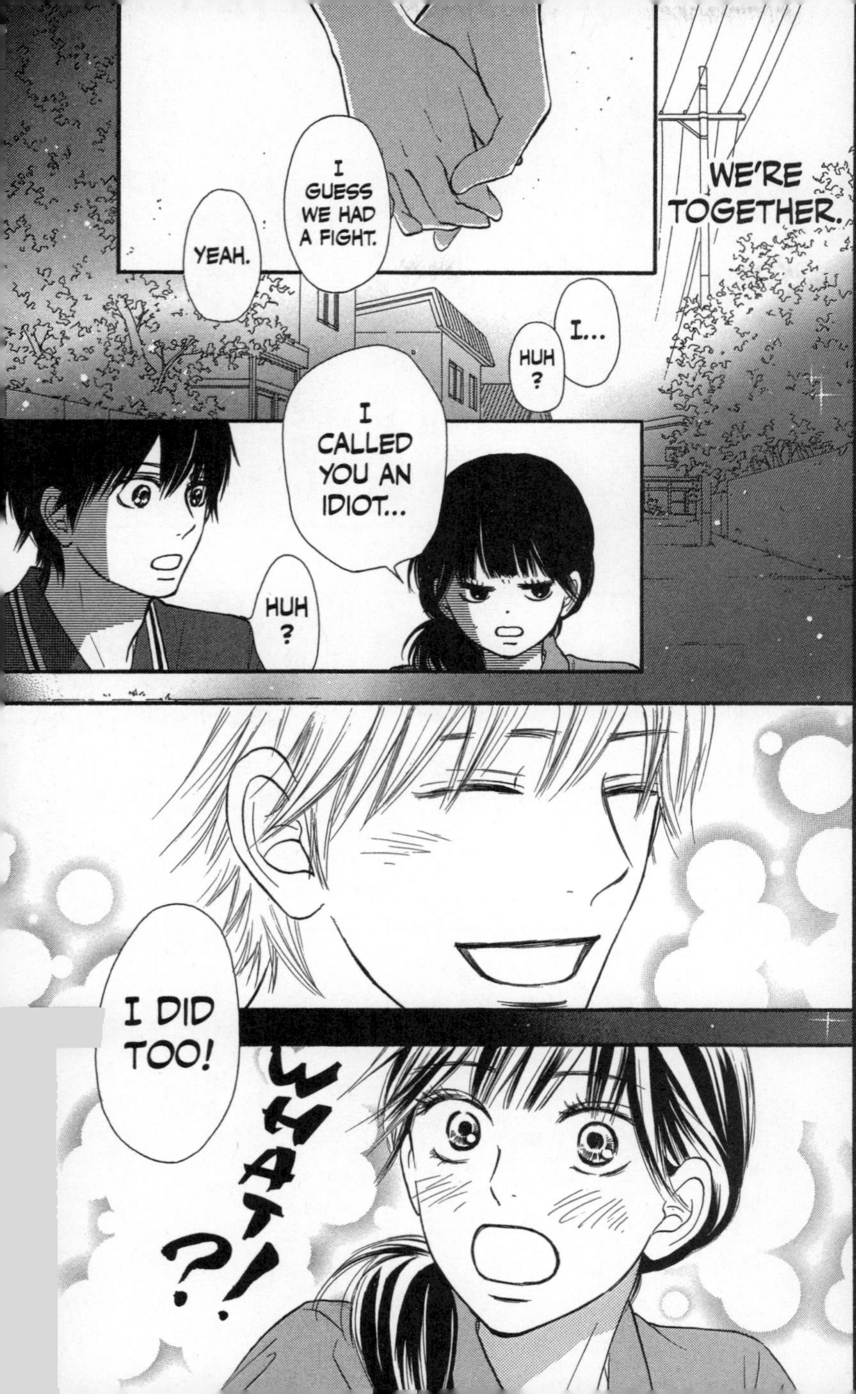
WE'RE TOGETHER.
I GUESS WE HAD A FIGHT.
YEAH.
I...
HUH?
I CALLED YOU AN IDIOT...
HUH?
I DID TOO!
WHAT?!

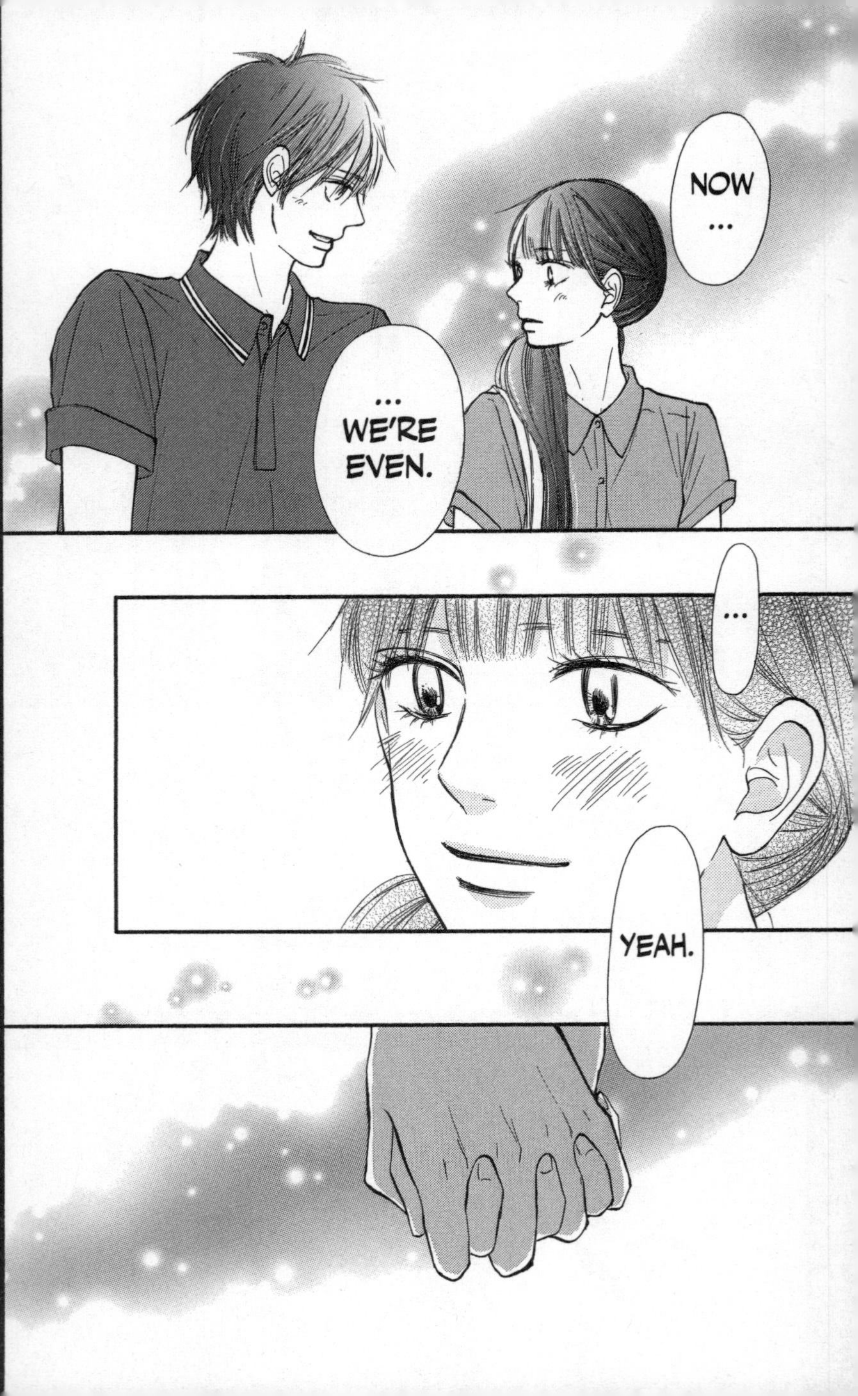
NOW ...
... WE'RE EVEN.
...
YEAH.

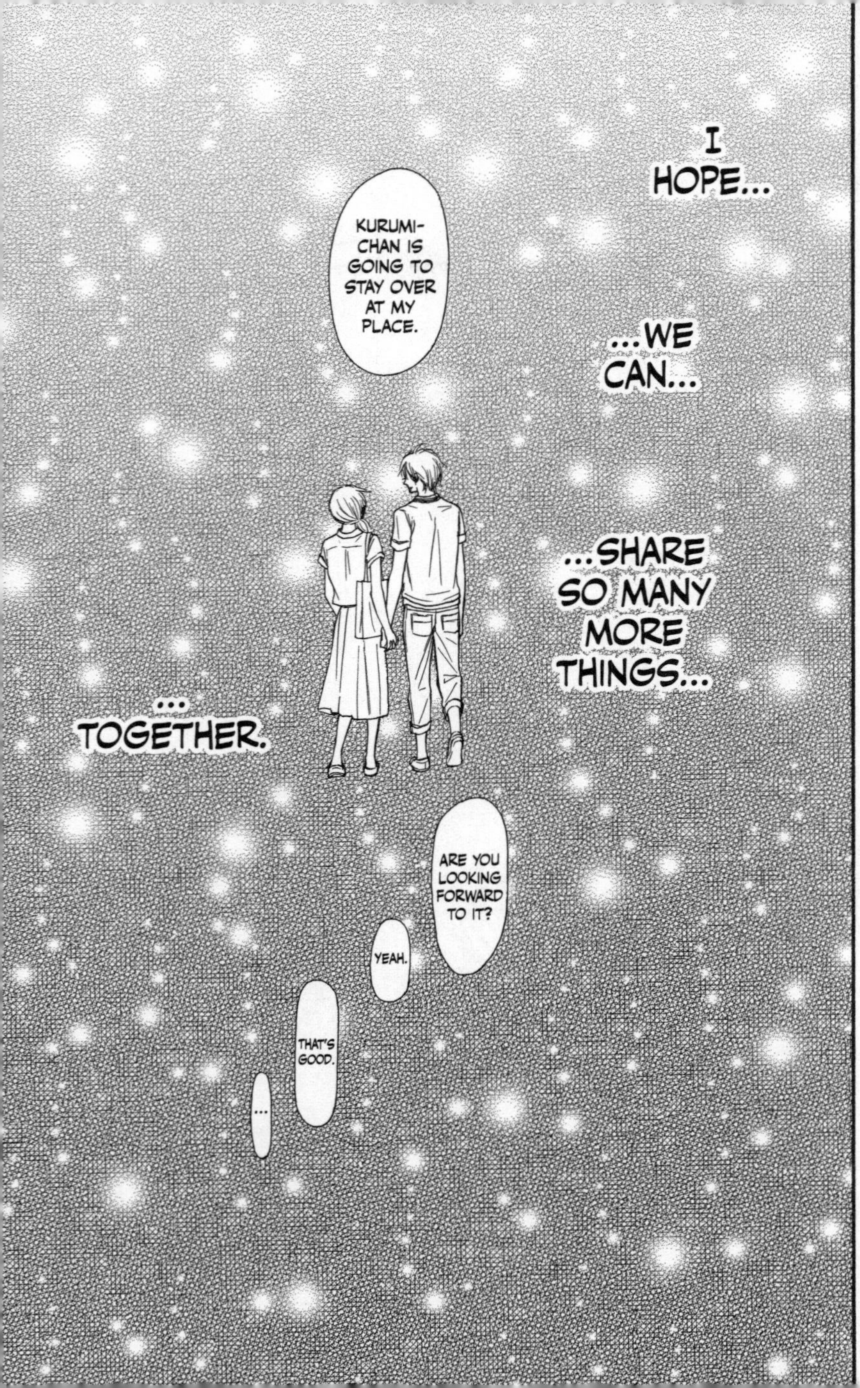
I HOPE...
KURUMI-CHAN IS GOING TO STAY OVER AT MY PLACE.
...WE CAN...
...SHARE SO MANY MORE THINGS...
... TOGETHER.
ARE YOU LOOKING FORWARD TO IT?
YEAH.
THAT'S GOOD.
...

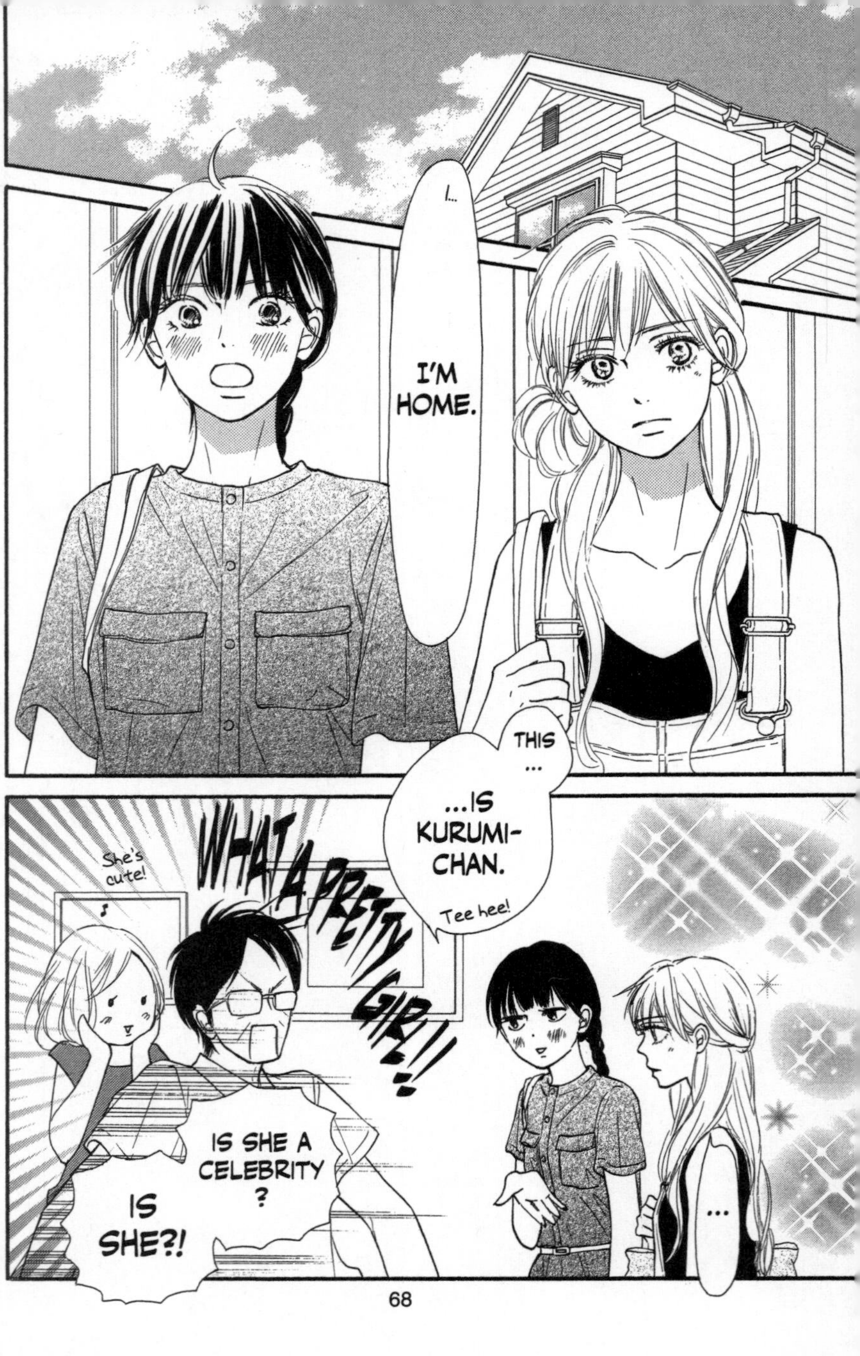
I...
I'M HOME.
THIS ...
...IS KURUMI-CHAN.
Tee hee!
WHAT A PRETTY GIRL!!
She's cute!
...
IS SHE A CELEBRITY?
IS SHE?!

KARUPIN on JAPAN 2

I'm going to drink those teas while I work!

By the way, something good happened recently. I got to work with Puré Gummy! I was so happy, since I eat them when I'm working and I crave something sour. Thank you for all the fun times!

I've never had a star-shaped Puré Gummy... No such luck!

My snacks at work are chinmi and Puré Gummy.

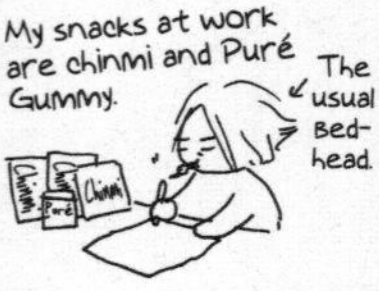

The usual Bed-head.
Chinmi
Puré
Chinmi

Anyway, this is turning into a long story. I don't know how many volumes are out anymore... Is this volume 26?

Seriously, if I could write better, it would have been more concise. Sorry about that...

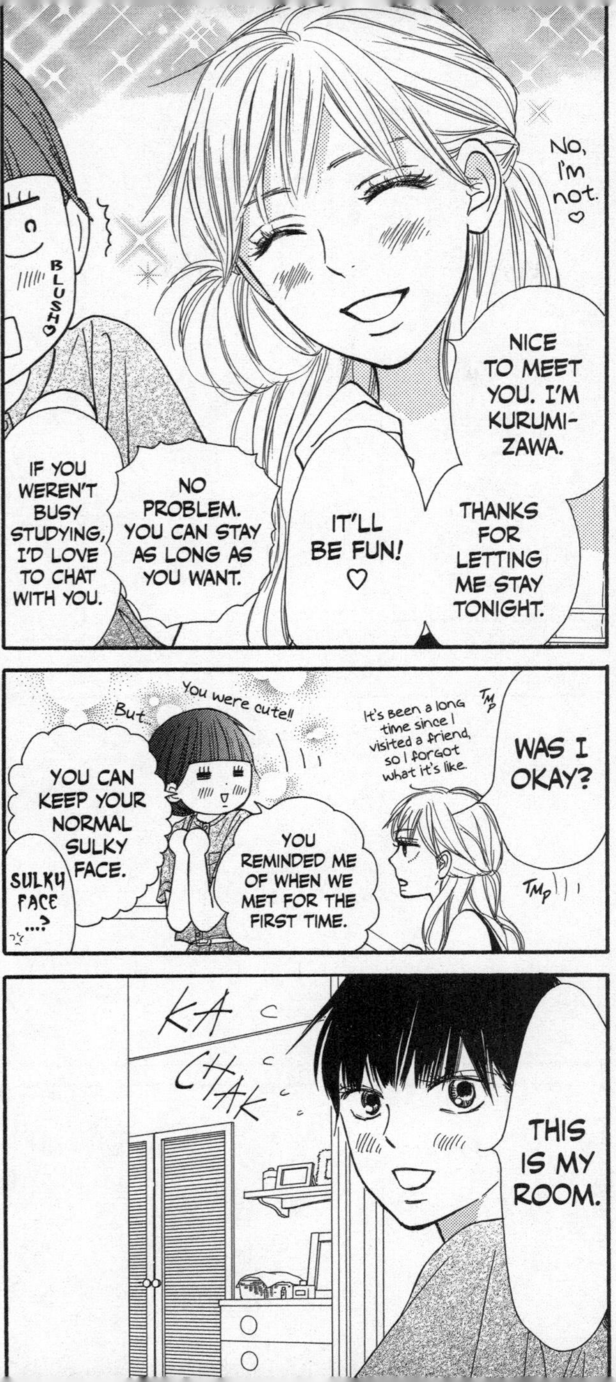

No, I'm not. ♡
NICE TO MEET YOU. I'M KURUMIZAWA.
THANKS FOR LETTING ME STAY TONIGHT.
IT'LL BE FUN! ♡
NO PROBLEM. YOU CAN STAY AS LONG AS YOU WANT.
IF YOU WEREN'T BUSY STUDYING, I'D LOVE TO CHAT WITH YOU.
BLUSH ♡
TMP
WAS I OKAY?
It's been a long time since I visited a friend, so I forgot what it's like.
TMP
You were cute!!
YOU REMINDED ME OF WHEN WE MET FOR THE FIRST TIME.
But...
YOU CAN KEEP YOUR NORMAL SULKY FACE.
SULKY FACE...?
THIS IS MY ROOM.
KA CHAK

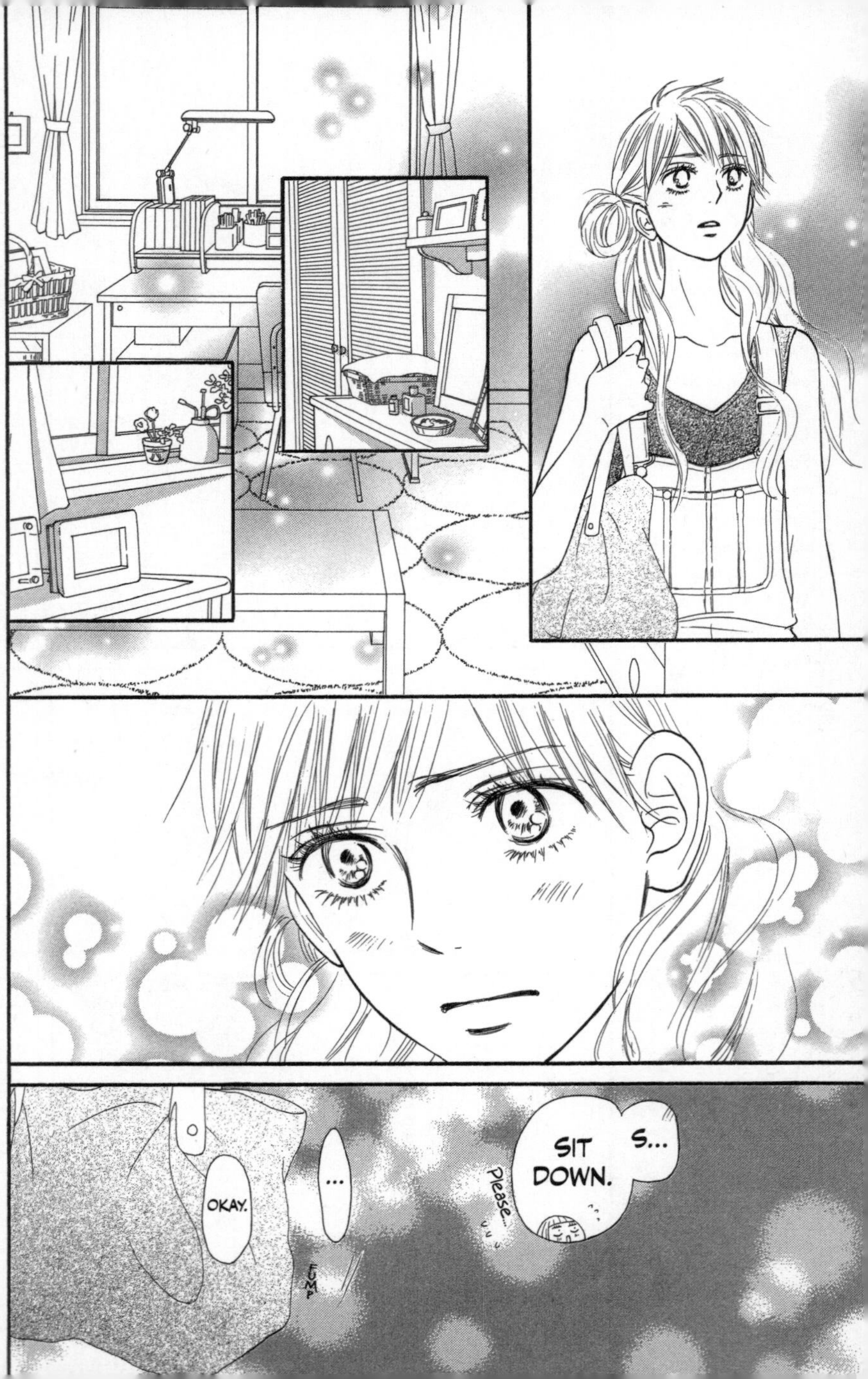
S...
SIT DOWN.
Please...
...
OKAY.
FUMP

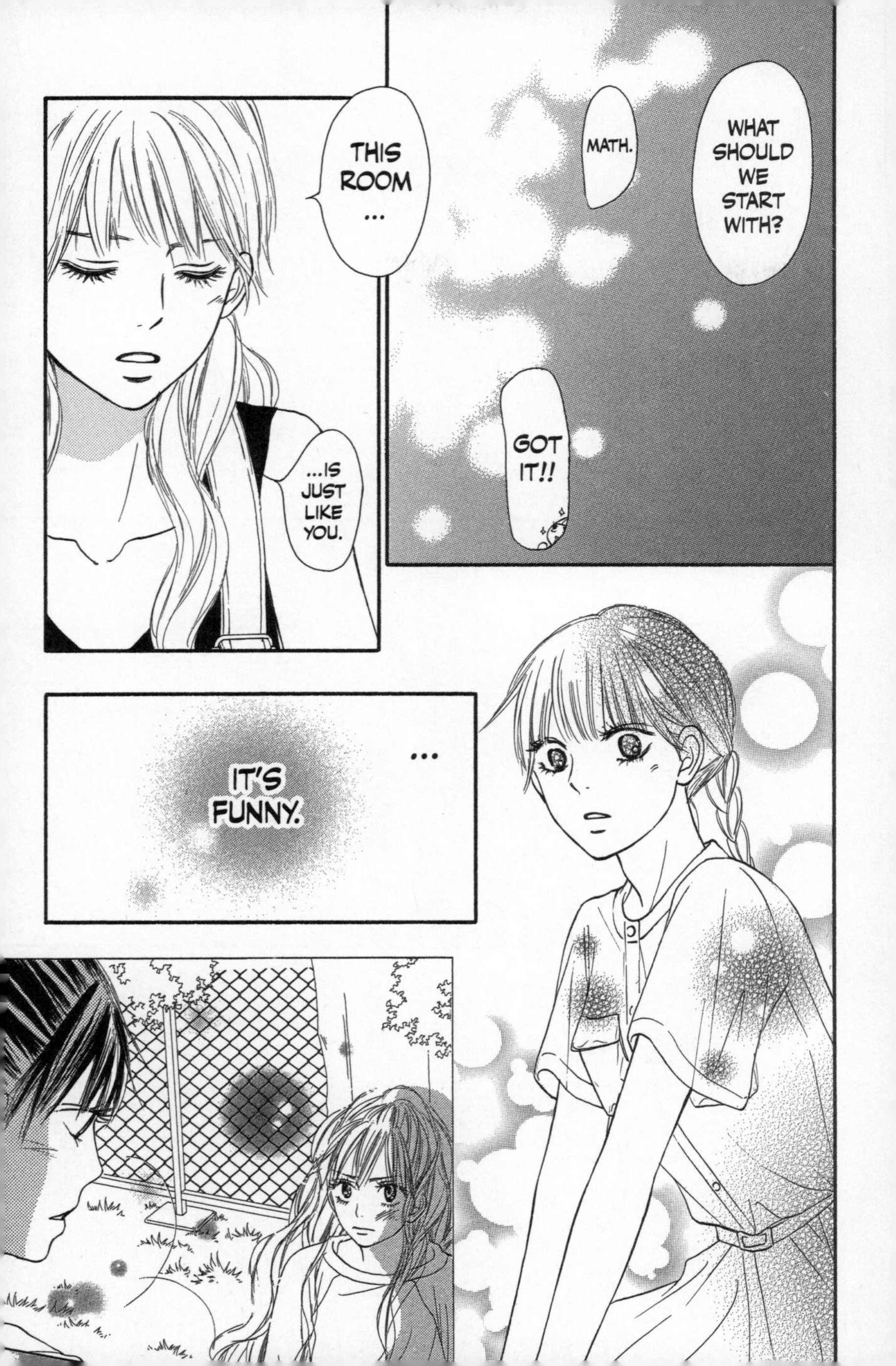
WHAT SHOULD WE START WITH?
MATH.
GOT IT!!
THIS ROOM ...
...IS JUST LIKE YOU.
...
IT'S FUNNY.

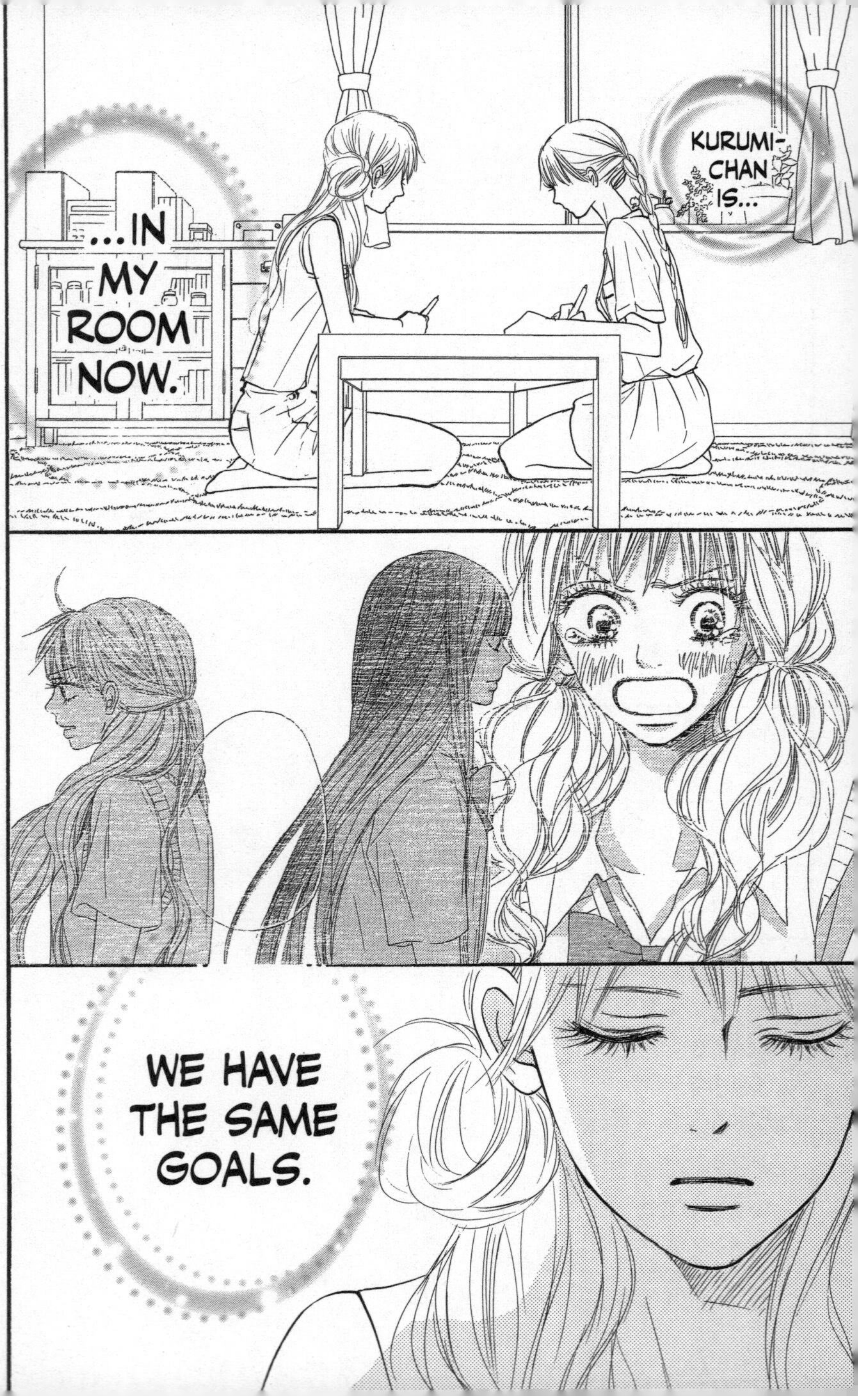
KURUMI-CHAN IS...
...IN MY ROOM NOW.
WE HAVE THE SAME GOALS.

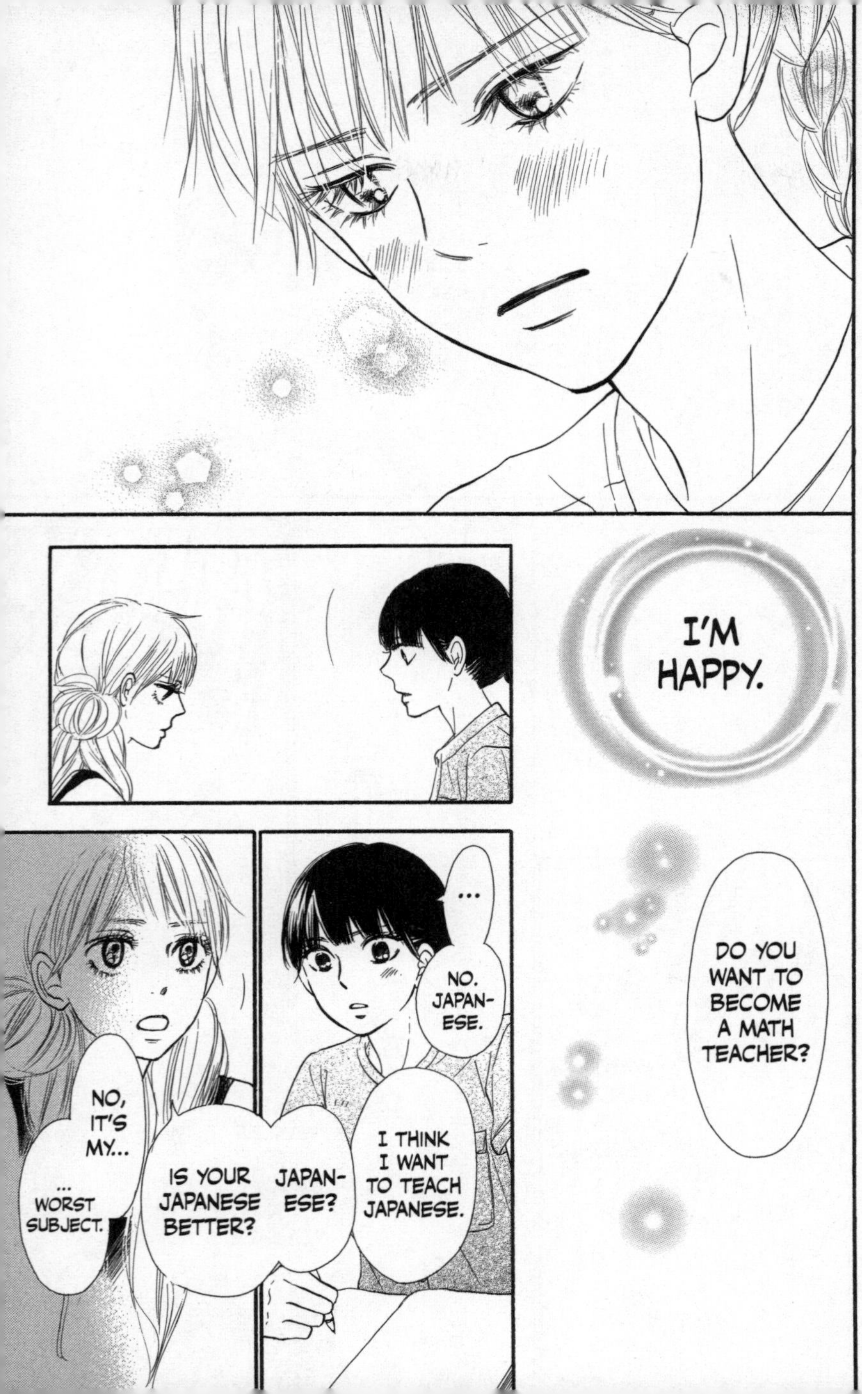
I'M HAPPY.
DO YOU WANT TO BECOME A MATH TEACHER?
...
NO. JAPANESE.
I THINK I WANT TO TEACH JAPANESE.
JAPANESE?
IS YOUR JAPANESE BETTER?
NO, IT'S MY...
... WORST SUBJECT.

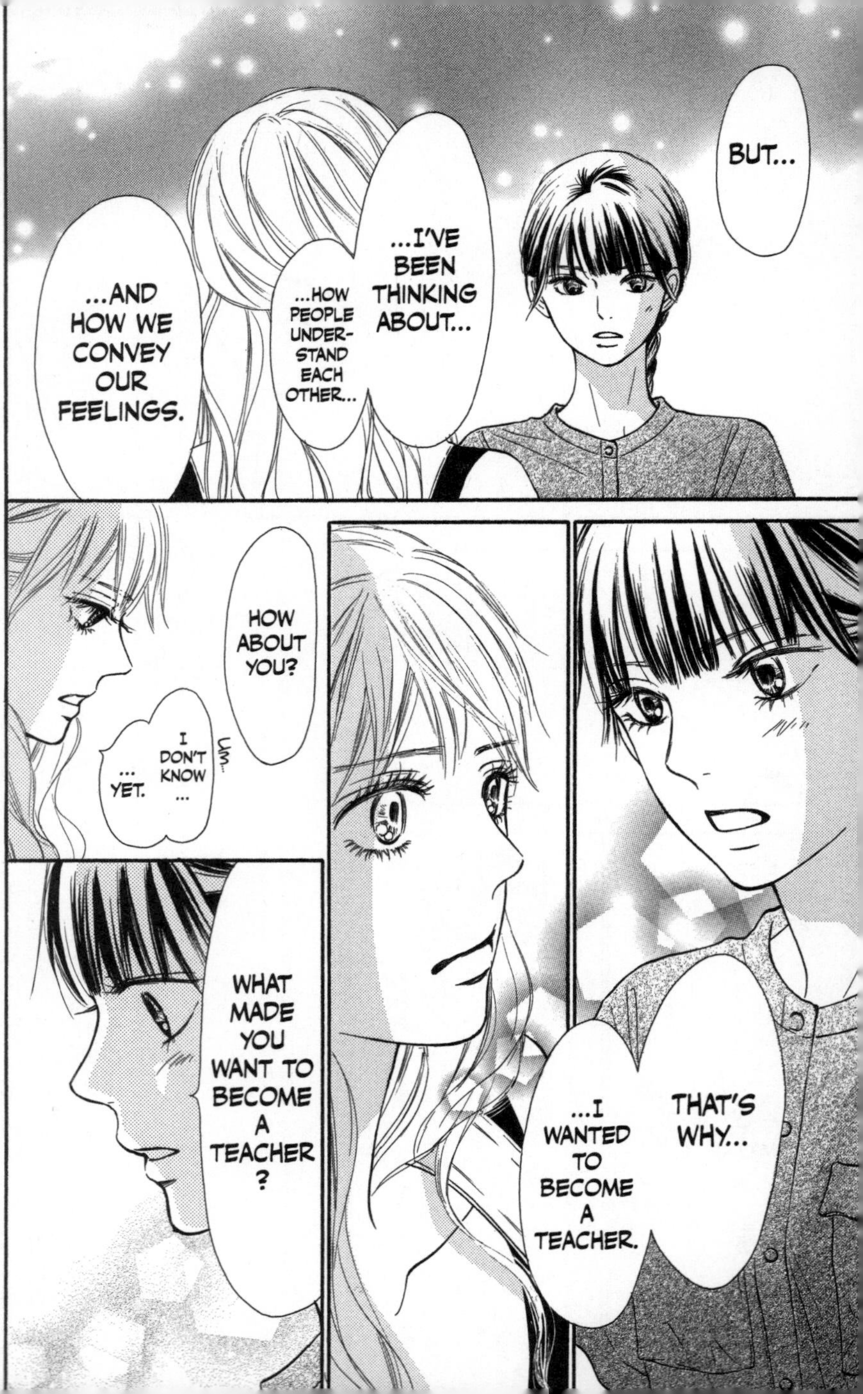
BUT...
...I'VE BEEN THINKING ABOUT...
...HOW PEOPLE UNDER-STAND EACH OTHER...
...AND HOW WE CONVEY OUR FEELINGS.
THAT'S WHY...
...I WANTED TO BECOME A TEACHER.
HOW ABOUT YOU?
Um...
I DON'T KNOW ...
... YET.
WHAT MADE YOU WANT TO BECOME A TEACHER?

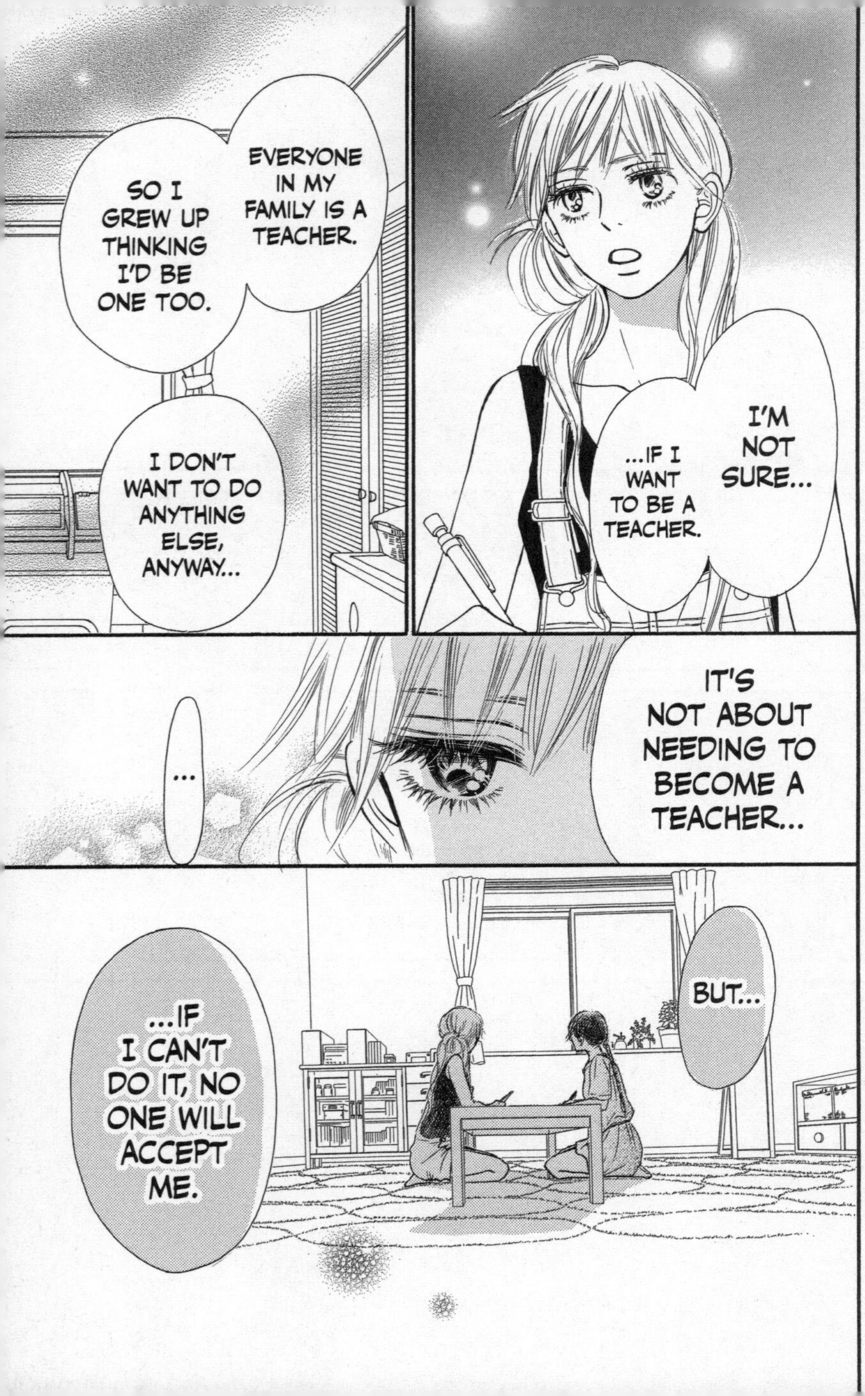
I'M NOT SURE...
...IF I WANT TO BE A TEACHER.
EVERYONE IN MY FAMILY IS A TEACHER.
SO I GREW UP THINKING I'D BE ONE TOO.
I DON'T WANT TO DO ANYTHING ELSE, ANYWAY...
IT'S NOT ABOUT NEEDING TO BECOME A TEACHER...
...
BUT...
...IF I CAN'T DO IT, NO ONE WILL ACCEPT ME.

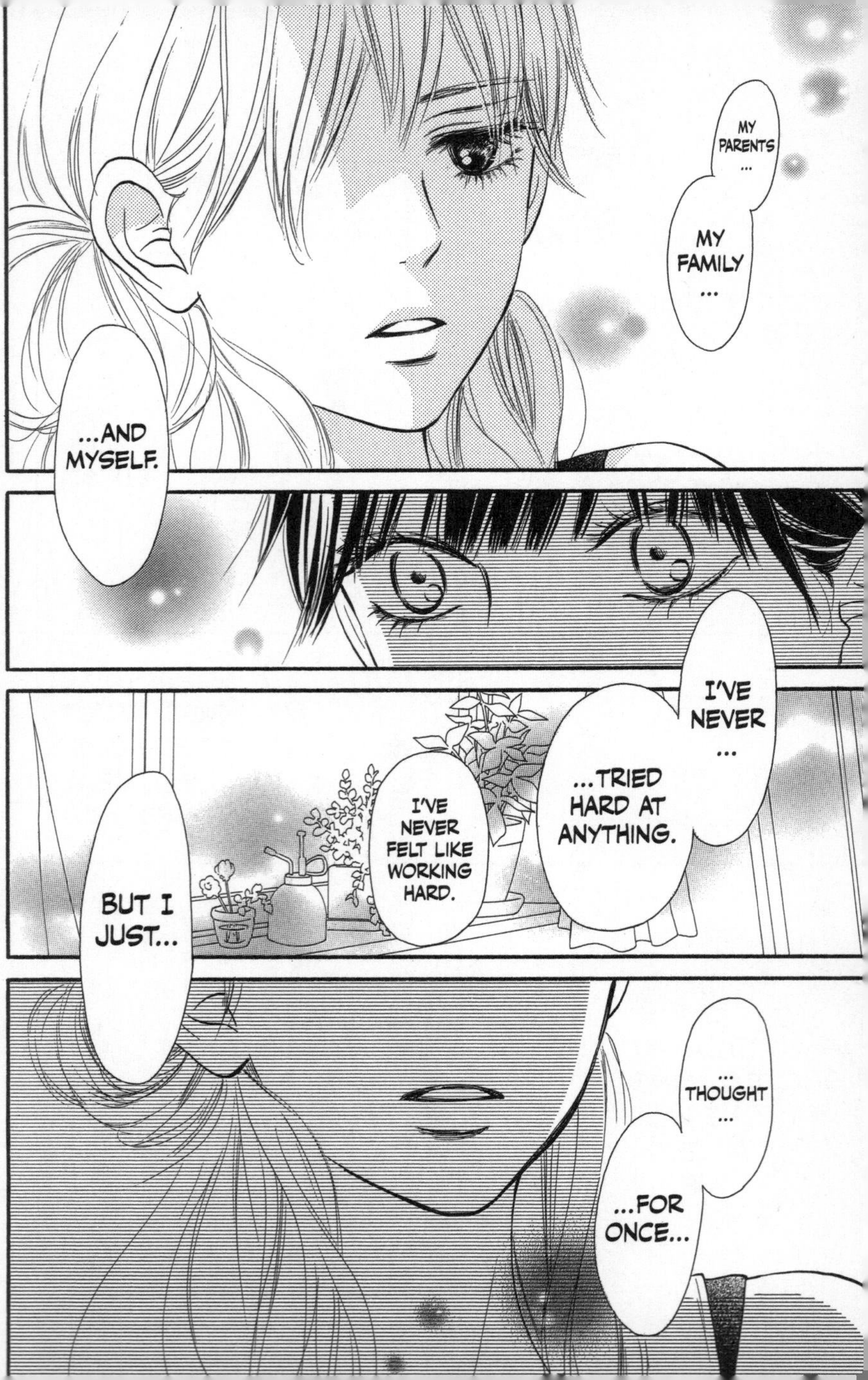
MY PARENTS ...
MY FAMILY ...
...AND MYSELF.
I'VE NEVER ...
...TRIED HARD AT ANYTHING.
I'VE NEVER FELT LIKE WORKING HARD.
BUT I JUST...
... THOUGHT ...
...FOR ONCE...

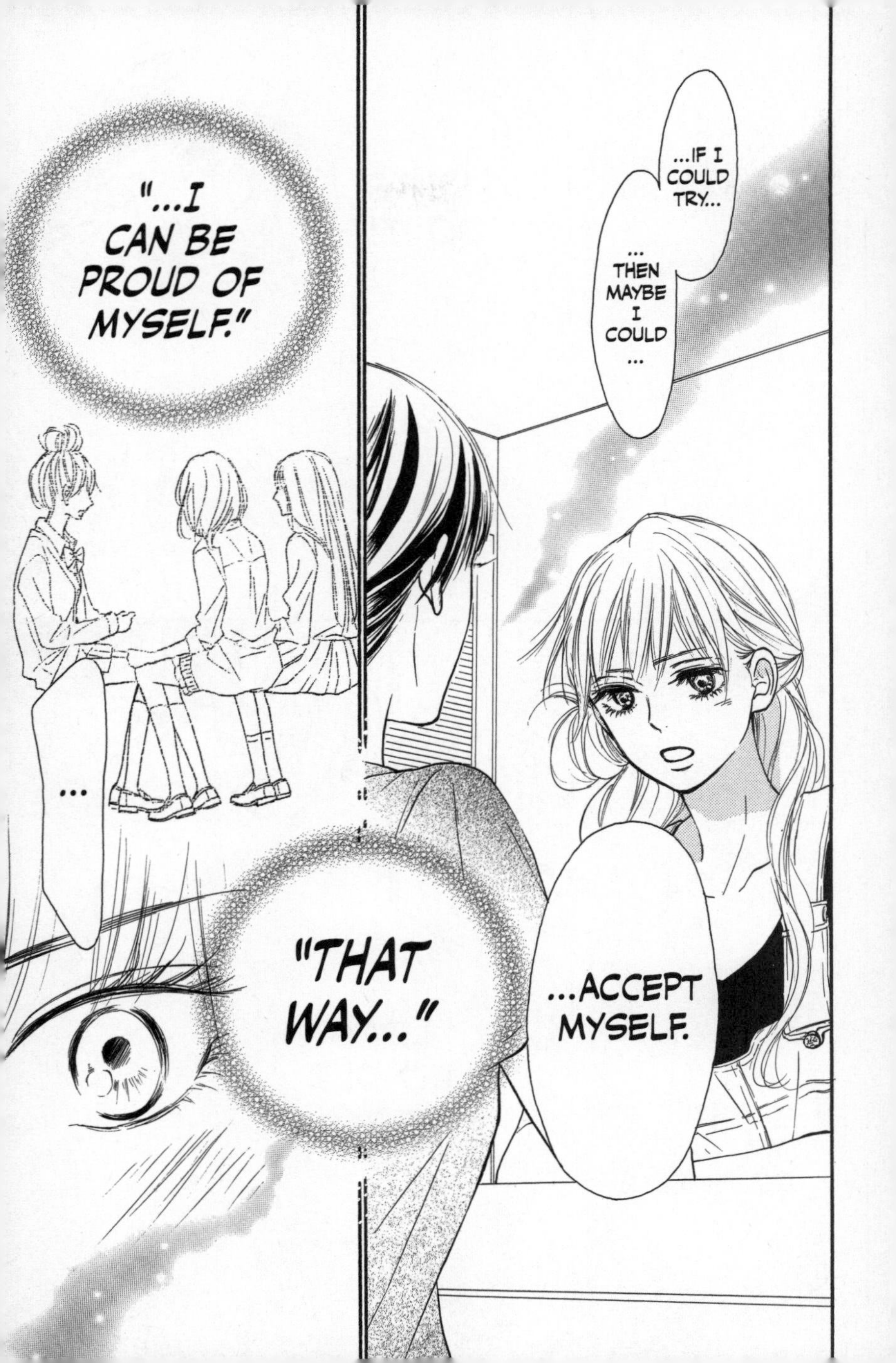
...IF I COULD TRY...
... THEN MAYBE I COULD ...
...ACCEPT MYSELF.
"...I CAN BE PROUD OF MYSELF."
...
"THAT WAY..."

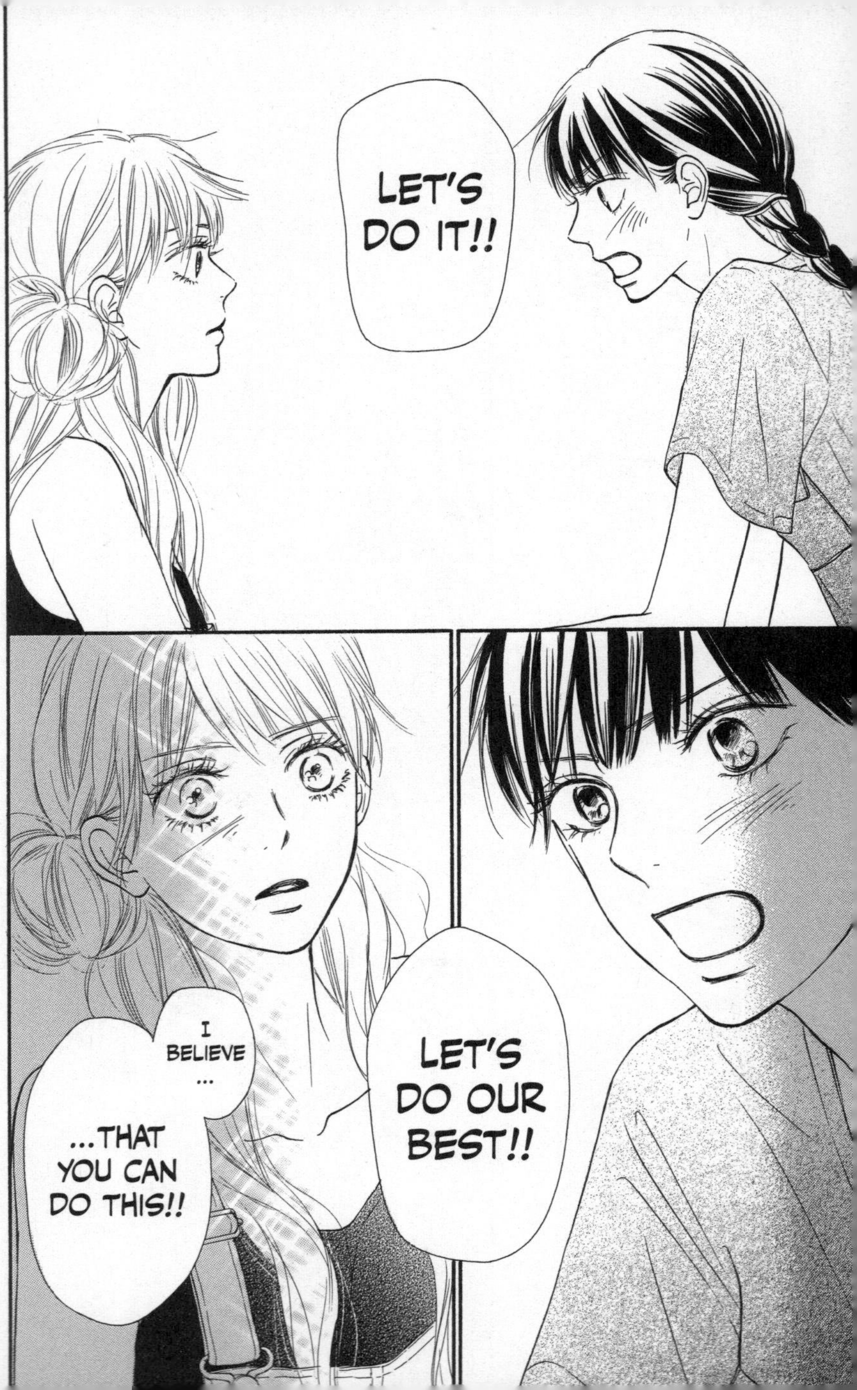
LET'S DO IT!!
LET'S DO OUR BEST!!
I BELIEVE...
...THAT YOU CAN DO THIS!!

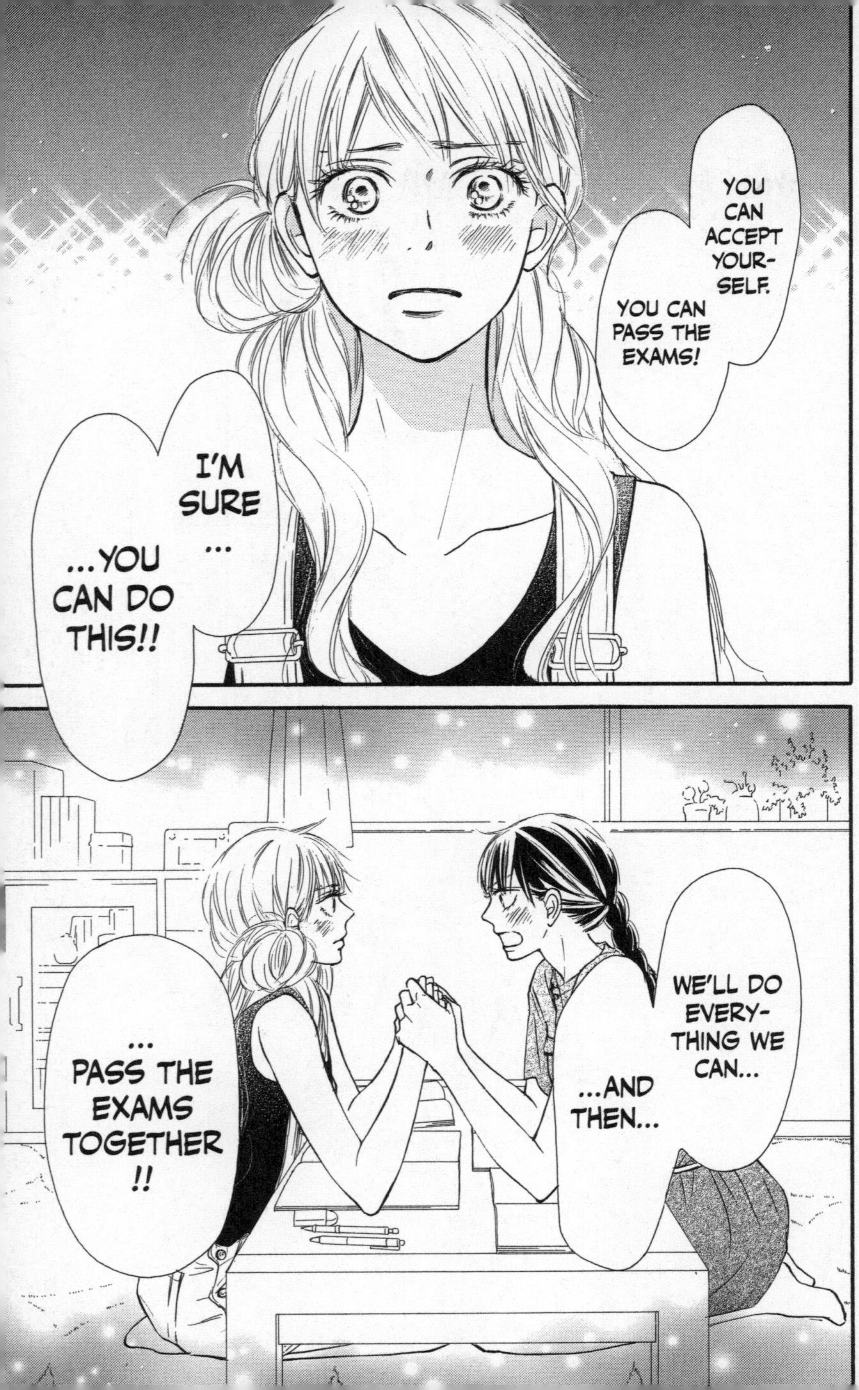
YOU CAN ACCEPT YOUR-SELF.
YOU CAN PASS THE EXAMS!
I'M SURE ...
...YOU CAN DO THIS!!
WE'LL DO EVERY-THING WE CAN...
...AND THEN...
... PASS THE EXAMS TOGETHER !!

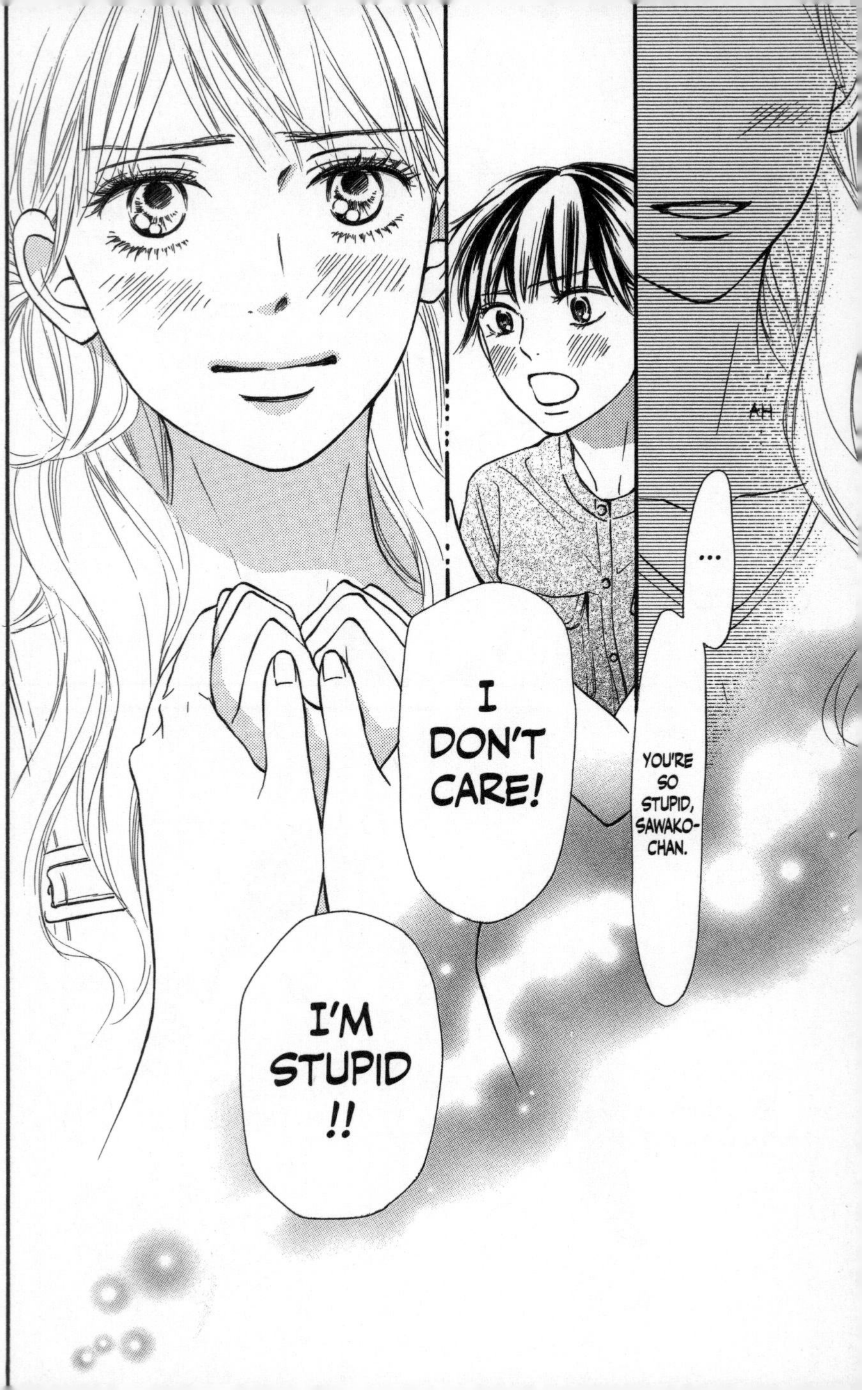
AH
...
YOU'RE SO STUPID, SAWAKO-CHAN.
I DON'T CARE!
I'M STUPID!!

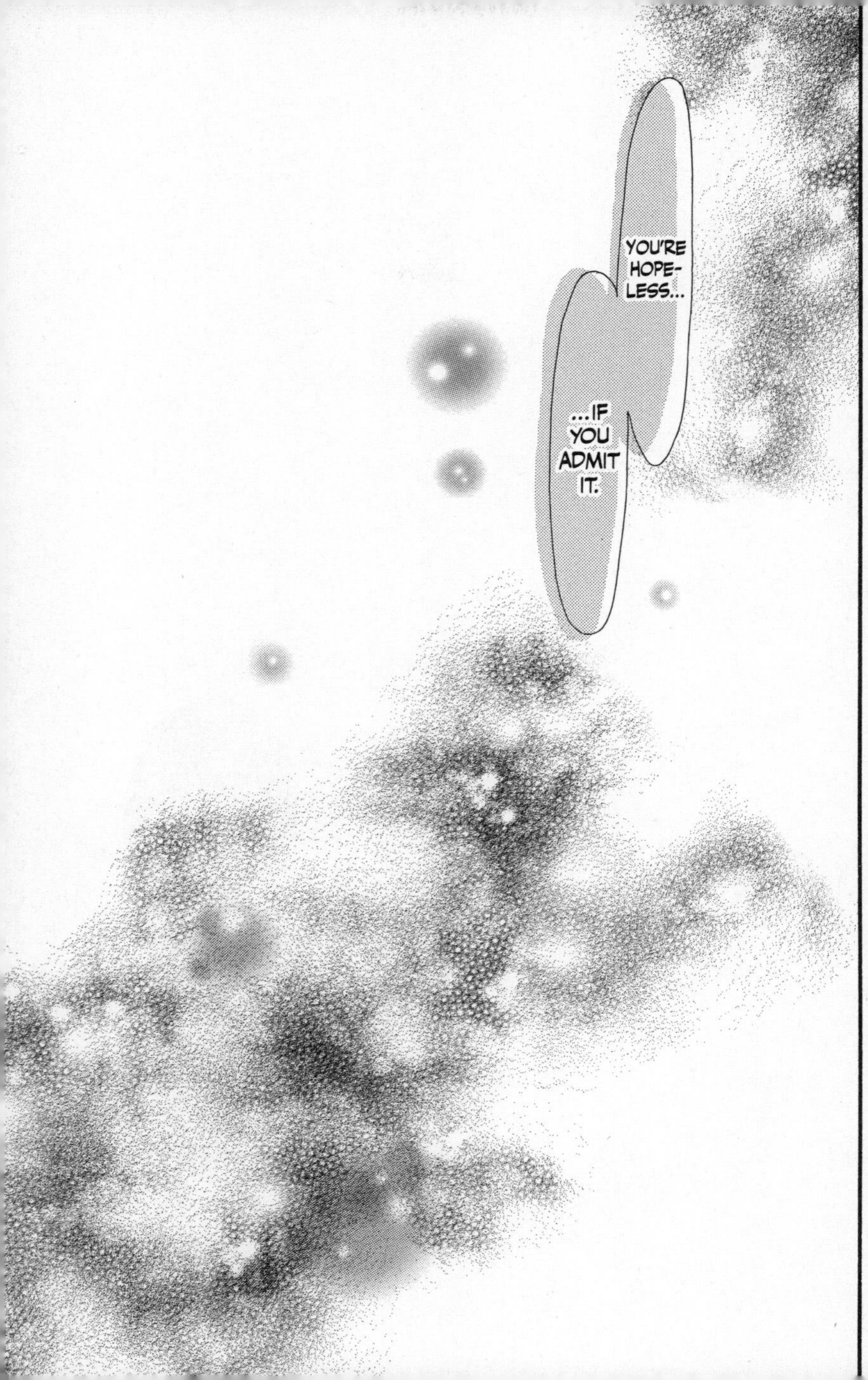
YOU'RE HOPE-LESS...
...IF YOU ADMIT IT.

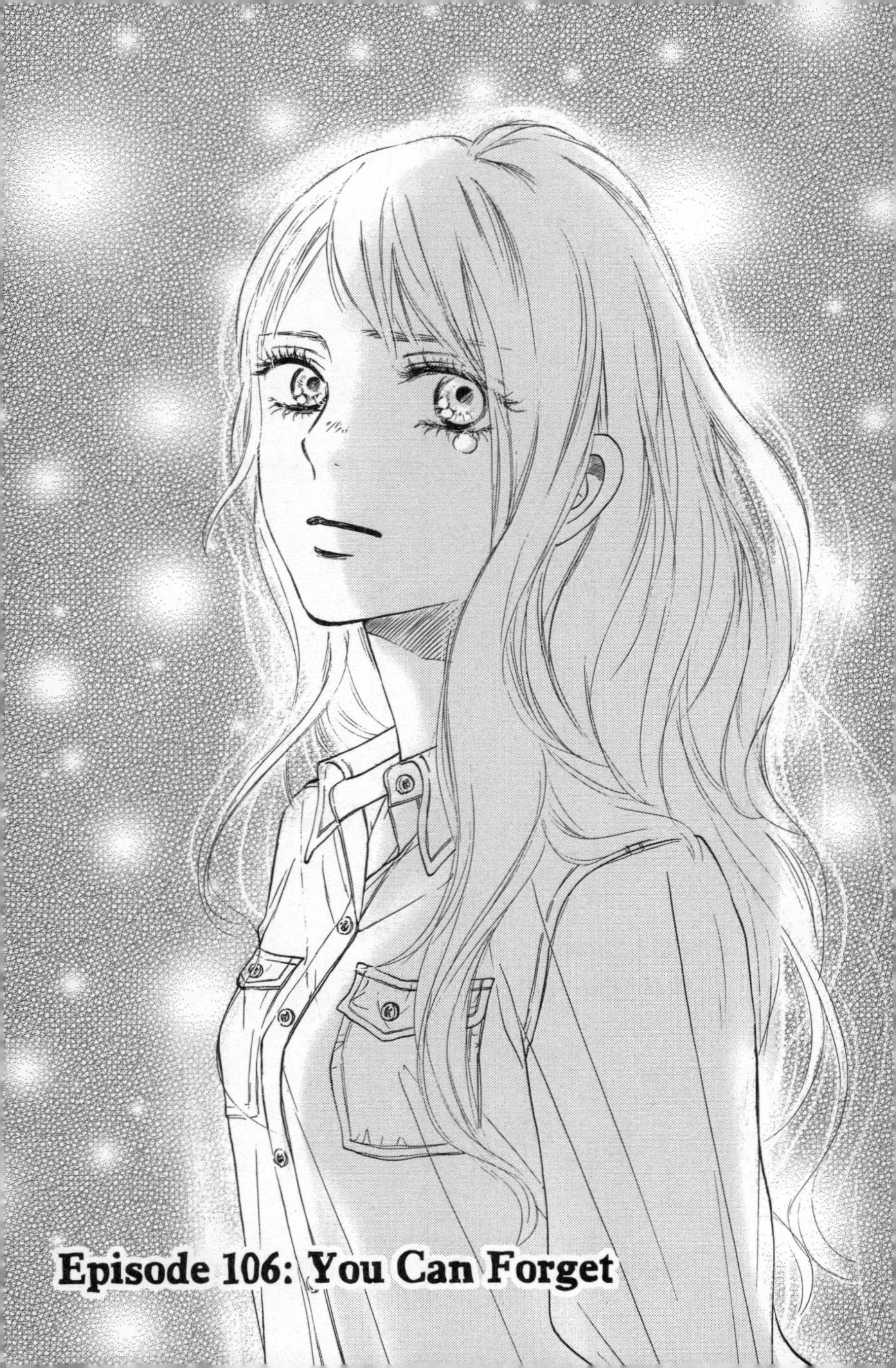

Episode 106: You Can Forget

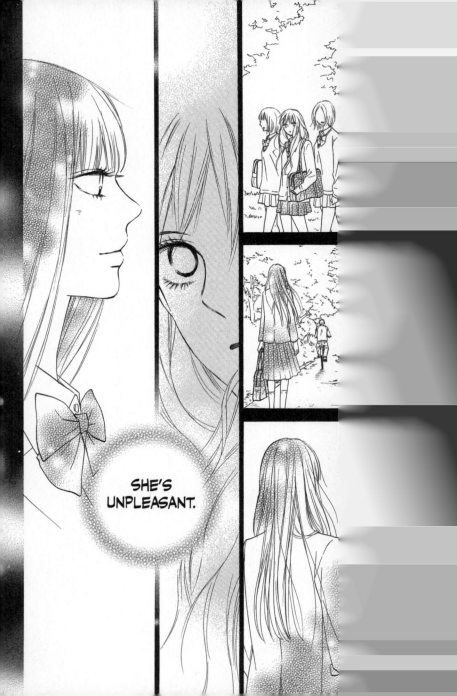

SHE'S UNPLEASANT.

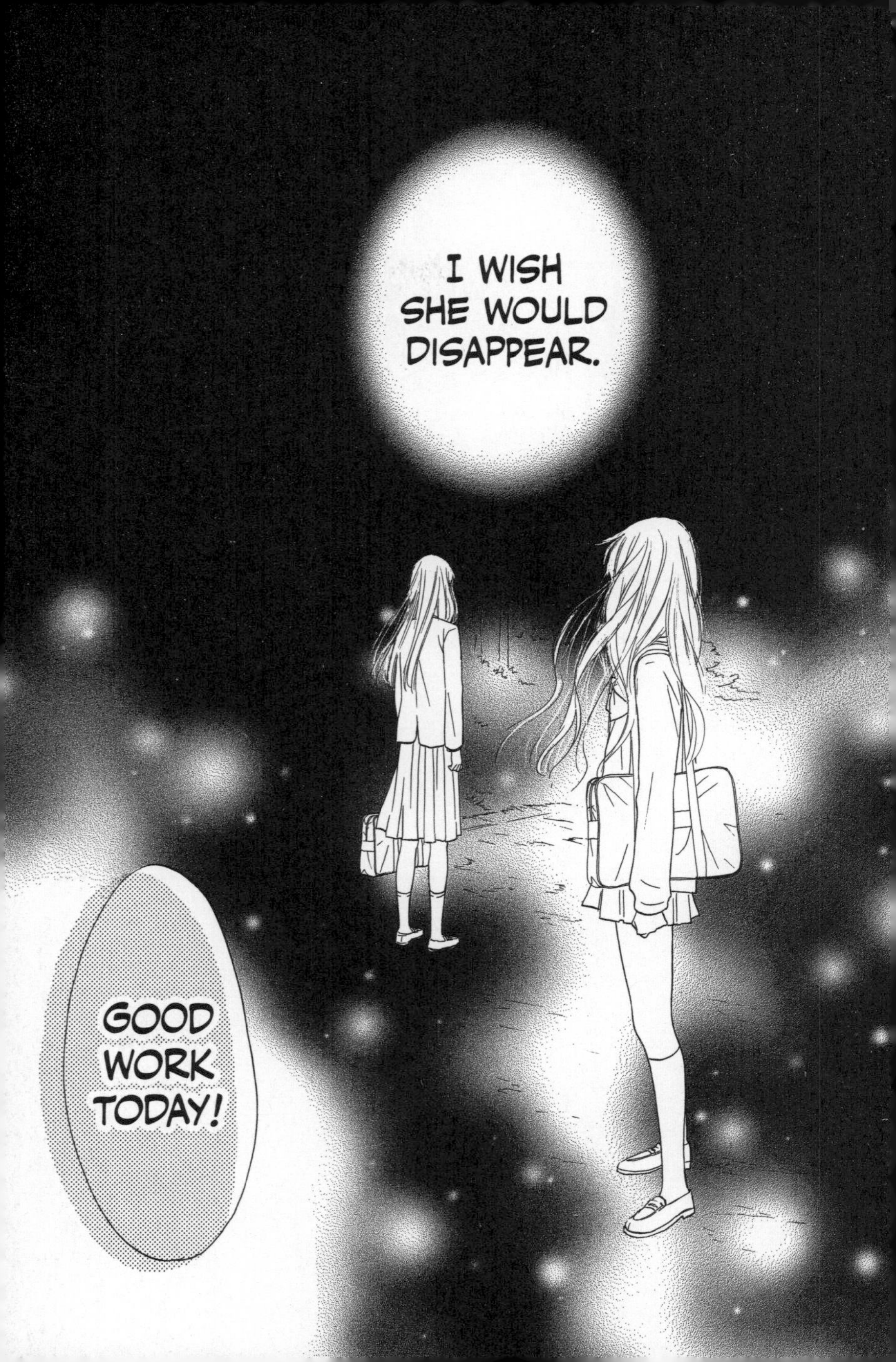
I WISH SHE WOULD DISAPPEAR.
GOOD WORK TODAY!

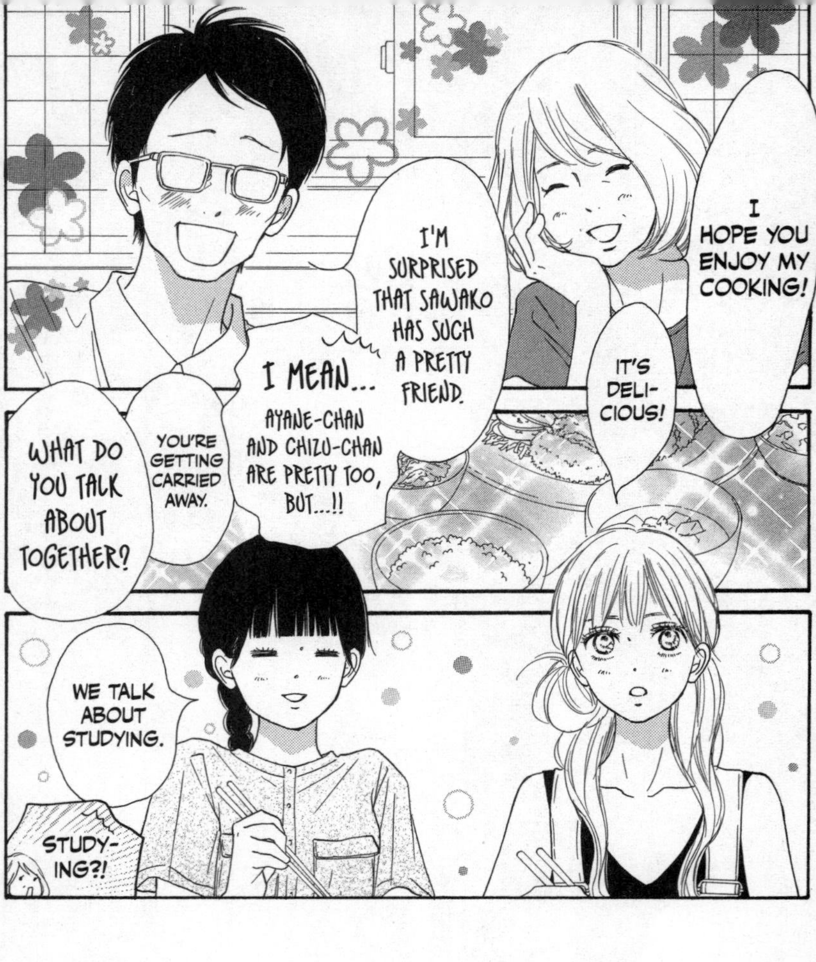
I HOPE YOU ENJOY MY COOKING!
IT'S DELI-CIOUS!
I'M SURPRISED THAT SAWAKO HAS SUCH A PRETTY FRIEND.
I MEAN... AYANE-CHAN AND CHIZU-CHAN ARE PRETTY TOO, BUT...!!
YOU'RE GETTING CARRIED AWAY.
WHAT DO YOU TALK ABOUT TOGETHER?
WE TALK ABOUT STUDYING.
STUDY-ING?!

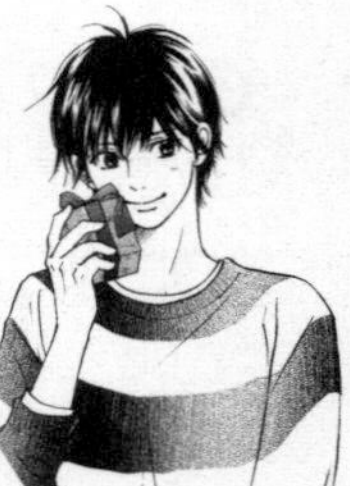

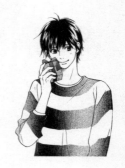

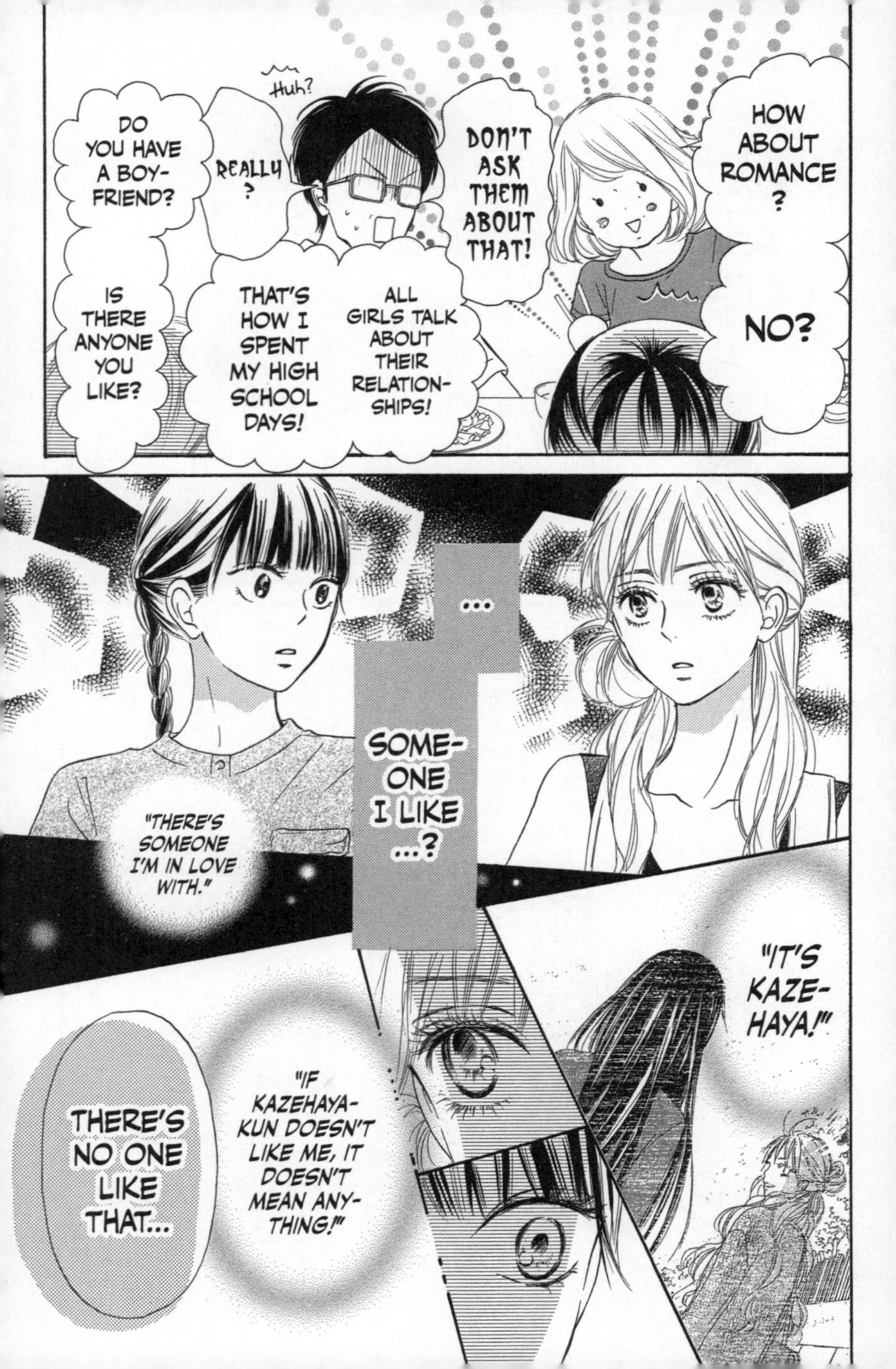
HOW ABOUT ROMANCE?
NO?
DON'T ASK THEM ABOUT THAT!
Huh?
REALLY?
ALL GIRLS TALK ABOUT THEIR RELATION-SHIPS!
THAT'S HOW I SPENT MY HIGH SCHOOL DAYS!
DO YOU HAVE A BOY-FRIEND?
IS THERE ANYONE YOU LIKE?
...
SOME-ONE I LIKE ...?
"THERE'S SOMEONE I'M IN LOVE WITH."
"IT'S KAZE-HAYA!"
"IF KAZEHAYA-KUN DOESN'T LIKE ME, IT DOESN'T MEAN ANY-THING!"
THERE'S NO ONE LIKE THAT...

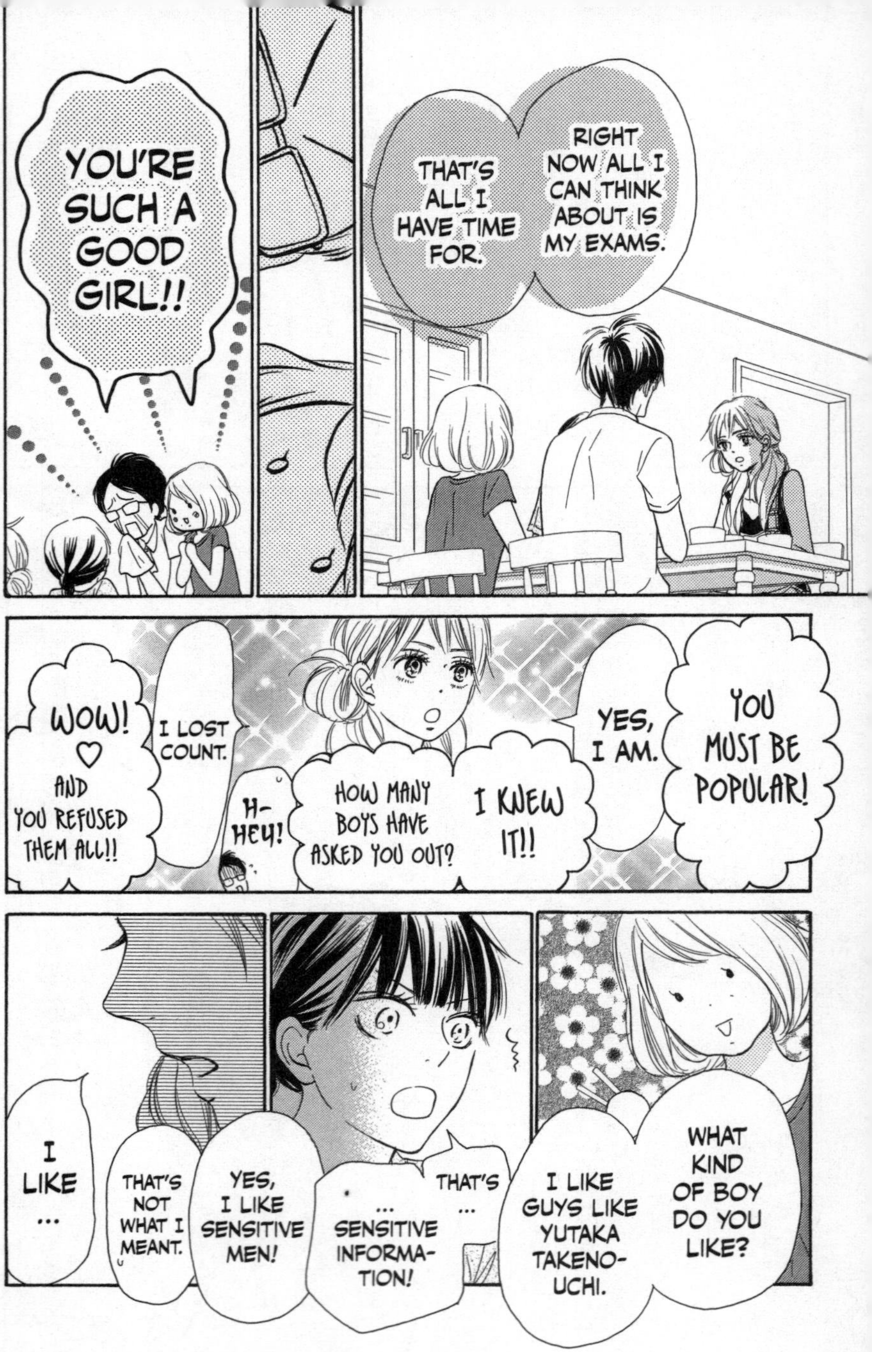
RIGHT NOW ALL I CAN THINK ABOUT IS MY EXAMS.
THAT'S ALL I HAVE TIME FOR.
YOU'RE SUCH A GOOD GIRL!!
YOU MUST BE POPULAR!
YES, I AM.
I KNEW IT!!
HOW MANY BOYS HAVE ASKED YOU OUT?
H-HEY!
I LOST COUNT.
WOW! ♥ AND YOU REFUSED THEM ALL!!
WHAT KIND OF BOY DO YOU LIKE?
I LIKE GUYS LIKE YUTAKA TAKENO-UCHI.
THAT'S ...
... SENSITIVE INFORMA-TION!
YES, I LIKE SENSITIVE MEN!
THAT'S NOT WHAT I MEANT.
I LIKE ...

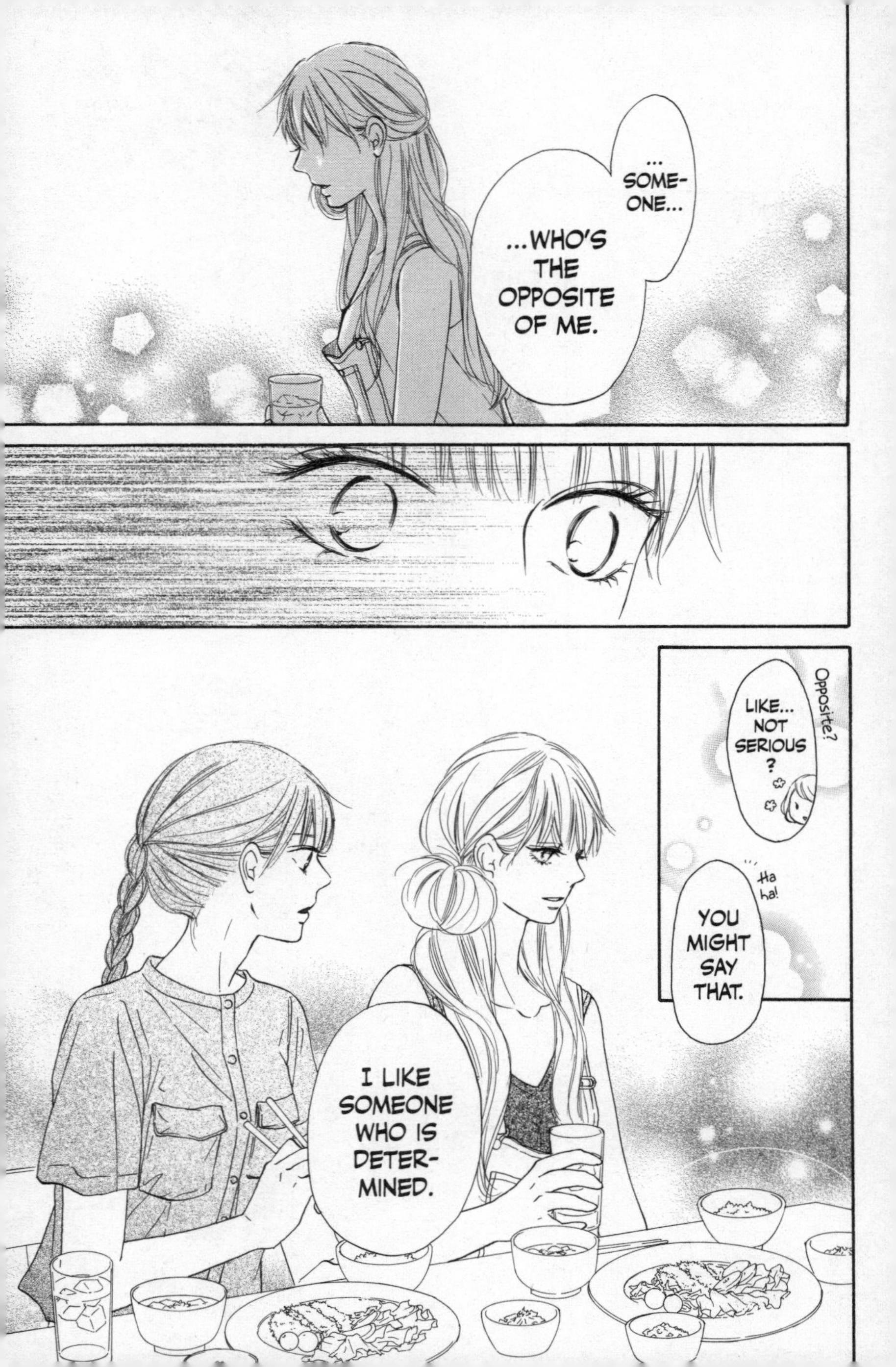

... SOME-ONE...
...WHO'S THE OPPOSITE OF ME.
Opposite?
LIKE... NOT SERIOUS?
Ha ha!
YOU MIGHT SAY THAT.
I LIKE SOMEONE WHO IS DETER-MINED.

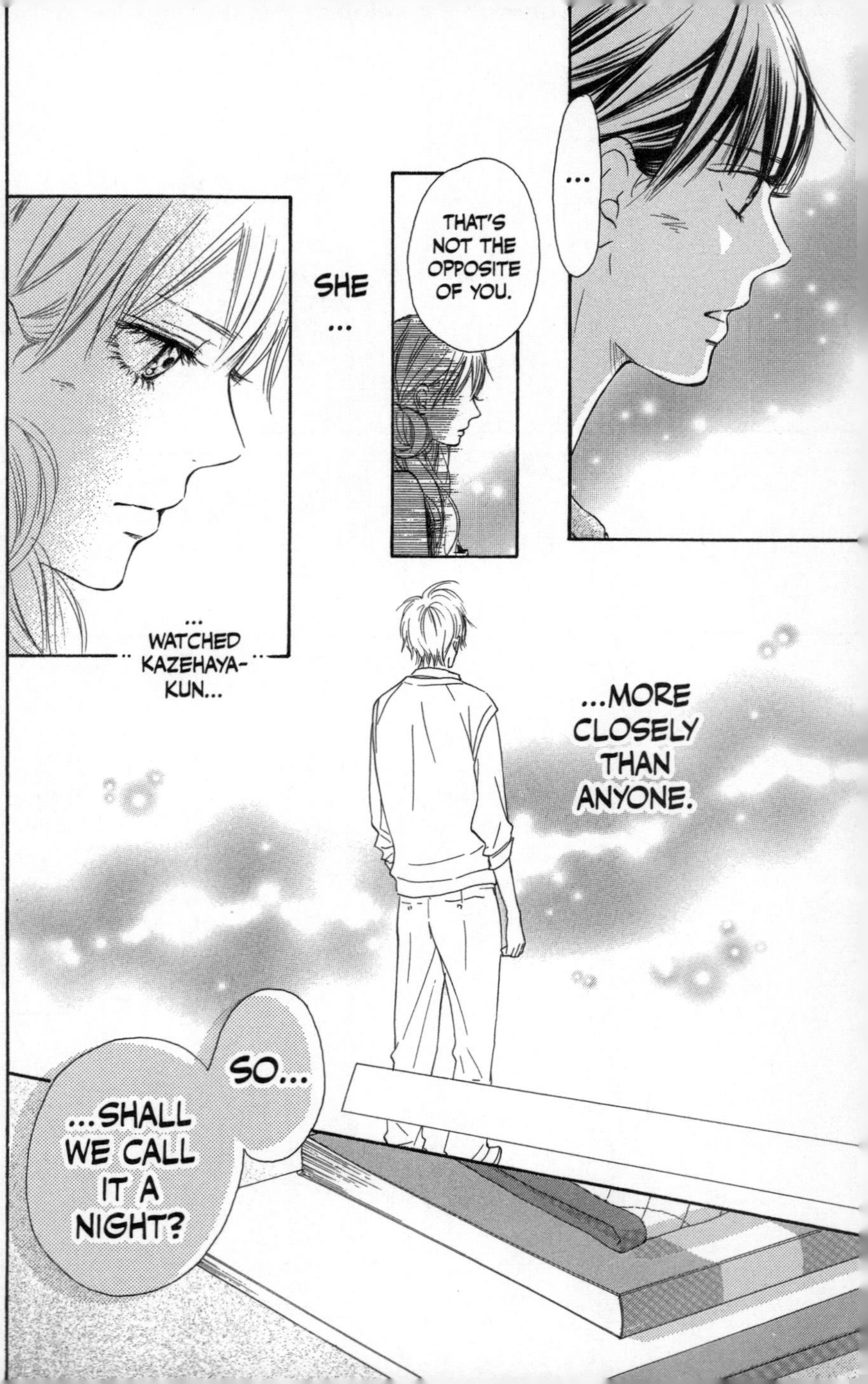
...
THAT'S NOT THE OPPOSITE OF YOU.
SHE ...
... WATCHED KAZEHAYA-KUN...
...MORE CLOSELY THAN ANYONE.
SO...
...SHALL WE CALL IT A NIGHT?

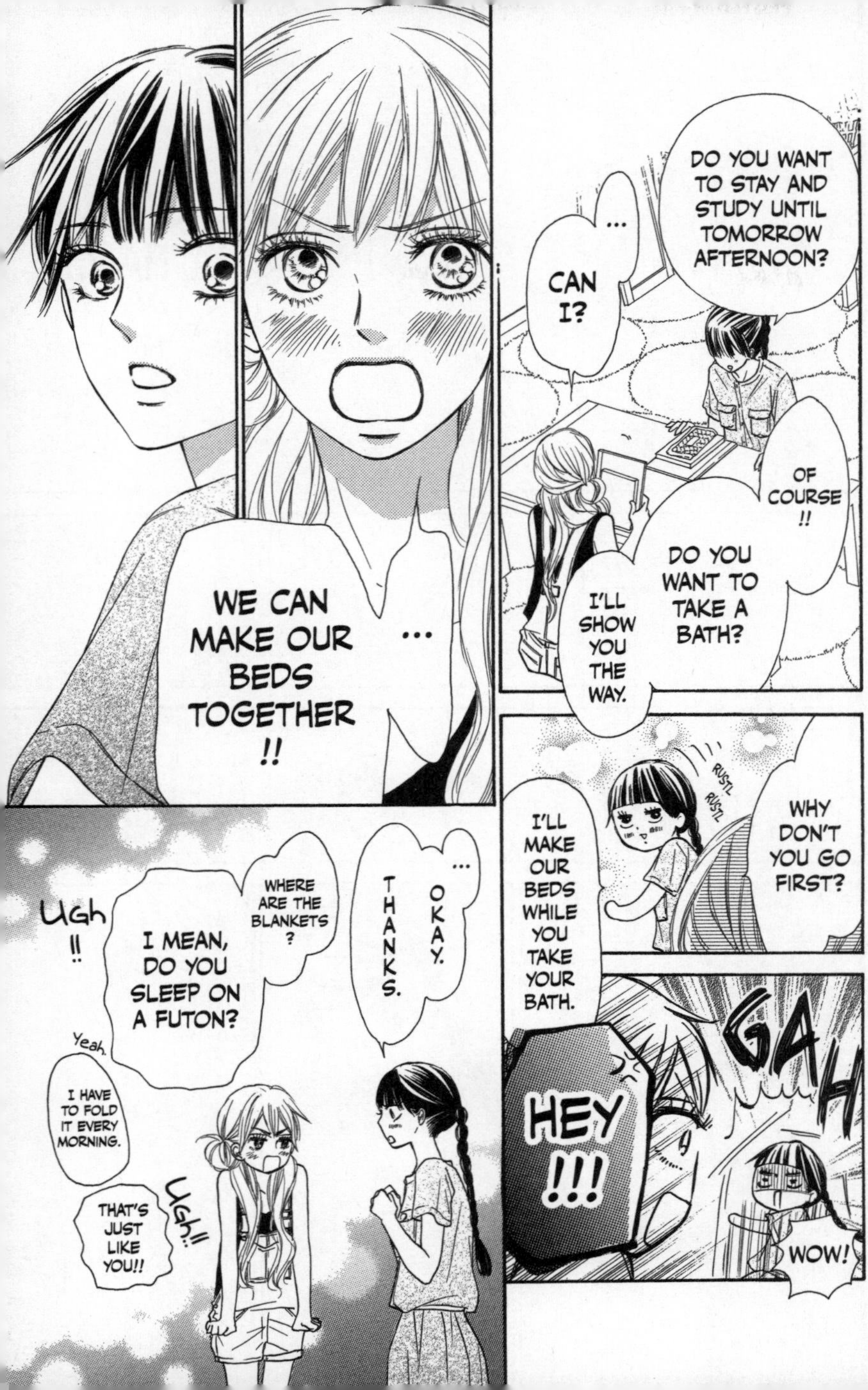
DO YOU WANT TO STAY AND STUDY UNTIL TOMORROW AFTERNOON?
... CAN I?
OF COURSE !!
DO YOU WANT TO TAKE A BATH?
I'LL SHOW YOU THE WAY.
WHY DON'T YOU GO FIRST?
RUSTL RUSTL
I'LL MAKE OUR BEDS WHILE YOU TAKE YOUR BATH.
GAH
HEY !!!
WOW!
WE CAN MAKE OUR BEDS TOGETHER !!
...
... OKAY.
THANKS.
WHERE ARE THE BLANKETS?
I MEAN, DO YOU SLEEP ON A FUTON?
Ugh !!
Yeah.
I HAVE TO FOLD IT EVERY MORNING.
Ugh!!
THAT'S JUST LIKE YOU!!

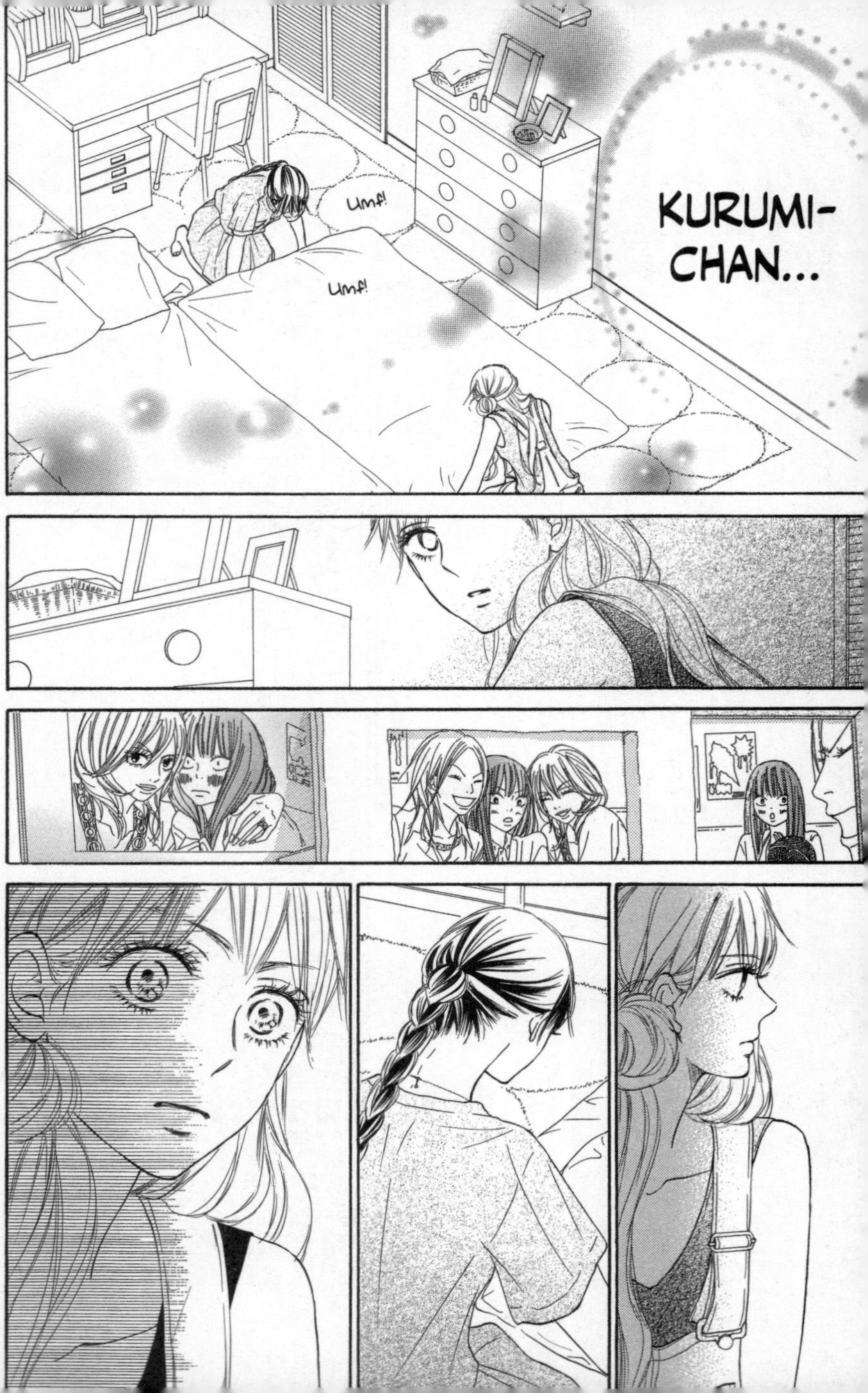
KURUMI-CHAN...
Umf!
Umf!

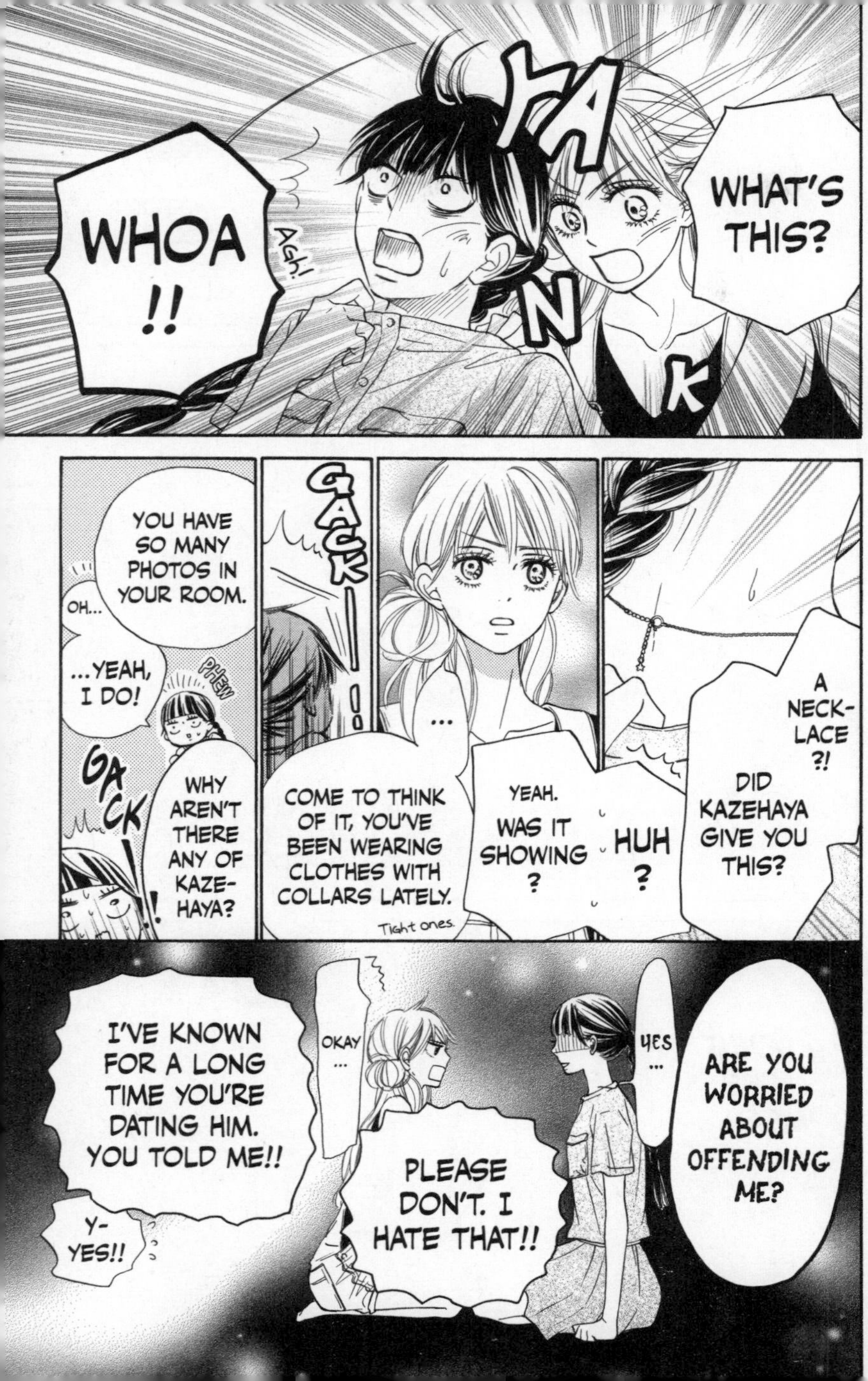
WHAT'S THIS?
YANK
Agh!
WHOA!!
A NECKLACE?!
DID KAZEHAYA GIVE YOU THIS?
HUH?
YEAH.
WAS IT SHOWING?
...
COME TO THINK OF IT, YOU'VE BEEN WEARING CLOTHES WITH COLLARS LATELY.
Tight ones.
GACK!!
YOU HAVE SO MANY PHOTOS IN YOUR ROOM.
OH...
...YEAH, I DO!
PHEW
WHY AREN'T THERE ANY OF KAZEHAYA?
GACK!
ARE YOU WORRIED ABOUT OFFENDING ME?
YES...
OKAY...
PLEASE DON'T. I HATE THAT!!
I'VE KNOWN FOR A LONG TIME YOU'RE DATING HIM. YOU TOLD ME!!
Y-YES!!

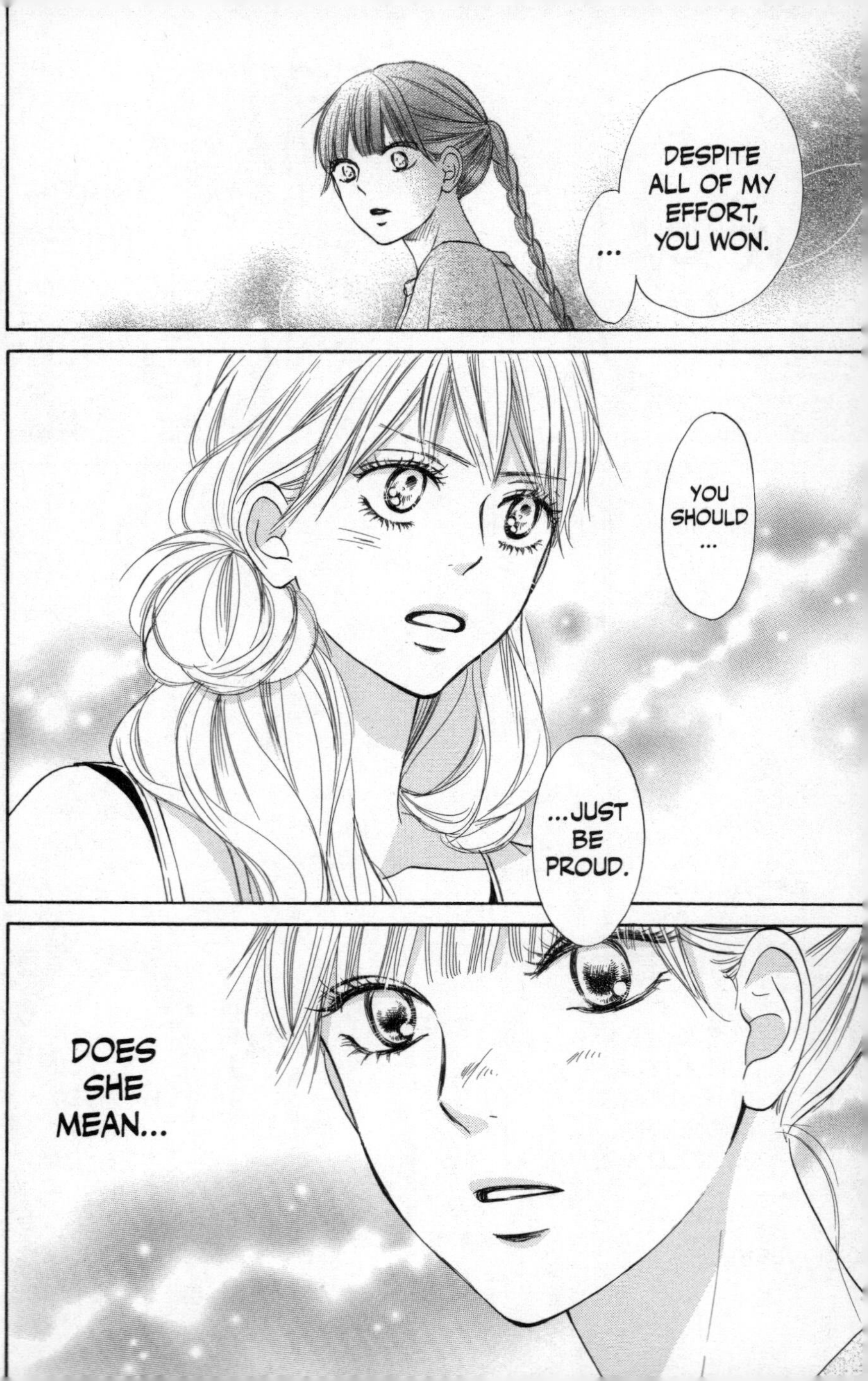
DESPITE ALL OF MY EFFORT, YOU WON.
...
YOU SHOULD ...
...JUST BE PROUD.
DOES SHE MEAN...

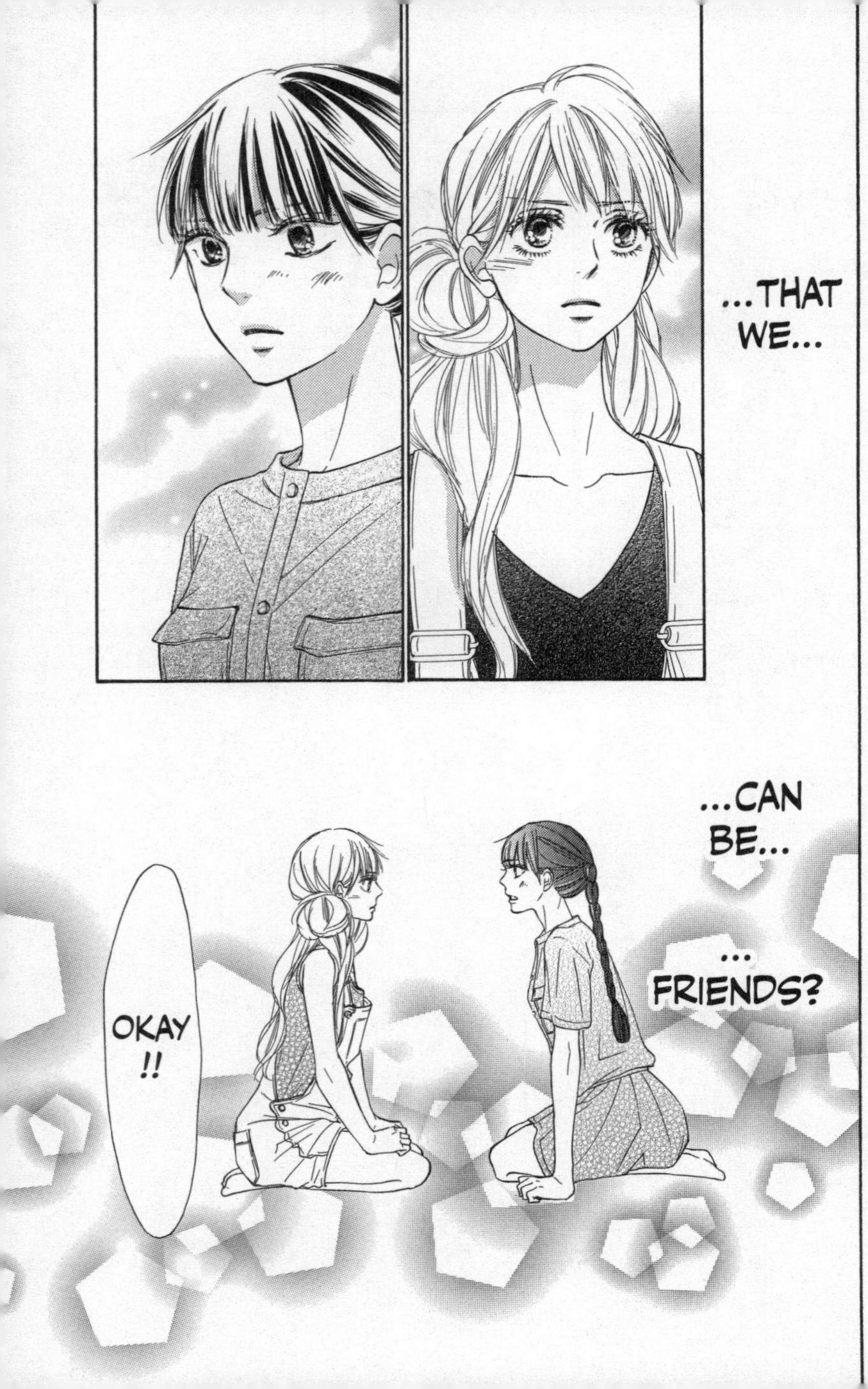
...THAT WE...
...CAN BE...
... FRIENDS?
OKAY !!

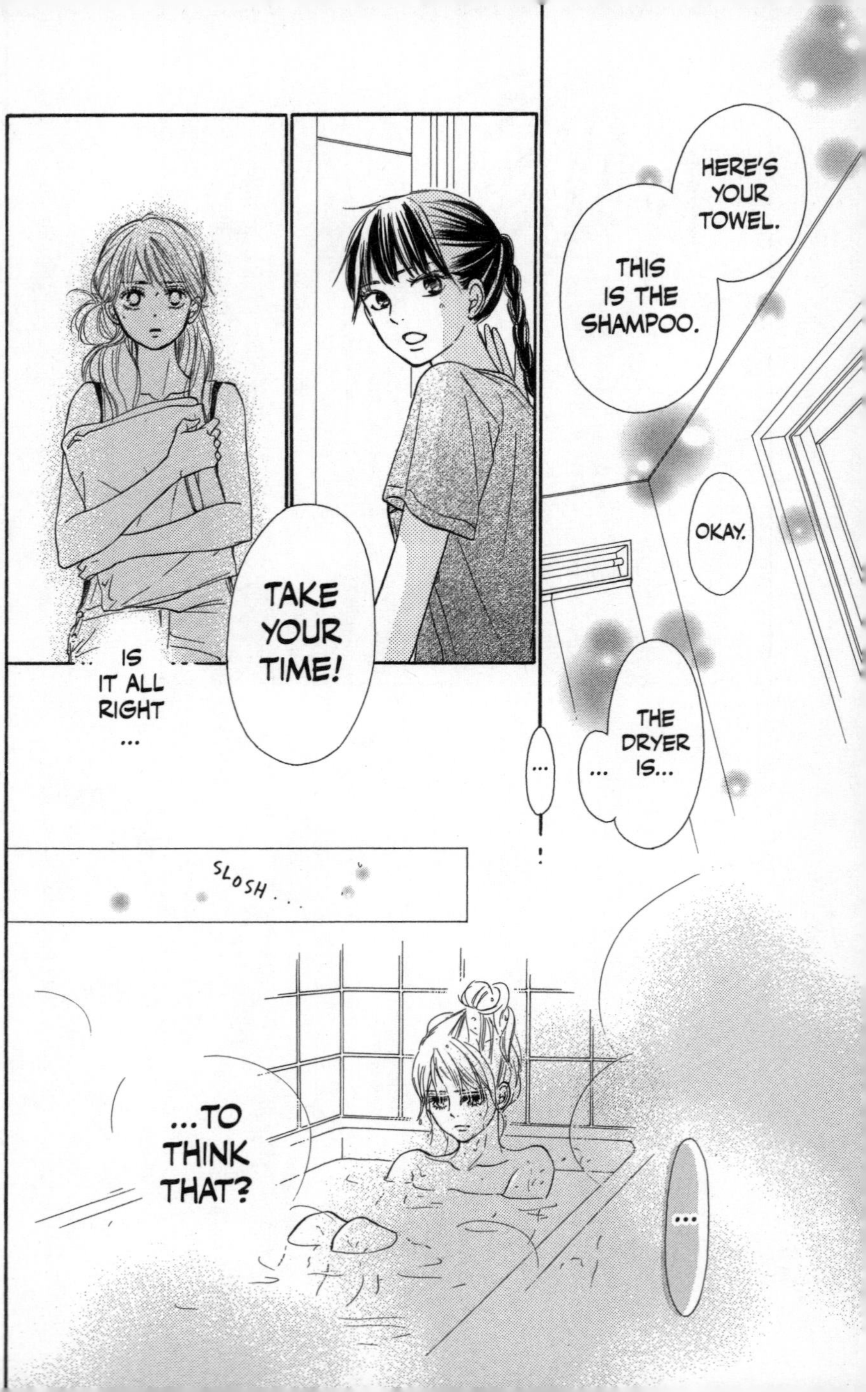
HERE'S YOUR TOWEL.
THIS IS THE SHAMPOO.
OKAY.
THE DRYER IS... ...
...
TAKE YOUR TIME!
IS IT ALL RIGHT ...
SLOSH...
...
...TO THINK THAT?

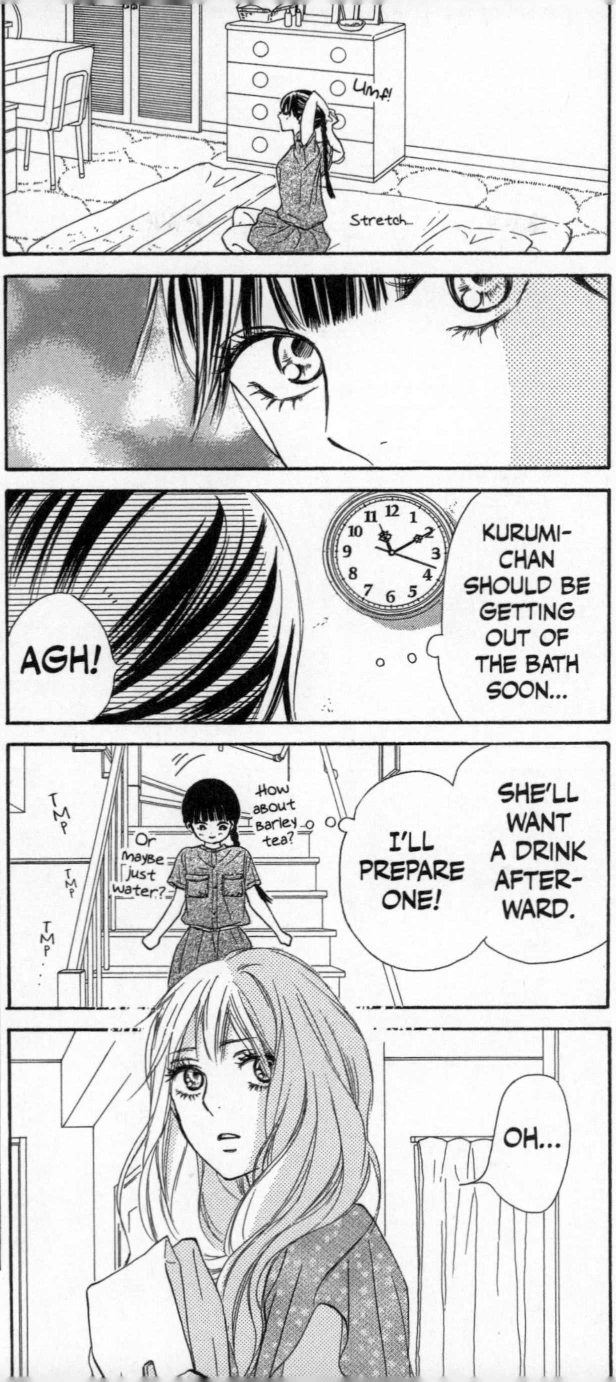
Umf!
Stretch...
KURUMI-CHAN SHOULD BE GETTING OUT OF THE BATH SOON...
AGH!
SHE'LL WANT A DRINK AFTER-WARD.
I'LL PREPARE ONE!
How about Barley tea?
Or maybe just water?
TMP
TMP
TMP
OH...

KARUPIN on JAPAN 3

Thank you to all of the fans who follow this series!

It's nearing the end. I think it will take a few more volumes? That's my sense of it anyway...

I'm very grateful to everyone who has followed this for so long. I'm also thankful for everyone who just read it even once. I also want to thank everyone who let me write whatever I wanted to!

But this isn't over yet...

I should've saved that speech for when the series actually finishes!

Maybe I feel like this because it's graduation season...?

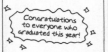

Congratulations to everyone who graduated this year!

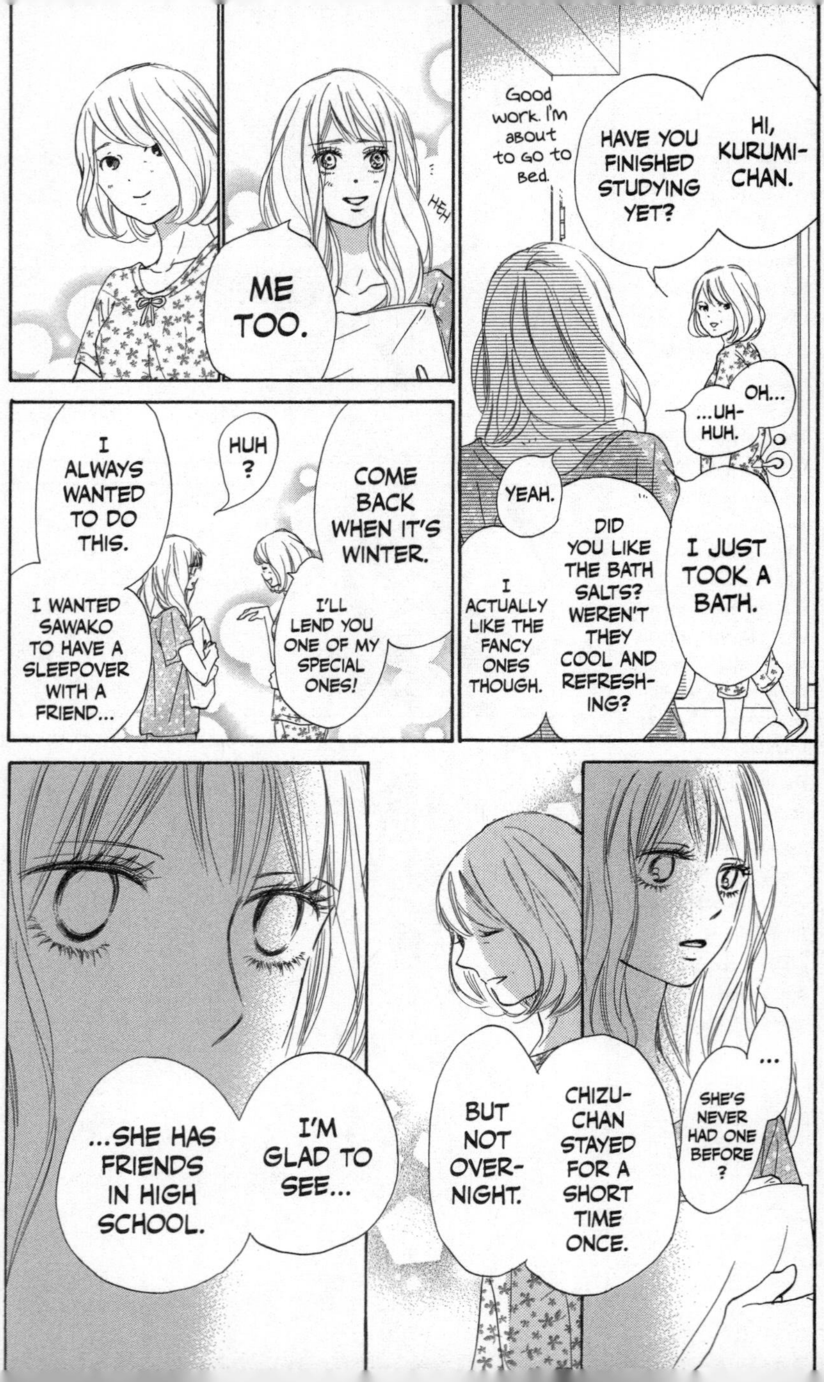
HI, KURUMI-CHAN.
HAVE YOU FINISHED STUDYING YET?
Good work. I'm about to go to bed.
OH...
...UH-HUH.
I JUST TOOK A BATH.
YEAH.
DID YOU LIKE THE BATH SALTS? WEREN'T THEY COOL AND REFRESH-ING?
I ACTUALLY LIKE THE FANCY ONES THOUGH.
HEH
ME TOO.
COME BACK WHEN IT'S WINTER.
HUH?
I'LL LEND YOU ONE OF MY SPECIAL ONES!
I ALWAYS WANTED TO DO THIS.
I WANTED SAWAKO TO HAVE A SLEEPOVER WITH A FRIEND...
...
SHE'S NEVER HAD ONE BEFORE?
CHIZU-CHAN STAYED FOR A SHORT TIME ONCE.
BUT NOT OVER-NIGHT.
I'M GLAD TO SEE...
...SHE HAS FRIENDS IN HIGH SCHOOL.

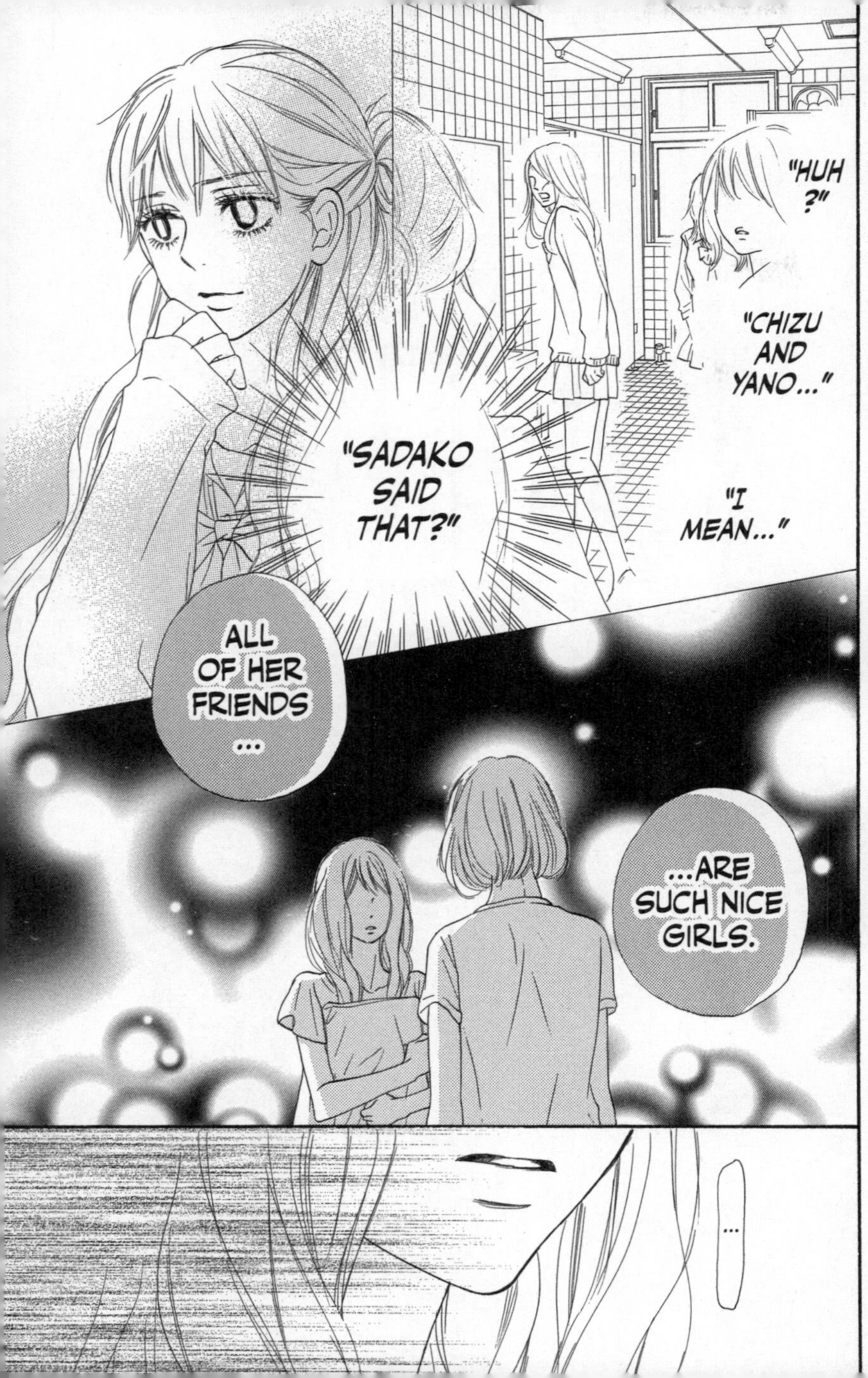
"HUH?"
"CHIZU AND YANO..."
"I MEAN..."
"SADAKO SAID THAT?"
ALL OF HER FRIENDS...
...ARE SUCH NICE GIRLS.
...

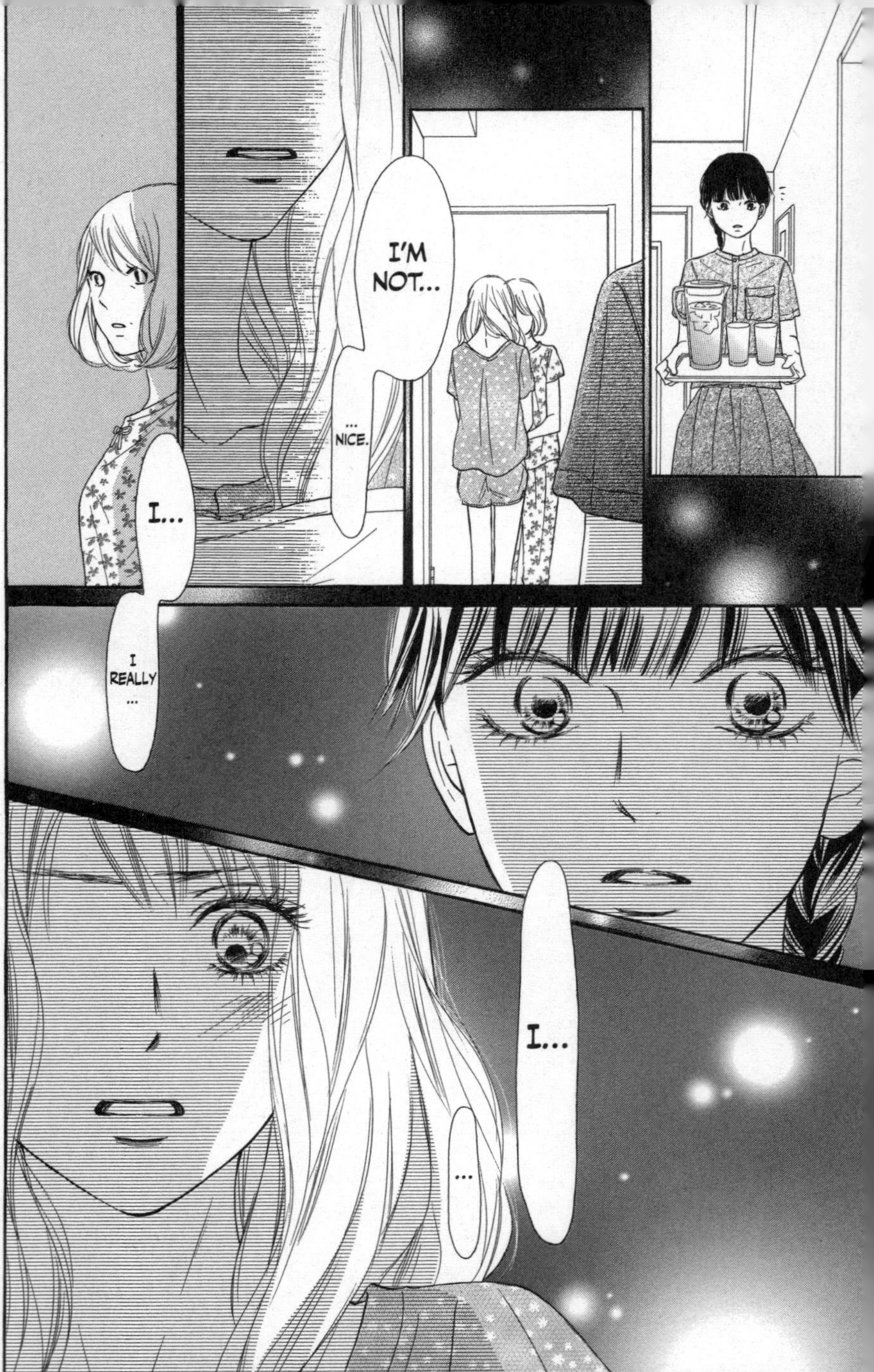
I'M NOT...
...NICE.
I...
I REALLY ...
I...
...

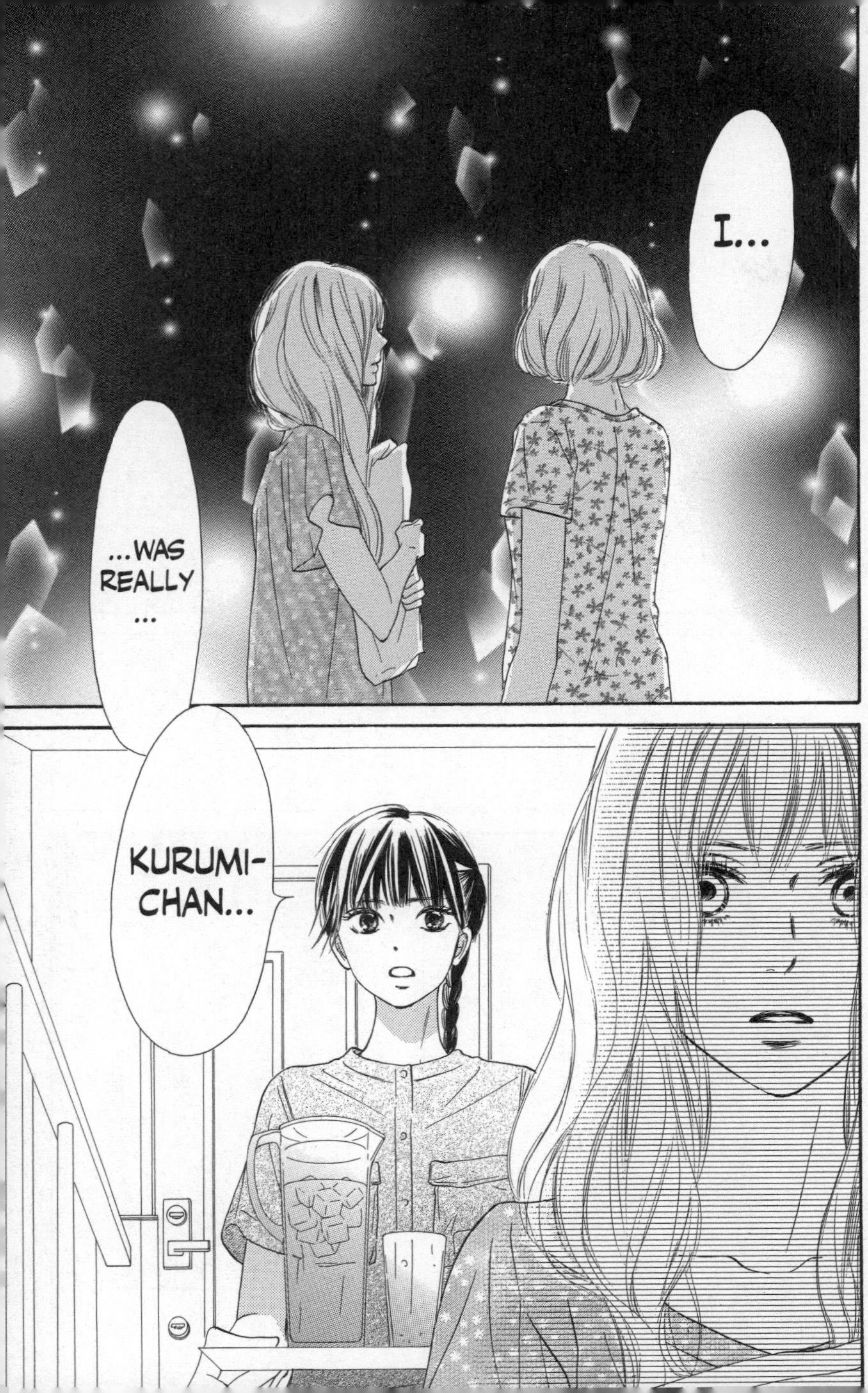
I...
...WAS REALLY ...
KURUMI-CHAN...

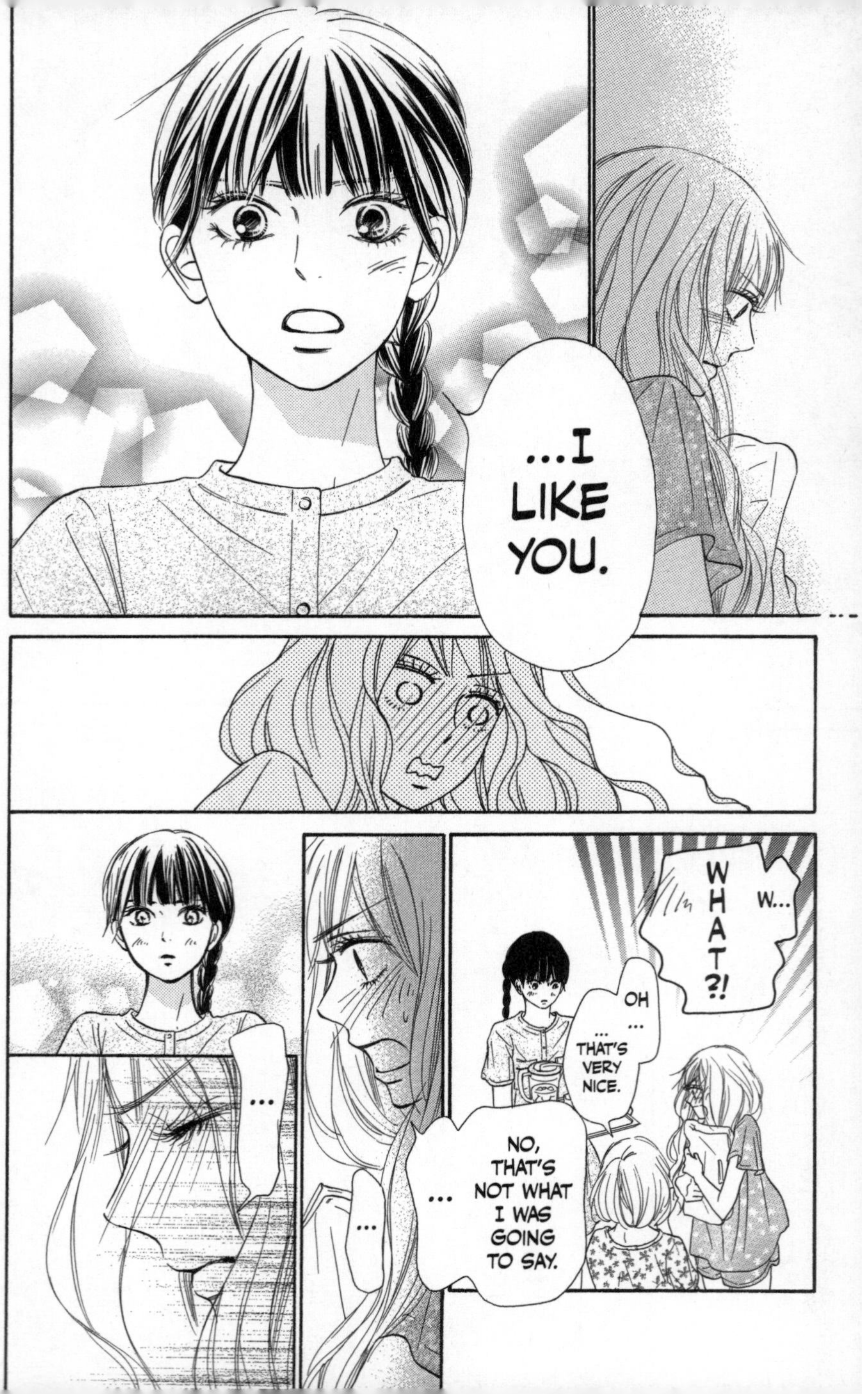
...I LIKE YOU.
W... WHAT?!
OH ... THAT'S VERY NICE.
NO, THAT'S NOT WHAT I WAS GOING TO SAY.
...
...
...

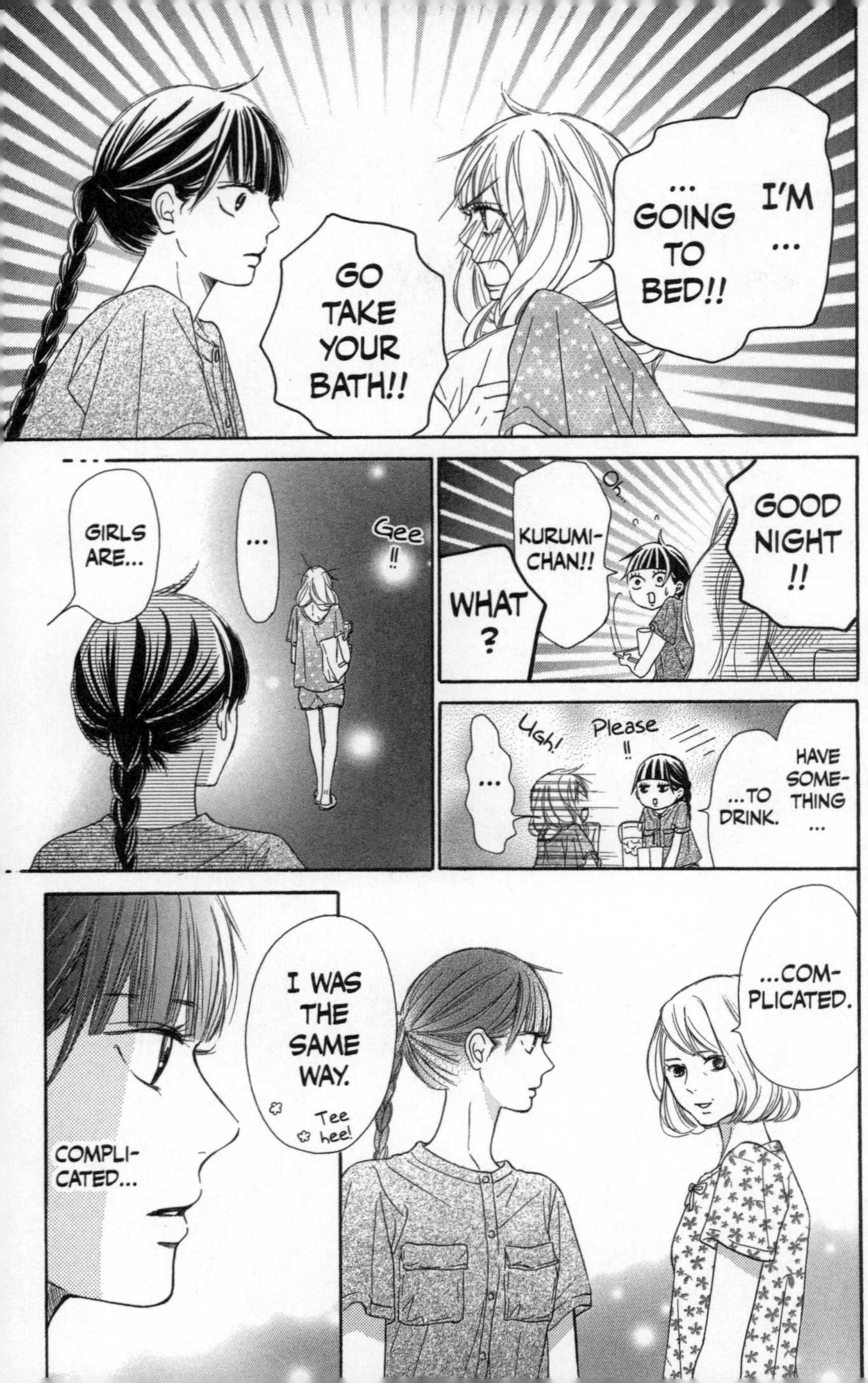
I'M ...
... GOING TO BED!!
GO TAKE YOUR BATH!!
GOOD NIGHT!!
KURUMI-CHAN!!
Oh
WHAT?
HAVE SOME-THING ...
...TO DRINK.
Please!!
Ugh!
...
Gee!!
...
GIRLS ARE...
...COM-PLICATED.
I WAS THE SAME WAY.
Tee hee!
COMPLI-CATED...

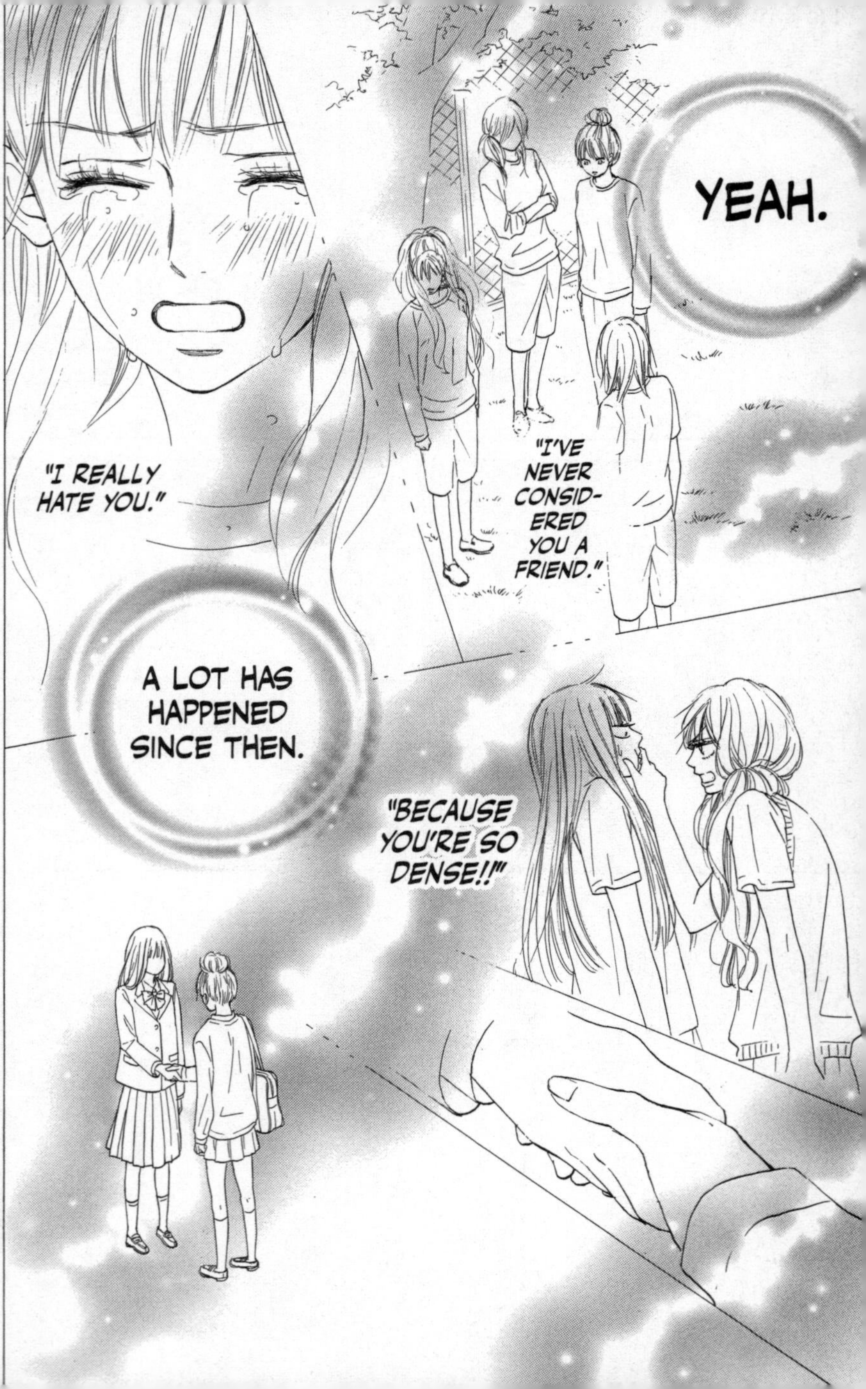
YEAH.
"I'VE NEVER CONSID-ERED YOU A FRIEND."
"I REALLY HATE YOU."
A LOT HAS HAPPENED SINCE THEN.
"BECAUSE YOU'RE SO DENSE!!"

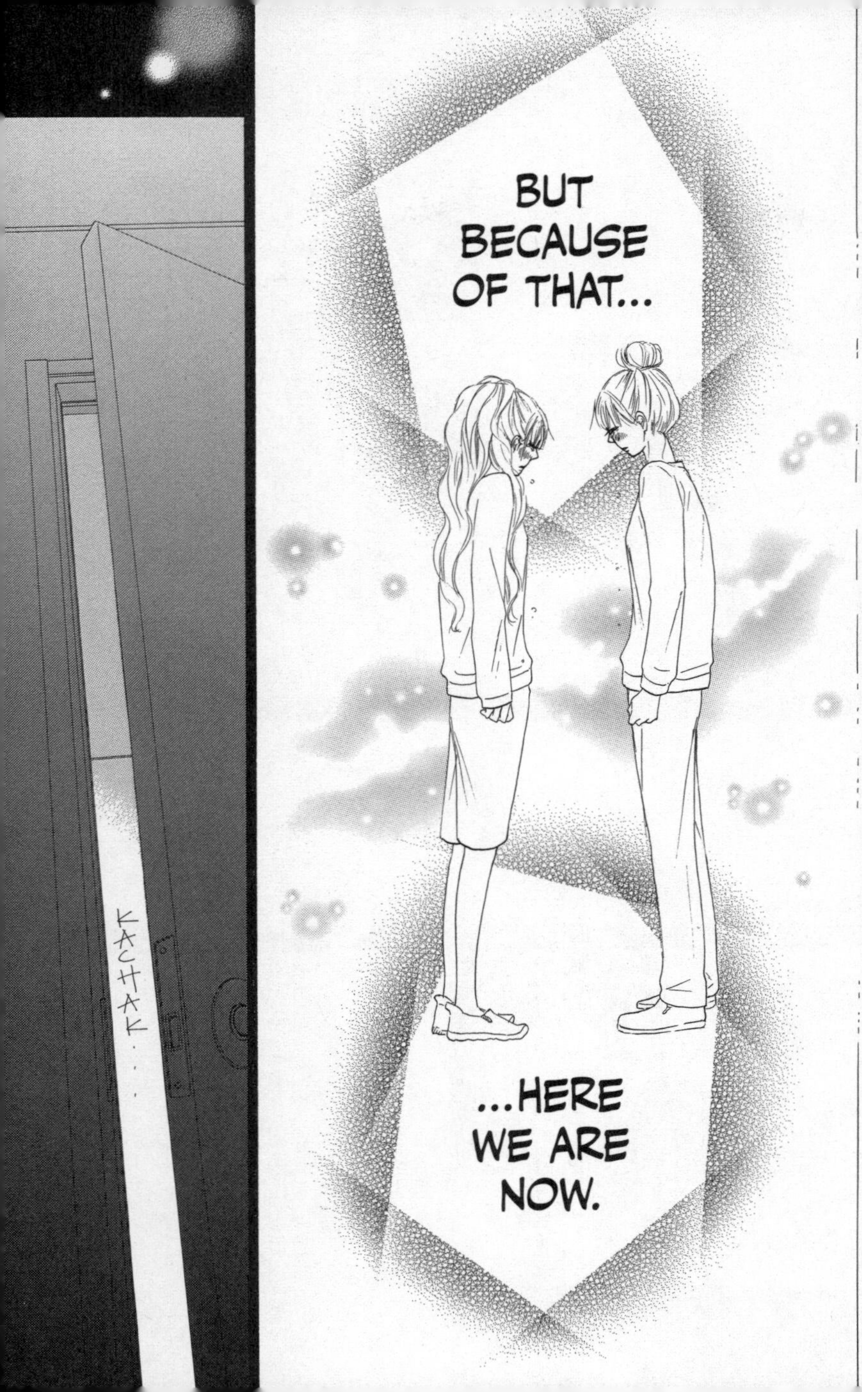
BUT BECAUSE OF THAT...
...HERE WE ARE NOW.
KACHAK...

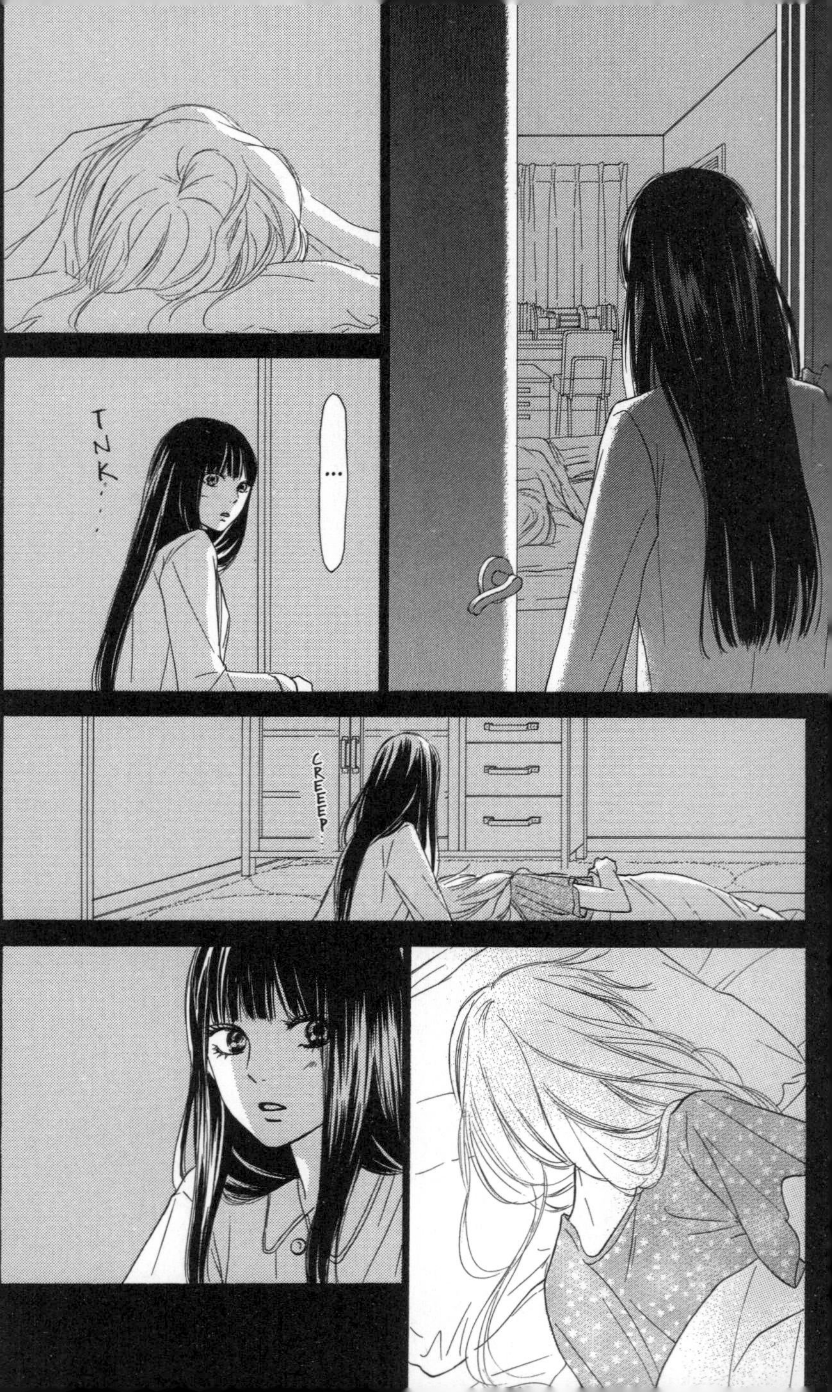

...
TNK...
CREEEP...

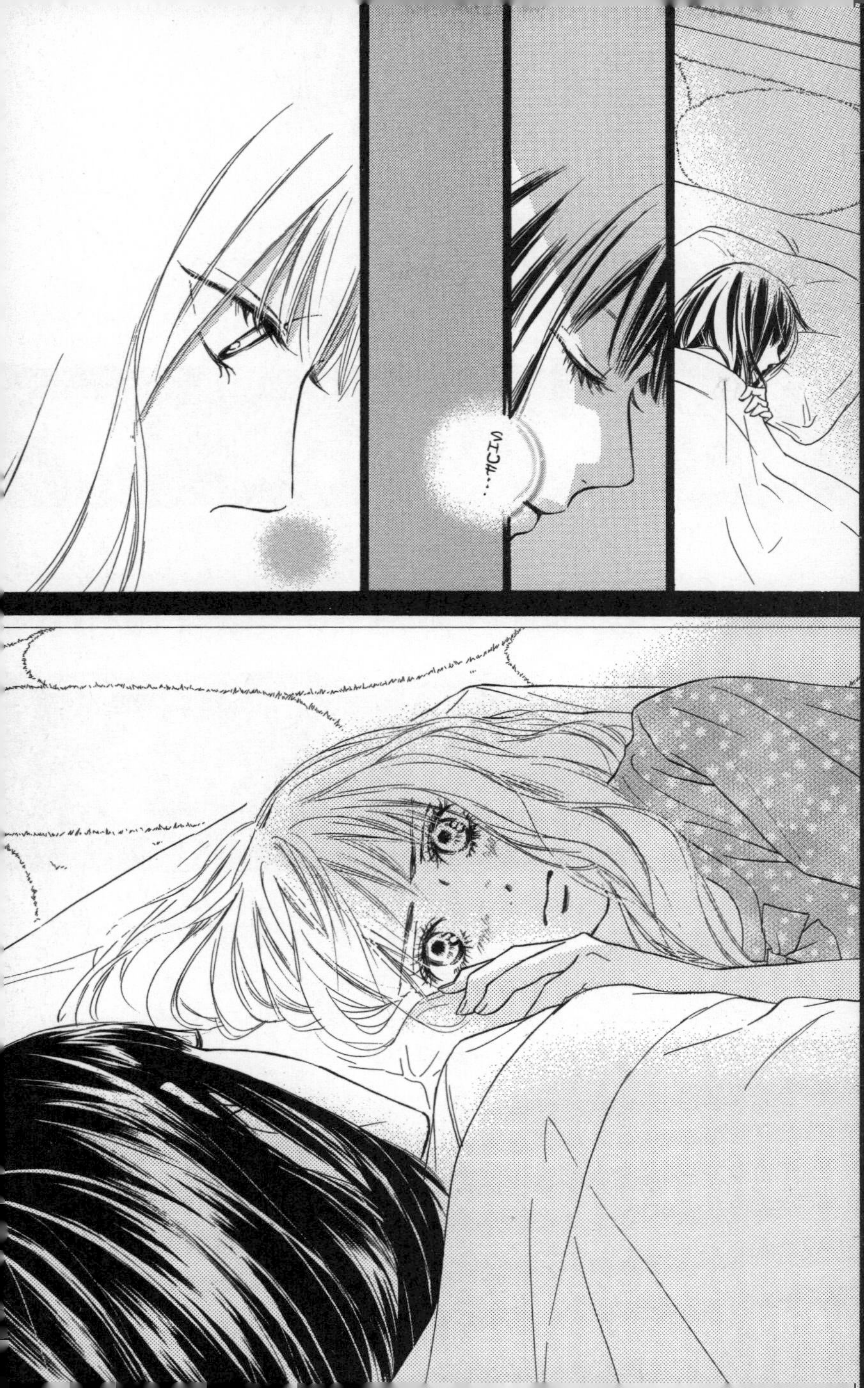

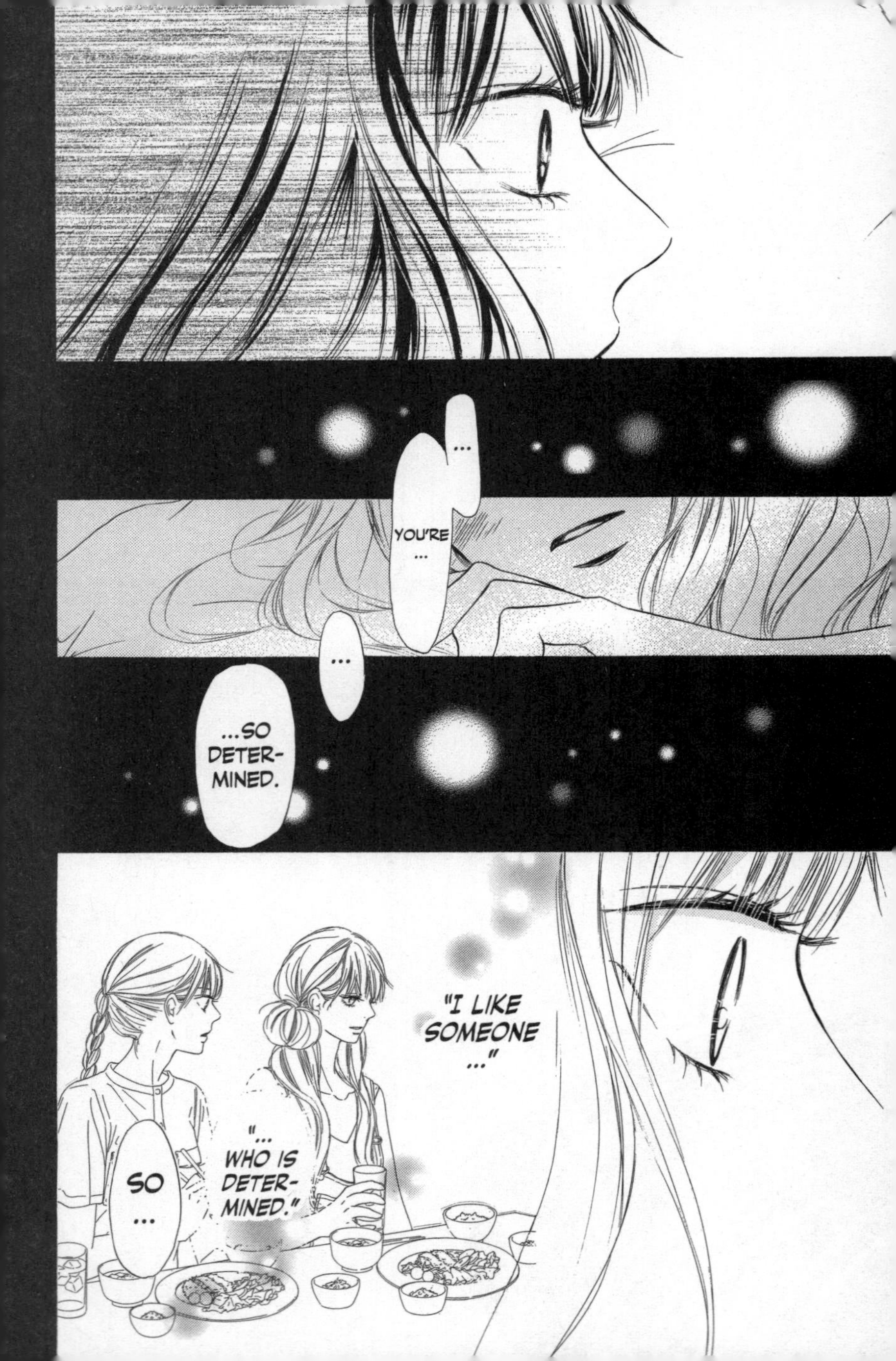
...
YOU'RE ...
...
...SO DETERMINED.
"I LIKE SOMEONE ..."
"... WHO IS DETERMINED."
SO ...

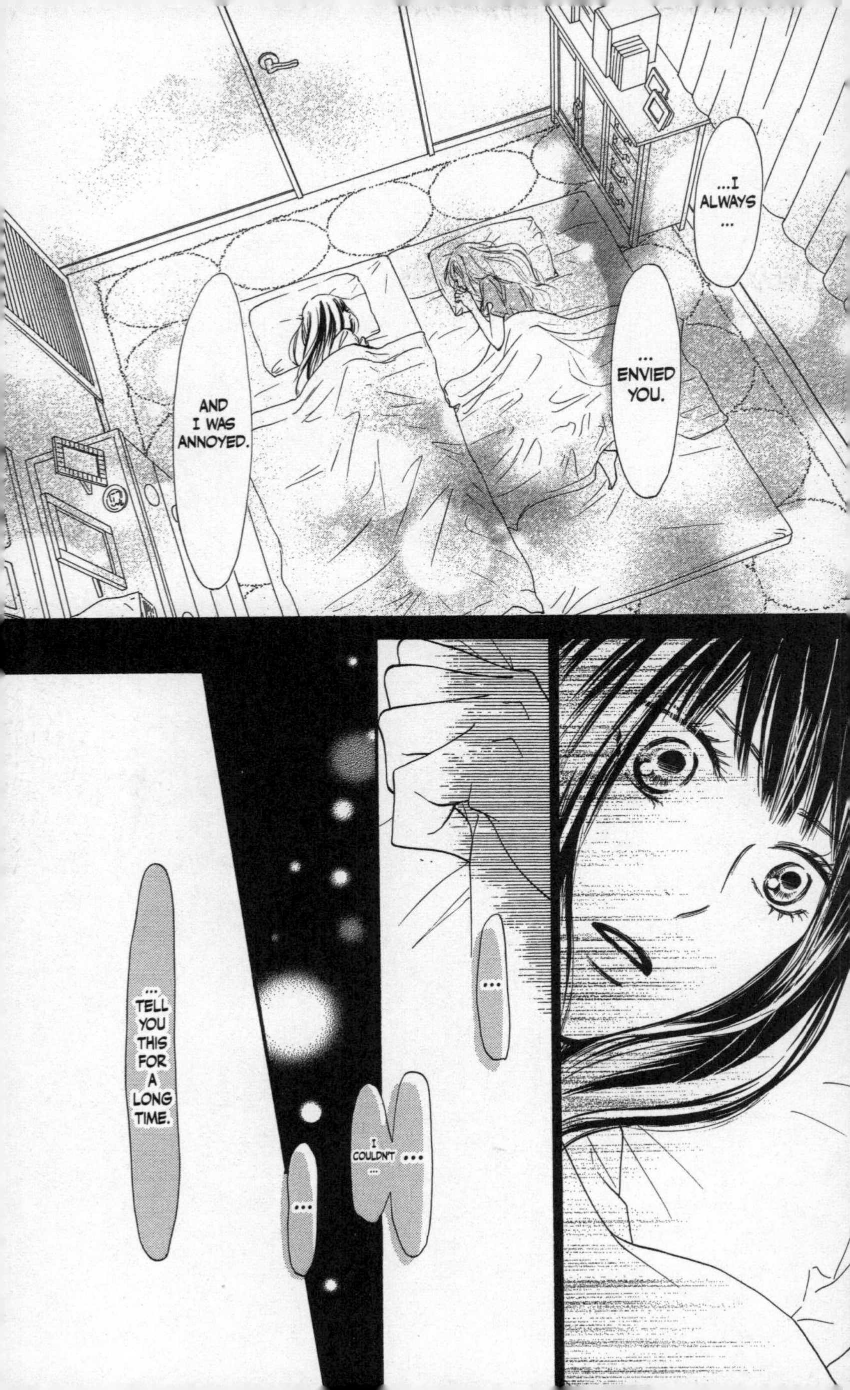
...I ALWAYS ...
... ENVIED YOU.
AND I WAS ANNOYED.
...
...
I COULDN'T ...
...
... TELL YOU THIS FOR A LONG TIME.

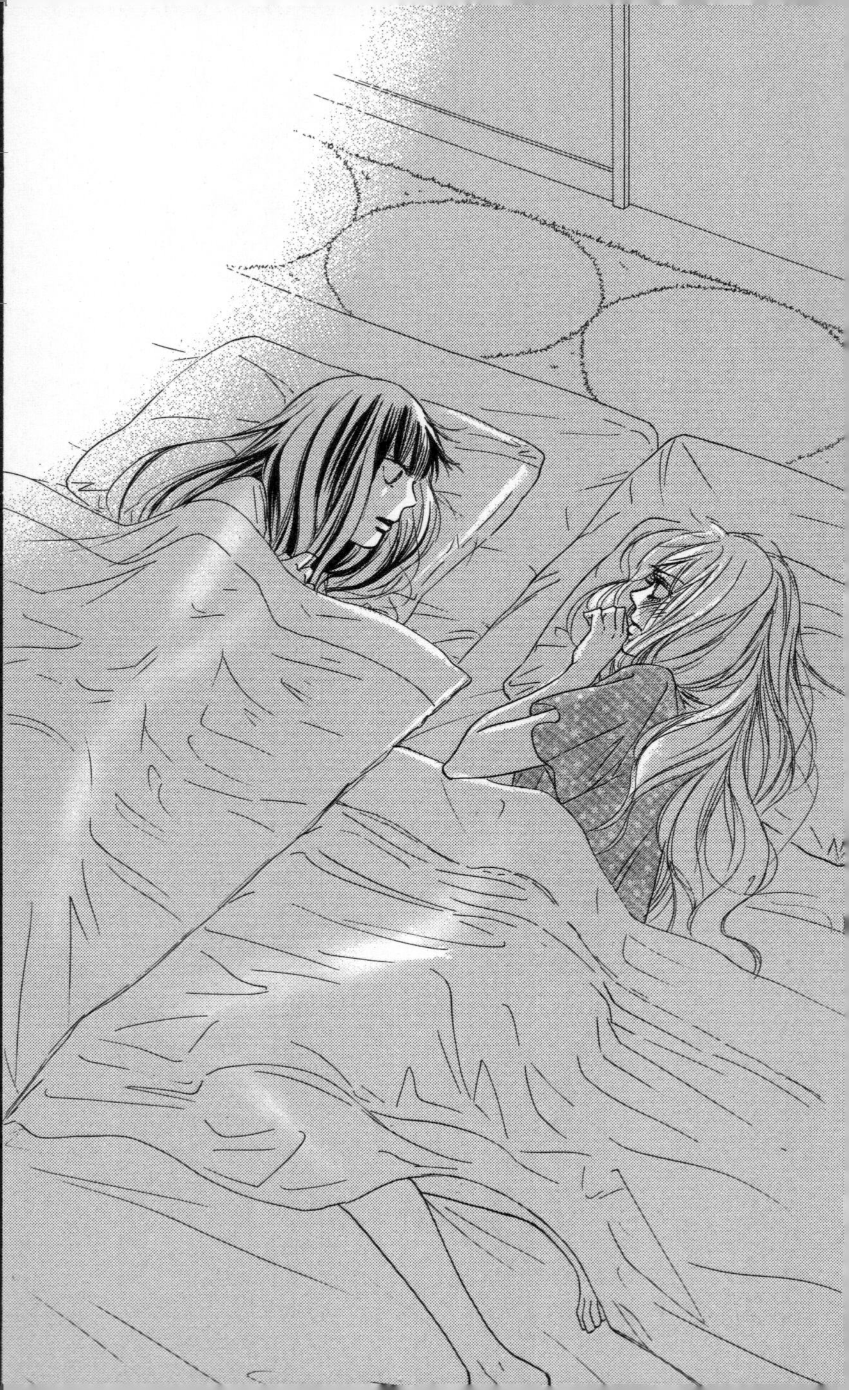

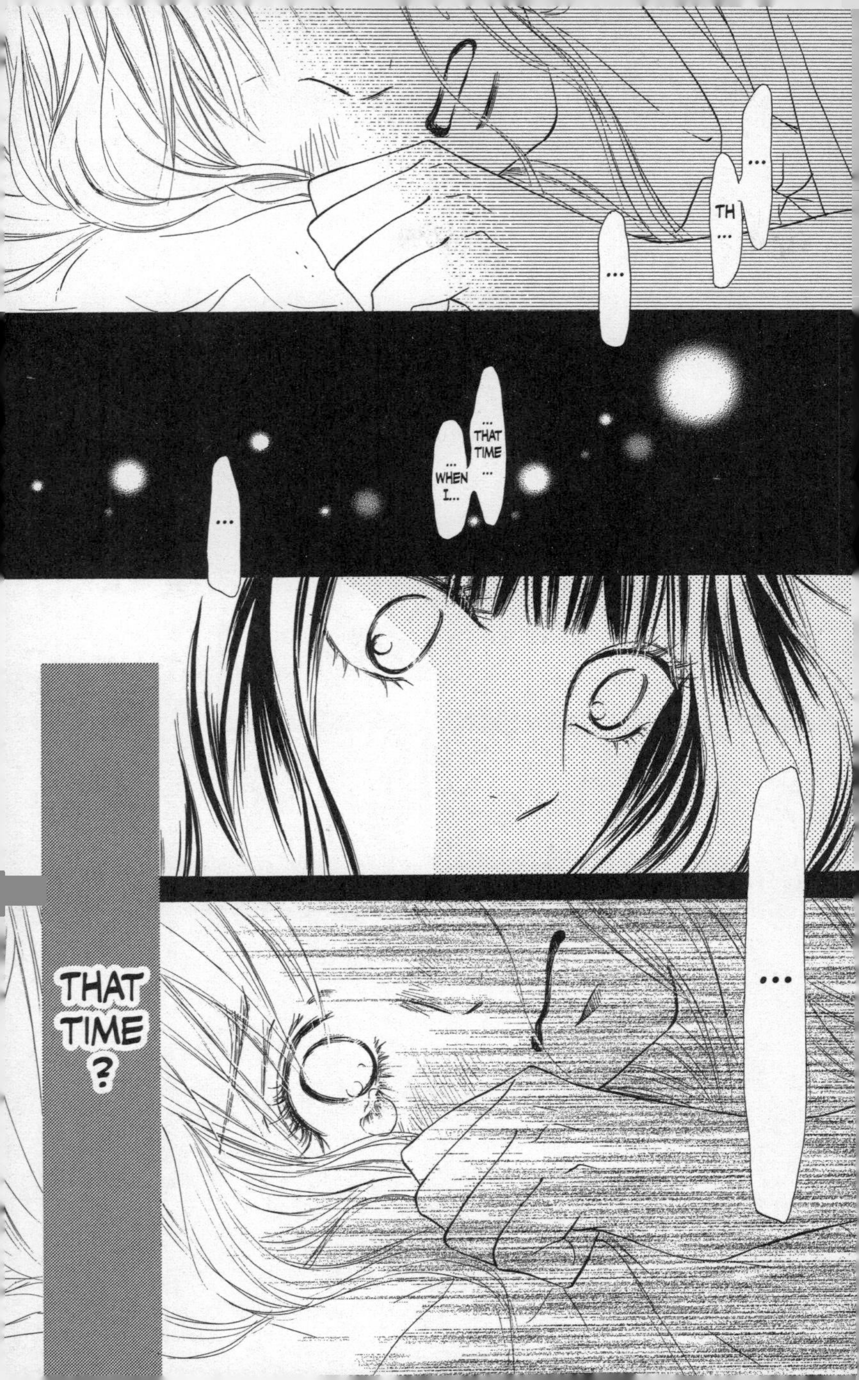
…
TH…
…
…THAT TIME…
…WHEN I…
…
…
THAT TIME?

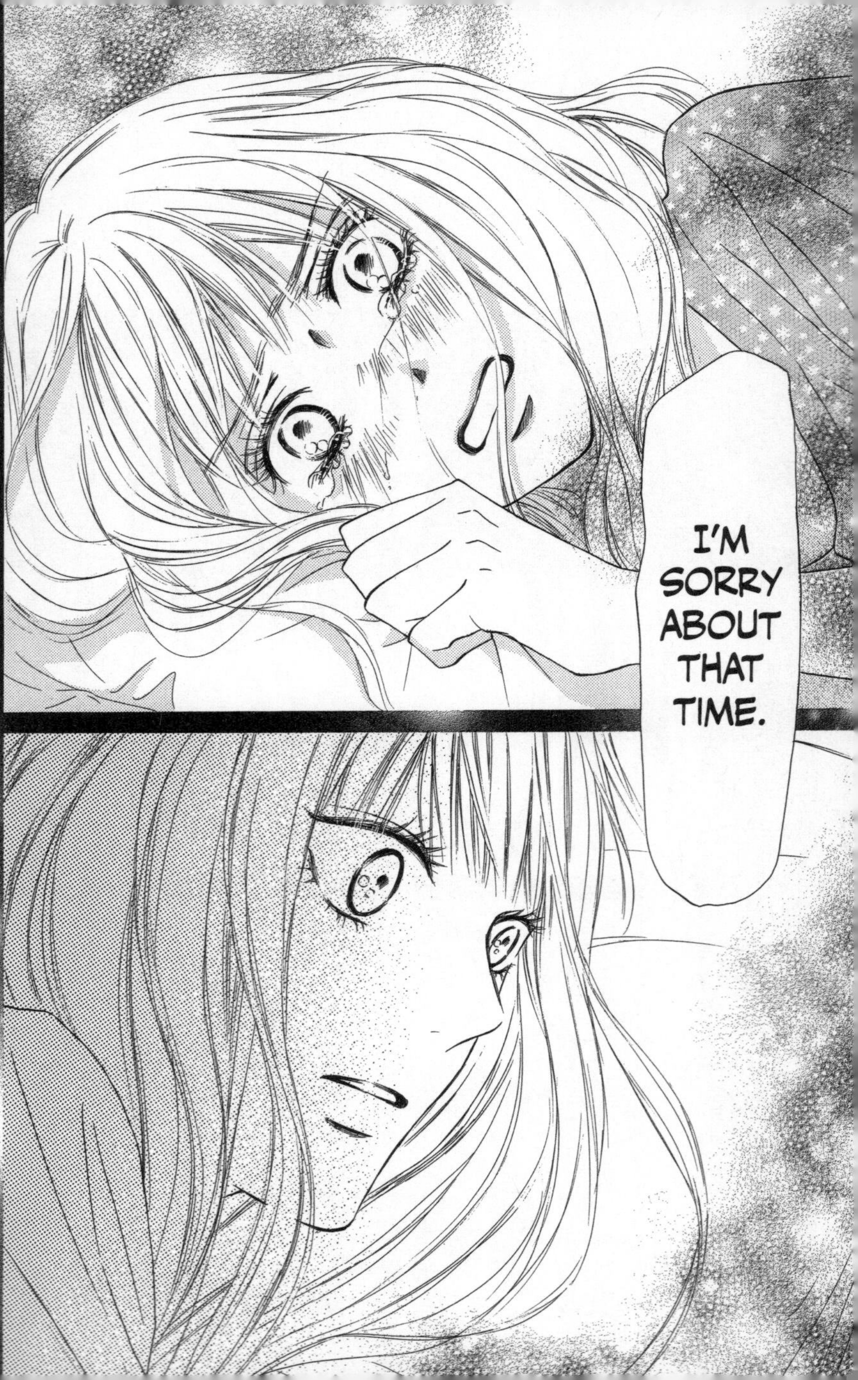
I'M SORRY ABOUT THAT TIME.

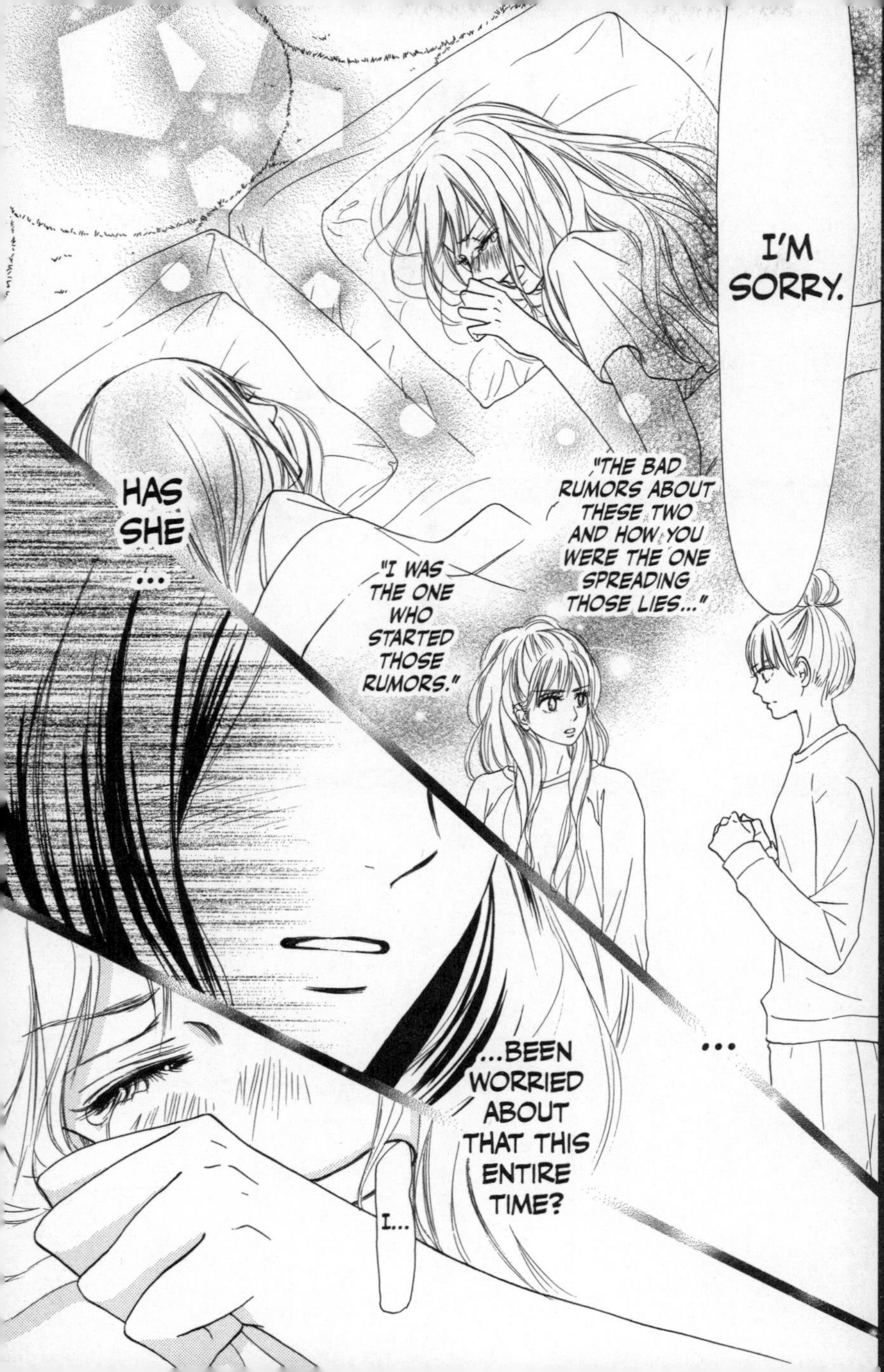
I'M SORRY.
"THE BAD RUMORS ABOUT THESE TWO AND HOW YOU WERE THE ONE SPREADING THOSE LIES..."
"I WAS THE ONE WHO STARTED THOSE RUMORS."
...
HAS SHE
...
...BEEN WORRIED ABOUT THAT THIS ENTIRE TIME?
I...

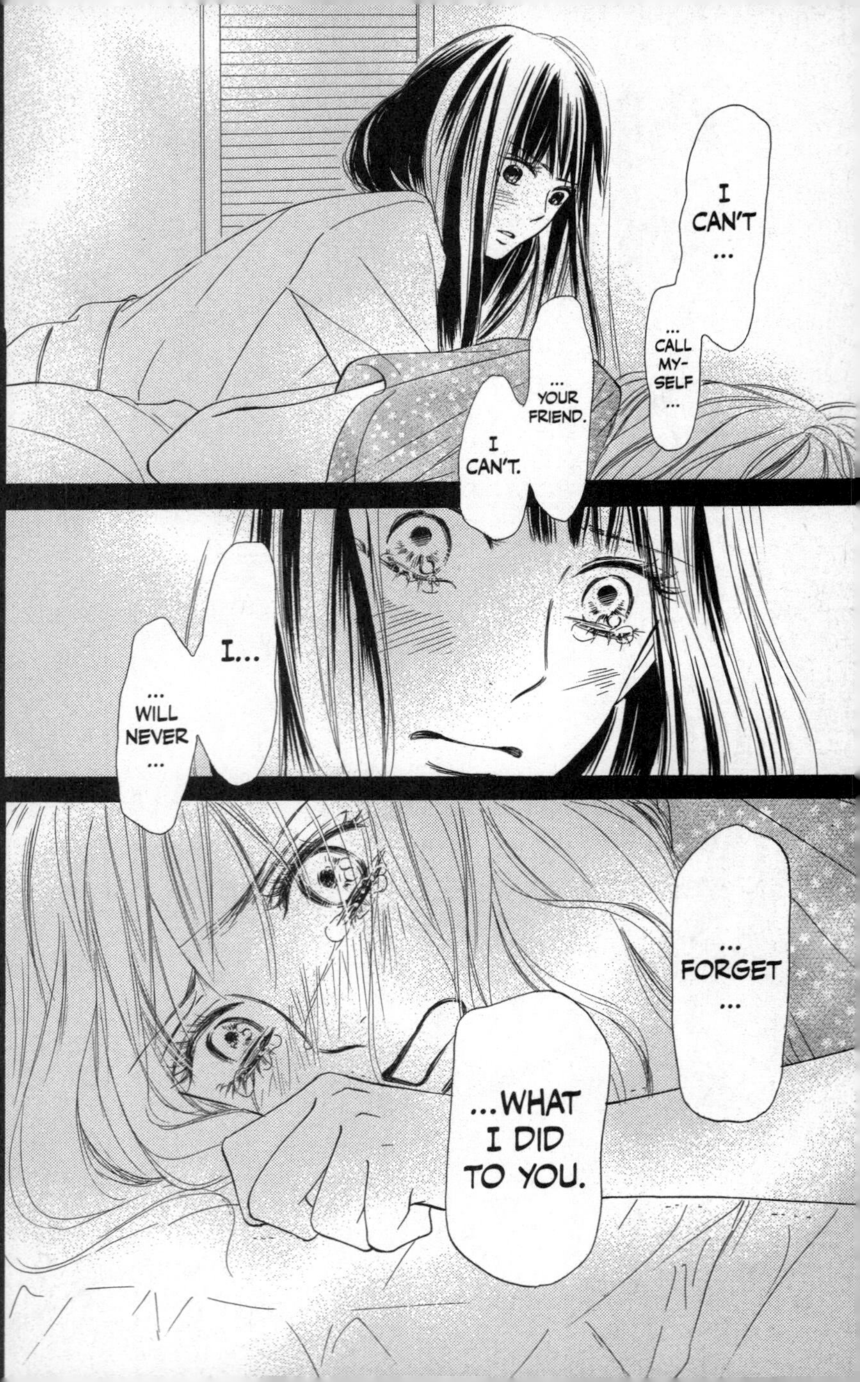
I CAN'T ...
... CALL MY-SELF ...
... YOUR FRIEND.
I CAN'T.
I...
... WILL NEVER ...
... FORGET ...
...WHAT I DID TO YOU.

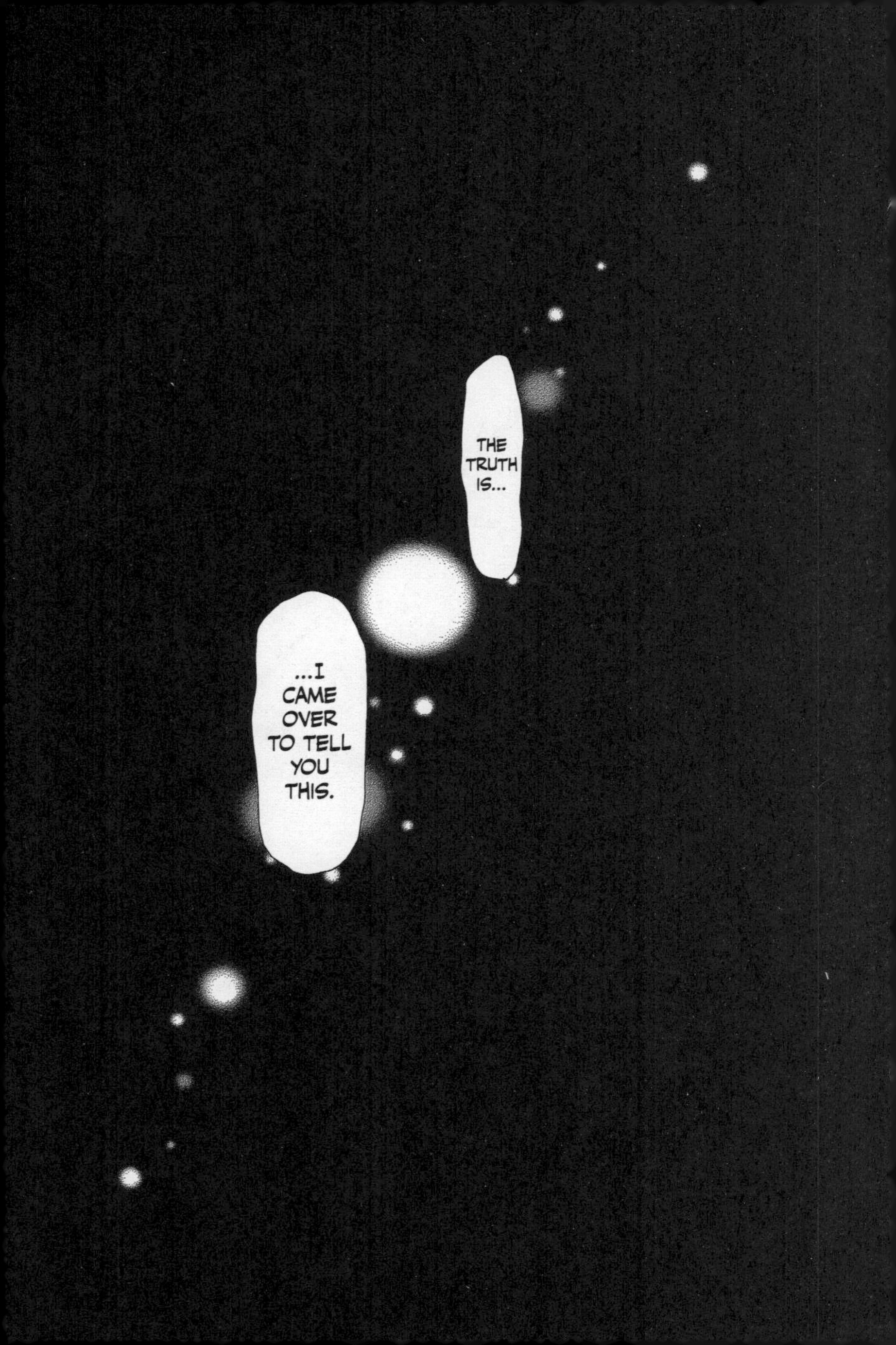
THE TRUTH IS...
...I CAME OVER TO TELL YOU THIS.

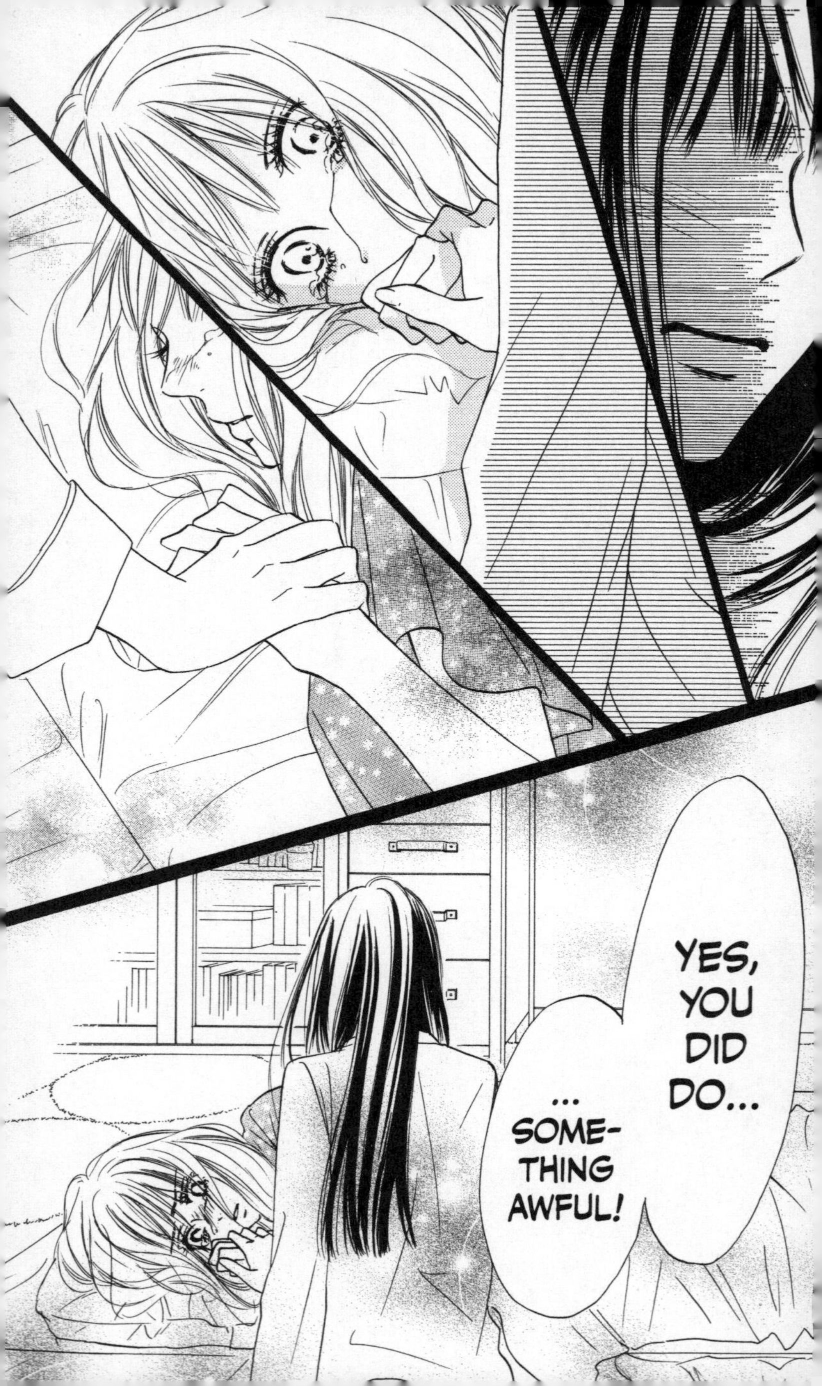
YES, YOU DID DO...
... SOME-THING AWFUL!

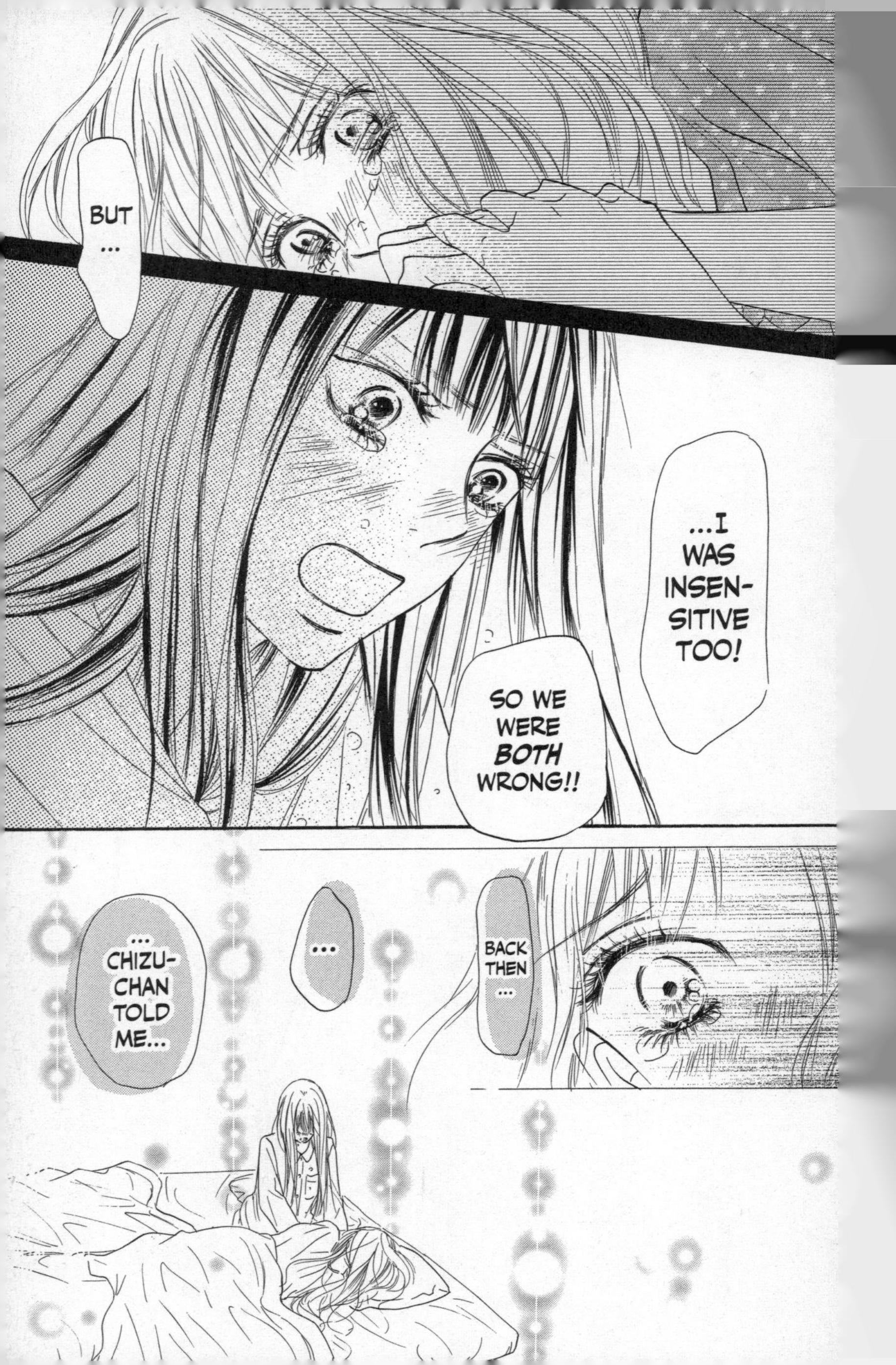
BUT ...
...I WAS INSEN-SITIVE TOO!
SO WE WERE *BOTH* WRONG!!
BACK THEN ...
...
... CHIZU-CHAN TOLD ME...

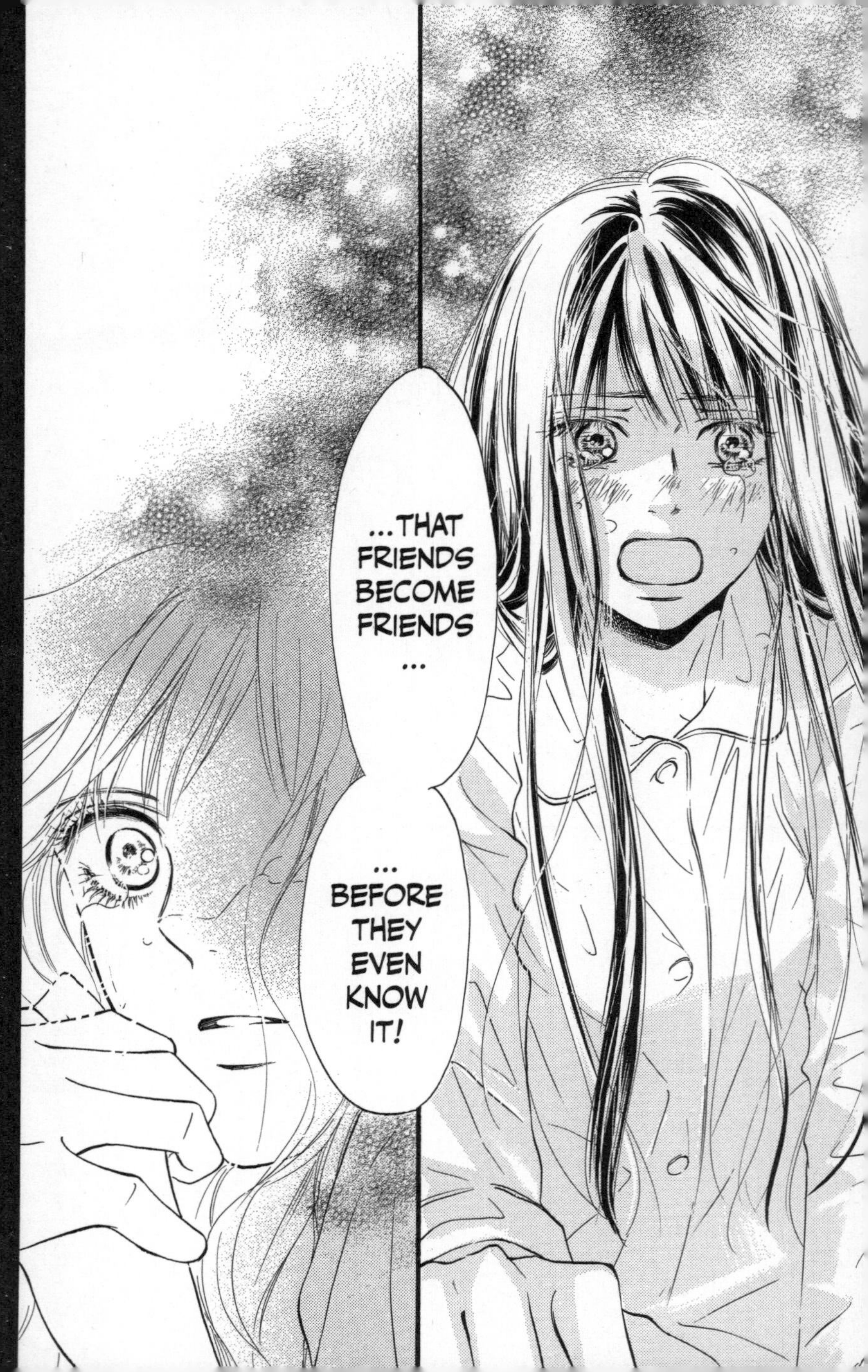
...THAT FRIENDS BECOME FRIENDS ...
... BEFORE THEY EVEN KNOW IT!

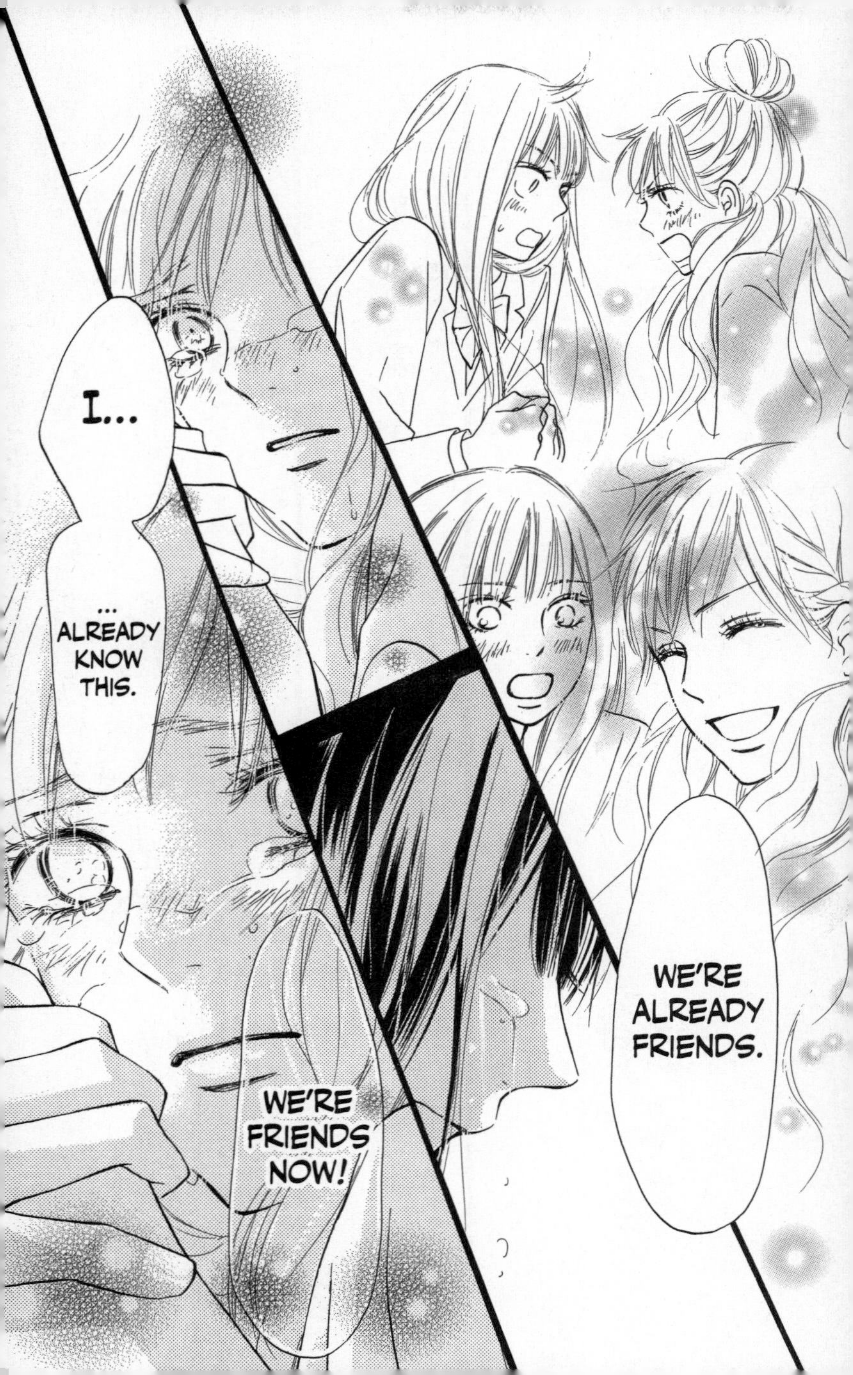
WE'RE ALREADY FRIENDS.
WE'RE FRIENDS NOW!
I...
...ALREADY KNOW THIS.

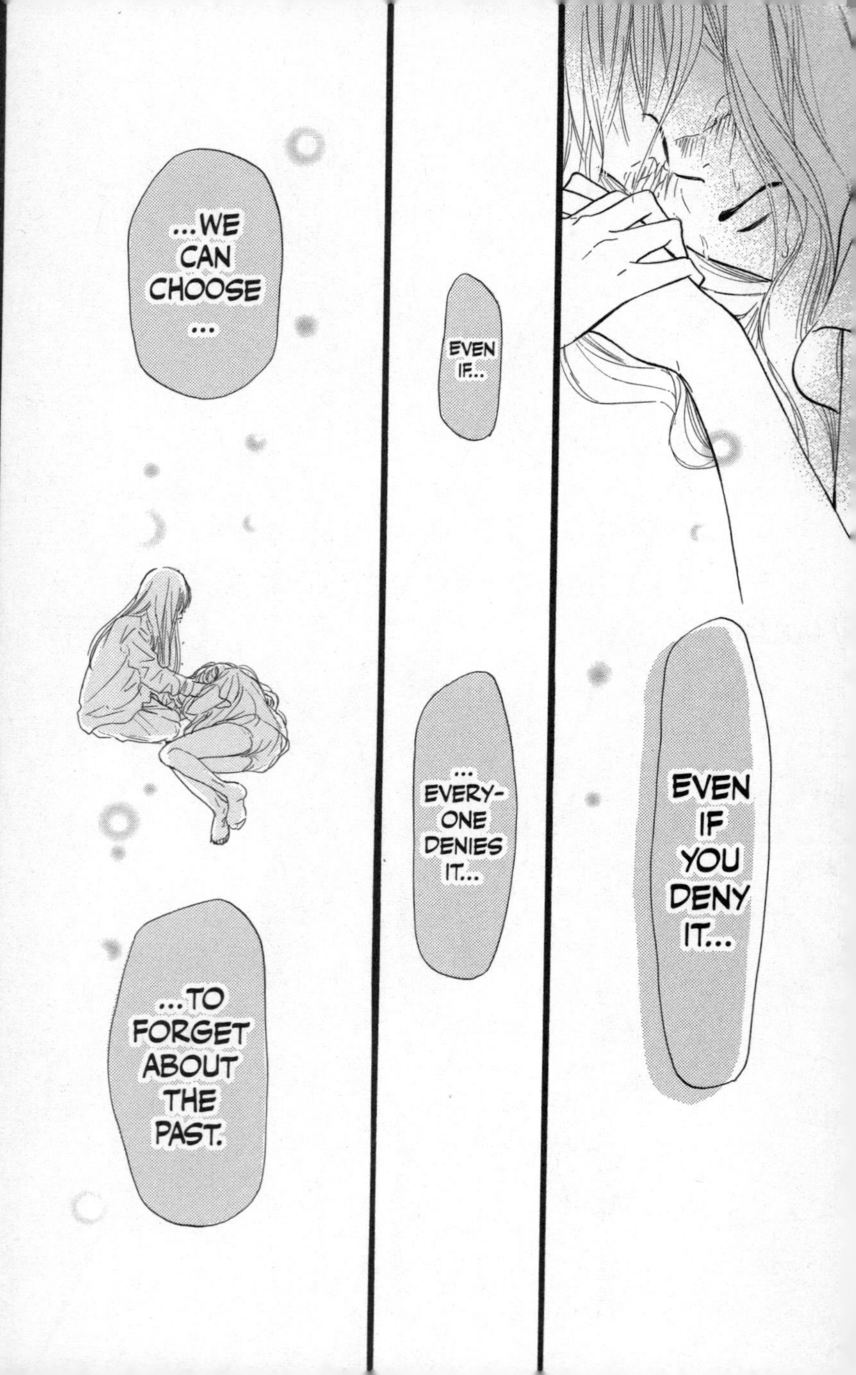
EVEN IF YOU DENY IT...
EVEN IF...
...EVERYONE DENIES IT...
...WE CAN CHOOSE...
...TO FORGET ABOUT THE PAST.

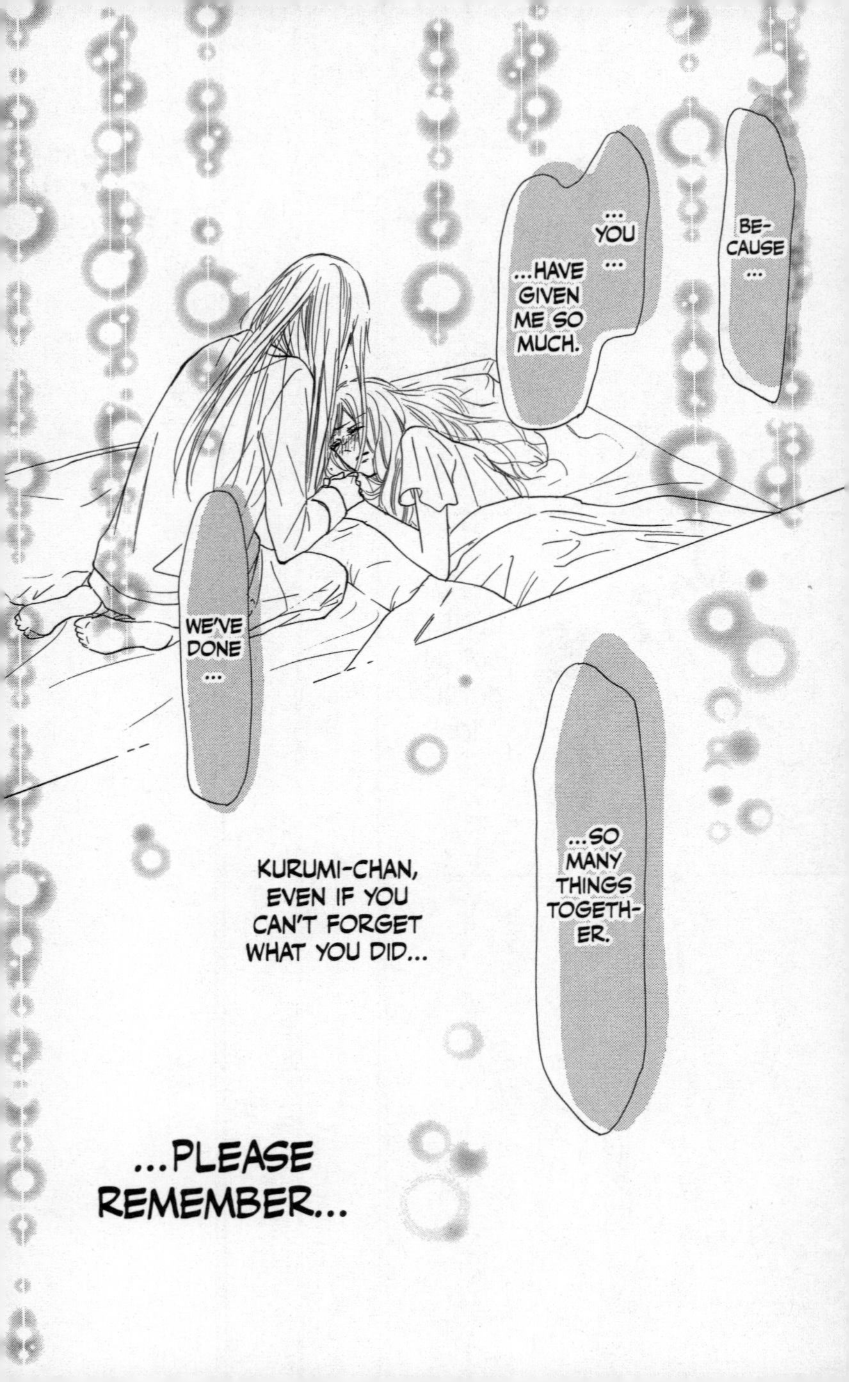
BE-CAUSE...
...YOU...
...HAVE GIVEN ME SO MUCH.
WE'VE DONE...
...SO MANY THINGS TOGETH-ER.
KURUMI-CHAN, EVEN IF YOU CAN'T FORGET WHAT YOU DID...
...PLEASE REMEMBER...

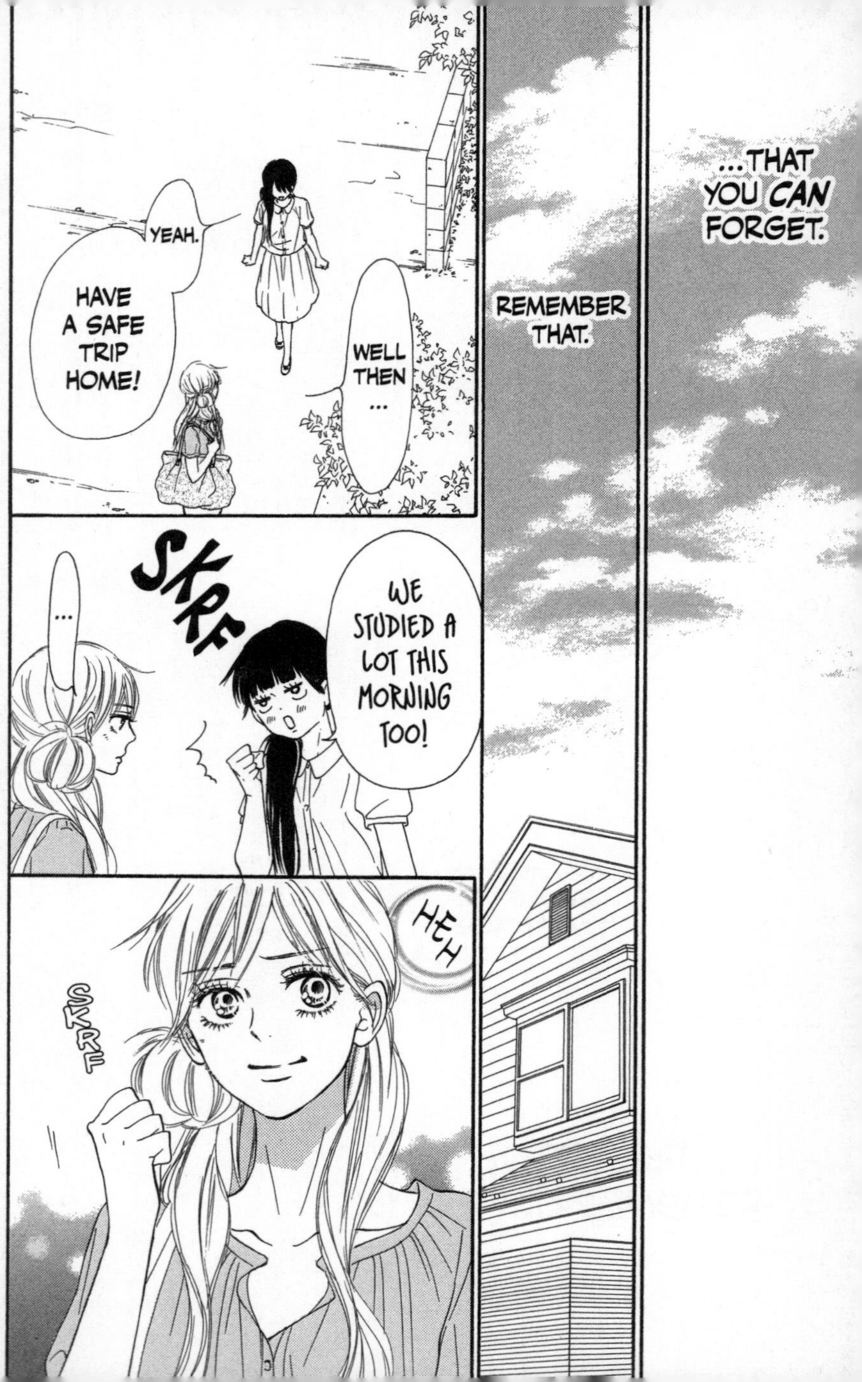
...THAT YOU CAN FORGET.
REMEMBER THAT.
WELL THEN ...
YEAH.
HAVE A SAFE TRIP HOME!
SKRF
WE STUDIED A LOT THIS MORNING TOO!
...
HEH
SKRF

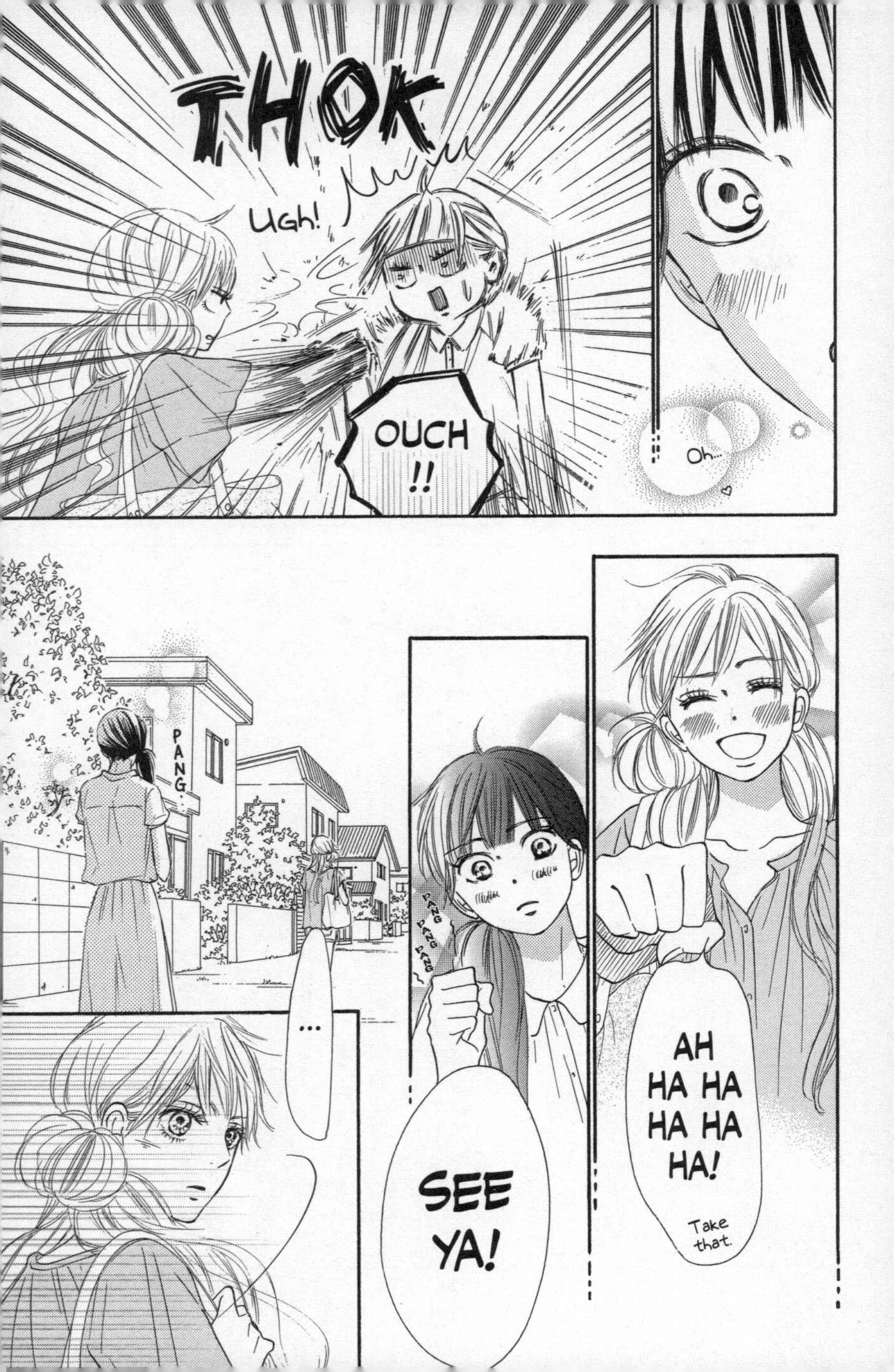
Oh...
THOK
Ugh!
OUCH!!
AH HA HA HA HA HA!
Take that.
PANG PANG PANG
SEE YA!
PANG...
...

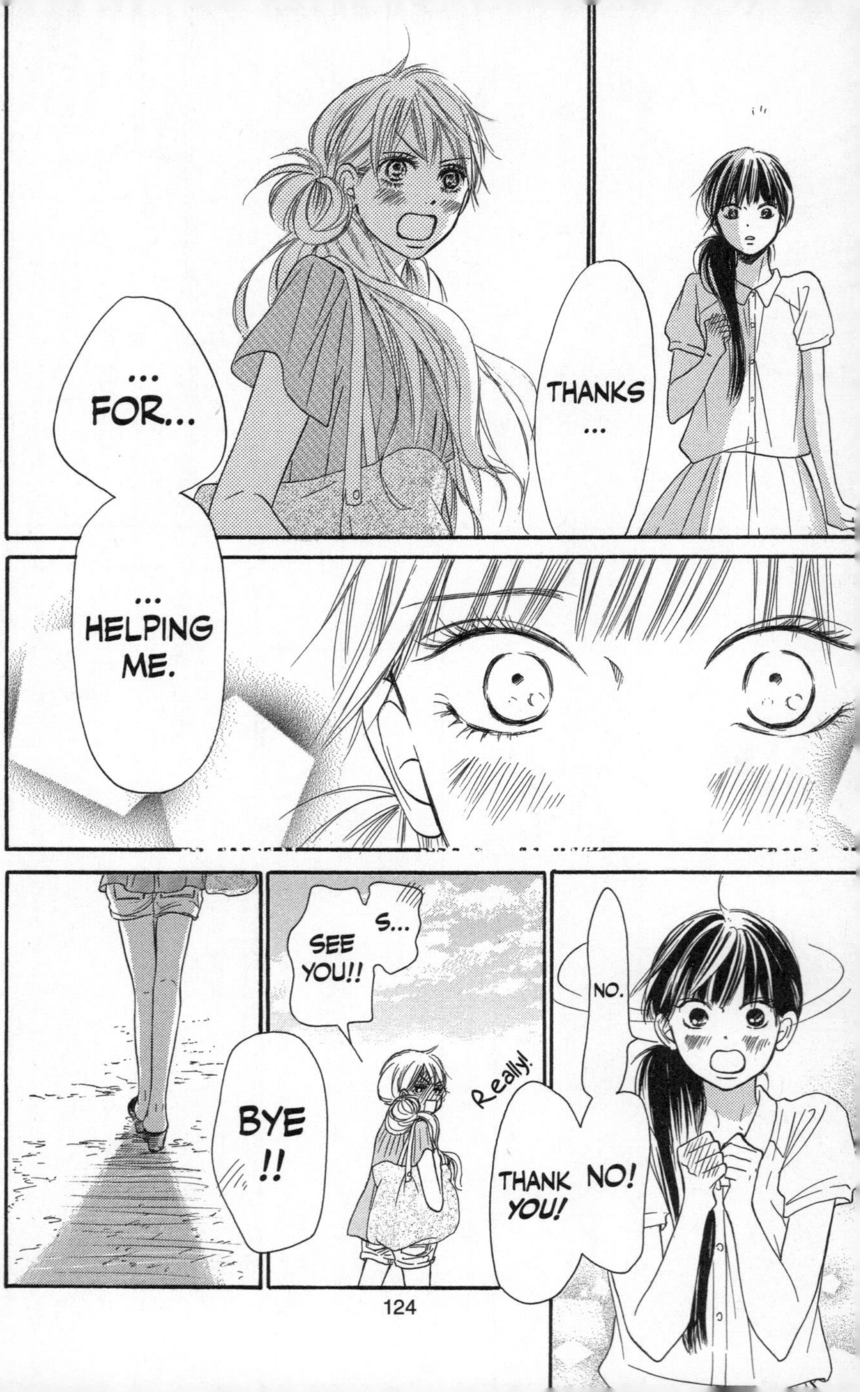
THANKS ...
... FOR...
... HELPING ME.
NO.
Really!
NO! THANK YOU!
S... SEE YOU!!
BYE !!

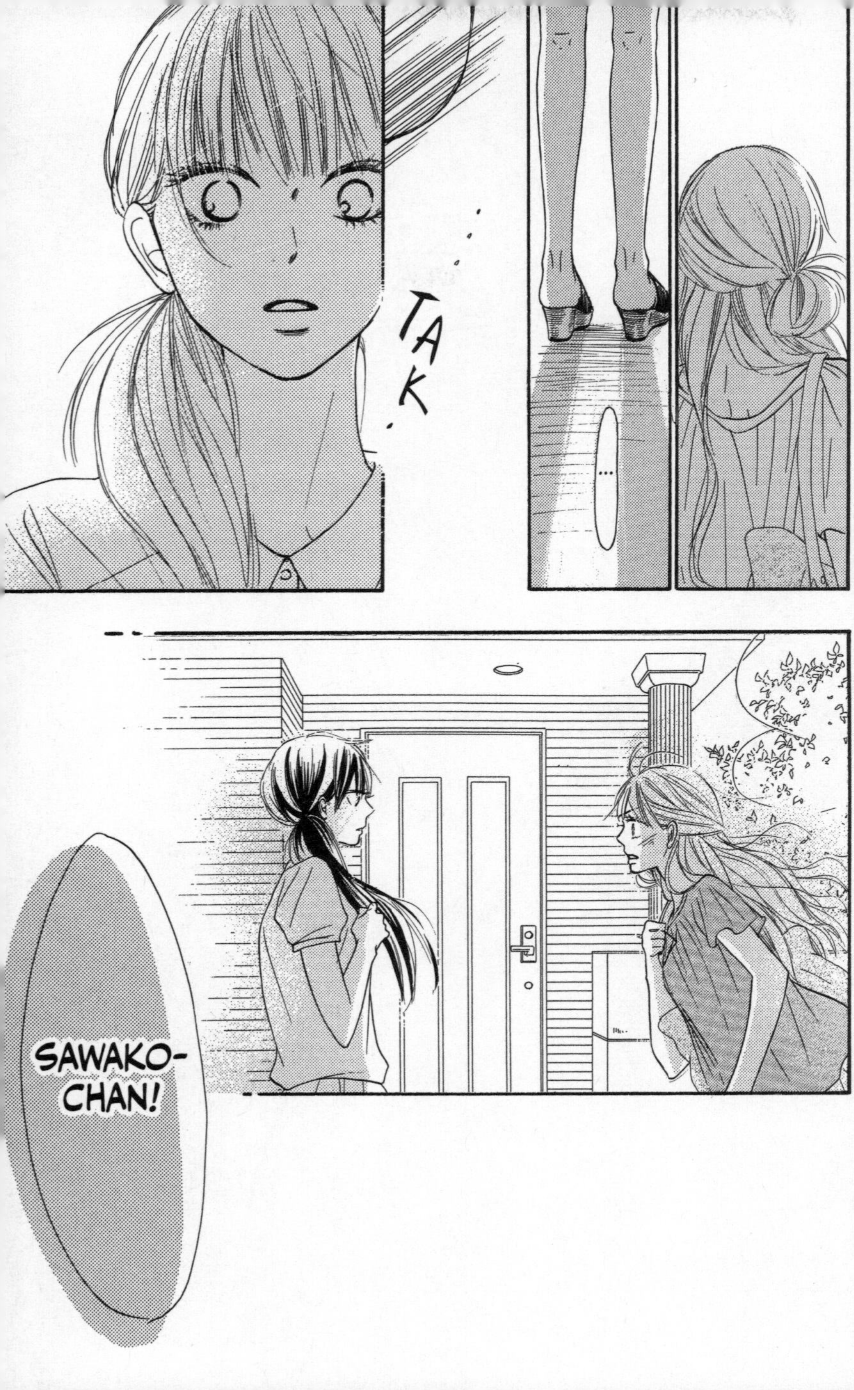
...
TAK
SAWAKO-CHAN!

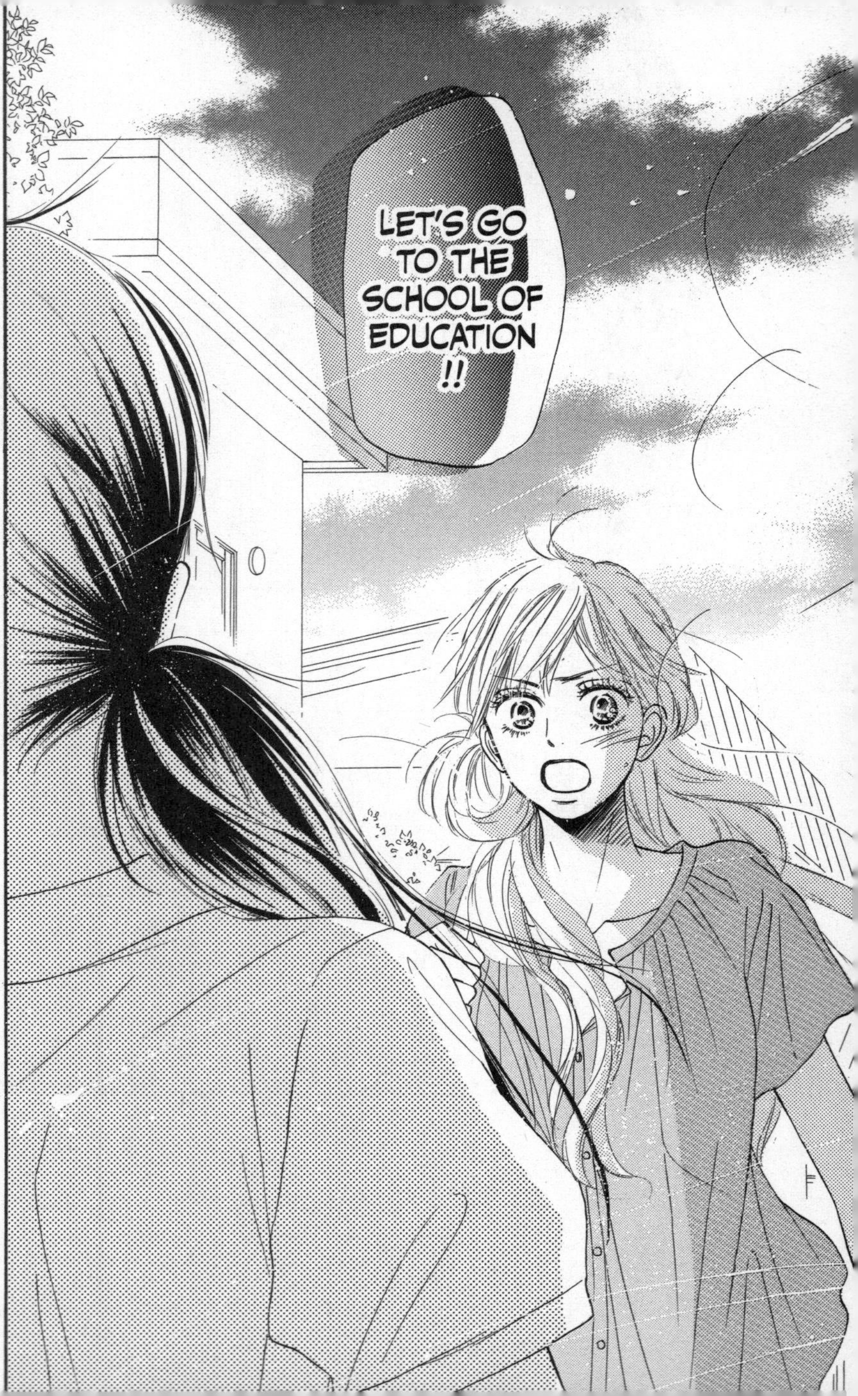
LET'S GO TO THE SCHOOL OF EDUCATION !!

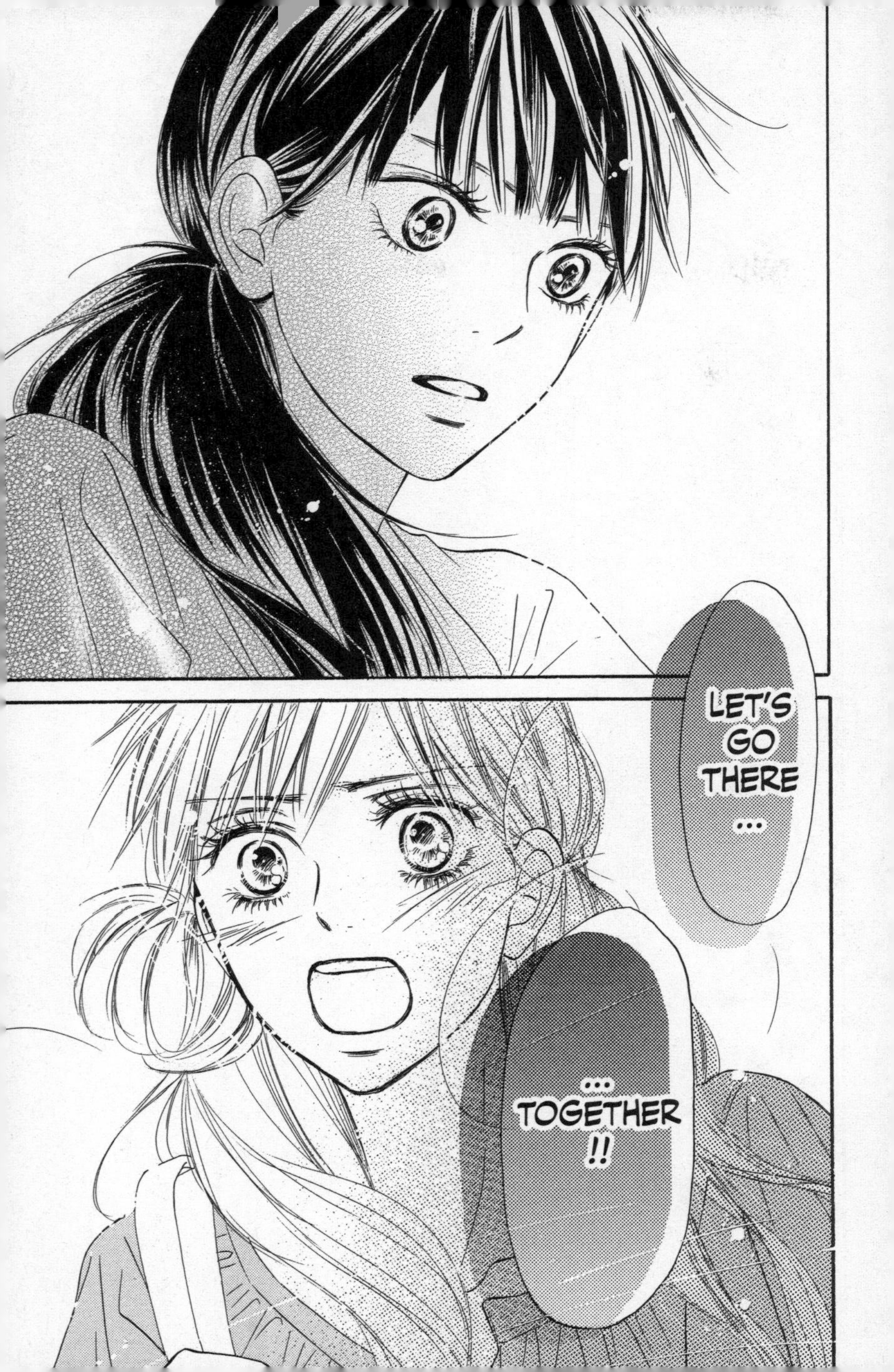
LET'S GO THERE ...
... TOGETHER !!

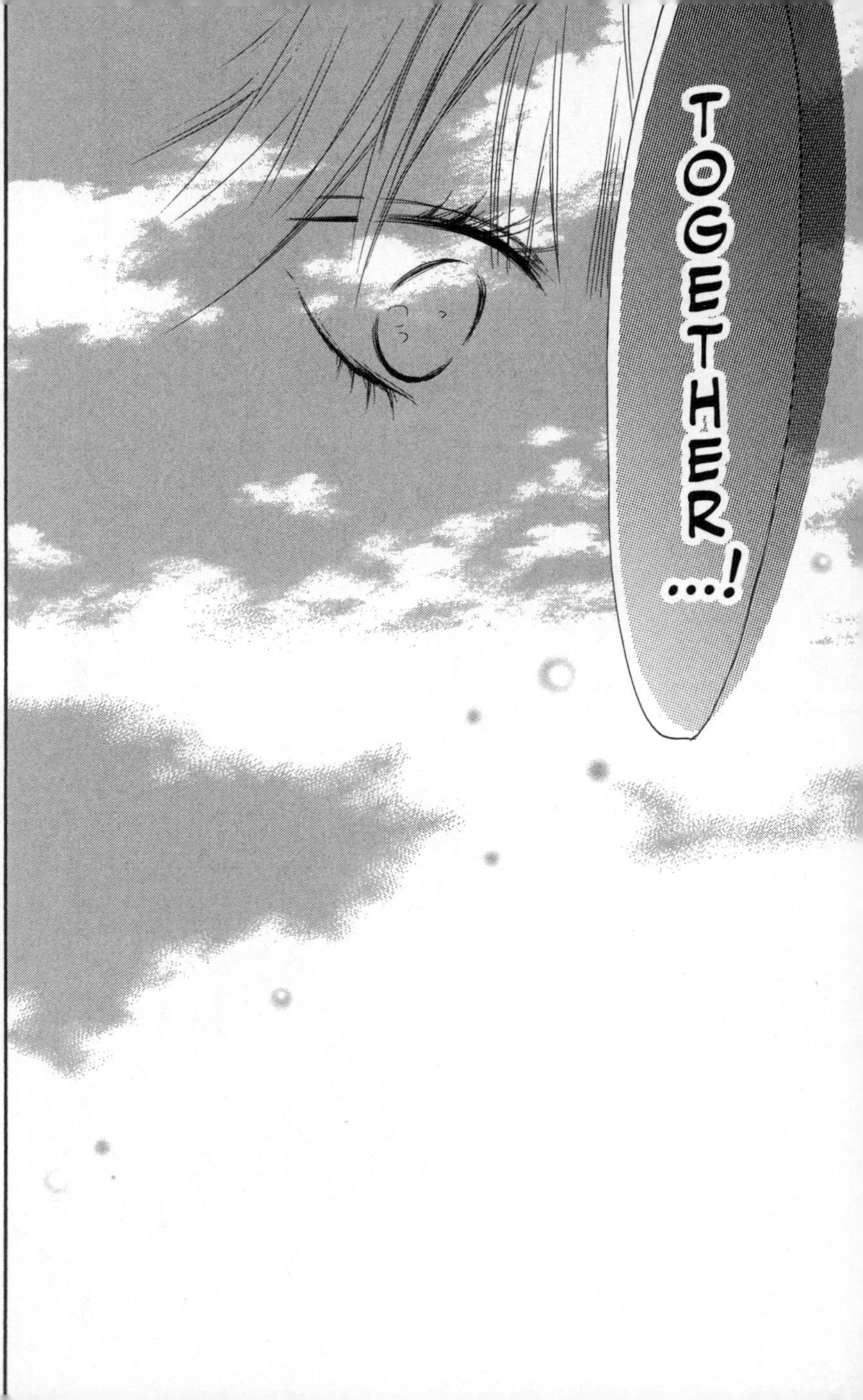
TOGETHER...!

Episode 107: First Love

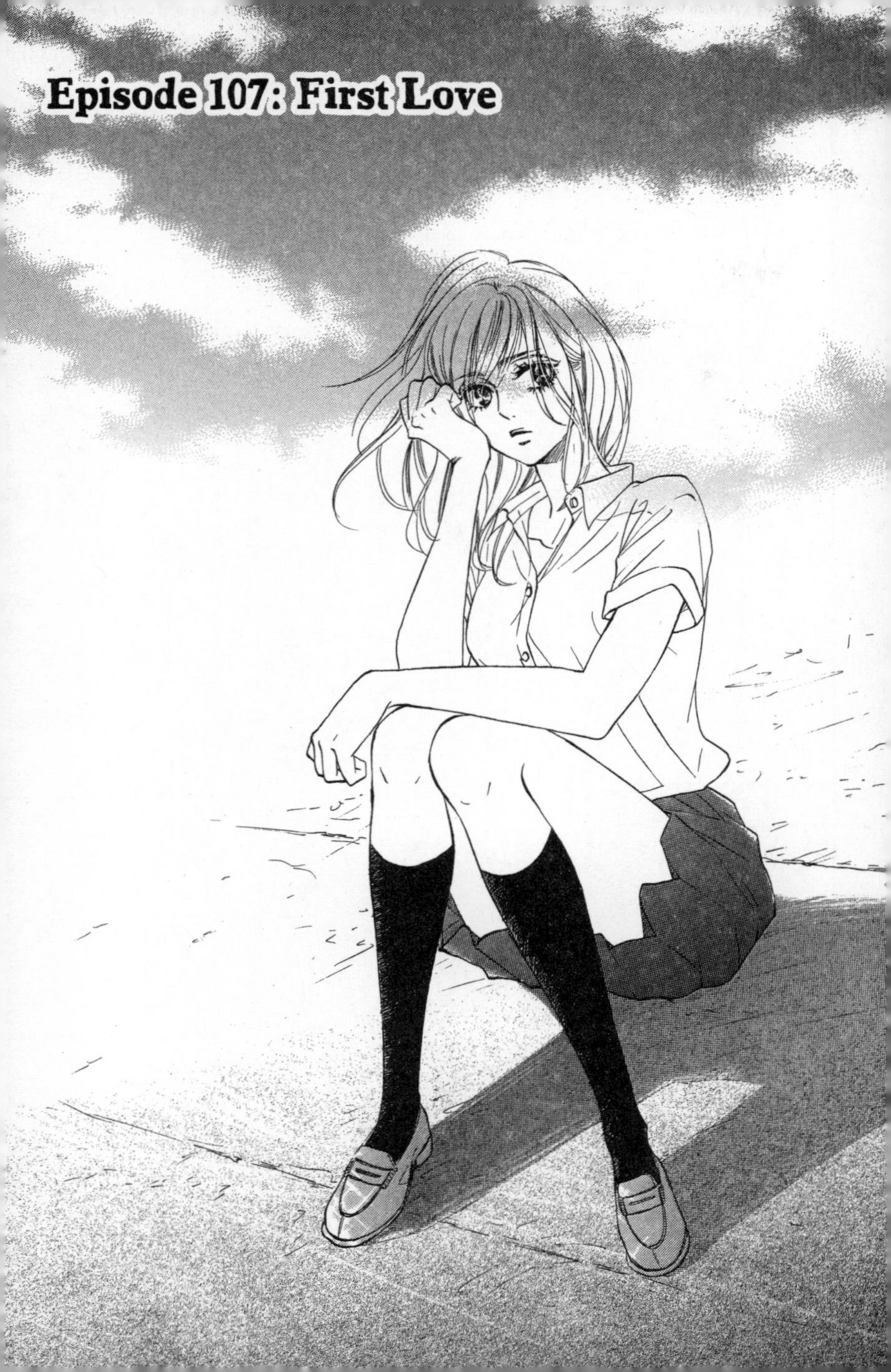

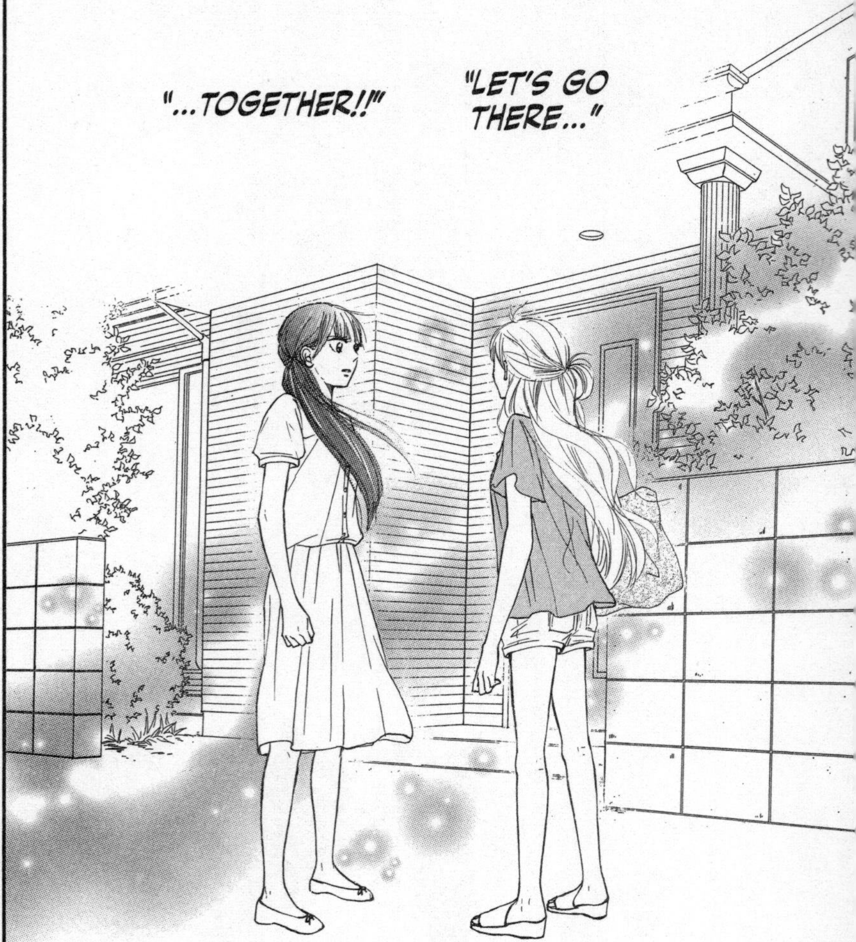
"LET'S GO THERE..."
"...TOGETHER!!"

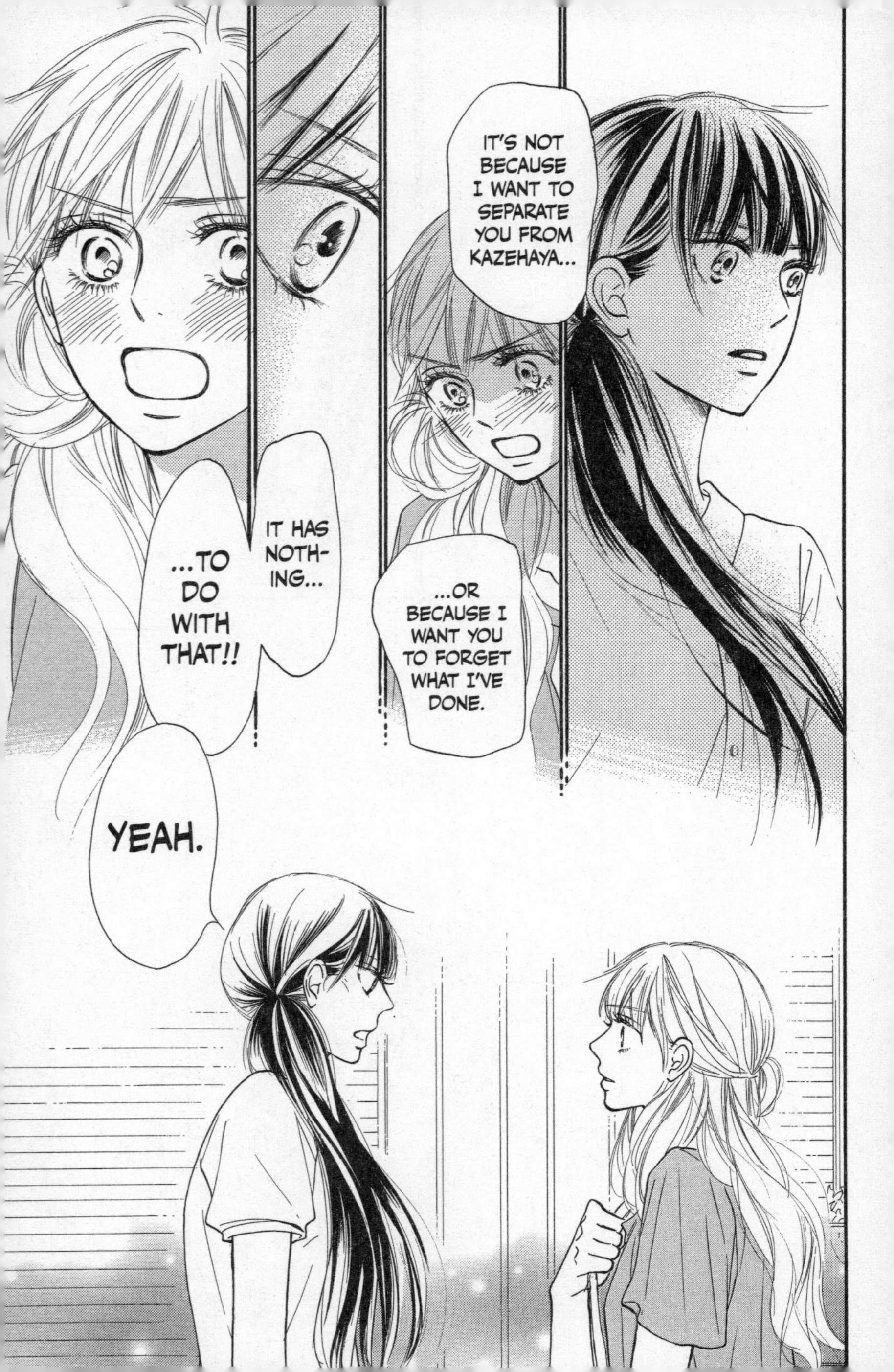
IT'S NOT BECAUSE I WANT TO SEPARATE YOU FROM KAZEHAYA...
...OR BECAUSE I WANT YOU TO FORGET WHAT I'VE DONE.
IT HAS NOTH-ING...
...TO DO WITH THAT!!
YEAH.

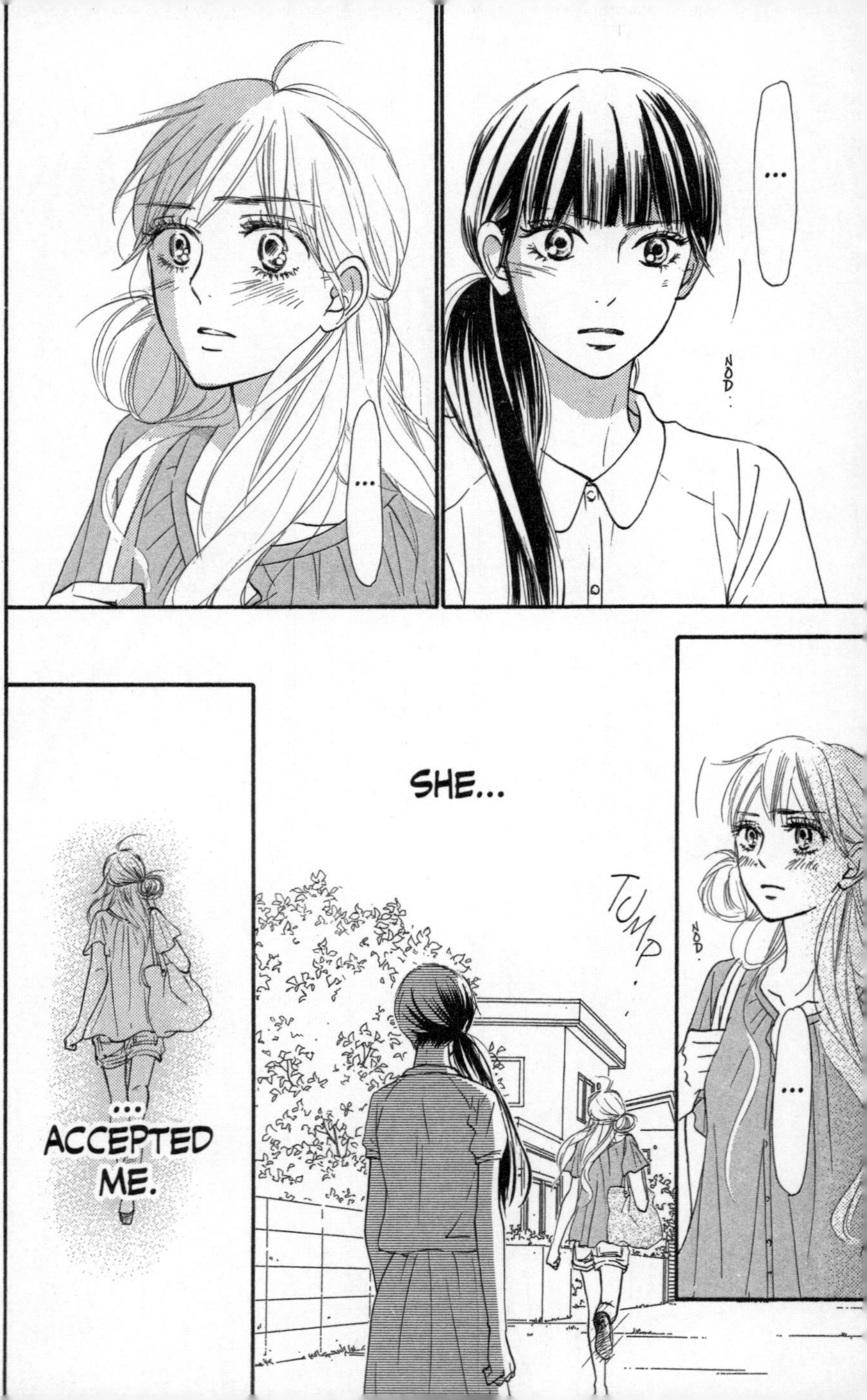
...
NOD..
...
NOD.
...
SHE...
TUMP..
...ACCEPTED ME.

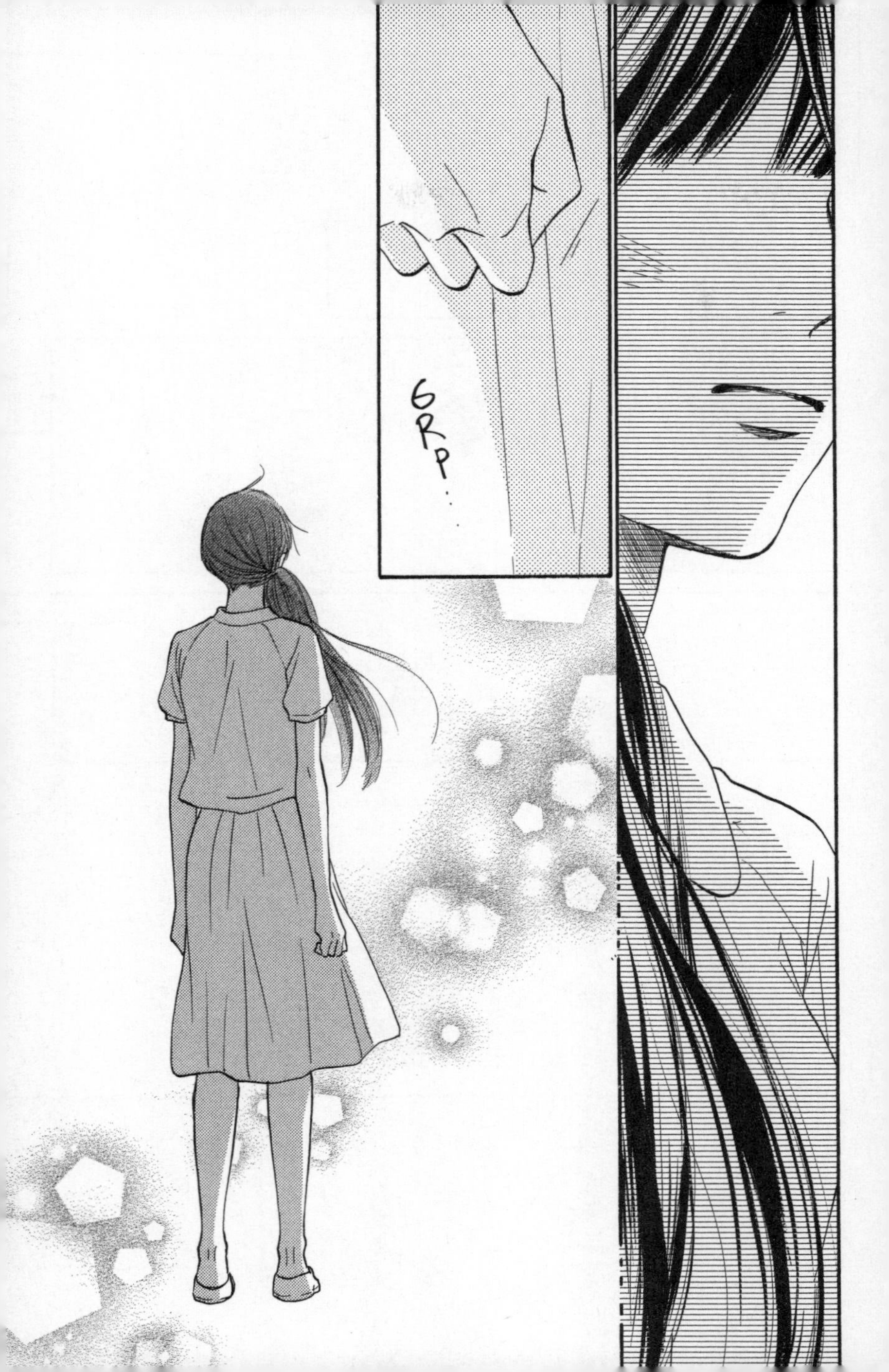
GRP...

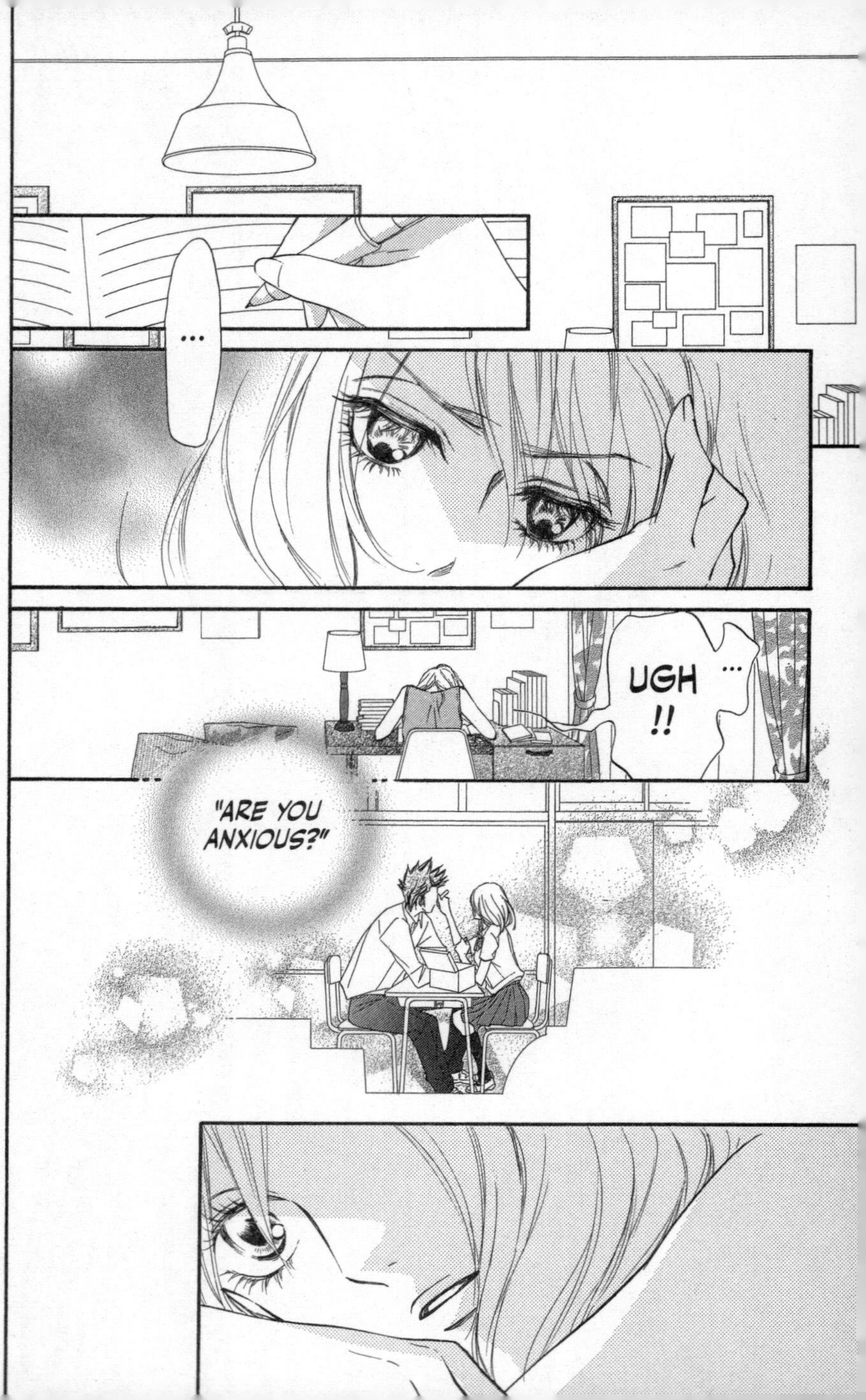
...
UGH... !!
"ARE YOU ANXIOUS?"

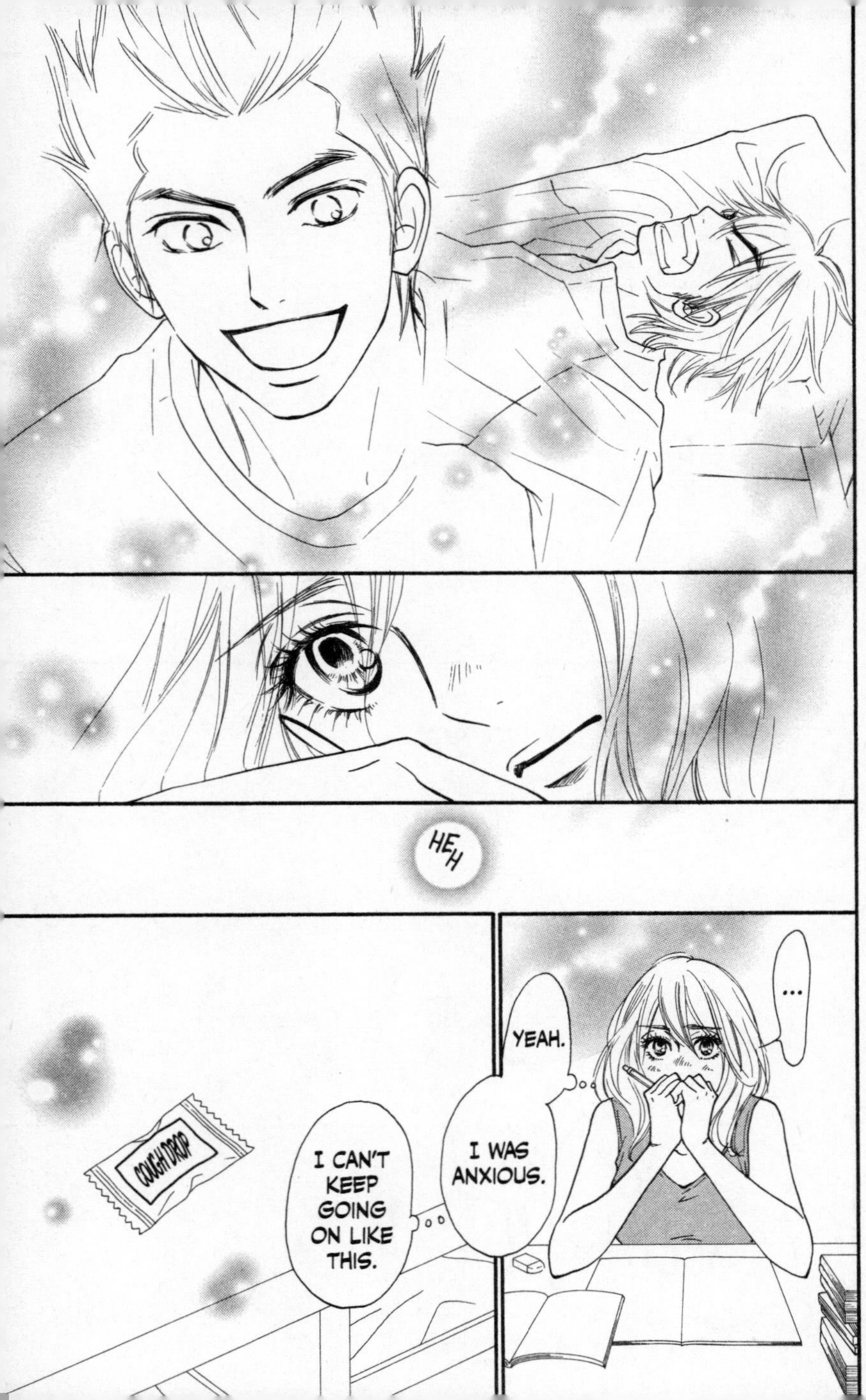
HEH
...
YEAH.
I WAS ANXIOUS.
I CAN'T KEEP GOING ON LIKE THIS.
COUGH DROP

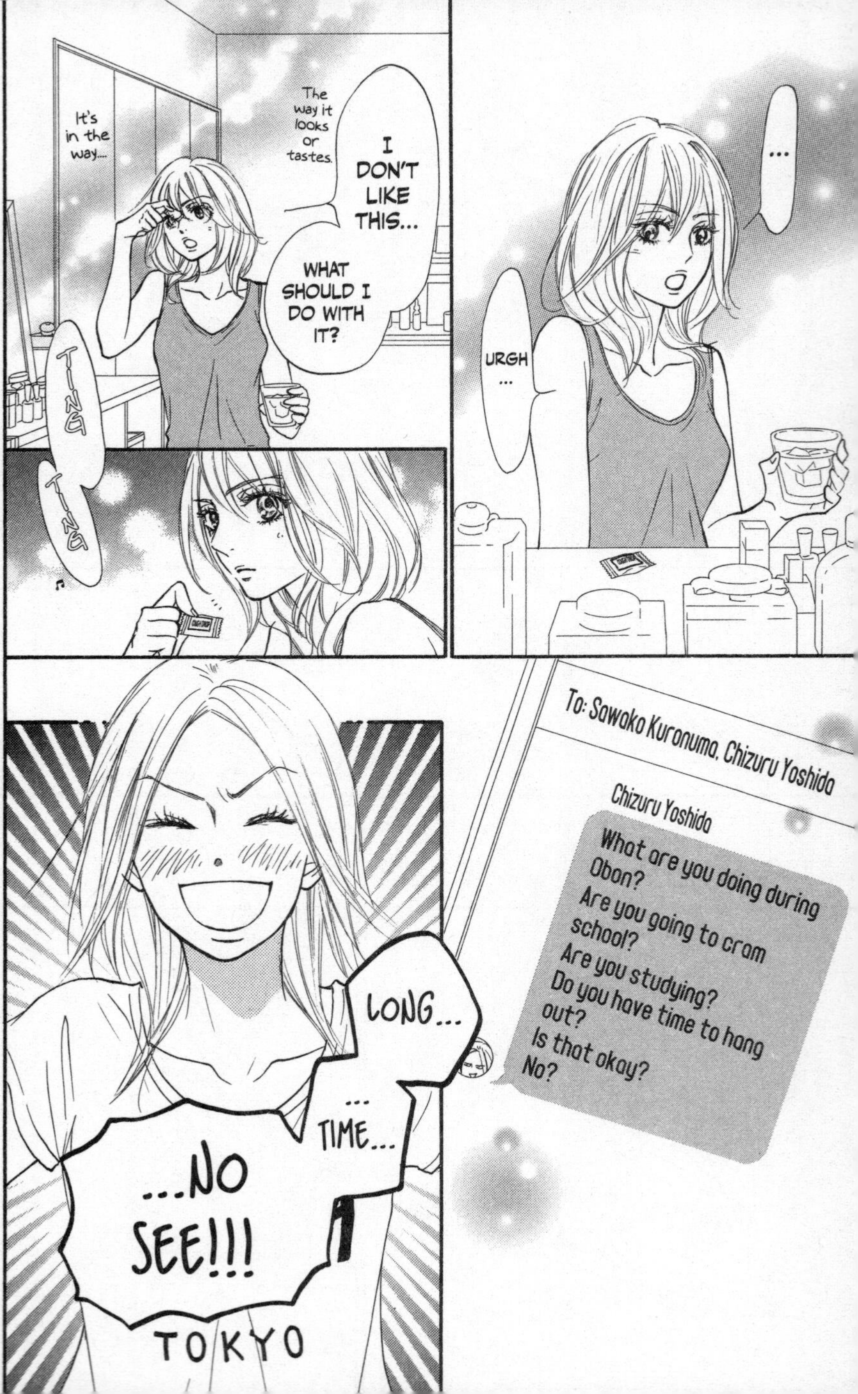
...
URGH...
It's in the way....
The way it looks or tastes.
I DON'T LIKE THIS...
WHAT SHOULD I DO WITH IT?
TING TING
TING TING
To: Sawako Kuronuma, Chizuru Yoshida
Chizuru Yoshida
What are you doing during Obon?
Are you going to cram school?
Are you studying?
Do you have time to hang out?
Is that okay?
No?
LONG...
...TIME...
...NO SEE!!!
TOKYO

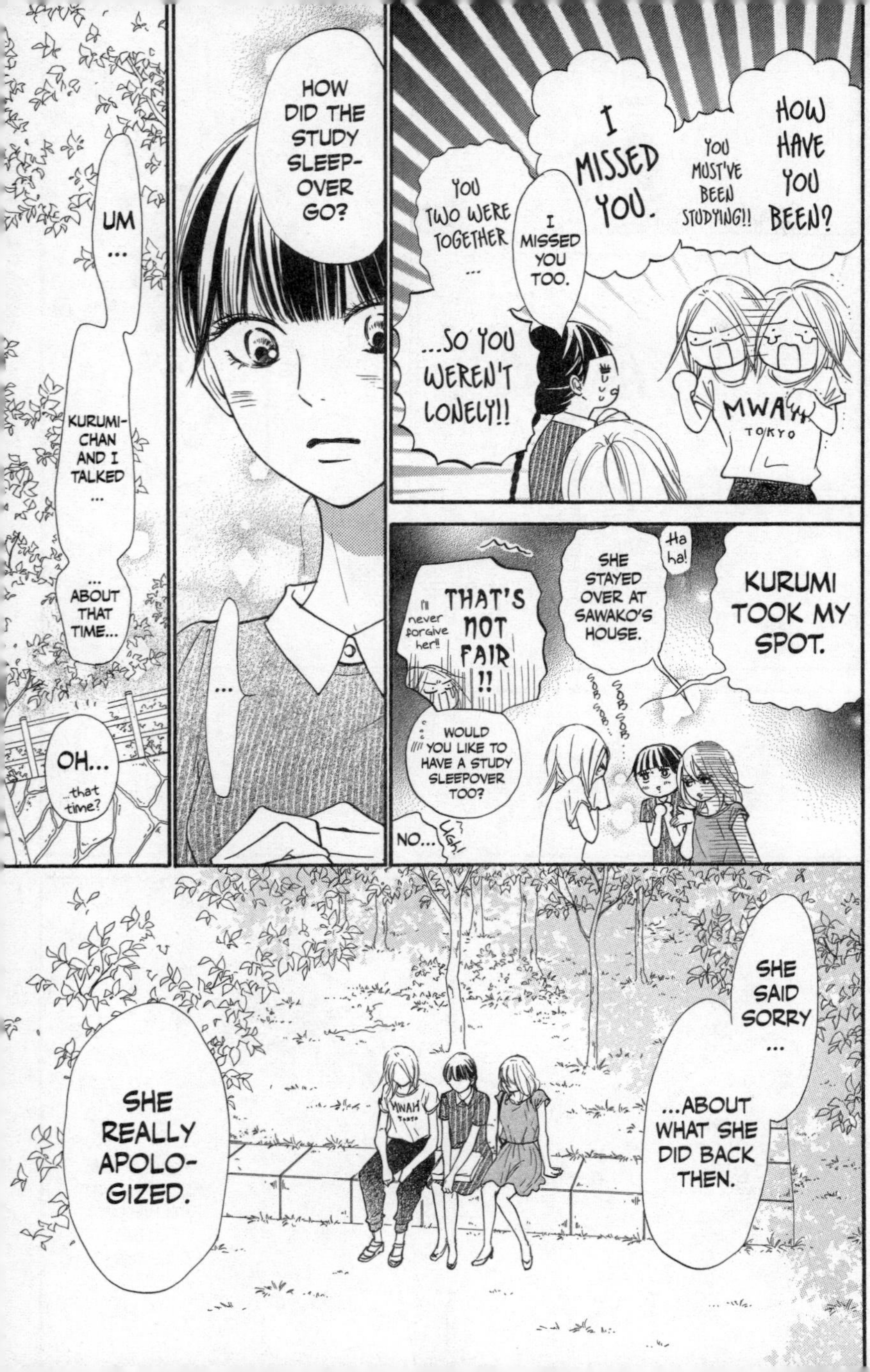
HOW HAVE YOU BEEN?
YOU MUST'VE BEEN STUDYING!!
I MISSED YOU.
I MISSED YOU TOO.
YOU TWO WERE TOGETHER...
...SO YOU WEREN'T LONELY!!
KURUMI TOOK MY SPOT.
Ha ha!
SHE STAYED OVER AT SAWAKO'S HOUSE.
THAT'S NOT FAIR!!
I'll never forgive her!!
SOB SOB...
SOB SOB...
WOULD YOU LIKE TO HAVE A STUDY SLEEPOVER TOO?
Ugh!
NO...
HOW DID THE STUDY SLEEP-OVER GO?
...
UM...
KURUMI-CHAN AND I TALKED...
...ABOUT THAT TIME...
OH...
...that time?
SHE SAID SORRY...
...ABOUT WHAT SHE DID BACK THEN.
SHE REALLY APOLOGIZED.

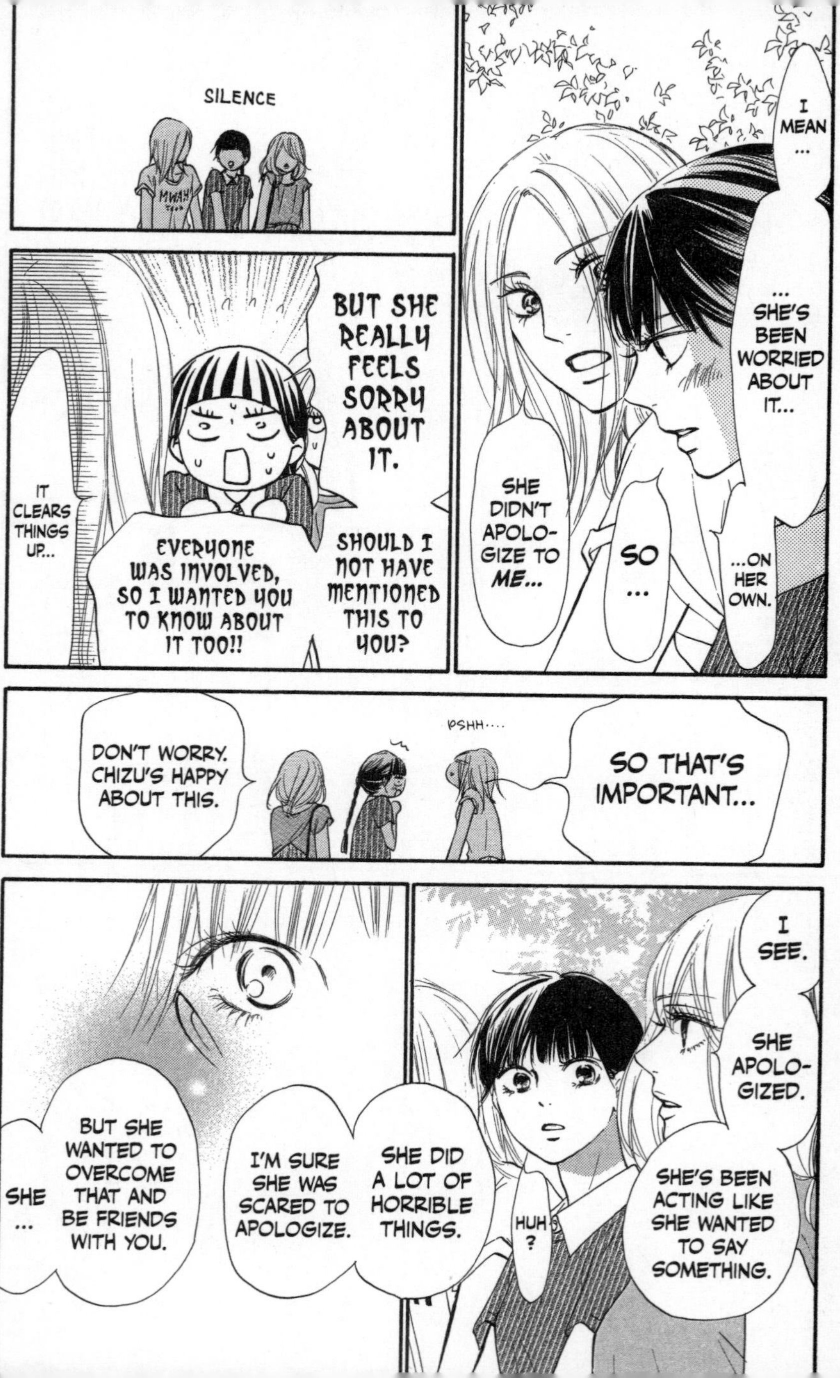
I MEAN ...
... SHE'S BEEN WORRIED ABOUT IT...
...ON HER OWN.
SO ...
SHE DIDN'T APOLOGIZE TO *ME*...
SILENCE
MWAH
BUT SHE REALLY FEELS SORRY ABOUT IT.
SHOULD I NOT HAVE MENTIONED THIS TO YOU?
EVERYONE WAS INVOLVED, SO I WANTED YOU TO KNOW ABOUT IT TOO!!
IT CLEARS THINGS UP...
SO THAT'S IMPORTANT...
PSHH....
DON'T WORRY. CHIZU'S HAPPY ABOUT THIS.
I SEE.
SHE APOLOGIZED.
SHE'S BEEN ACTING LIKE SHE WANTED TO SAY SOMETHING.
HUH ?
SHE DID A LOT OF HORRIBLE THINGS.
I'M SURE SHE WAS SCARED TO APOLOGIZE.
BUT SHE WANTED TO OVERCOME THAT AND BE FRIENDS WITH YOU.
SHE ...

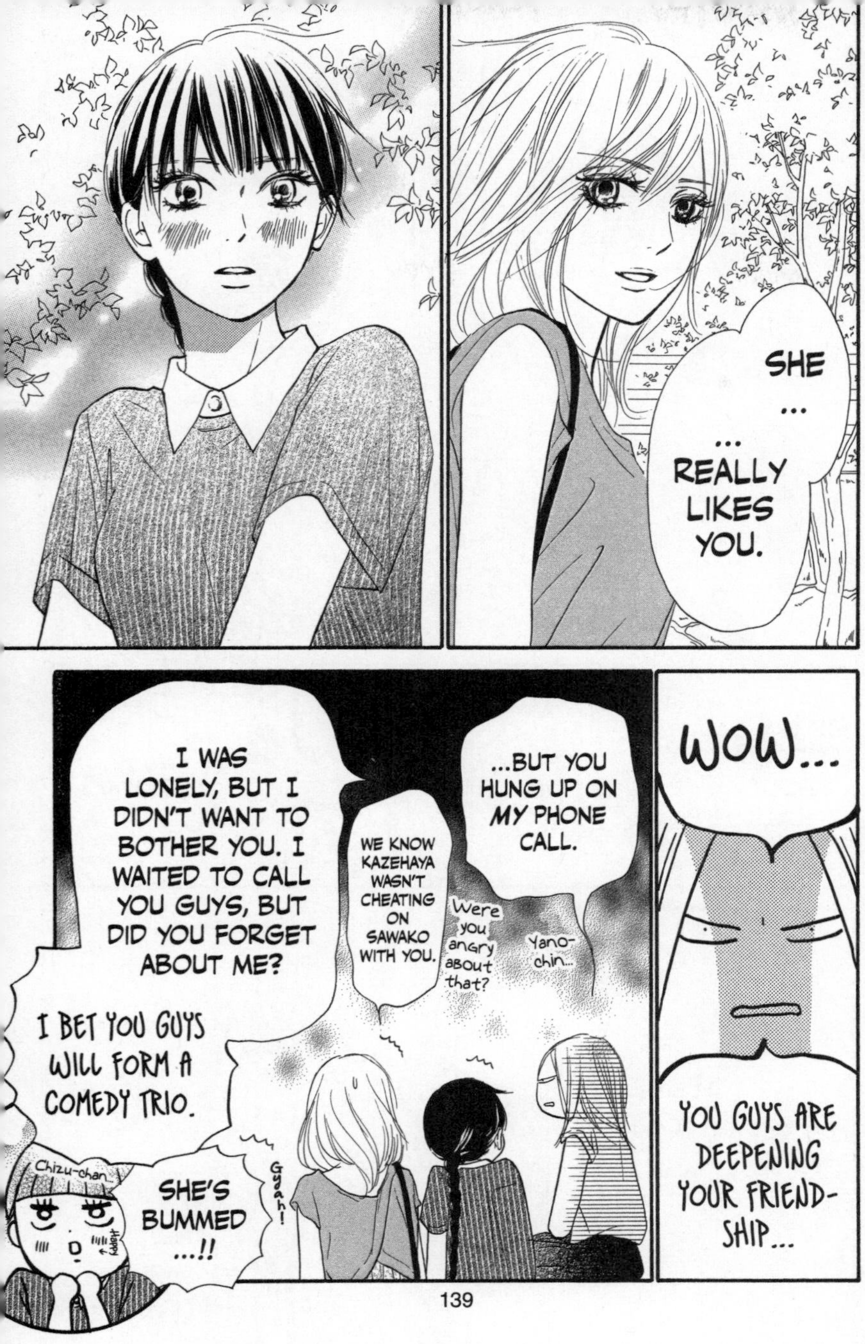
SHE ... ... REALLY LIKES YOU.
WOW...
YOU GUYS ARE DEEPENING YOUR FRIEND-SHIP...
...BUT YOU HUNG UP ON MY PHONE CALL.
Yano-chin...
Were you angry about that?
WE KNOW KAZEHAYA WASN'T CHEATING ON SAWAKO WITH YOU.
I WAS LONELY, BUT I DIDN'T WANT TO BOTHER YOU. I WAITED TO CALL YOU GUYS, BUT DID YOU FORGET ABOUT ME?
I BET YOU GUYS WILL FORM A COMEDY TRIO.
Gyah!
SHE'S BUMMED ...!!
Happy
Chizu-chan...

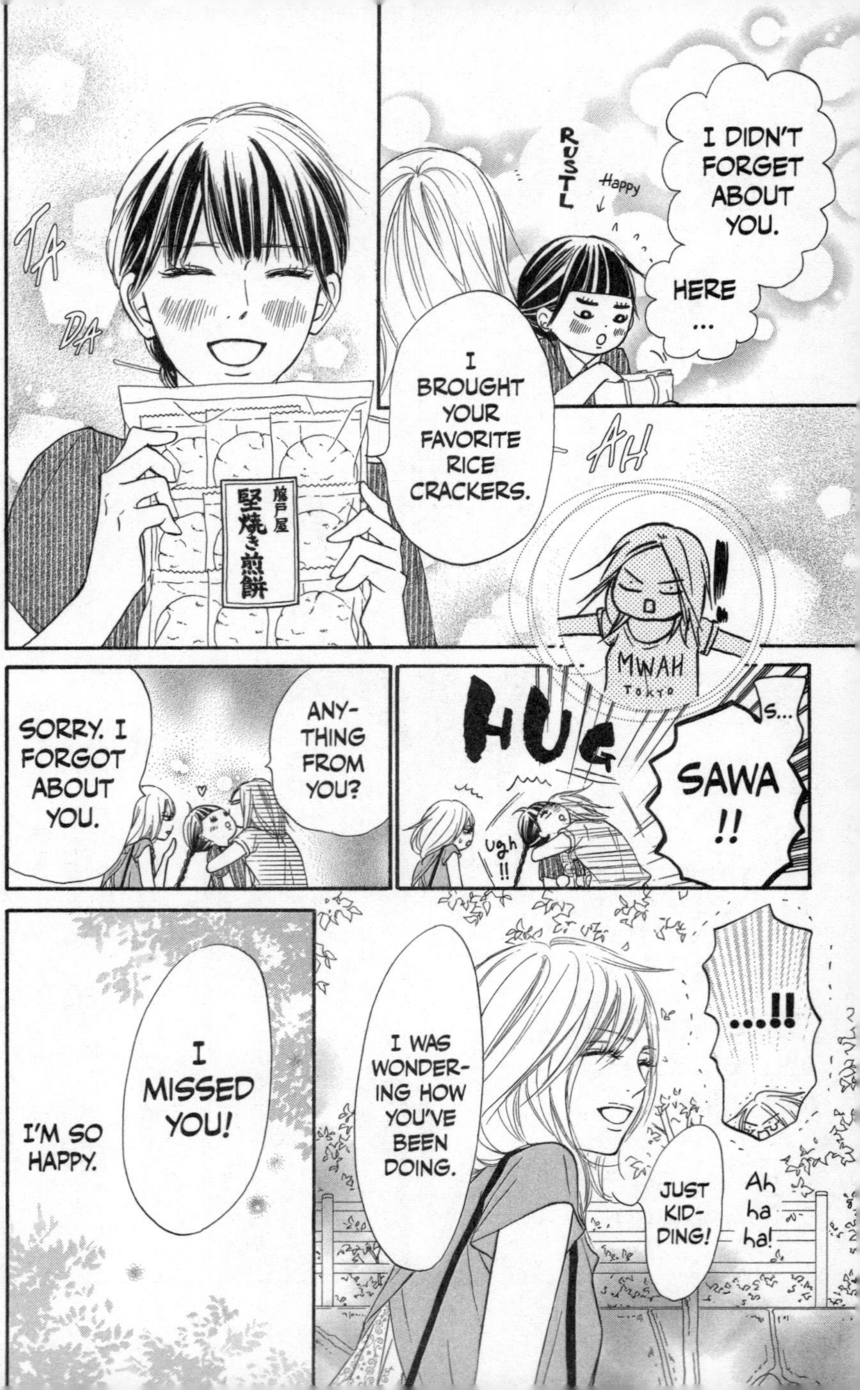
RUSTL
Happy
I DIDN'T FORGET ABOUT YOU.
HERE ...
AH
!
MWAH
TOKYO
TA
DA
I BROUGHT YOUR FAVORITE RICE CRACKERS.
堅焼き煎餅
S...
SAWA !!
HUG
Ugh !!
ANY-THING FROM YOU?
SORRY. I FORGOT ABOUT YOU.
...!!
Ah ha ha!
JUST KID-DING!
I WAS WONDER-ING HOW YOU'VE BEEN DOING.
I MISSED YOU!
I'M SO HAPPY.

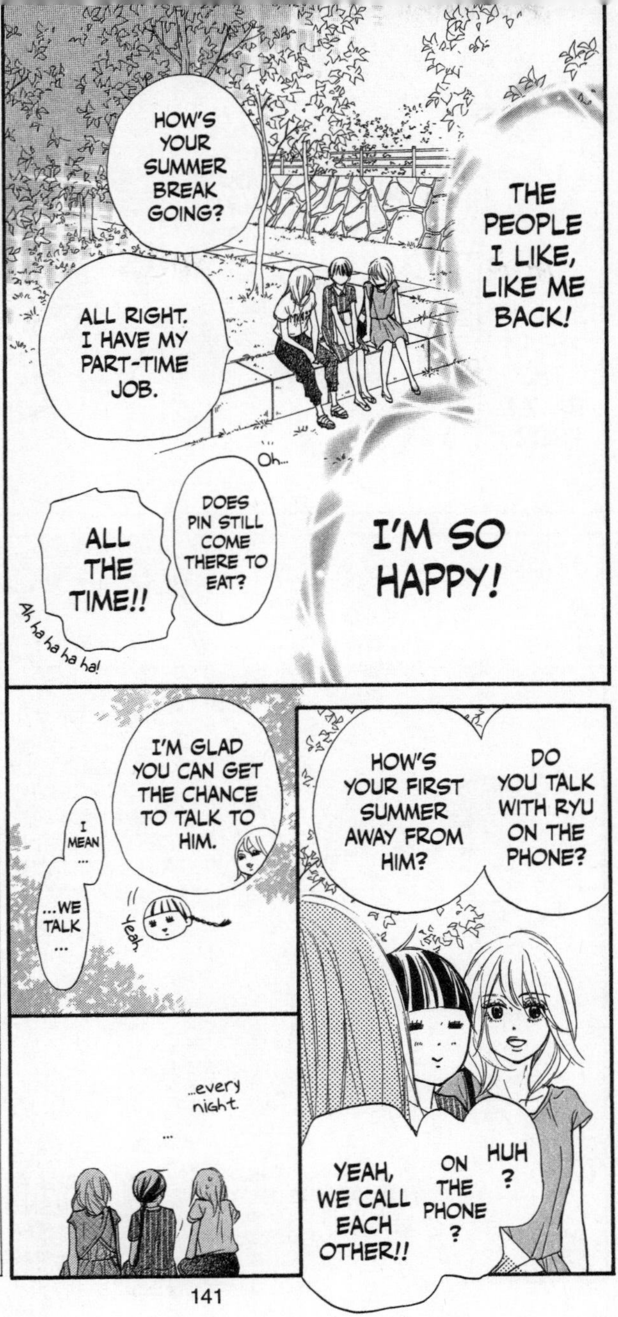
THE PEOPLE I LIKE, LIKE ME BACK!
HOW'S YOUR SUMMER BREAK GOING?
ALL RIGHT. I HAVE MY PART-TIME JOB.
I'M SO HAPPY!
Oh...
DOES PIN STILL COME THERE TO EAT?
ALL THE TIME!!
Ah ha ha ha ha!
DO YOU TALK WITH RYU ON THE PHONE?
HOW'S YOUR FIRST SUMMER AWAY FROM HIM?
HUH?
ON THE PHONE?
YEAH, WE CALL EACH OTHER!!
I'M GLAD YOU CAN GET THE CHANCE TO TALK TO HIM.
Yeah.
I MEAN...
...WE TALK...
...every night.
...

KARUPIN on JAPAN 4

So, the story is coming along. I'd be happy if you would continue following for a little longer.

It's already volume 26! Thanks so much!

I'm Shiina and I really want salty and greasy foods after eating healthy for so long!

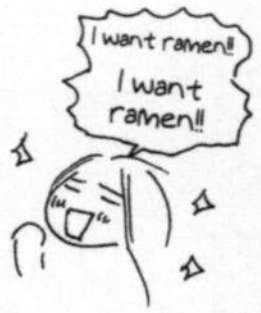
I want ramen!!
I want ramen!!

I really want to eat ramen...

Ramen...

March 2016
Karuho Shiina

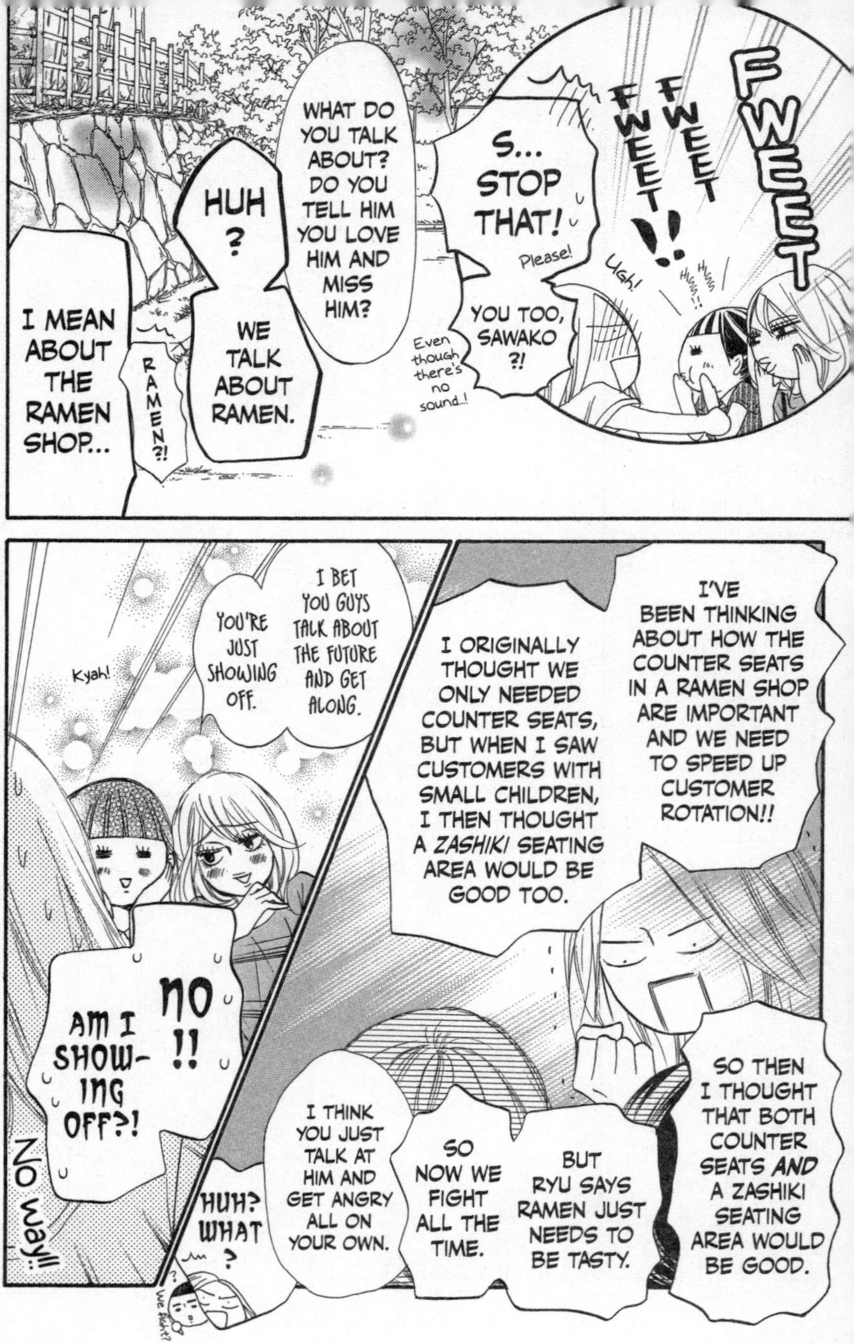
FWEET
FWEET
FWEET!!
HISS HISS!!
Ugh!
S... STOP THAT!
Please!
YOU TOO, SAWAKO?!
Even though there's no sound...!
WHAT DO YOU TALK ABOUT? DO YOU TELL HIM YOU LOVE HIM AND MISS HIM?
HUH?
WE TALK ABOUT RAMEN.
RAMEN?!
I MEAN ABOUT THE RAMEN SHOP...
I'VE BEEN THINKING ABOUT HOW THE COUNTER SEATS IN A RAMEN SHOP ARE IMPORTANT AND WE NEED TO SPEED UP CUSTOMER ROTATION!!
I ORIGINALLY THOUGHT WE ONLY NEEDED COUNTER SEATS, BUT WHEN I SAW CUSTOMERS WITH SMALL CHILDREN, I THEN THOUGHT A *ZASHIKI* SEATING AREA WOULD BE GOOD TOO.
SO THEN I THOUGHT THAT BOTH COUNTER SEATS *AND* A ZASHIKI SEATING AREA WOULD BE GOOD.
BUT RYU SAYS RAMEN JUST NEEDS TO BE TASTY.
SO NOW WE FIGHT ALL THE TIME.
I THINK YOU JUST TALK AT HIM AND GET ANGRY ALL ON YOUR OWN.
HUH? WHAT?
We fight?
I BET YOU GUYS TALK ABOUT THE FUTURE AND GET ALONG.
YOU'RE JUST SHOWING OFF.
Kyah!
NO!!
AM I SHOWING OFF?!
No way!!

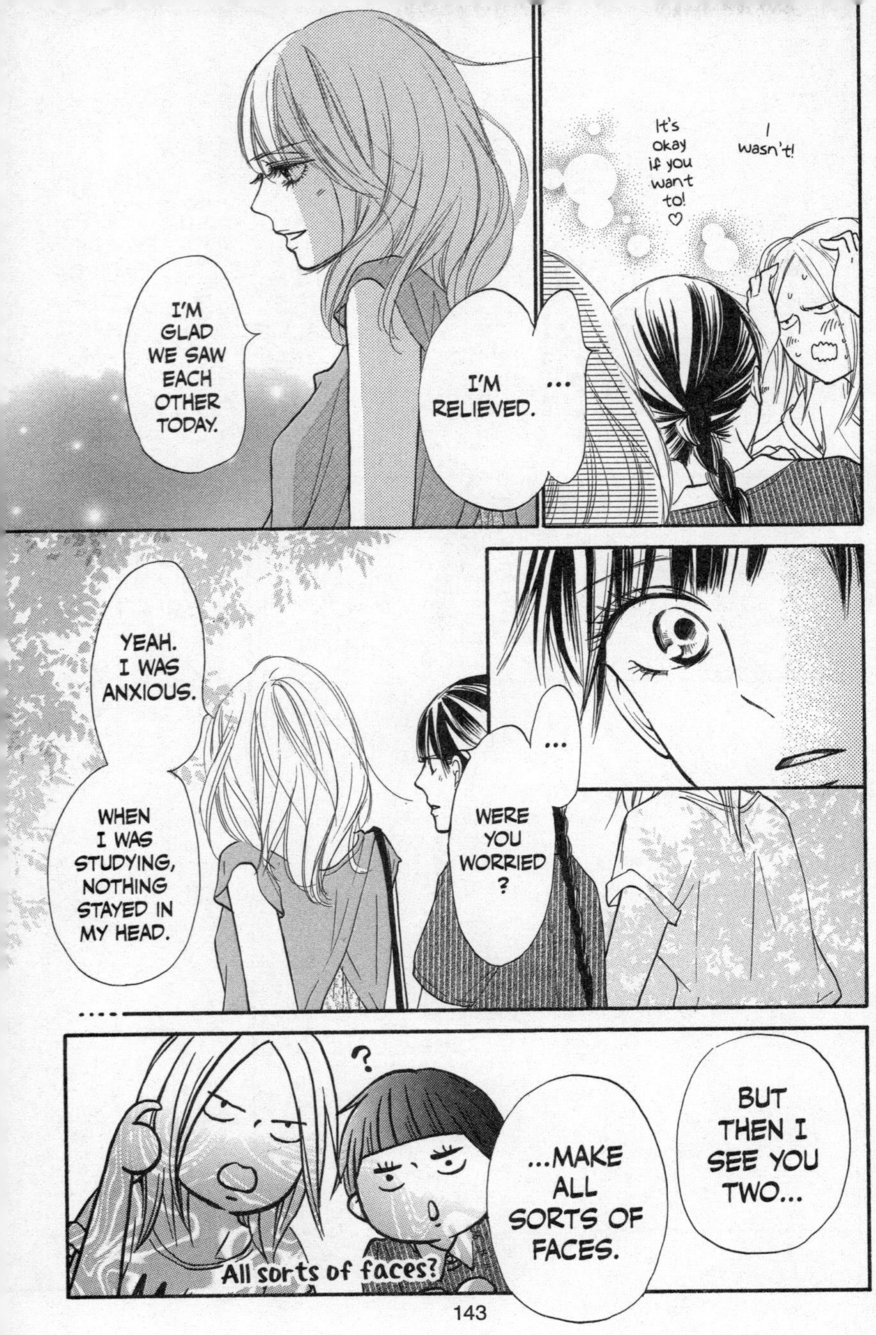
It's okay if you want to! ♡
I wasn't!
...
I'M RELIEVED.
I'M GLAD WE SAW EACH OTHER TODAY.
...
WERE YOU WORRIED?
YEAH. I WAS ANXIOUS.
WHEN I WAS STUDYING, NOTHING STAYED IN MY HEAD.
....
BUT THEN I SEE YOU TWO...
...MAKE ALL SORTS OF FACES.
?
All sorts of faces?

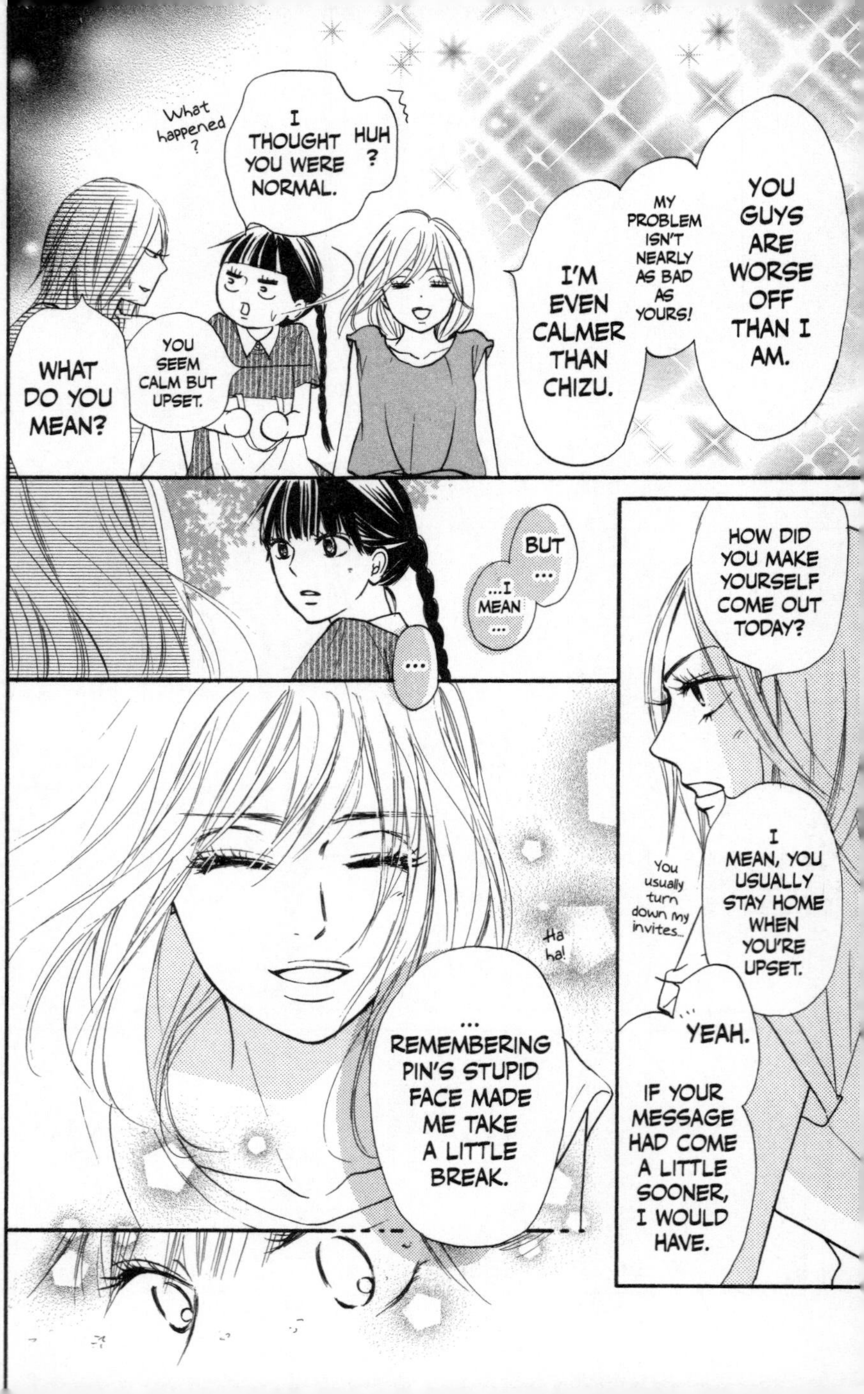
YOU GUYS ARE WORSE OFF THAN I AM.
MY PROBLEM ISN'T NEARLY AS BAD AS YOURS!
I'M EVEN CALMER THAN CHIZU.
HUH?
I THOUGHT YOU WERE NORMAL.
What happened?
YOU SEEM CALM BUT UPSET.
WHAT DO YOU MEAN?
HOW DID YOU MAKE YOURSELF COME OUT TODAY?
I MEAN, YOU USUALLY STAY HOME WHEN YOU'RE UPSET.
You usually turn down my invites...
...YEAH.
IF YOUR MESSAGE HAD COME A LITTLE SOONER, I WOULD HAVE.
BUT...
...I MEAN...
...
Ha ha!
...REMEMBERING PIN'S STUPID FACE MADE ME TAKE A LITTLE BREAK.

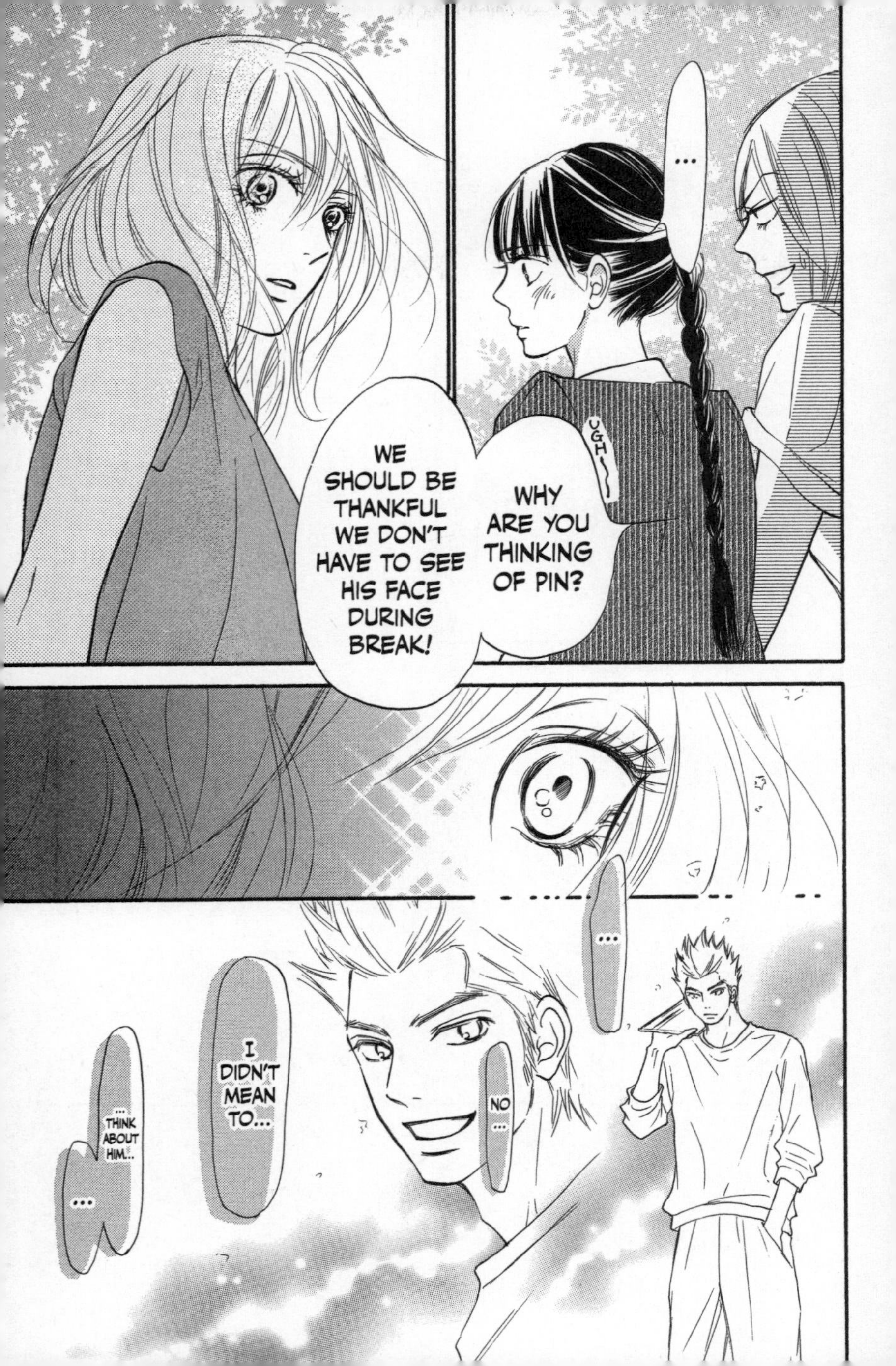
...
UGH~
WHY ARE YOU THINKING OF PIN?
WE SHOULD BE THANKFUL WE DON'T HAVE TO SEE HIS FACE DURING BREAK!
...
NO ...
I DIDN'T MEAN TO...
...THINK ABOUT HIM...
...

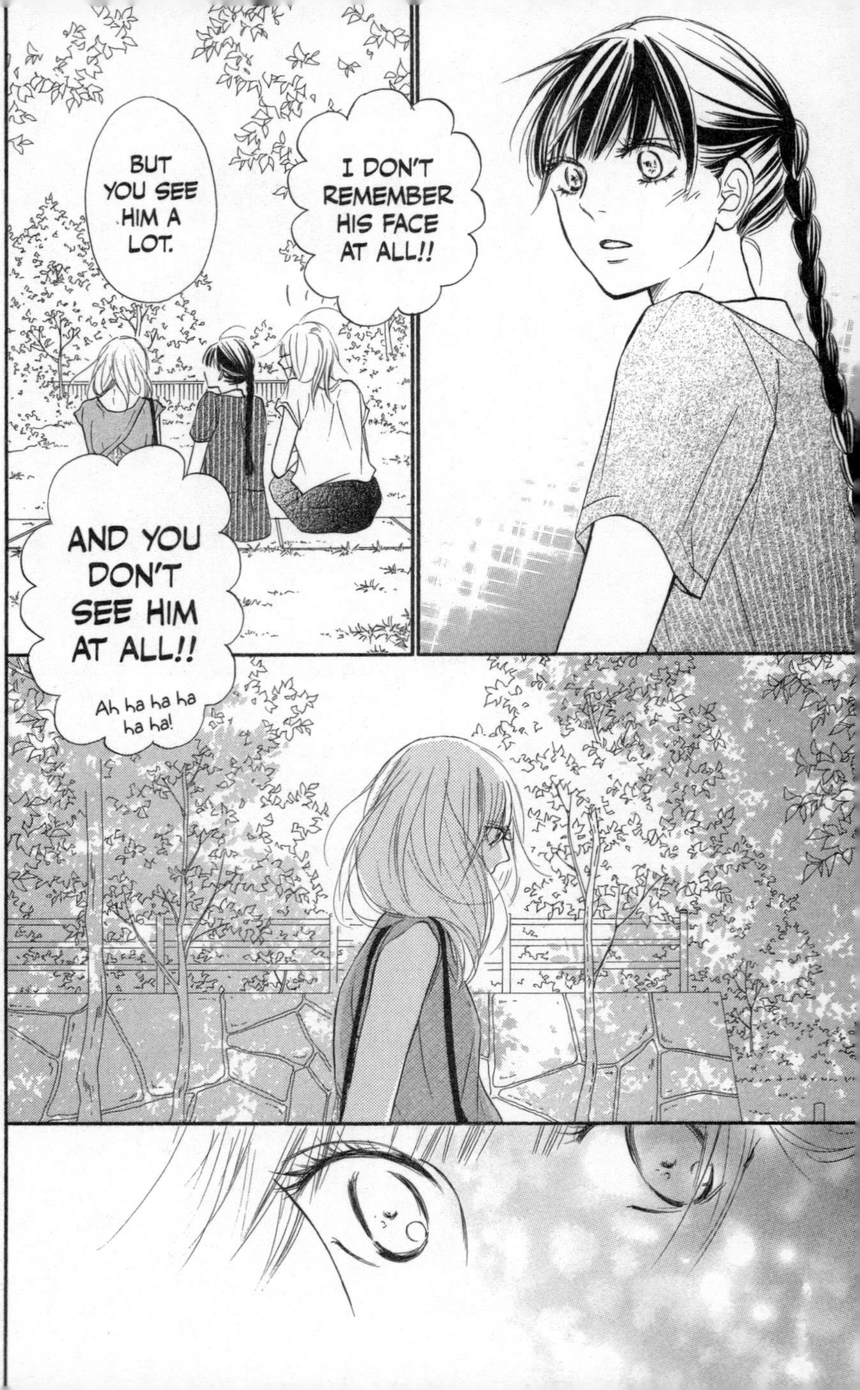
I DON'T REMEMBER HIS FACE AT ALL!!
BUT YOU SEE HIM A LOT.
AND YOU DON'T SEE HIM AT ALL!!
Ah ha ha ha ha ha!

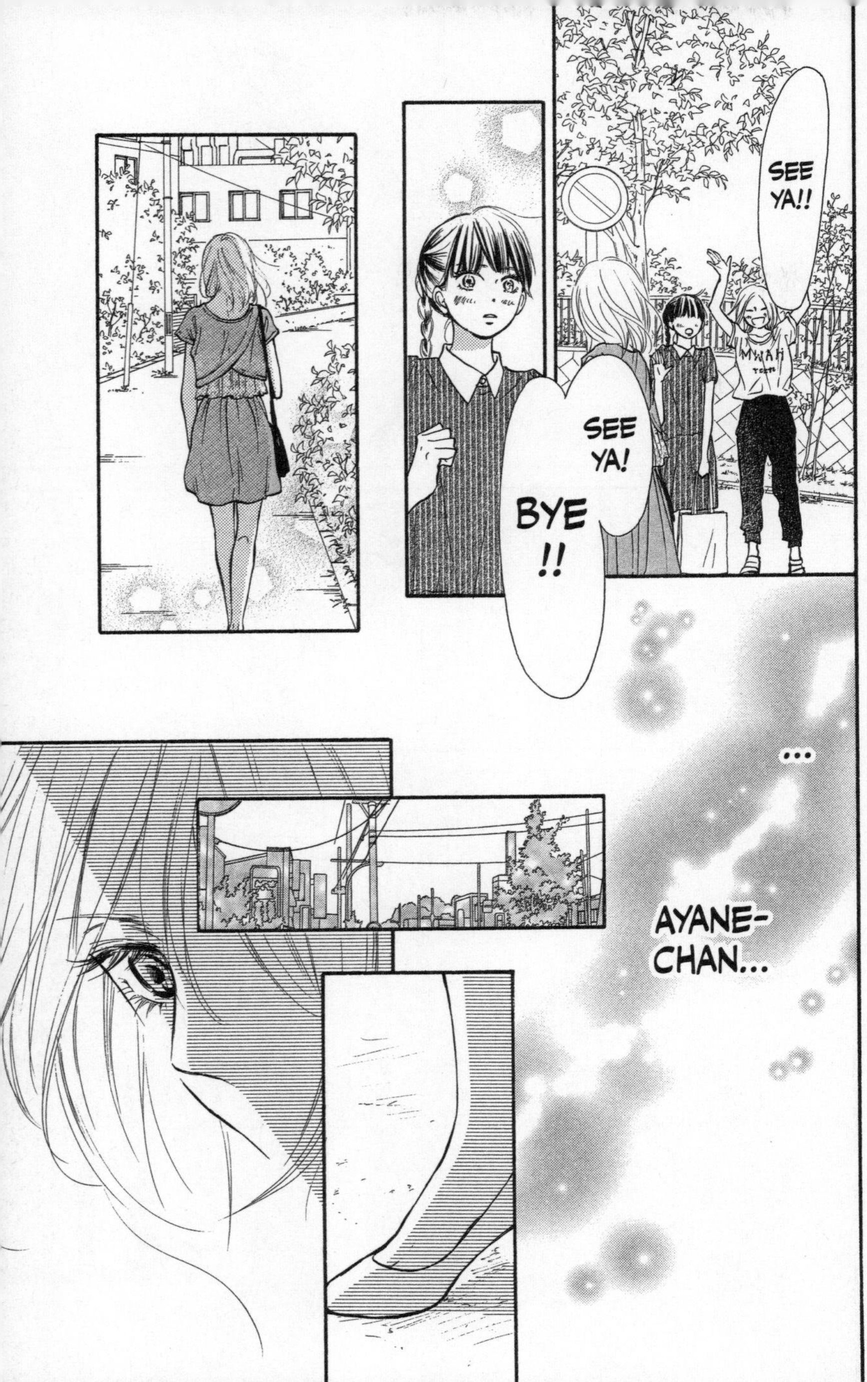
SEE YA!!
SEE YA!
BYE !!
...
AYANE-CHAN...

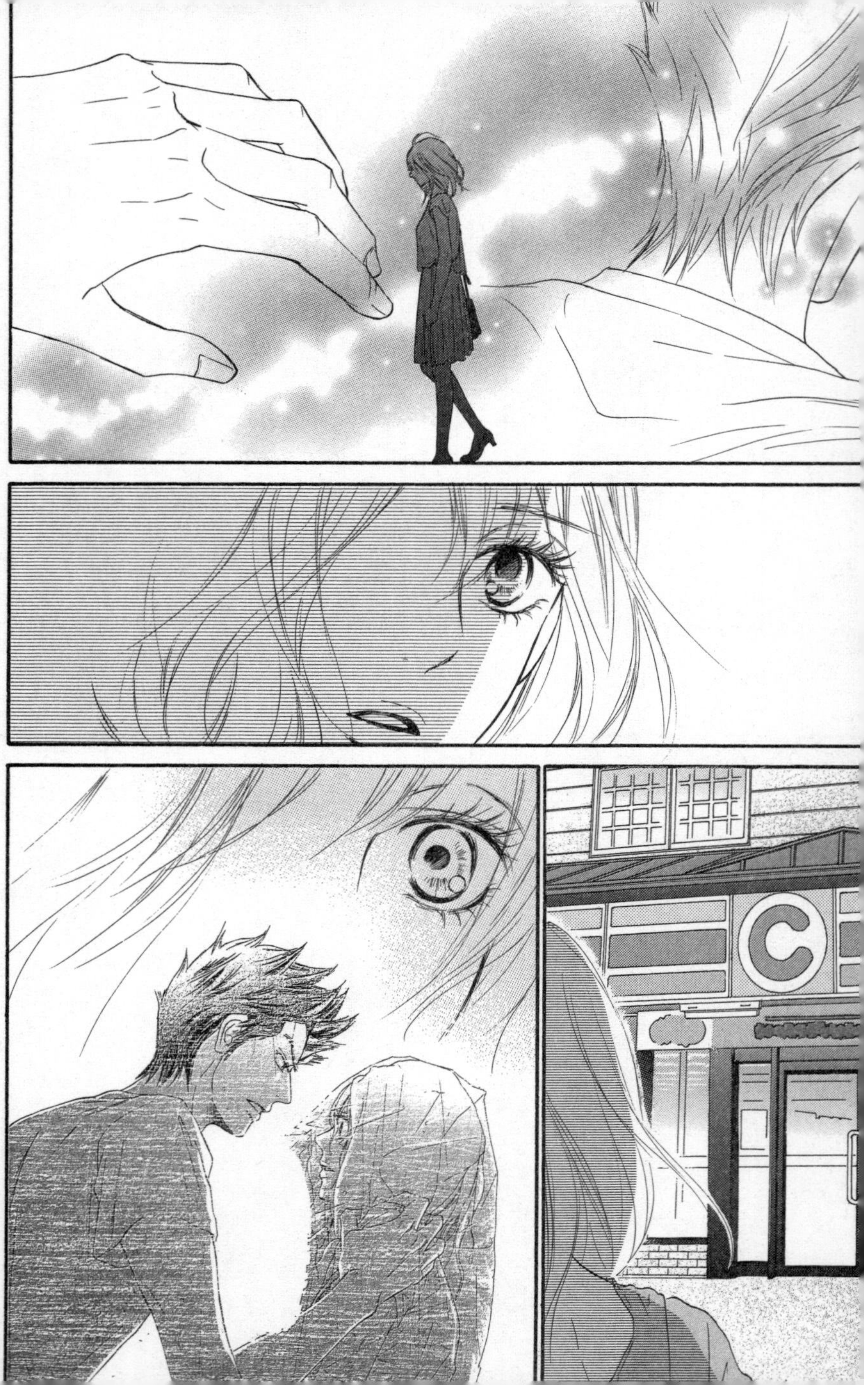

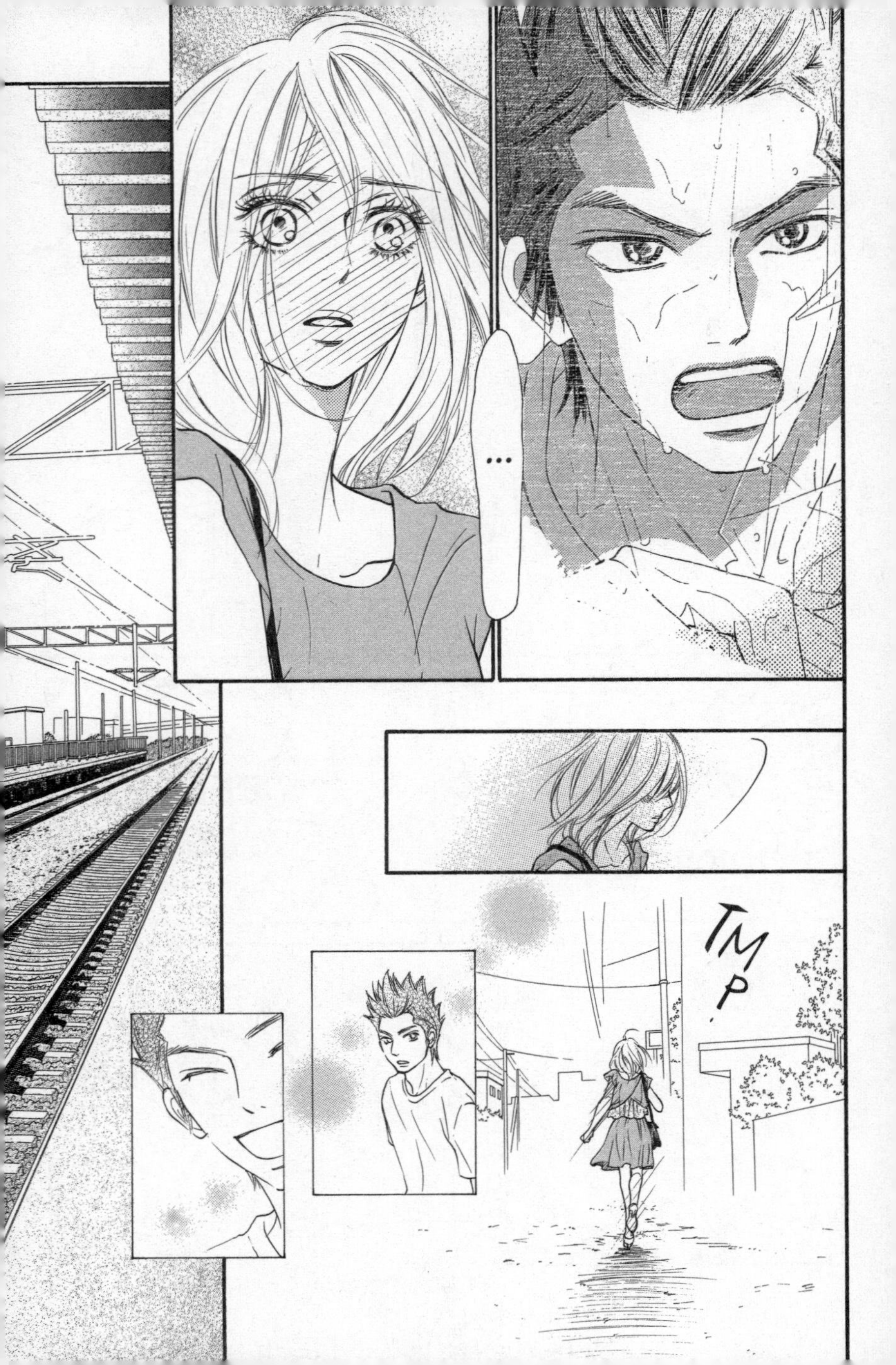
...
TMP!

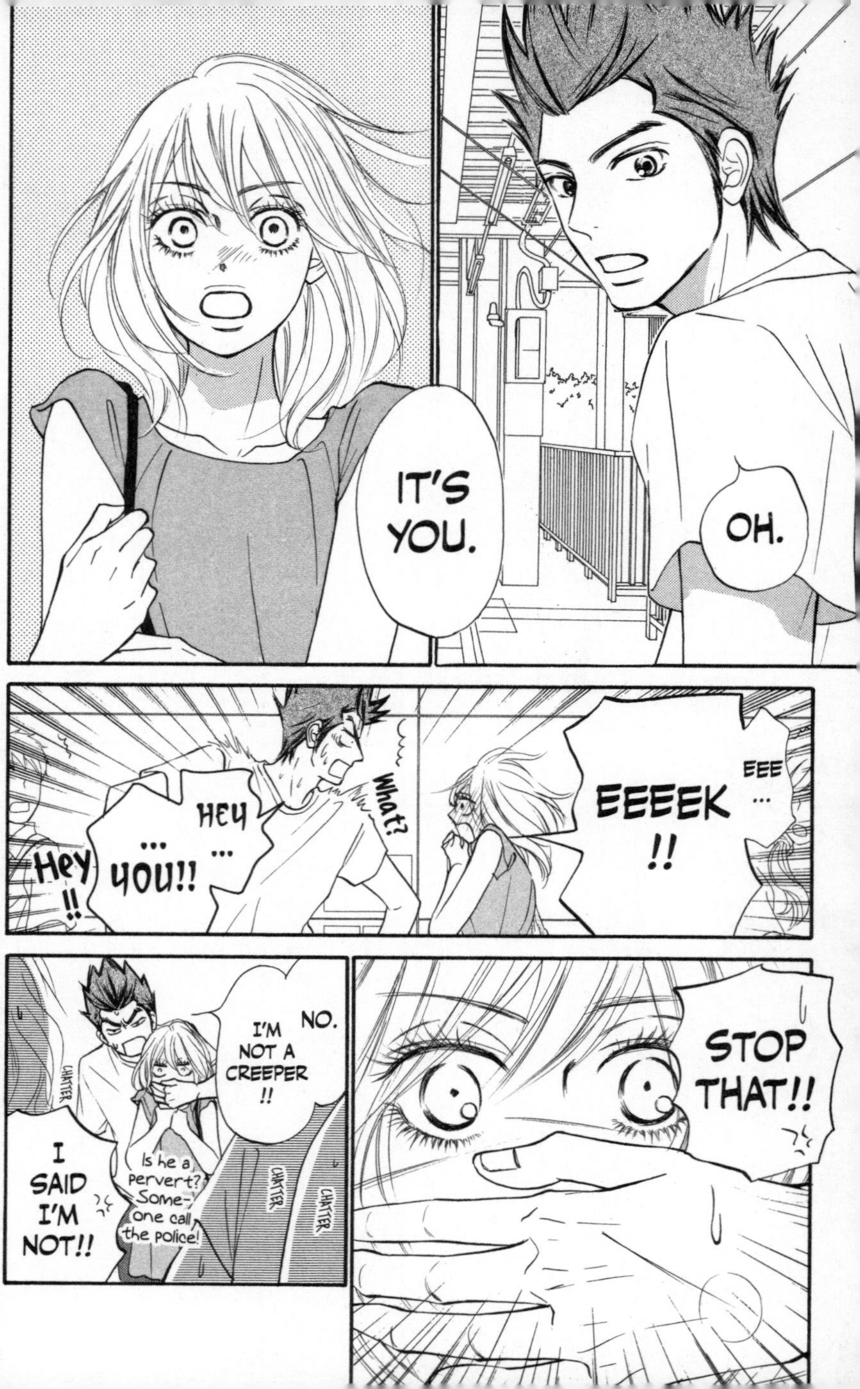
OH.
IT'S YOU.
EEEEK!!
EEE...
What?
HEY... YOU!!
Hey!!
STOP THAT!!
NO.
I'M NOT A CREEPER!!
CHATTER
CHATTER
CHATTER
Is he a pervert? Some-one call the police!
I SAID I'M NOT!!

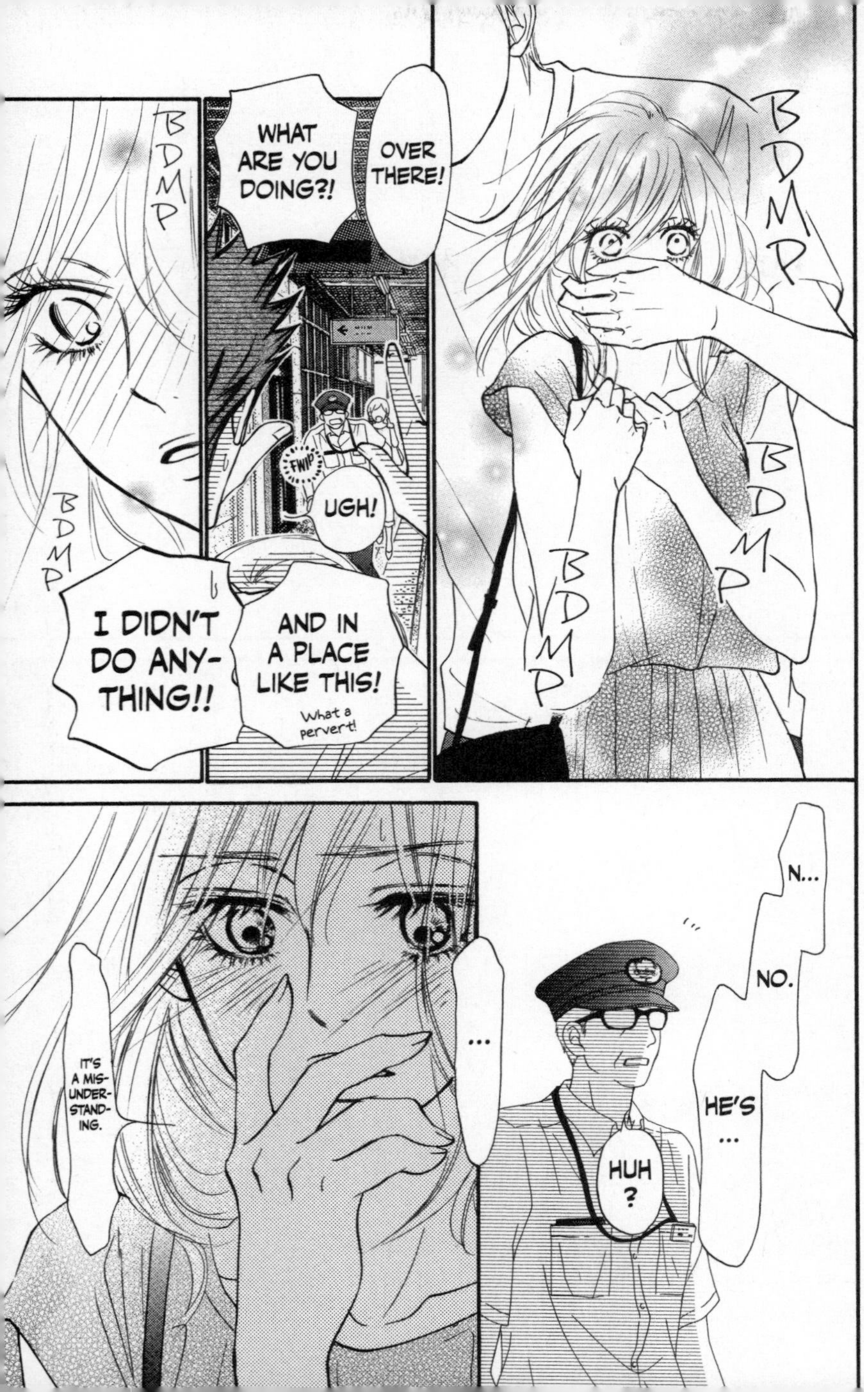
BDMP
BDMP
BDMP
BDMP
OVER THERE!
WHAT ARE YOU DOING?!
FWIP
UGH!
AND IN A PLACE LIKE THIS!
What a pervert!
BDMP
BDMP
I DIDN'T DO ANY-THING!!
N...
NO.
HE'S...
HUH?
...
IT'S A MIS-UNDER-STAND-ING.

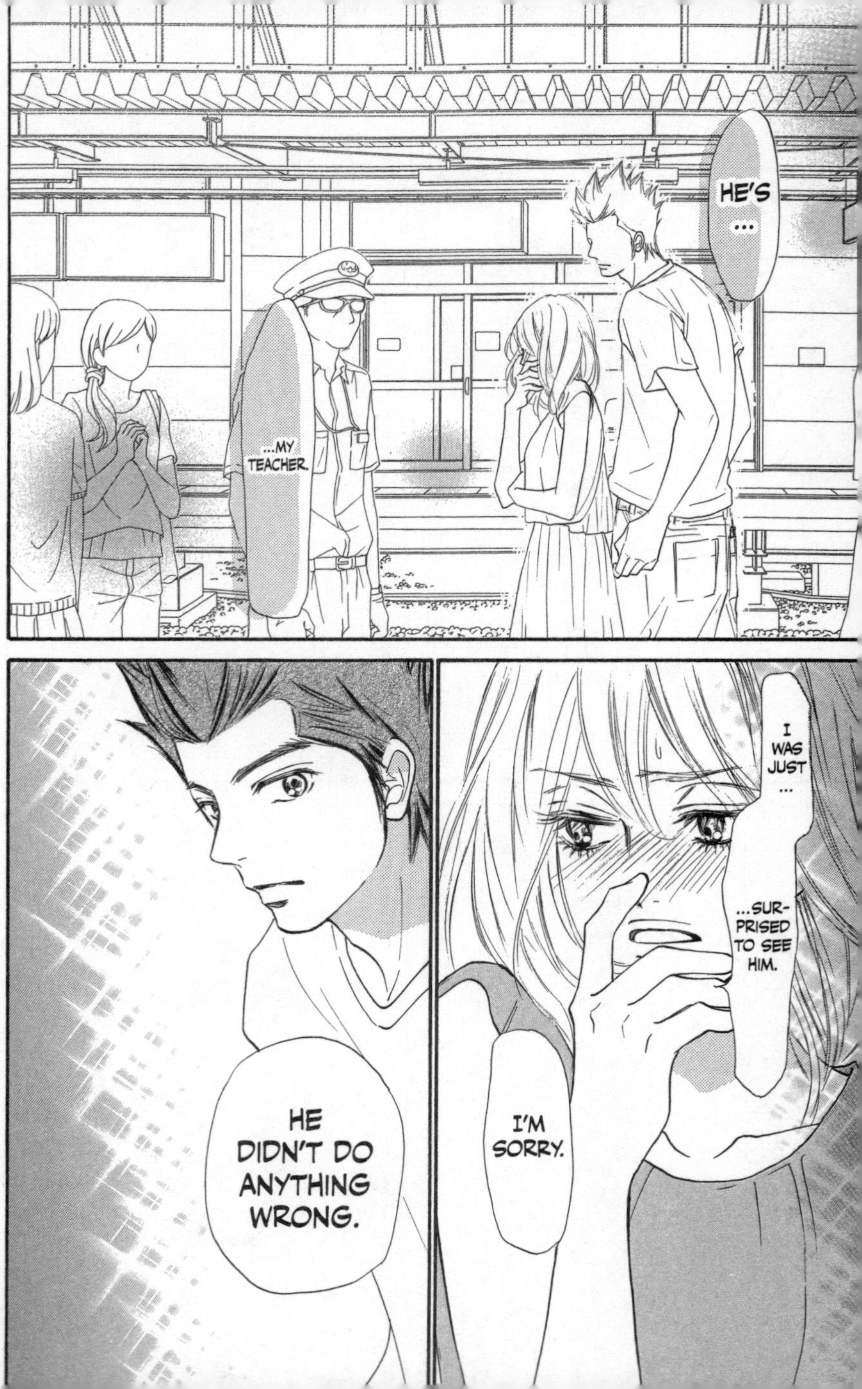
HE'S ...
...MY TEACHER.
I WAS JUST ...
...SUR-PRISED TO SEE HIM.
I'M SORRY.
HE DIDN'T DO ANYTHING WRONG.

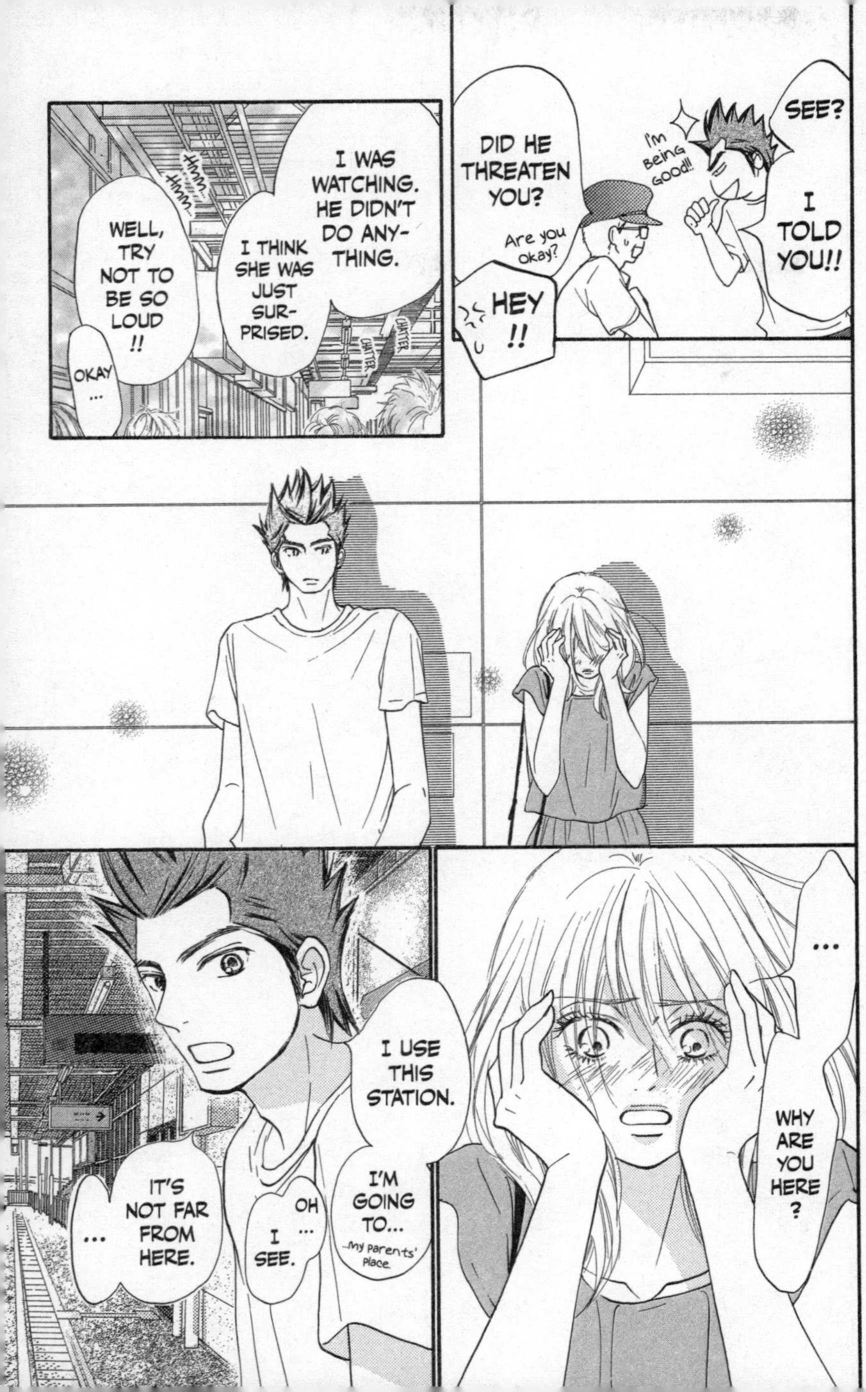
SEE?
I TOLD YOU!!
I'm Being Good!!
DID HE THREATEN YOU?
Are you okay?
HEY !!
I WAS WATCHING. HE DIDN'T DO ANY-THING.
I THINK SHE WAS JUST SUR-PRISED.
CHATTER CHATTER
Hmm... Hmm...
WELL, TRY NOT TO BE SO LOUD !!
OKAY ...
...
WHY ARE YOU HERE ?
I USE THIS STATION.
I'M GOING TO...
...my parents' place.
OH ... I SEE.
IT'S NOT FAR FROM HERE.
...

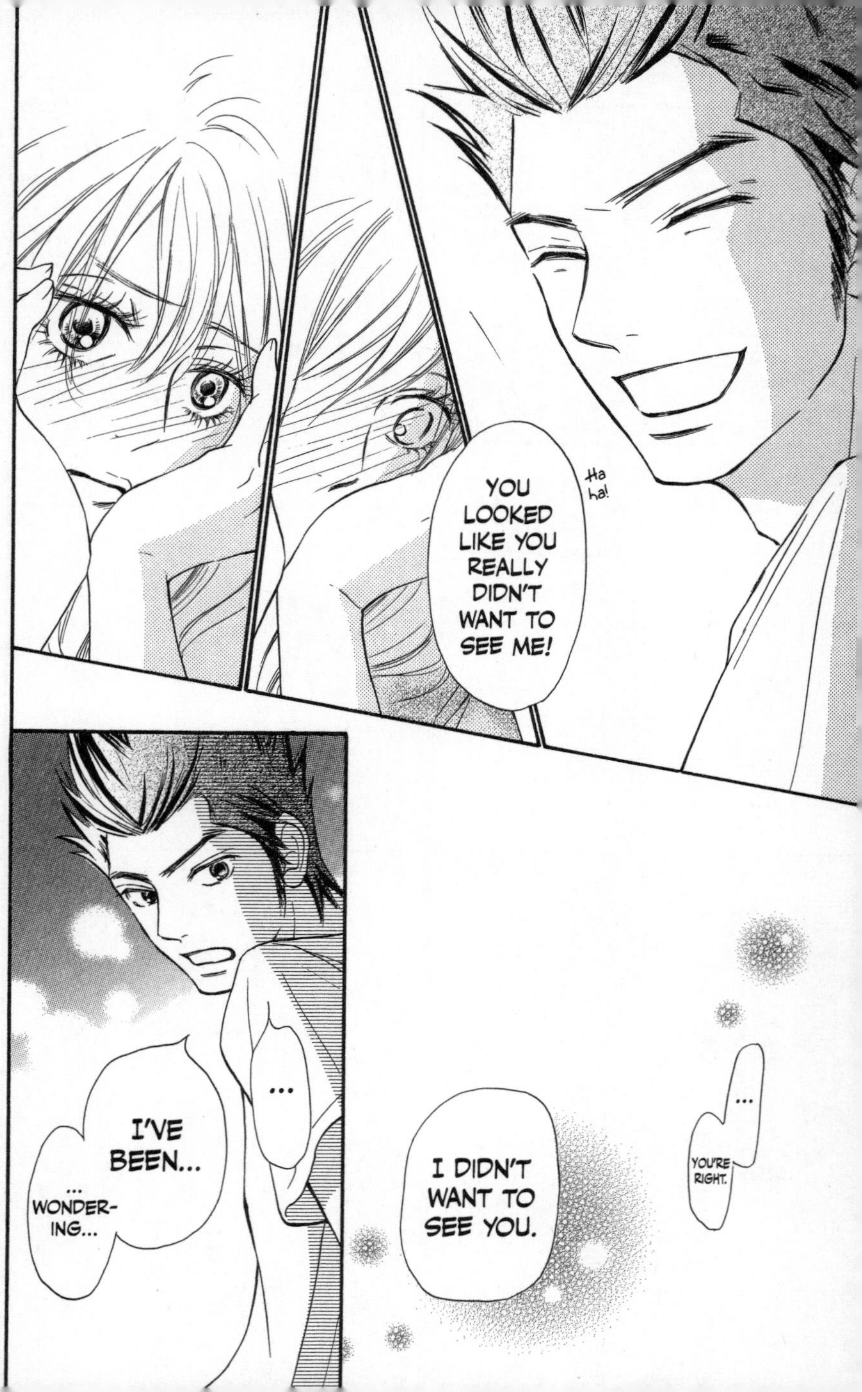
Ha ha!
YOU LOOKED LIKE YOU REALLY DIDN'T WANT TO SEE ME!
...
YOU'RE RIGHT.
I DIDN'T WANT TO SEE YOU.
...
I'VE BEEN... ... WONDERING...

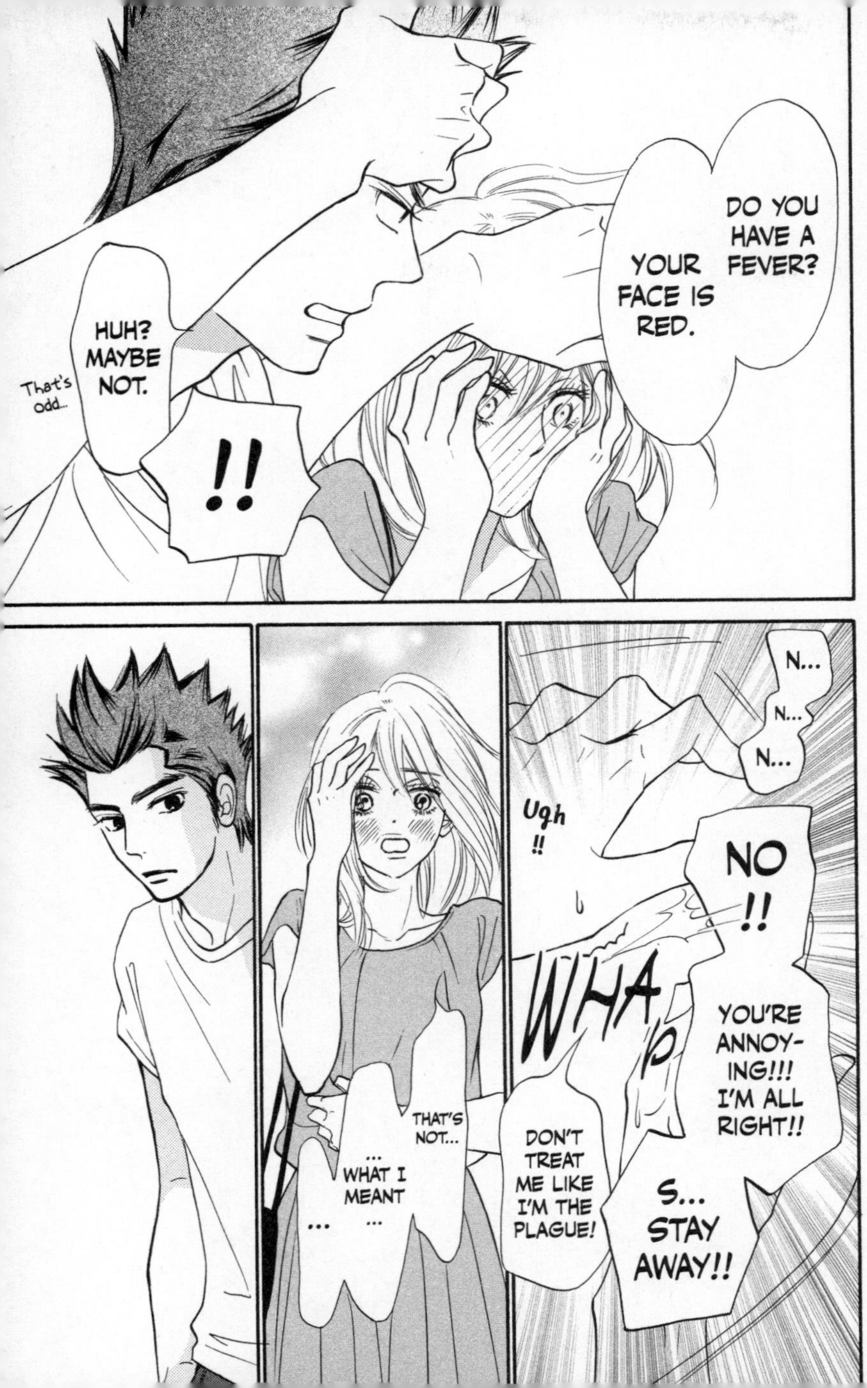
DO YOU HAVE A FEVER?
YOUR FACE IS RED.
!!
HUH? MAYBE NOT.
That's odd...
N...
N...
N...
Ugh !!
NO !!
WHAP
YOU'RE ANNOY-ING!!! I'M ALL RIGHT!!
S... STAY AWAY!!
DON'T TREAT ME LIKE I'M THE PLAGUE!
THAT'S NOT...
... WHAT I MEANT ...
...

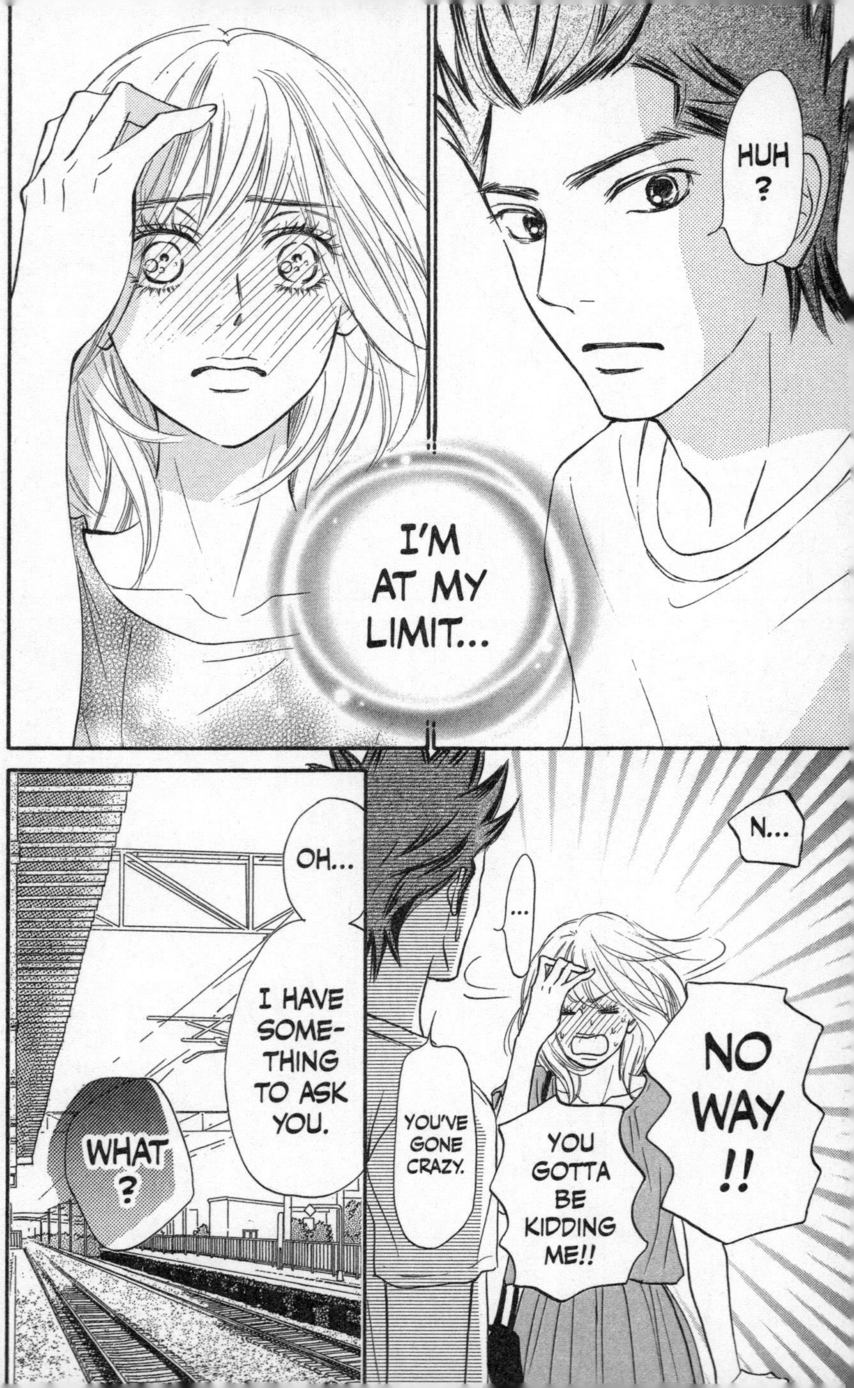
HUH?
I'M AT MY LIMIT...
N...
...
NO WAY!!
YOU GOTTA BE KIDDING ME!!
YOU'VE GONE CRAZY.
OH...
I HAVE SOMETHING TO ASK YOU.
WHAT?

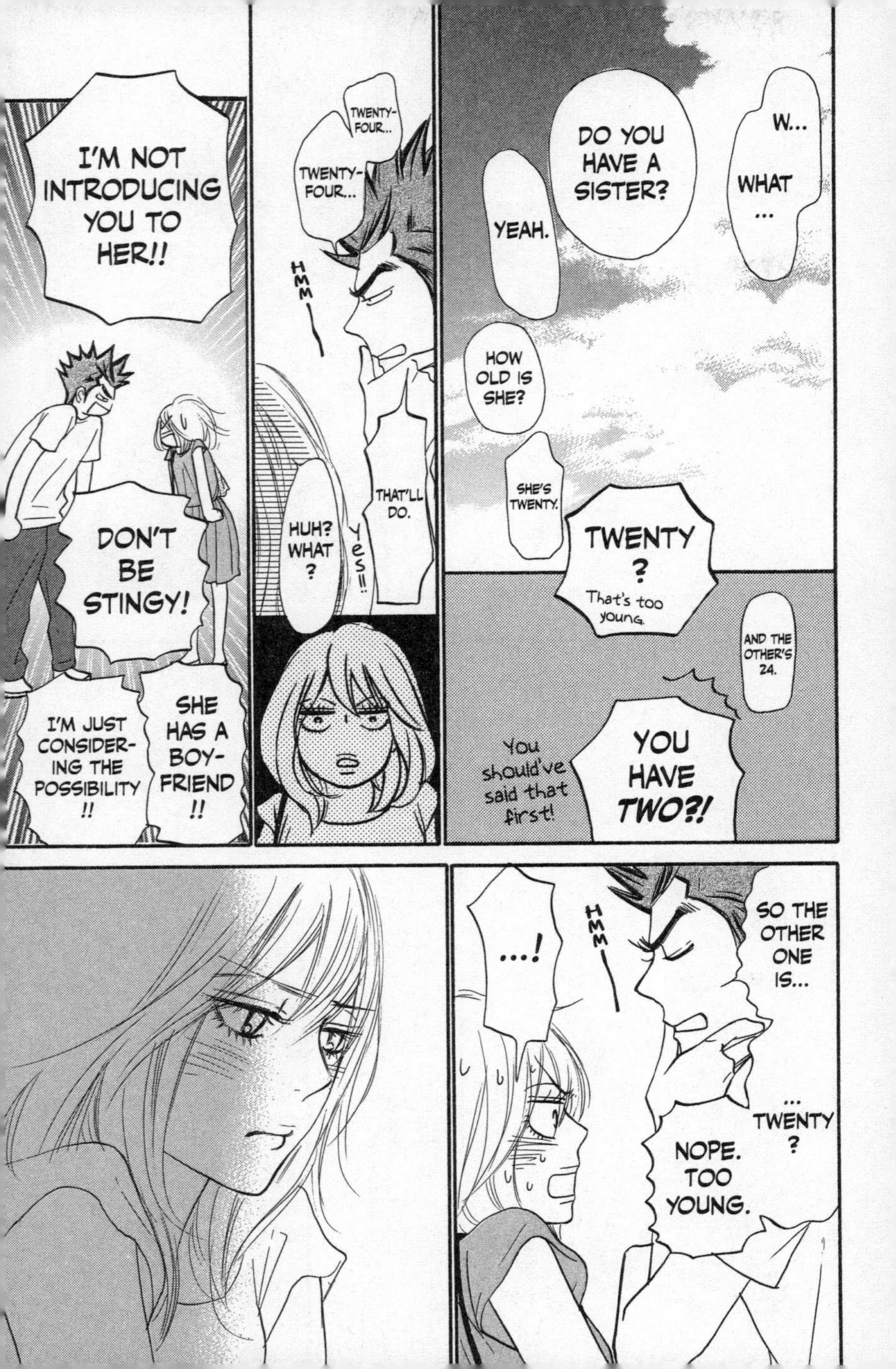
W... WHAT ...
DO YOU HAVE A SISTER?
YEAH.
HOW OLD IS SHE?
SHE'S TWENTY.
TWENTY? That's too young.
AND THE OTHER'S 24.
YOU HAVE TWO?!
You should've said that first!
TWENTY-FOUR..
TWENTY-FOUR...
HMM—
THAT'LL DO.
Yes!!
HUH? WHAT?
I'M NOT INTRODUCING YOU TO HER!!
DON'T BE STINGY!
SHE HAS A BOYFRIEND!!
I'M JUST CONSIDERING THE POSSIBILITY!!
SO THE OTHER ONE IS...
HMM—
...!
...TWENTY?
NOPE. TOO YOUNG.

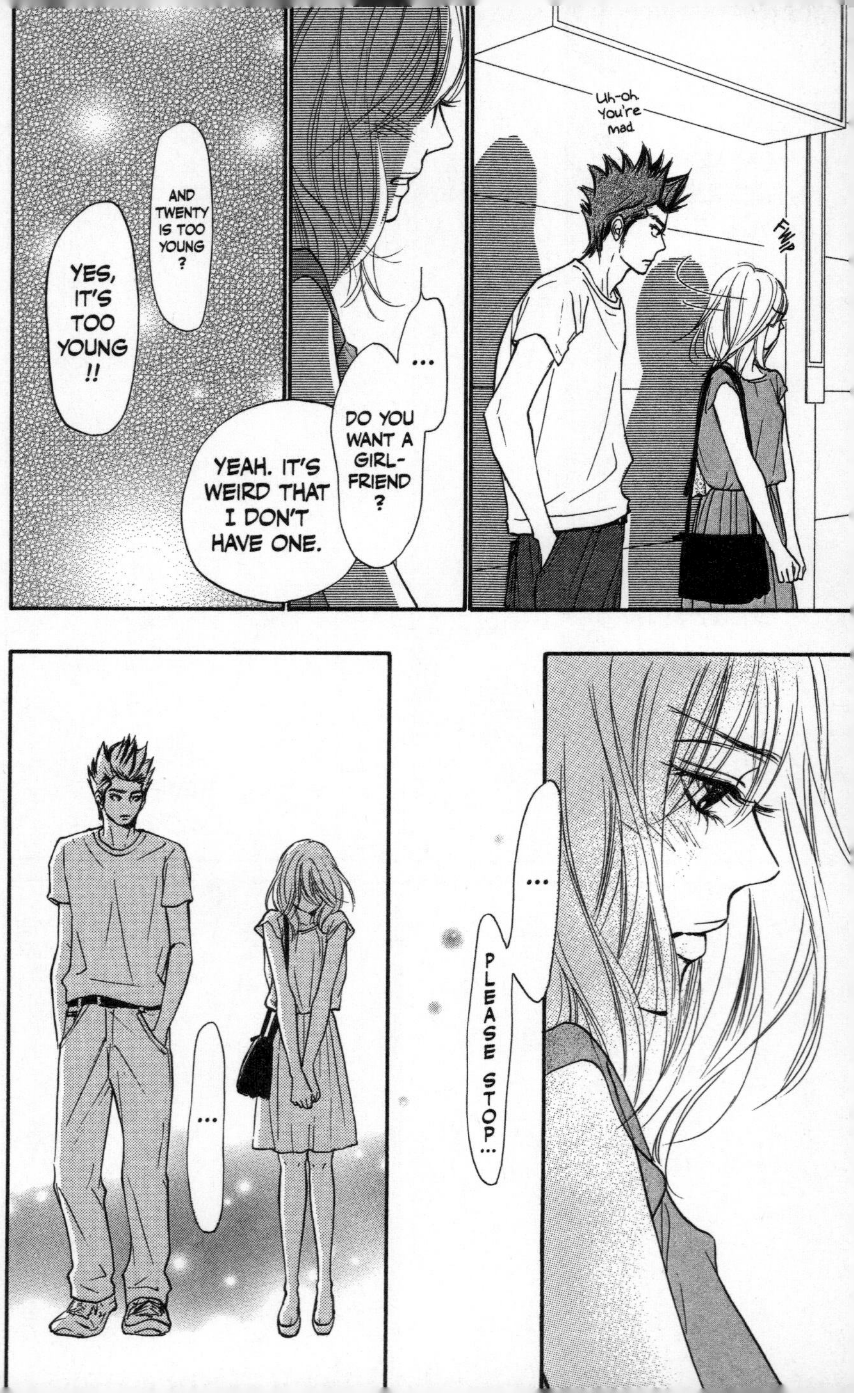
Uh-oh. You're mad.
FWIP
...
DO YOU WANT A GIRL-FRIEND?
YEAH. IT'S WEIRD THAT I DON'T HAVE ONE.
AND TWENTY IS TOO YOUNG?
YES, IT'S TOO YOUNG!!
...
PLEASE STOP...
...

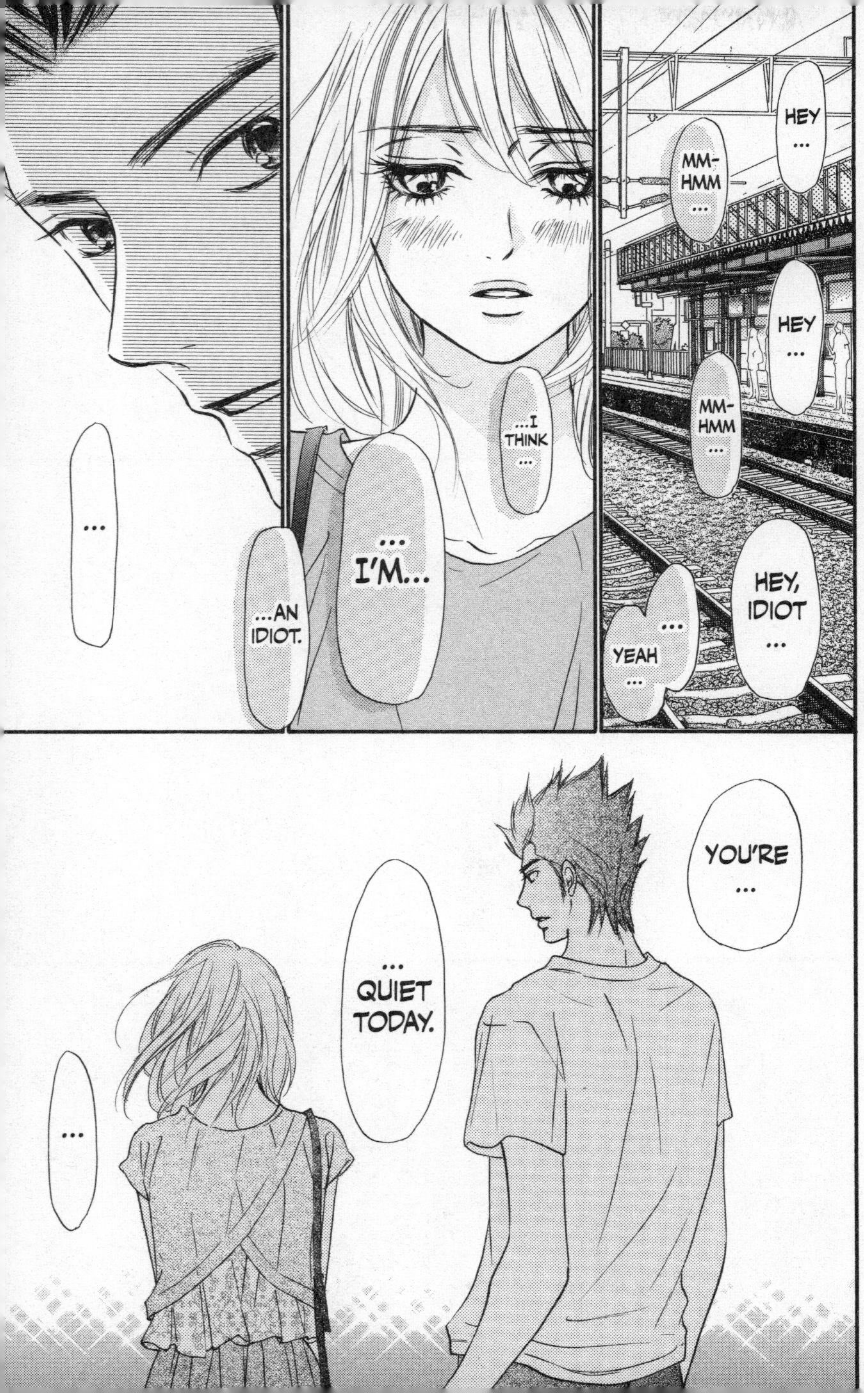
HEY ...
MM-HMM ...
HEY ...
MM-HMM ...
HEY, IDIOT ...
... YEAH ...
...I THINK ...
... I'M...
...AN IDIOT.
...
YOU'RE ...
... QUIET TODAY.
...

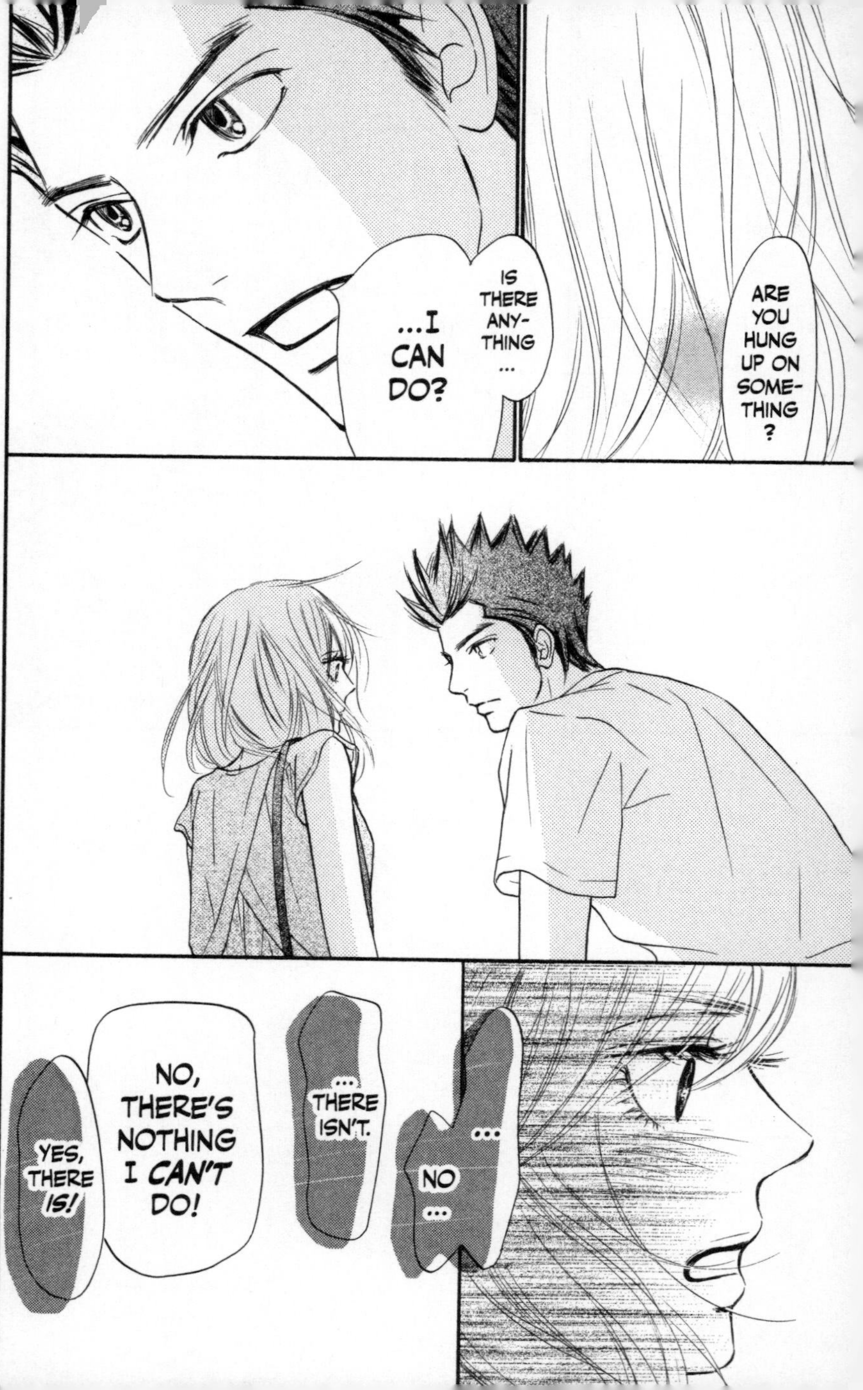
ARE YOU HUNG UP ON SOMETHING?
IS THERE ANYTHING...
...I CAN DO?
...NO...
...THERE ISN'T.
NO, THERE'S NOTHING I *CAN'T* DO!
YES, THERE *IS!*

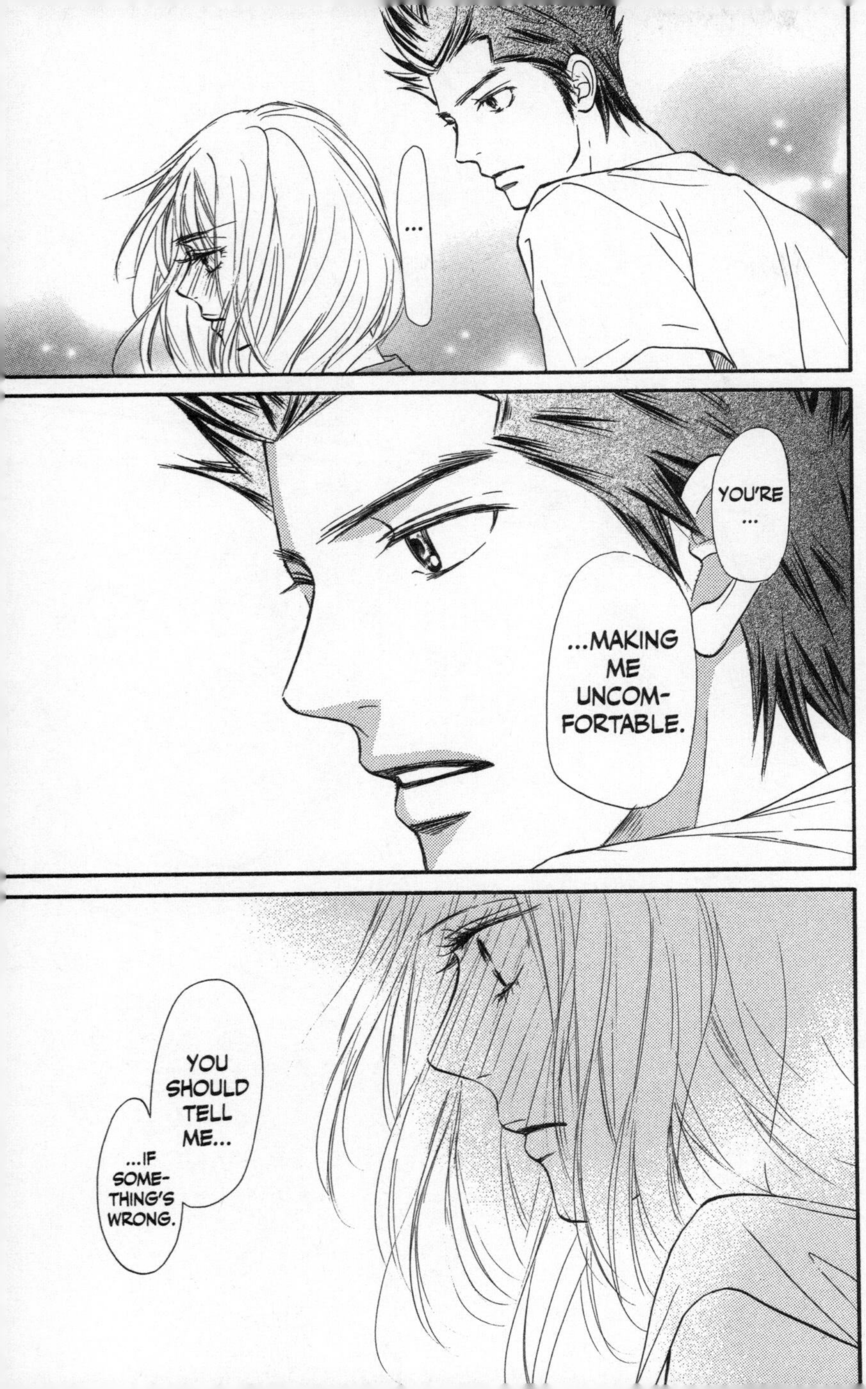
...
YOU'RE ...
...MAKING ME UNCOMFORTABLE.
YOU SHOULD TELL ME...
...IF SOMETHING'S WRONG.

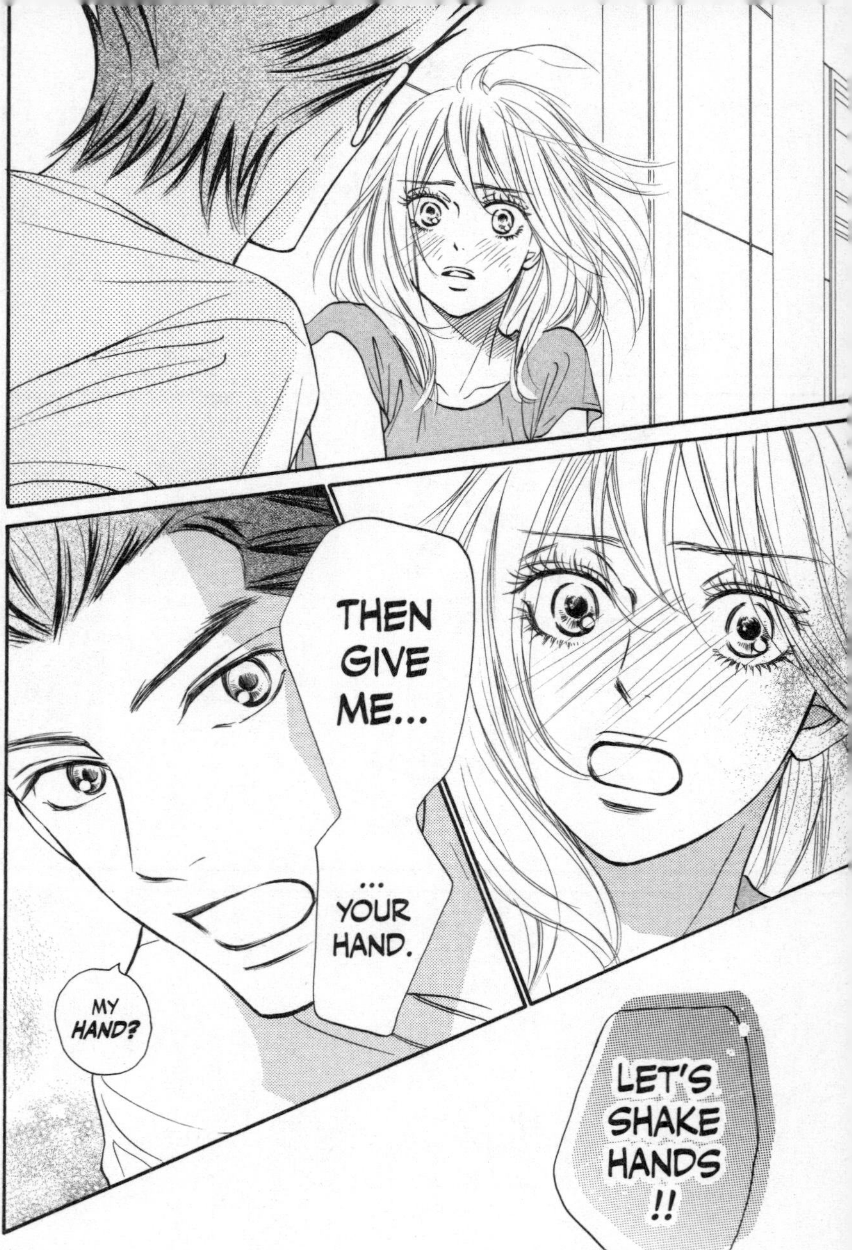
THEN GIVE ME...
...YOUR HAND.
MY HAND?
LET'S SHAKE HANDS!!

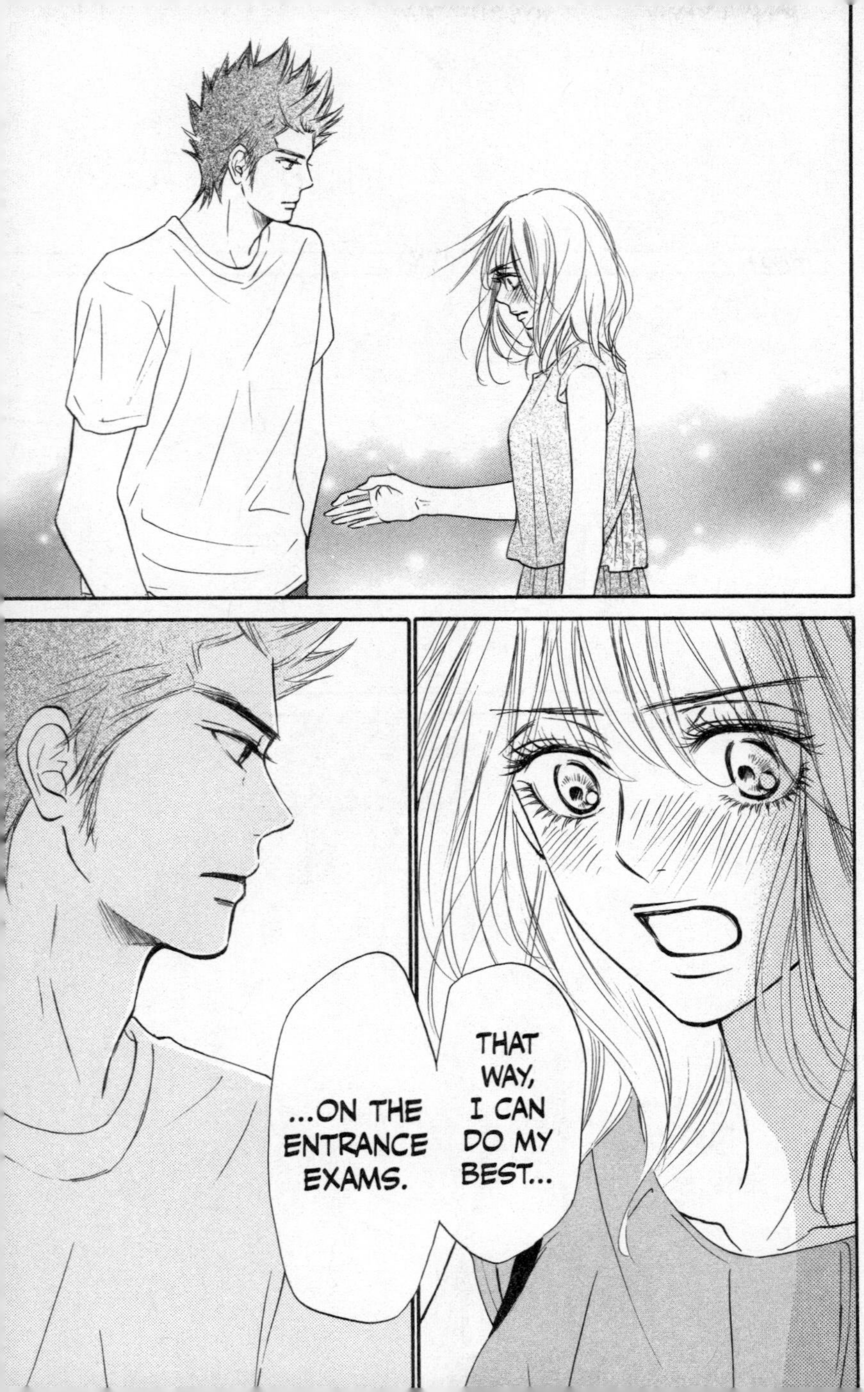
THAT WAY, I CAN DO MY BEST...
...ON THE ENTRANCE EXAMS.

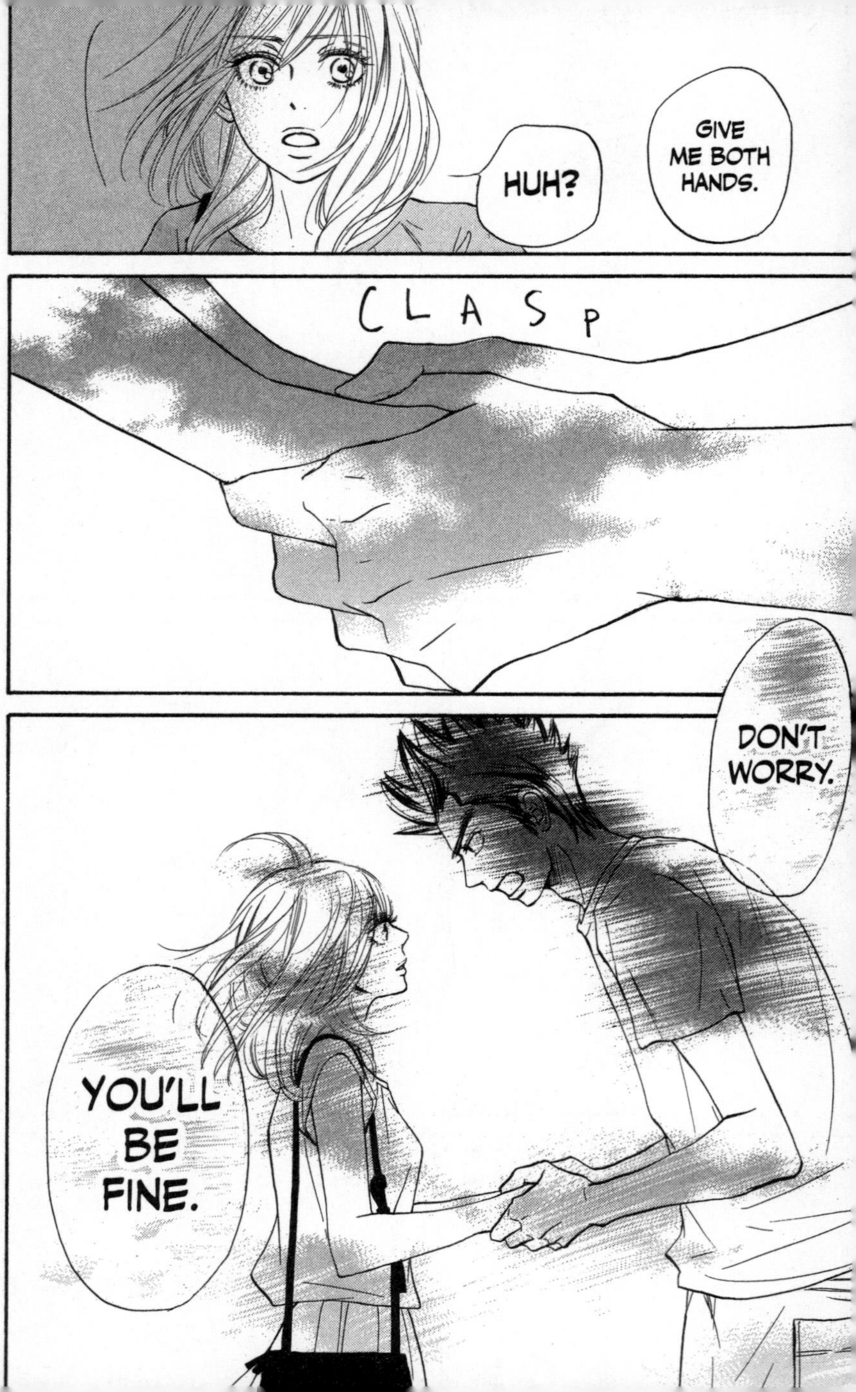
GIVE ME BOTH HANDS.
HUH?
CLASP
DON'T WORRY.
YOU'LL BE FINE.

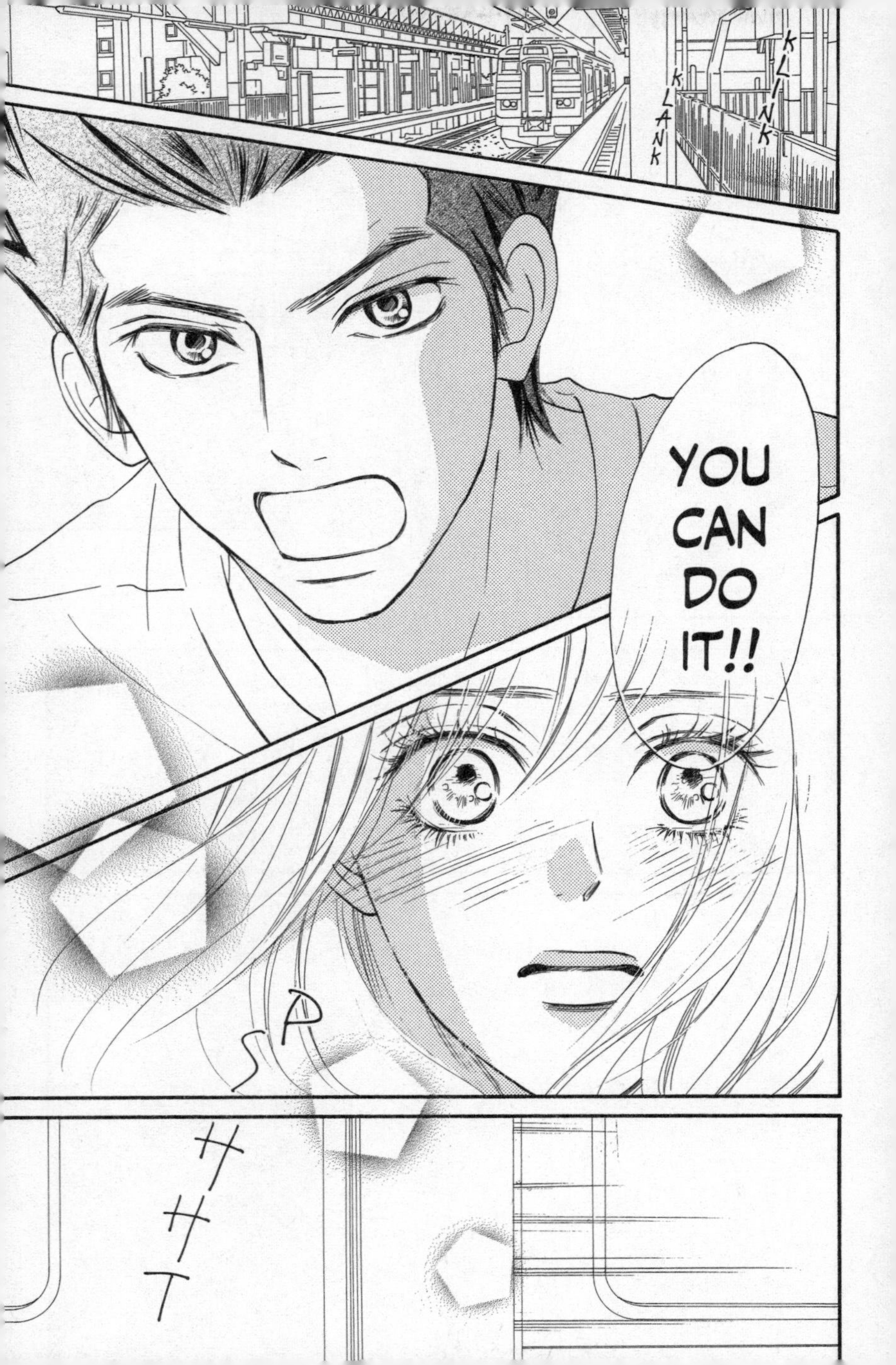
KLINK
KLANK
YOU CAN DO IT!!
SP

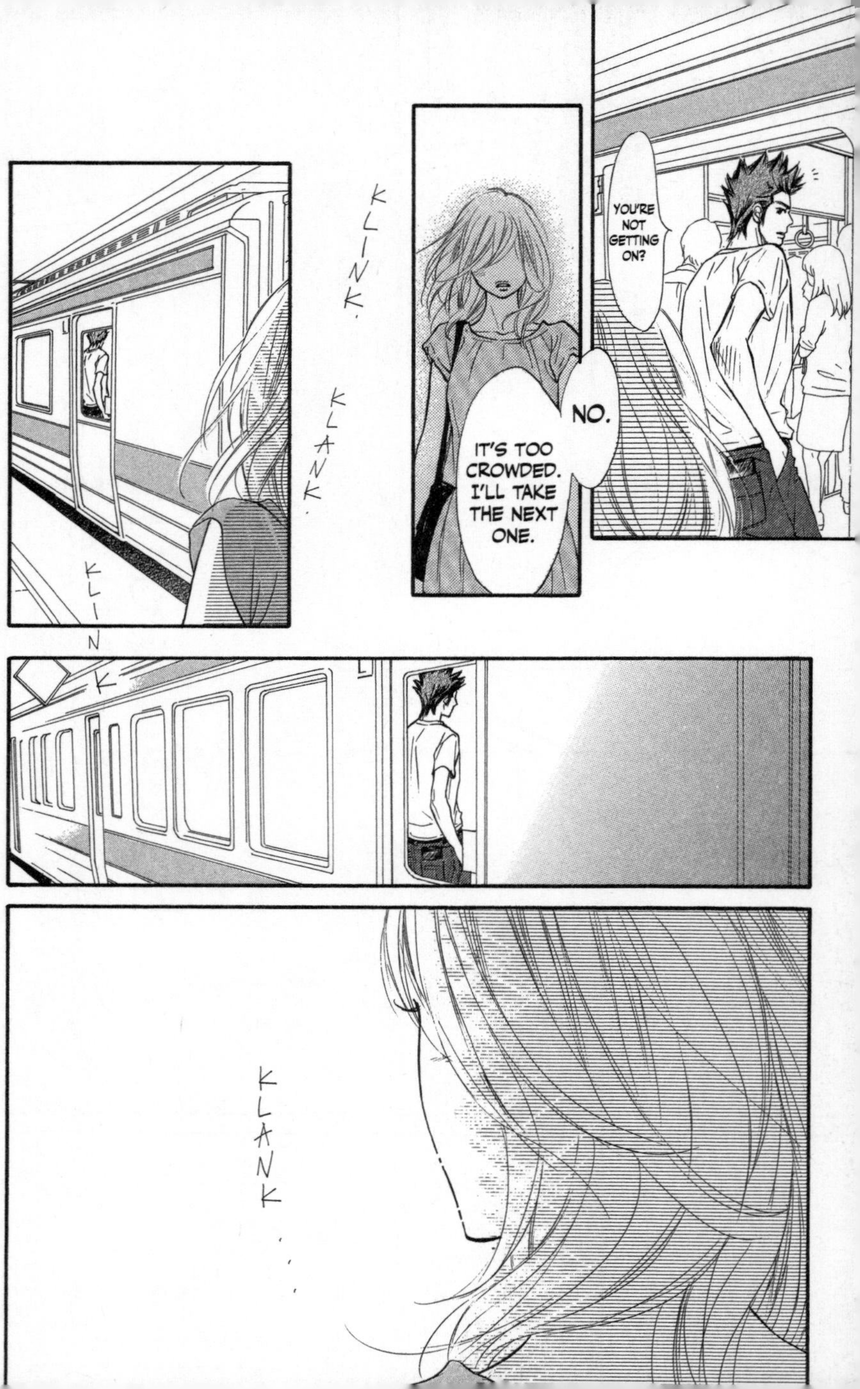

YOU'RE NOT GETTING ON?
NO.
IT'S TOO CROWDED. I'LL TAKE THE NEXT ONE.
KLINK.
KLANK.
KLINK
KLANK . . .

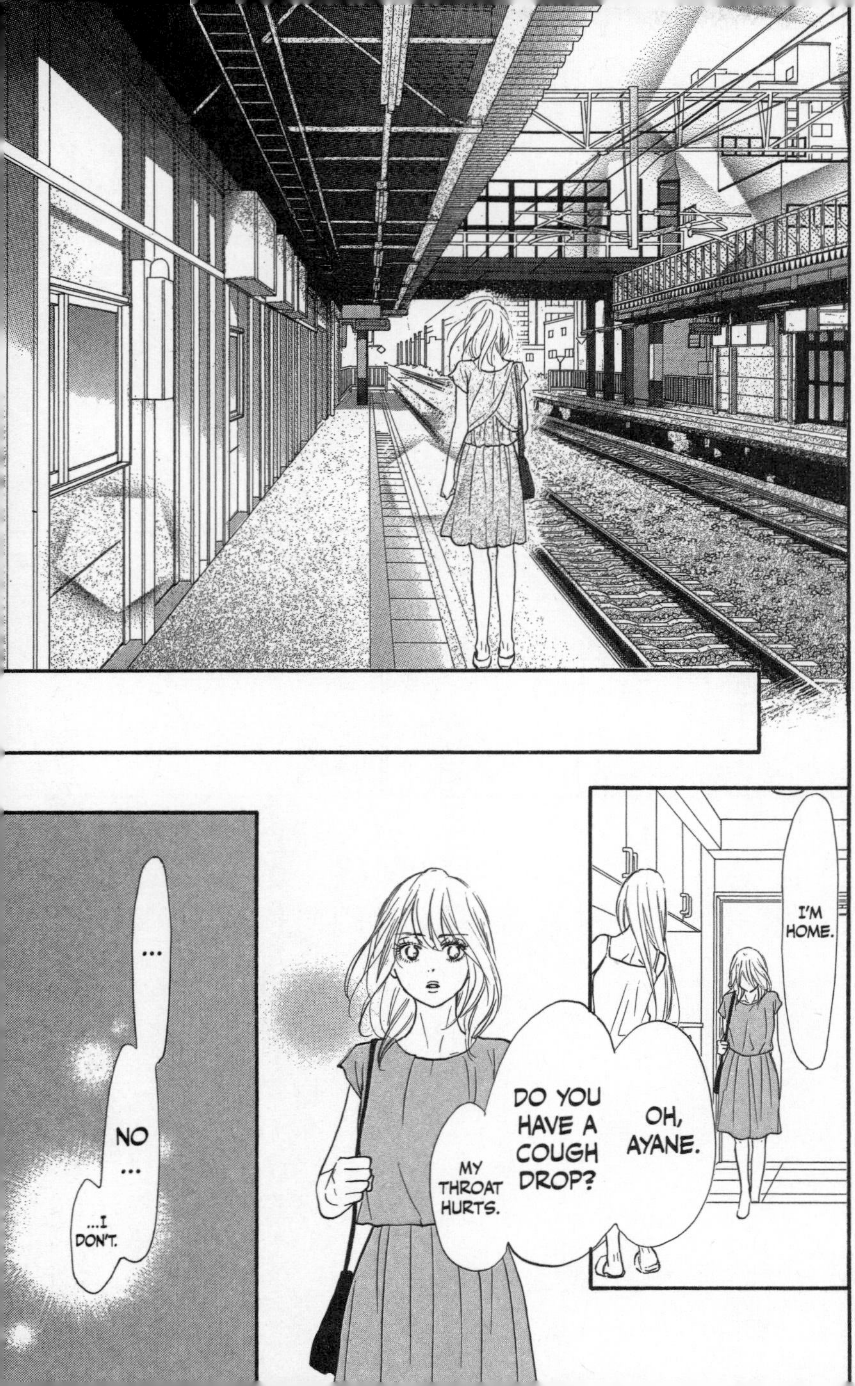
I'M HOME.
OH, AYANE.
DO YOU HAVE A COUGH DROP?
MY THROAT HURTS.
...
NO ...
...I DON'T.

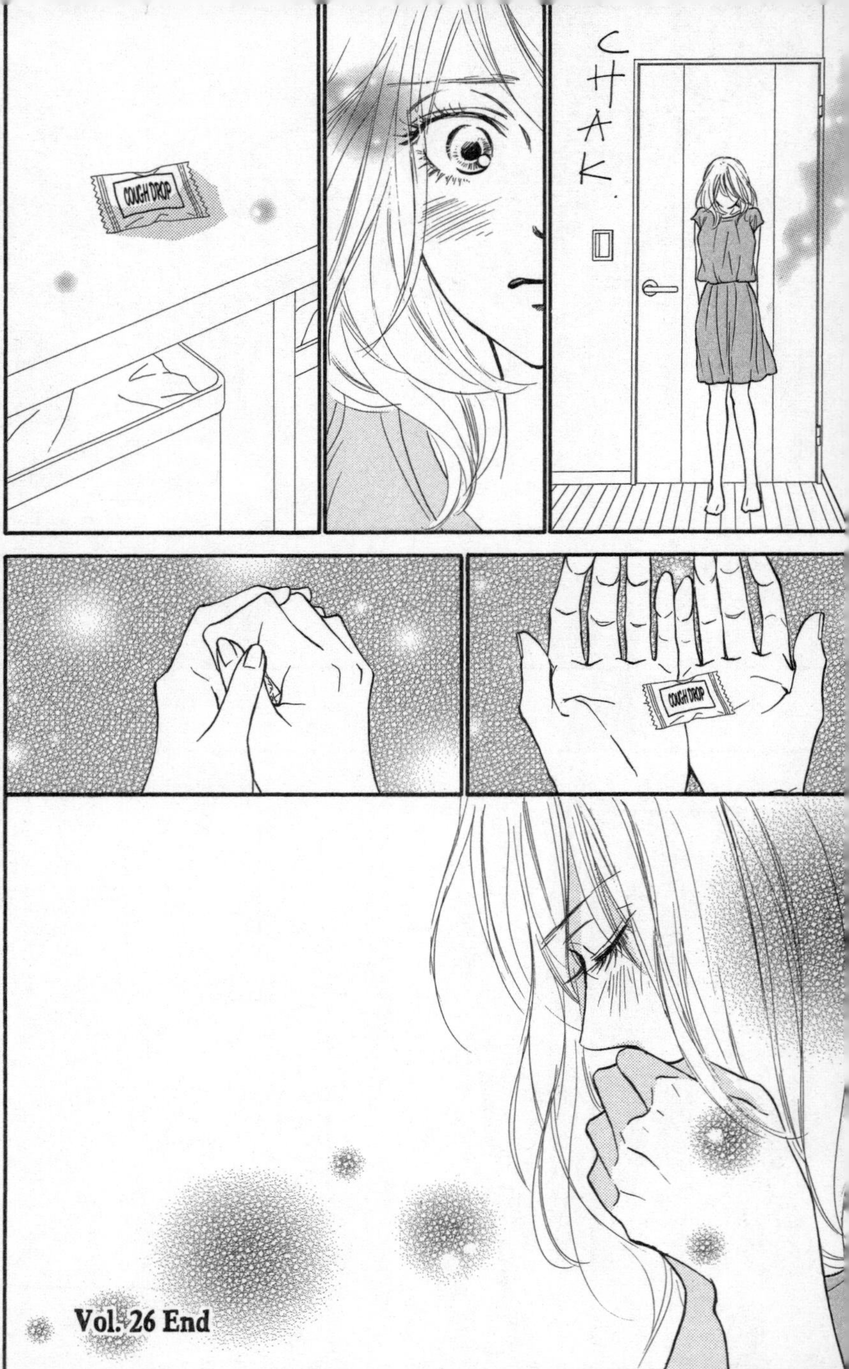
CHAK.
COUGH DROP
COUGH DROP
Vol. 26 End

From me (the editor) to you (the reader).

Here are some Japanese culture explanations that will help you better understand the references in the *Kimi ni Todoke* world.

Honorifics:
When saying someone's name in Japanese, a suffix is often attached to indicate how familiar the speaker is with the person. Some are more polite and respectful, while others are endearing. Calling someone by just their first name is the most informal.
-kun is used for young men or boys, usually someone you are familiar with.
-chan is used for young women, girls or young children and can be used as a term of endearment.
-san is used for someone you respect or are not close to, or to be polite.

Page 11, My Margaret:
The My Margaret exhibition was an event held in Japan for the fiftieth anniversary of the manga magazine *Margaret*, which is the magazine *Kimi ni Todoke* is serialized in in Japan.

Page 14, Obon:
A Japanese Buddhist festival that honors the spirits of one's ancestors. It lasts for three days and is a national holiday in Japan.

Page 69, Puré Gummy:
A gummy snack in Japan. While the gummies aren't usually star shaped, rumor has it that if you run across one that is, it will bring you good luck.

Page 69, chinmi:
Chinmi generally refers to local delicacies. They are usually some form of pickled seafood.

Page 88, Yutaka Takenouchi:
A Japanese actor who regularly appears in commercials.

Page 142, zashiki:
A seating area with tatami floor mats and low tables with no chairs.

I like rapeseed blossoms. I eat them!
They're tasty when boiled with soy sauce,
mustard or sesame sauce. I want to use
them for tempura in the spring. The truth
is, I prefer to eat food that others prepare
for me, but sometimes I have no choice
but to make food for myself. And of course
fresh steamed rice is delicious!!

--Karuho Shiina

Karuho Shiina was born and raised in
Hokkaido, Japan. Though *Kimi ni Todoke*
is only her second series following many
one-shot stories, it has already racked
up accolades from various "Best Manga
of the Year" lists. Winner of the 2008
Kodansha Manga Award for the shojo
category, *Kimi ni Todoke* also placed
fifth in the first-ever Manga Taisho
(Cartoon Grand Prize) contest in 2008. In
Japan, an animated TV series debuted in
October 2009, and a live-action film was
released in 2010.

Kimi ni Todoke
VOL. 26

Shojo Beat Edition

STORY AND ART BY
KARUHO SHIINA

Translation/Ari Yasuda, HC Language Solutions, Inc.
Touch-up Art & Lettering/Vanessa Satone
Design/Nozomi Akashi
Editor/Marlene First

Printed in the U.S.A.

Published by VIZ Media, LLC
P.O. Box 77010
San Francisco, CA 94107

10 9 8 7 6 5 4 3 2 1
First printing, March 2017

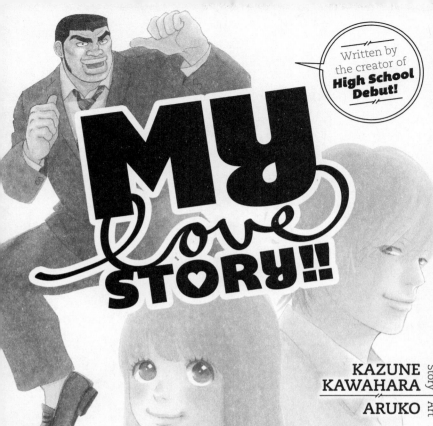

Written by the creator of **High School Debut!**

MY love STORY!!

KAZUNE KAWAHARA *Story*

ARUKO *Art*

Takeo Goda is a GIANT guy with a GIANT *heart*

Too bad the girls don't want him!
(They want his good-looking best friend, Sunakawa.)

Used to being on the sidelines, Takeo simply stands tall and accepts his fate. But one day when he saves a girl named Yamato from a harasser on the train, his (love!) life suddenly takes an incredible turn!

Surprise!

You may be reading the wrong way!

It's true: In keeping with the original Japanese comic format, this book reads from right to left—so action, sound effects, and word balloons are completely reversed. This preserves the orientation of the original artwork—plus, it's fun! Check out the diagram shown here to get the hang of things, and then turn to the other side of the book to get started!

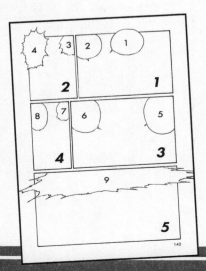